THE GLOBAL GOV
OF KNOWLEDGE

Patent offices around the world have granted millions of patents to multinational companies. Patent offices are rarely studied and yet they are crucial agents in the global knowledge economy. Based on a study of forty-five rich and poor countries that takes in the world's largest and smallest offices, Peter Drahos argues that patent offices have become part of a globally integrated private governance network that serves the interests of multinational companies. He shows that the Trilateral Offices of Europe, the USA and Japan make developing-country patent offices part of the network through the strategic fostering of technocratic trust. By analysing the obligations of patent offices under the patent social contract and drawing on a theory of nodal governance, the author proposes innovative approaches to patent office administration that would allow developed and developing countries to recapture the public spirit of the patent social contract.

PETER DRAHOS is a professor at the Regulatory Institutions Network in the Australian National University and holds a Chair in Intellectual Property at Queen Mary, University of London.

THE GLOBAL GOVERNANCE OF KNOWLEDGE

Patent Offices and their Clients

PETER DRAHOS

CAMBRIDGE
UNIVERSITY PRESS

CAMBRIDGE UNIVERSITY PRESS
Cambridge, New York, Melbourne, Madrid, Cape Town, Singapore,
São Paulo, Delhi, Dubai, Tokyo

Cambridge University Press
The Edinburgh Building, Cambridge CB2 8RU, UK

Published in the United States of America by Cambridge University Press, New York

www.cambridge.org
Information on this title: www.cambridge.org/9780521195669

First published 2010

Printed in the United Kingdom at the University Press, Cambridge

A catalogue record for this publication is available from the British Library

Library of Congress Cataloguing in Publication data
Drahos, Peter, 1955–
The global governance of knowledge : patent offices and their clients / Peter Drahos.
p.   cm.
ISBN 978-0-521-19566-9 (hardback)
1. Patent laws and legislation.   2. Globalization.   I. Title.
K1505.D73 2010
346.04′86–dc22
2009042030

ISBN 978-0-521-19566-9 Hardback
ISBN 978-0-521-14436-0 Paperback

To Julie

CONTENTS

DIAGRAMS AND TABLES

Diagrams

Tables

LIST OF ABBREVIATIONS

AIPN	Asian Industrial Property Network
ANVISA	National Sanitary Surveillance Agency of Brazil
APEC	Asia-Pacific Economic Cooperation
ARIPO	African Regional Intellectual Property Organization
ASEAN	Association of Southeast Asian Nations
Asian Trilaterals	Chinese PO, Japanese PO, Korean Intellectual Property Office
CIS	Commonwealth of Independent States
EAPC	Eurasian Patent Convention
EAPO	Eurasian Patent Organization
ECAP	European Community-ASEAN Intellectual Property Rights Co-operation Programme
EEC	European Economic Community
EPC	European Patent Convention
EPO	European Patent Office
EU	European Union
EPAC	External Patent Audit Committee
FDI	Foreign Direct Investment
FTA	Free Trade Agreement
GATT	General Agreement on Tariffs and Trade
GCC	Gulf Cooperation Council
ICC	International Chamber of Commerce
IP	Intellectual Property
IPEA	International Preliminary Examining Authority
ISA	International Searching Authority
ISO	International Standards Organization
JPO	Japanese Patent Office
KIPO	Korean Intellectual Property Office
NGO	Non-government Organization
MFN	Most Favoured Nation
NIIP	National Institute of Industrial Property
OAPI	Organisation Africaine de la Propriété Intellectuelle
OECD	Organisation for Economic Co-operation and Development

Paris Convention	Paris Convention for the Protection of Industrial Property, 1883 as revised
PATCOM	Patent Committee
PCT	Patent Cooperation Treaty, 1970 as revised
PLT	Patent Law Treaty, 2000
PO	Patent Office
PPH	Patent Prosecution Highway
SIPO	State Intellectual Property Office of China
SMEs	Small to medium enterprises
TNCs	Transnational corporations
Trilateral Offices (or Trilaterals)	European PO, Japanese PO, US Patent and Trademark Office
TRIPS	Agreement on Trade-Related Aspects of Intellectual Property Rights, 1994
UNCTAD	United Nations Conference on Trade And Development
USPTO	United States Patent and Trademark Office
USTR	United States Trade Representative
WIPO	World Intellectual Property Organization
WTO	World Trade Organization

PREFACE

Patent office administration would strike many a person as a dull topic. In fact this is wrong, for it is an excruciatingly dull topic. Yet like many such technical topics it explains why our world is the way that it is. States need tax bureaucracies to collect taxes, otherwise they would not last long as states. Multinationals need patent offices to grant patents, otherwise they could not raise private taxes. They would have to find other ways in which to gain monopolies over medicines, chemicals, seeds and software.

The importance of the topic, along with the realization that patent offices had largely been neglected in the regulatory literature, led me to undertake the study. My focus was not on one office in particular but rather on the interaction amongst patent offices and in particular between developed and developing-country patent offices. The development effects of intellectual property rights have become a major area of study, but we do not know much about how developing-country patent offices administer the standards of patentability that arrive in their countries through various treaty processes.

Administering a patent system is one of the few areas of intellectual property over which developing countries have considerable sovereign discretion. Patent offices might be one place in which one might find developing-country resistance to the hegemony that the US, EU and Japan exercise over patent standard-setting processes. Instead, I found that developing-country patent offices were being deeply integrated into a system of patent office administration that was being led by the patent offices of the US, EU and Japan. So while developing-country negotiators would contest the standard-setting games of the US, EU and Japan in places like the World Trade Organization (WTO) and the World Intellectual Property Organization, their patent offices were closely and quietly cooperating with the patent offices of these three countries. Much of the practical impact of the patent system is better understood by looking at what happens in patent offices than in a WTO negotiating room or the language of a patent statute. The world's patent offices are participating in what one of my interviewees described as an 'invisible' process of harmonization. Driving this process are pressures and demands coming from the multinational users of the system. They will benefit from this emerging system of global patent governance.

My home base, the Regulatory Institutions Network at the Australian National University, was an ideal place in which to undertake the study. With colleagues like John Braithwaite, Valerie Braithwaite, Neil Gunningham, Peter Grabosky and Hilary Charlesworth, one never has to wander too far for insightful comment on an issue. The work of Chris Arup and William van Caenegem, as well as their friendship and support, are continuing sources of help for me. My conversations with Michael Blakeney about intellectual property, as always, gave me insights and helped me to understand the dynamics of patent administration. Luigi Palombi and Hazel Moir were always prepared to give up their time to listen to my attempts to articulate an argument. Their suggestions improved this book. My thanks also go to Dr Ian Heath, the Director General of IP Australia until his retirement in 2007. His office was a research partner in this project under the Australian Research Council's Linkage scheme. Dr Heath and the members of IP Australia were of great support to me. They helped to arrange for access to other patent offices and always met my requests for assistance and data with polite and unfailing cooperation. They will probably not agree with my analysis, but Ian Heath's view was that independent long-term research was needed. If only universities understood the research process so well. I would also like to thank the patent examiners I spoke to who helped me to understand the job. It is a very important one, for which they do not receive sufficient recognition.

My Research Associate for most of this project was Ms Cecily Stewart. She was simply the best assistant that anyone could ask for, helping to track down material, organizing data, creating wonderful PowerPoint slides and generally bringing structure to chaos.

I have dedicated this book to my wife Julie Ayling. She had to listen to too many monologues from me concerning patent office administration. Somehow she was able to feign interest. Acting beyond the call of duty she read sections of the book. Her patient and loving support enabled me to start and finish the project.

Patent offices and the global governance of knowledge

The patent ocean: Kiribati

It is a little surprising that one can apply for a patent in Kiribati. More surprising though is that there are twenty or so mainly pharmaceutical patents registered in its patent office.[1] No-one in Kiribati much cares about the few patent files languishing in a filing cabinet since, if the predictions about climate change are right, they are destined for Davey Jones' locker. Almost all of Kiribati is less than two metres above sea level and so its inhabitants are experiencing what happens when an ocean begins to rise up and wash over settled land. The furthest thing from anyone's mind on Kiribati is pharmaceutical patents and yet someone could be bothered to apply for them.

If one had to guess where one could not lodge a patent, Kiribati would have been a plausible choice. Given another guess one might opt for some deeply war-torn country such as Iraq or Afghanistan. In the case of Iraq it is a case of 'nice try, but no cigar'. Prior to the US invasion of Iraq, there was a patent law in place. After the US invasion, the Administrator of the Coalition Provisional Authority, Paul Bremer, promulgated an order that brought aspects of Iraq's patent law up to international standards.[2] Patenting activity in the Iraq Patent Office (PO) is not great.[3] The cigar is tantalizingly in reach with Afghanistan. But Afghanistan did become a member of the World Intellectual Property Organization (WIPO) in 2005[4] and since then has been working closely with WIPO on developing its laws and establishing a patent office. The Director General of

---

[1] Fiona Ey, 'Institutional Framework and Procedures Regulating Access to Pharmaceutical Products to Address Public Health Problems', Paper prepared for Commonwealth Secretariat, December 2005, 17.

[2] 'Coalition Provisional Authority Order Number 81: Patent, Industrial Design, Undisclosed Information, Integrated Circuits and Plant Variety Law', 26 April 2004. Available at www.trade.gov/static/iraq_memo81.pdf.

[3] See the entry for Iraq in Table A1 in the *World Patent Report*, 2008, WIPO, Geneva, 63.

[4] See www.wipo.int/about-ip/en/ipworldwide/pdf/af.pdf.

Afghanistan's Intellectual Property Board did get up and thank WIPO at a meeting of patent offices in 2007 in Singapore for all its assistance in helping to set up a patent office.[5]

In fact it is hard to identify a country where one cannot register a patent. Of course one can get into debates over what counts as a country for the purpose of the question. Is the Holy See a country? Whether it is or not, according to WIPO Italian patent law applies and it has an industrial property office (industrial property includes patents).[6] Even if one is brave enough to ask a rugby-loving Welshman whether Wales really is a country, the fact that Wales does not have its own patent office does not mean that it is a patent-free zone. The UK PO, which is located in Wales, issues patents for the UK.

Depending on how one defines and counts countries, there appear to be about 195 countries in the world. There are probably less than five countries where one cannot obtain a patent. Timor Leste is one such country. Some countries, such as Somalia, have a patent office, but whether it is open for business is another question. Since there are about fifty least-developed countries in the world (meaning they have a gross national income per capita of under US$750[7]) and patent law is a form of law linked to technological affluence, one might have expected it to be easy to identify countries without patent law and offices.[8] It turns out that most of the poor countries of the world have acquired patent law and patent offices as a result of processes of colonization or more recently globalization. Patent law in these countries is 'imported law' or, perhaps more accurately, imposed law.[9] For example, we will see in Chapter 10 that Kiribati acquired its patent law when it was a British colony. Similarly, the integration of African countries into the international patent framework began during colonial times. Today the only continent to have two regional patent organizations is Africa (see Chapter 10).

Once the patent institution takes hold in a country it has proved to have a viral-like resilience, reproducing itself in ever more sophisticated

---

[5] WIPO Asia-Pacific Forum of Heads of Intellectual Property Offices, Singapore, 4–6 December 2007. The author attended this meeting as an observer.

[6] See www.wipo.int/about-ip/en/ipworldwide/pdf/va.pdf.

[7] See www.un.org/special-rep/ohrlls/ldc/ldc%20criteria.htm.

[8] See www.wipo.int/ldcs/en/statistics/number_ldcs.html.

[9] The term 'imported law' comes from Nobuyuki Yasuda, 'Law and Development from the Southeast Asian Perspective: Methodology, History, and Paradigm Change' in Christoph Antons (ed.), *Law and Development in East and Southeast Asia*, Routledge Curzon, London and New York, 2003, 25, 27.

ways and in the unlikeliest places. The remarkable spread of the patent institution throughout the world provides the foundation for a global system of patent governance of the world's technological markets. The next section outlines this system of governance.

Global patent governance

The study began with the hypothesis that patent offices around the world are cooperating to integrate their administrative procedures and technical systems, thereby building a system for the global governance of knowledge. For present purposes, cooperative behaviour is behaviour aimed at facilitating some common purpose, an example being the exchange of examiners between offices in order to better understand the other office's examination procedures. Integration refers to the adoption of a system or standard by two or more offices that leads those offices to have similar work outcomes in relation to patent applications. For example, offices can be said to be integrating if they adopt the same technical systems for searching the patent and non-patent literature, if they adopt the same patent system for classifying patent applications, or if they establish a procedure for sharing or recognizing the work results of other offices.

This hypothesis was derived from the findings of an earlier, much broader study of the globalization of business regulation in more than twenty different regulatory domains that I did with John Braithwaite.[10] Amongst our conclusions were that hegemony within the world system had come to depend profoundly upon the commodification and control of abstract objects by means of intellectual property rights. Related findings were that multinationals, in particular US multinationals, had been crucial actors in re-shaping the intellectual property regime by linking it to the trade regime and that US multinationals were the most recurrently effective actors in enrolling the power of states and influential international organizations when it came to achieving their global regulatory agendas.

When it comes to the patent system, the regulatory agenda of multinationals is to have in all significant markets a set of largely uniform patent rules that make it cheap to obtain patents, that maximize the scope of patentable subject matter and that minimize state control over the use of the patented technology (see Chapter 6). Standing in the way of this agenda is

---

[10] John Braithwaite and Peter Drahos, *Global Business Regulation*, Cambridge University Press, Cambridge, 2000.

the fact that patent systems remain predominantly national institutions with a small number of regional arrangements. At the level of rules and procedures, patent harmonization has a long way to go and negotiations amongst states to harmonize patent rules have over the decades, like glaciers, only inched forward.[11] Moreover, historically states had moved very cautiously in giving up sovereignty over their patent systems, using them in various ways as tools to protect their industries and allowing for selective free-riding. Patent offices were absolutely fundamental to such state strategies because much can be hidden in the detail of administration. Given the territorial, protectionist origins of patent offices one would not have necessarily predicted the emergence of high levels of cooperation amongst them.

One way in which to progress the patent harmonization agenda is for patent offices to cooperate in the recognition of each other's work results and procedures. We will see that the gains to multinational companies of patent office cooperation are high. It follows that multinationals have strong incentives to encourage such cooperation amongst offices. As my work with John Braithwaite showed, multinational companies also have a successful track record of being able to enrol national and international organizations to meet their global regulatory goals. In the remaining chapters of this book we will see that patent offices are, through cooperation at the level of administration, helping to create a system for the global governance of knowledge. This governance system represents a private power of taxation based on the use of patents. Those best placed to use this system of governance are multinationals with large patent portfolios. In the section following this one, we will see that the taxing power of patents enables patent owners to regulate the world's technology markets. The taxing power of patents does not depend on just one patent, but large patent portfolios, as well as complementary strengths such as power over distribution networks and brand identity. Under these conditions the taxation power of patents comes into its own. Multinationals with large patent portfolios use those portfolios to constitute a private fiscal base. Through patents they build a system of private taxation of the world's technology markets. Small players, such as universities, that send their staff chasing after patents generally end up selling or licensing

---

[11] For an account of some of the problems see Susan K. Sell, *Power and Ideas: North-South Politics of Intellectual Property and Antitrust*, State University of New York Press, Albany NY, 1998. On the differences of detail see Harold C. Wegner, *Patent Harmonization*, Sweet and Maxwell, London, 1993.

their patents (usually on poor terms) because they do not have complementary strengths of branding and distribution.[12] They have patents but not a system of patent governance and so end up as cogs in other players' systems.

National and regional patent offices of developed and developing countries play a vital role in the nuts and bolts of this system of governance. In fact we will see that patent offices, at the level of technical cooperation, have been able to advance the case of global patent governance further than have states at the level of treaty negotiation. Much has been achieved in the construction of a global system of patent governance by patent offices through quiet technocratic cooperation. This governance system should not, however, be confused with the idea of a world patent. In order to better understand this system of governance the next section provides some definitional clarifications. Before moving on we should note that this patent-based governance system for knowledge is not the only one under construction. Other systems based on ideas of shared ownership of resources are much discussed these days, but patent-based governance of knowledge is arguably the most advanced in terms of a global administrative infrastructure.[13]

Definitional clarifications

There is no global patent system in the sense of a patent office to which one can apply for the grant of a single patent that will apply in all the countries of the world. Patent law remains deeply territorial. There is US patent law, Japanese patent law, South African patent law, Chinese patent law and so on. In order to get a patent in the US, for example, the United States Patent and Trademark Office (USPTO) must grant that patent. As is always the case with patent law, there are qualifications and nuances to even the most basic propositions. So, for example, in order to acquire a patent in the US one does not have to start the patent application in the USPTO.

---

[12] For the wide variations in profitability of patenting by US universities see Dennis R. Trune and Lewis N. Goslin, 'University Technology Transfer Programs: A Profit/Loss Analysis', 57 (1998) *Technological Forecasting and Social Change*, 197. For a study that shows that returns from patenting are skewed towards a small number of universities see A.D. Heher, 'Return on Investment in Innovation: Implications for Institutions and National Agencies', 31 (2006) *Journal of Technology Transfer*, 403.

[13] For an excellent survey of the politics of movements that are launching alternatives to patent-based governance see Amy Kapczynski, 'The Access to Knowledge Mobilization and the New Politics of Intellectual Property', 117 (2008) *Yale Law Journal*, 804.

Under international treaty rules one can start the application process in another office, but ultimately it is the USPTO that has to grant the patent. The deep territoriality of patent law also has qualifications since there are regional arrangements for the grant of patents in some parts of the world. The most well known of these arrangements is the one constituted by the European Patent Convention (EPC). However, these regional arrangements for the most part build on the national territoriality of patents. The European Patent Office (EPO), for example, grants what is termed a European patent, but under the EPC that patent has the effect of being a national patent in contracting states.[14] Enforcement under the EPC system is left to national courts.

Even though one cannot speak of a global patent system in the legal sense of a single granted patent that applies in all the jurisdictions of the world, one can speak of the globalization of patent systems to refer to the fact that more and more countries have or are in the process of acquiring a national patent system. The phrase *patent system* is used to refer to patent law as administered by various actors such as patent offices, courts and the patent attorney profession. The *patent law* of a country is made up of legislation (usually a patent statute or code), including various forms of delegated legislation, and the interpretation of that legislation by authoritative bodies (these may include courts, tribunals, patent offices etc.). The national patent law of countries has been the subject of international coordination and harmonization through international agreements. The term *international patent framework* will be used here to refer to the multilateral treaties and agreements that deal with patents, the most important of these being the Paris Convention for the Protection of Industrial Property, 1883 (Paris Convention), the Patent Cooperation Treaty, 1970 (PCT) and the Agreement on Trade-Related Aspects of Intellectual Property Rights, 1994 (TRIPS). Included in the international patent framework are also regional treaties such as the EPC along with hundreds of bilateral agreements (for example, free trade agreements (FTAs)) that deal with intellectual property standards, including patents.[15] One might also use the term *international patent regime* to refer to the various treaties and agreements, but the term *regime* comes out of a set of theoretical debates in international relations and so for the most part the more descriptive term *international*

[14] See Article 2 of the European Patent Convention.
[15] On the role of those bilateral agreements see Peter Drahos, 'BITS and BIPS: Bilateralism in Intellectual Property', 4 (2001) *Journal of World Intellectual Property*, 791.

patent framework will be used. The term *patent institution* follows the economist's use of the term institution and simply refers to a discrete set of rules that shape the responses and behaviour of interacting human beings in particular contexts.[16] Patent system and patent institution in this book function as interchangeable terms, the use of institution providing a convenient link to the literature on the importance of institutions to economic progress.

Patents as private taxation

Following Macaulay's suggestion in 1841 that copyright is a 'tax on readers', one might also say that patents are a tax on consumers of technology.[17] In much the same way that the category of readers includes potential authors, consumers also includes innovators. This leads to an ancillary claim that patents are a tax on innovators.

Conceiving of patents as a form of private tax is generally useful because it brings the costs of patents sharply into focus. Characterizing the patent monopoly as a private property right has a certain cloaking effect when it comes to understanding the real-world cost of patents. The ideological appeal of property rights can sometimes obscure the cost issue when it comes to making decisions about whether or not to strengthen intellectual property rights. Arguments for raising taxes on the other hand rarely escape notice or scrutiny. Thinking about intellectual property rights as a form of tax brings into obvious sight the possibility that, just as one can have too many taxes, one can have too much intellectual property. It also leads into a discussion about the compliance burden generated by this private system of taxation. John Thomas nicely captures its scale in the US by pointing out that in 2000 the US government issued about 83,000 pages of regulations, guidelines etc. in its Federal Register, whereas the USPTO in its *Official Gazette* was generating about 40,000 pages per week, essentially generating in two weeks what the rest of the

---

[16] See Douglass C. North, *Institutions, Institutional Change and Economic Performance*, Cambridge University Press, Cambridge, 1990, 3.

[17] For the quote and its context see Mark Rose, 'Nine-Tenths of the Law: the English Copyright Debates and the Rhetoric of the Public Domain', 66 (2003) *Law and Contemporary Problems*, 75, 83. In nineteenth-century debates over the patent system, some of those against the system argued that patents were a tax on manufacturers. See Moureen Coulter, *Property in Ideas: The Patent Question in Mid-Victorian Britain*, Thomas Jefferson University Press, Kirksville, Missouri, 1991, 89–90.

US government generated in a year.[18] This staggering statistic captures another point about patent offices. They are massive sources of administrative regulation of the economy.

The reason for characterizing patents as a form of tax is not, however, to begin discussion about the costs and benefits of the patent system but rather to help explain why large corporations take so keen an interest in the reform of patent office administration. Each time a patent office grants a patent, in effect, it issues a right to collect taxes. This right may take the form of a licensing agreement in which a licensee agrees to pay royalties or in the form of the monopoly price that the patent owner is able to charge consumers. Broadly speaking, states emerge when sovereigns are able to enclose resources within a territorial boundary and, through law, tax those resources. The use of taxes represents the last stage of the fiscal evolution of the state, an evolution in which the use of monopolies to raise revenue features prominently.[19] States acting rationally will seek to enclose as many resources as possible in order to create a large fiscal base. Preserving the integrity of their fiscal base is one of the primary goals of modern states. Multinationals operating in the global knowledge economy face a situation not dissimilar to states. Patent portfolios offer a means of enclosing knowledge assets for potential exploitation. A patent gives a private right of command over a resource that takes the form of a bundle of rights which when exercised by the patent owner creates a stream of private revenue. The size of the revenue will be determined by various factors including demand for the technology and the availability of substitutes.

Patents perform a double function in terms of the fiscal base of multinationals. They help to define the scope of the fiscal base and at the same time they create the possibility of revenue streams from that base. So, for example, it matters profoundly to pharmaceutical multinationals whether chemical compounds are part of patentable subject matter. Patents do not just define the scope of a multinational's fiscal base through patentable subject matter definitions, but also through territorial reach. A country that did not have a patent law would not form part of a multinational's private taxation system since a company could not lodge patents there. It would have no private right of taxation that was

---

[18] John R. Thomas, 'The Responsibility of the Rulemaker: Comparative Approaches to Patent Administration Reform', 17 (2002) *Berkeley Technology Law Journal*, 727, 740.

[19] On the history of the use of state monopolies for revenue raising purposes see C.F. Bastable, 'Taxation Through Monopoly', 1 (1891) *The Economic Journal*, 307.

backed by patent law and the courts. For multinationals there is a strong incentive to ensure that all countries have a patent system because it means that those countries become part of the patent-based system of taxation, as well as reducing the number of countries that can in this private system of taxation play the role of patent havens. In a world where capital and scientific skill are highly mobile there is some chance, admittedly small, that a small island country might end up in the role of a patent haven. Large pharmaceutical companies have probably never given much thought to registering their patents in Malta, but this has seen at least one generic company build a large plant there in order to take advantage of the pharmaceutical patent free environment.[20] Large pharmaceutical companies do not like this kind of surprise. This, in part, helps to explain why even the smallest countries in the world are being integrated into a system of patent governance. Malta is now a member of the EPC.

Understanding the global patent regime as a system of private taxation also enables us to see more clearly the importance of patent offices to multinationals. In essence, a system of private taxation, just like a system of public taxation, depends on massive bureaucracy. The global integration of patent offices is creating just such a bureaucracy. To begin with, it is important that a country has a patent office that issues patents for that country. A patent law without a patent office is of little use to companies since without a patent office there would be noone to issue the patents, i.e. the instruments of private taxation. A country need not have a national office as long as there is an office that issues a patent for the territory of that country. In much the same way that sovereign states have automated the collection of taxes, so too multinationals as private sovereigns have sought a high degree of regulatory automation of the patent application process. Instead of complex and distinctive national procedures of application, multinationals want simple and common application procedures (see, for example, the position of the Industry Trilateral described in Chapter 6). We will also see that multinationals want a multilateral approach to patent office administration in which, for instance, the examination work of one office is used or recognized by other offices leading to a saving of work and time by these other offices. There is some irony in this, for in the area of public taxation, multinationals have been more supportive of bilateral

---

[20] See 'Malta's lack of pharma patents seemed positive', www.maltamedia.com/artman2/publish/financial/article_2189.shtml.

models of state taxation in which states are more likely to compete against each other to the benefit of multinationals.[21]

Collective action, co-evolution and diffusion: explaining the changes in patent office administration

The globalization of the patent institution is an example of regulatory globalization. One explanation for processes of regulatory globalization, an explanation that John Braithwaite and I have advanced, is that globalization is best understood in terms of actors using mechanisms at their disposal to support some principles of regulation and to oppose others. Regulatory globalization becomes a contest of principles in which there are winners and losers. By way of example, states or multinationals with large trade gains from intellectual property have supported the principle of national treatment and the principle of harmonization (in the direction of higher standards) while net importers of intellectual property have sought to minimize the operation of these principles using the principle of state sovereignty. Economic coercion, such as the use of threats of trade sanctions, has been a dominant mechanism deployed by powerful coalitions of the US and multinational companies.[22]

The patent institution is in practical terms a fully globalized (but not harmonized) institution. At the level of principle, a deep convergence has occurred in patent law. TRIPS requires its members to recognize patents for inventions that are new, inventive and have industrial application.[23] But principles are in their nature abstract and open-ended and can through interpretation be adapted to suit local circumstances and context. TRIPS, for example, does not define what is invention, meaning that there is some scope for national interpretation. Similarly, it does not define a level of inventiveness, it merely requires inventiveness for the purposes of patentability. Even more importantly, TRIPS says virtually nothing about how a country is to administer its patent system. It does not require or prohibit, for example, a system of pre-grant opposition. It leaves it open to a country to have a system of deferred or mandatory examination of patent applications. At the level of interpretation of principles and in the

---

[21] Braithwaite and Drahos, *Global Business Regulation*, 106–9.
[22] Peter Drahos with John Braithwaite, *Information Feudalism*, Earthscan, London, 2002, Ch. 6.
[23] Article 27.1.

way that one runs a system of patent administration, the principle of state sovereignty remains strong.

For actors that have been on the losing end of contests of principles, sovereignty over patent administration offers a chance to re-contest the outcome or to at least adapt the winning principles at the national level in ways that minimize the costs. Along similar lines, the winners in the global regulatory contests cannot rest on their laurels. They have to ensure that the interpretive possibilities of principles are not used to create a set of rules that quietly rob them of a victory that was gained at the level of principles. For example, India in its patent law has enacted a definition of patentable subject matter that mitigates some of the consequences of having to recognize under TRIPS the patentability of pharmaceutical products (see Chapter 7). Of course, this definition itself has to be interpreted. This is one example of a much broader truth about patent offices – they are crucial sites of interpretation of patent law. It is a patent examiner who will first make interpretive judgements about whether the patent application meets standards of novelty, inventiveness and utility, and whether it has sufficiently disclosed the invention to the public. In most cases the examiner's judgement is also the last judgement because only a tiny fraction of patent cases end up being finally decided by a court. In the US the average patent litigation rate is a little less than 2% and in European countries it is about 1%.[24] Many patent cases, however, are settled by the parties prior to judgement.[25] It is the national courts that decide the patent law of a country, but patent offices have to turn that law into bureaucratic routines of decision-making in order to process the thousands of patent applications that they receive each year. What happens in patent offices around the world is just as important to the multinational users of the patent system as what happens in the courts.

[24] See Stuart J. H. Graham, Bronwyn H. Hall, Dietmar Harhoff and, David C. Mowery, 'Patent Quality Control: A Comparison of U.S. Patent Re-examinations and European Patent Oppositions' in Wesley M. Cohen and Stephen A. Merrill (eds.), *Patents in the Knowledge-Based Economy*, National Academies Press, Washington DC, 2003, 74, 89. Lanjouw and Schankerman find an average litigation rate of 19 suits per 1,000 patents. Jean O. Lanjouw and Mark Schankerman, 'Enforcement of Patent Rights in the United States' in Wesley M. Cohen and Stephen A. Merrill (eds.), *Patents in the Knowledge-Based Economy*, National Academies Press, Washington DC, 2003, 145, 146.

[25] Kesan and Ball find that about 80% of patent cases settle. See Jay P. Kesan and Gwendolyn G. Ball, 'How are Patent Cases Resolved? An Empirical Examination of the Adjudication and Settlement of Patent Disputes', University of Illinois College of Law, Law and Economics Working Papers, Paper 52, 2006, 1, 18.

Summarizing the argument so far we have seen that patents are building blocks that can be used to construct a system of private taxation, a system that can, by virtue of the spread of the patent institution, be a genuinely global system. Patent offices are critical to this system because they decide the fate of patent applications. The logic of collective action would lead to the prediction that those firms with the most to gain from this patent governance of knowledge would organize to influence patent offices in directions that supported the evolution of this governance.[26] Collective action is more likely to emerge where there are concentrated interests that will gain a benefit from such action, because concentrated interests face lower costs of organization and greater individual gains. Diffuse interests face the reverse problem.

Is there evidence of concentrated interests when it comes to patent systems? One way in which to answer this question is to investigate the patterns of ownership of patents in major patenting countries. For example, is it the case that a few companies own many patents or is patent ownership very widely spread? In a recent analysis Hazel Moir points out that somewhat unexpectedly there is little work on this issue.[27] Her own analysis suggests a concentration of ownership. Comparing US and Australian patent ownership data she points out that for the period 1990–2001 the top 100 corporate patenters in the US owned 35% of the patents and in Australia the top 100 owned 34%.[28] Her study also helps to corroborate the studies that show that TRIPS was the product of collective action by multinational owners of intellectual property rights.[29] For example, thirteen multinationals were intimately involved in the business pressure and lobbying that led to TRIPS (which included but was not confined to patents). Ten of these companies were on the major patenters list in the US and four were companies that patented heavily in both the US and Australia during this period. There are other bits of evidence that

[26] Mancur Olson, *The Logic of Collective Action*, Harvard University Press, Cambridge, 1965.

[27] Hazel V. J. Moir, 'Who Benefits? An Empirical Analysis of Australian and US Patent Ownwership', Centre for the Governance of Knowledge and Development, Working Paper October 2008, available at http://cgkd.anu.edu.au/menus/workingpapers.php.

[28] Hazel V. J. Moir, 'Who Benefits? An Empirical Analysis of Australian and US Patent Ownwership', Centre for the Governance of Knowledge and Development, Working Paper October 2008, 11.

[29] Peter Drahos, 'Global Property Rights in Information: The Story of TRIPS at the GATT', 13 (1995) *Prometheus*, 6; Drahos with Braithwaite, *Information Feudalism*; Susan Sell, *Private Power, Public Law: The Globalization of Intellectual Property Rights*, Cambridge University Press, Cambridge, 2003.

suggest that patent ownership is concentrated. When the USPTO releases its table of top ten US universities obtaining patents the total is about 1,100, a number that any one of the top ten corporate patenters exceeds and the top corporate patenter usually triples.[30]

One of the findings of the fieldwork was that patent offices do not spend a lot of time drawing attention to the concentration of ownership of patents. When I put it to offices that it was a case of a few owning many patents with the rest forming a long tail they agreed that this was the pattern. As to why this was not made more evident from the endless statistics that are published on patents, the clearest answer came from the German PO to the effect that it was not the most politically saleable feature of the patent system. The German PO was the only office to admit without prompting the dominance of the patent system by a few large corporations. One can see why patent offices are reluctant to talk about this issue. Why advertise the fact, especially if you are the patent office of a developing or midsize developed country, that you spend most of your time granting lots of patent monopolies to a small group of mainly foreign multinationals? National patent offices would love to see more small to medium enterprises (SMEs) using the patent system, but these enterprises have to deal with the cost and complexity of the system.[31] For patent offices the use of the patent system by SMEs remains disappointingly low (but may be at an efficient level for those enterprises given alternative options such as trade secrets).[32] So patent offices keep plugging away trying to sell the virtues of the patent system to SMEs, or as the Austrian PO so nicely put it,

---

[30] See, for 2002, www.uspto.gov/web/offices/com/speeches/03–09.htm for the top ten universities and www.uspto.gov/web/offices/com/speeches/04–01.htm for the top ten patenters.

[31] For an analysis in the UK context see Stuart Macdonald, 'Exploring the Hidden Costs of Patents' in Peter Drahos and Ruth Mayne (eds.) *Global Intellectual Property Rights*, Palgrave Macmillan, Hampshire and NY, 2002, 13. For a comprehensive discussion of the literature and an analysis of the Australian context see 'Factors Affecting the Use of Intellectual Property (IP) Protection by Small and Medium Enterprises (SMEs) in Australia', A Report for the Commonwealth Department of Industry, Innovation and Resources, Intellectual Property Research Institute of Australia (IPRIA), April 2005, available at www.innovation.gov.au/Documents/IPprotectionbysmes20050725153926.pdf.

[32] See, for example, 'Utilisation of Patent Protection in Europe: Representative Survey Carried Out on Behalf of the European Patent Office, Munich', 17 (1995) *World Patent Information*, 100. The European Commission takes the view that much more can be done to encourage SMEs to use the patent system. See Commission of the European Communities, 'Enhancing the patent system in Europe', COM (2007) 165 final, Brussels, 3.4.2007.

helping those stuck in the long tail of owning a few patents 'to transition' to large-scale ownership.

Another incentive for collective action might come from those owning the most valuable patents, a group which may or may not overlap with the group that owns the most patents. Only a comparatively small number of patents are valuable in revenue terms.[33] One possibility is that these valuable patents are held by the relatively small number of players that can afford large patent portfolios. There may also be a sectoral bias here. Bessen and Meurer suggest that the economic benefits of patents fall to a few firms in the chemical and pharmaceutical industries: 'Over one-half of the value of worldwide patents accrues to a small number of large pharmaceutical firms; over two-thirds accrues to firms in the chemical and pharmaceutical industries'.[34]

One powerful interest group facing patent offices, then, is a small group of multinationals which patent frequently and hold valuable patents. This is not the only interest group that patent offices have to confront. The patent attorneys that represent inventors have their own interests and concerns, in part to do with ensuring that patent office reforms do not rob them of their lucrative national practices. Patent attorneys live in fear of deregulation. Small companies from sectors such as biotechnology or information technology that cannot afford to build patent portfolios on the scale of IBM, but which nevertheless have a patenting strategy, form another type of interest group. There is a complex interest group politics that surrounds patent office administration made up of corporate and non-corporate players, both large and small. But paying too much attention to this complexity is not seeing the forest for the trees. Where the forest lies is in the patenting activity of a comparatively few multinationals that dominate the patent system both in terms of the global ownership of patents and the economic benefits of ownership. As we noted earlier, this is not something to which patent offices by and large want to admit. As just mentioned it was only the German PO that spoke about this issue and that went on to observe that the real domination of the system by multinationals should be made much more transparent to the

---

[33] F.M. Scherer and Dietmar Harhoff, 'Technology Policy for a World of Skew-distributed Outcomes', 29 (2000) *Research Policy*, 559.

[34] James Bessen and Michael J. Meurer, *Patent Failure: How Judges, Bureaucrats, and Lawyers Put Innovators at Risk*, Princeton University Press, Princeton and Oxford, 2008, 109.

public.[35] Discussion of the relevance of the system to small and medium enterprises is to draw a veil of illusion over the real nature of the system. It is a small group of multinationals that have had the greatest hand in the globalization of the patent institution and it is they that take a deep interest in the way that patent offices administer their respective national systems. It is to their agendas that one has to look in order to explain the emerging system of global patent governance.

Regulatory globalization and the logic of collective action can explain why actors might organize and how they can achieve goals of global regulatory transformation. But these two theories do not explain the persistence of a patent institution over time. The patent system is a socio-economic institution that has its origins in the early medieval period. It has persisted over the centuries through great technological and social transformations such as the industrial revolution and the successive information technology revolutions of the twentieth century. One theoretical approach that focuses on the resilience of institutions over time is a co-evolutionary explanation and model of change. The idea that different groups of organisms interact in a process of reciprocal influence that generates change for both (plants increase their toxicity and insects adapt to the new level) has also been applied to explain the evolution of institutions.[36]

A theory of co-evolution that takes in multiple relationships such as the one that Johann Murmann, for example, develops in order to explain the loss of leadership of the synthetic dye industry by Britain and France to Germany is not attempted here.[37] But for present purposes it is important to identify the co-evolutionary relationship that exists between patent offices and the regular multinational users of the patent system, because that relationship helps to explain the persistence of the patent institution over time and, as we will see, the changes in patent administration. A co-evolutionary relationship is one in which two actors confer advantages on each other that assist them in their competitive struggles with others.[38]

---

[35] The German PO's Annual Report 2007 reports that of the roughly 12,000 patent applicants from Germany, 3.6% accounted for 60% of the applications. See Annual Report 2007, 17.

[36] See generally Elizabeth Garnsey and James McGlade (eds.), *Complexity and Co-Evolution: Continuity and Change in Socio-Economic Systems*, Edward Elgar, Cheltenham, UK, 2006.

[37] J. P. Murmann, *Knowledge and Competitive Advantage: The Coevolution of Firms, Technology, and National Institutions*, Cambridge University Press, Cambridge, 2003.

[38] This is along the lines of Murmann's definition. See Murmann, *Knowledge and Competitive Advantage*, p. 22.

Patent offices are a key actor within the patent system. They grant patents. As the succeeding chapters of this book make clear they can, through guidelines and interpretation, change or modify the operation of the patent system. The willingness of patent offices to adapt the patent system has its origins in the interaction between offices and their clients, with large industrial users of the system being a dominant influence in those interactions. The large patent offices with their thousands of employees interact on a daily basis with many thousands of patent applicants. Their interactions and communications are of a scale and regularity that courts and legislatures cannot rival. Through constant communication and exchange of information with their clients, patent offices come to understand their needs and so exercise their administrative discretion and power in ways that respond to those needs. In Chapter 2 we will see the importance to various industrial actors of patent offices recognizing particular claiming formats. The advantages to patent offices of this co-evolutionary relationship lie in an understanding of the patent office business model that is described in the next section.

The relationship between patent offices and the large industrial users of their services is a part of a broader national institutional and regulatory dynamic involving many other actors. While it is a dominant relationship that confers advantages upon both it is no guarantee of success in competitive struggles. For example, patent offices have done much to assist pharmaceutical multinationals by allowing claiming formats for pharmaceuticals products, but if states have strong systems of pharmaceutical price regulation in place the power of those multinationals to extract patent rents from those states will be reduced.

The co-evolutionary approach to institutional development hooks up with explanations of global regulatory capitalism that place the emphasis on diffusion processes in which actors learn by following others. David Levi-Faur has argued that horizontal mechanisms based on observation and learning by actors having to confront common regulatory problems in a world of interdependency and integrated markets can help to explain the patterns in global regulatory capitalism.[39] Horizontal diffusion mechanisms form an important part of the explanatory story for the rise and spread of patent offices in European countries. For example, those in the nineteenth-century UK who were interested in reforming patent

[39] David Levi-Faur, 'The Global Diffusion of Regulatory Capitalism' in David Levi-Faur and Jacint Jordana (eds.), *The Rise of Regulatory Capitalism: The Global Diffusion of a New Order*, 598 (2005) *The Annals of the American Academy of Political and Social Science*, 12.

administration looked to the experience of the US with its patent office, the office which had had the longest experience of any office in examining patents (see Chapter 3). Culture and history nudged learning along certain pathways. Countries that had acquired the French, English or German system of patent administration were slow to deviate from it. Horizontal processes of learning, however, do not explain the emergence of TRIPS. A big lever of economic coercion in the form of trade threats was pulled by a hegemonic power acting in concert with other powerful allies. Once developing countries realized that they would have to implement TRIPS as part of their WTO obligations, different kinds of diffusion processes began to operate in the case of patent office administration. Borrowing Levi-Faur's typology, there were top-down processes involving international organizations such as WIPO that saw patent models exported to some developing countries, bottom-up processes in which domestic interest group politics adjusted the received patent office model to better suit a local context (India, we will see, provides an example of this bottom-up process), as well as horizontal processes of learning and reciprocal coordination among the big developed-country offices (these processes explain the emergence of the Trilateral Offices of Europe, Japan and the US: see Chapter 6). In all this, succeeding generations of actors came to national patent institutions that had been co-evolving with national and then global industries, especially the chemical and pharmaceutical industries from the nineteenth century onwards. Each of these densely formed national patent institutions, acting with the invisibility of gravity, helped to shape the beliefs of new generations of actor groups about their opportunities within the institution to make adjustments to it that would bring them gains.

Explaining the changes in patent offices rests on an understanding of their co-evolutionary history and where they have featured in the sequences of actor-initiated mechanisms that operate in the globalization of regulation. Was the office an object of an actor-initiated mechanism (for example, the country was the subject of trade threats) or was it an initiator of a mechanism (for example, the provider of technical solutions in a top-down process of diffusion)? If the former, was the patent office part of a broader set of national institutions that had the capacity to respond with a counter-modelling strategy that regulated the effects of imposed law and models? India and China have that kind of capacity. Kiribati does not. Though whether actors in countries have the imagination and courage to develop bold models of resistance, ones that have an influence beyond the shores of their conception, is another question. We come back to the gravitational pull of co-evolution. The patent institution, more than most institutions, has functioned in the manner of a heavy dead hand from the past, weighing down upon actors seeking to embrace new ways of innovation.

Finally, the co-evolutionary processes within the patent system also ended up converging with ideological shifts within states over the direction of the general reform of public service administration. These shifts have brought great changes to public administration in many developed countries over the last three decades. In the next section we will see that patent offices have emerged from these reforms organizationally transformed.

Patent offices: the business model approach

Within Europe most patent offices begin life as part of a government bureaucracy, with the functions of processing patent applications and registering patents and collecting fees for their services (see Chapter 3). The functions of patent offices today are much the same as they were in the nineteenth century. They continue to process patent applications and register patents. As one would expect, patent offices have been part of organizational transformations and restructurings that have occurred in all governmental bureaucracies around the world. Broadly speaking, for some patent offices the result has been to achieve more independence. They have become independent governmental agencies, allowed to keep some or all of the fees that they collect rather than having to return those fees to general revenue. This was more or less true for all the offices interviewed, with some developing-country offices such as the Indonesian PO working towards that goal. The Banks Committee, which conducted a review of the British patent system that reported in 1970, noted that most patent offices around the world operated on the basis that the fees collected should more or less meet the cost of patent office services.[40] Federico in a 1954 survey showed that some offices were able to generate modest surpluses for their governments.[41] Many patent offices today would say that they continue to operate on a cost recovery basis, but because many of them have become self-funding their perception of what costs they have to recover has probably also changed.

---

[40] 'The British Patent System: Report of the Committee to Examine the Patent System and Patent Law (Chairman M A L Banks Esq)', Her Majesty's Stationery Office, London, 1970, 59.

[41] P. J. Federico, 'Renewal Fees and Other Patent Fees in Foreign Countries', 36 (1954), *Journal of the Patent Office Society*, 827, 848.

How cost recovery is implemented through fee structure is another matter. In the case of the British PO, the Banks Committee pointed out that the strategy was to make entry into the patent system cheap (the application fee at that time was one pound) and to recover the actual costs of searching and examining the patent application through annual renewal fees. Federico's 1954 survey showed that the system of annual patent fees was being used by most major patenting countries.[42] The US and Canada were at the time of his survey the only two major patenting countries that did not have a system of patent renewal fees.[43] At the time of the Banks Committee, renewal fees contributed about 66% of the costs of the British PO, with 19% coming from pre-grant fees.[44]

It remains true today that renewal fees for patents remain the single most important source of income for patent offices. It is also true that patent offices keep the costs of entry into the system low and look to recover their costs of operation through their renewal stream of revenue. Most of the developed-country offices I spoke to indicated that the initial application fee did not fully cover their costs in processing an application for grant. At the EPO interview, for example, the fees for search and examination were said to represent about 30% of the EPO's real costs. At the UK PO interview the fee structure was described as one of 'backend loading' in which it took about 12 years to recover the cost of search and examination. It follows that under this kind of model POs have to ensure that a significant number of patent applications make it to grant, otherwise there will not be enough of a renewal stream of income. Patent searches and examinations that do not lead to grants represent losses for an office.

Another important fact that patent offices must contend with in terms of their business model is that many patent owners decide that a patent is not worth renewing. Patent renewal data is country specific. But one big trend is that many patents do not make it to full term. For example, in the US about 45% of patents are allowed to lapse in the second stage of renewal (the end of the seventh year) and in France the data shows that about 50% of patents do not make it to the tenth year.[45] All patent offices

[42] Ibid., 827.
[43] This has changed. The US began applying renewal fees to granted patents for applications filed on or after 12 December 1980. See 35 U.S.C. 41(b). The Canadian PO also charges renewal fees.
[44] 'The British Patent System', 59.
[45] For the US see Stephen A. Merrill, Richard C. Levin, and Mark B. Myers, (eds), *A Patent System for the 21st Century*, National Academies Press, Washington, 2004, 31; and for France, see Mark Schankerman, 'How valuable is patent protection? Estimates by technology field', 29 (1998) *Rand Journal of Economics*, 77, 81–5.

have to take the rate of lack of renewal of patents into account. If they issue a small number of patents, using, for example, a much more stringent test of inventiveness, they will have to contend with a lower income.

There are economic arguments for using patent renewal fees much more robustly to provide incentives to firms that do R&D and to discourage those that do not from using the patent system.[46] But the politics of patent fees for the time being trumps efficiency arguments. Patent offices do raise fees, but since the nineteenth century the cost of patenting has fallen quite dramatically in real terms (see Chapter 3). Patent offices remain committed to the philosophy of cheap and easy entry into the system. This in turn has helped to produce large numbers of patent applications, with all the world's major offices having backlogs of patent applications in the hundreds of thousands. While patent offices will play around with using fees in an attempt to control, for example, the number of claims in a patent application, the use of very large fees as a regulatory instrument remains blocked by the strength of industry lobbies. Still, it was clear from the interviews that at least some patent offices saw potential in using fees to help stop the gaming of the system and to obtain better cooperation from the patent attorneys.

At the same time as patent offices have found ways to cooperate in order to solve their backlog problems, they also find themselves operating in an environment in which they are potential competitors. If the work of patent offices is broken up into three simple parts: (1) searching the patent and non-patent literature, (2) examining the patent application, and then (3) granting and maintaining the patent, it is in the first two stages that we can see competition beginning to increase. The great volume of patent applications and grants in the world (about 1.66 million applications were filed worldwide in 2005[47]) has generated a demand for patent searching and so patent offices have developed search services that they offer on a commercial basis. A market in examination services is also emerging. For example, some countries, Singapore being an example, have decided to outsource the examination of patents to other offices. In Singapore's case, the patent offices of Australia, Austria and Denmark have taken on this work. For the Singaporean office the use of these three offices provides some price competition, especially since there are other offices to which Singapore can outsource. The interviews revealed that Singapore was

---

[46] Francesca Cornelli and Mark Schankerman, 'Patent Renewals and R&D Incentives', 30 (1999) *RAND Journal of Economics*, 197.

[47] *WIPO Patent Report 2007*, WIPO, Geneva, 10.

happy with its arrangement. Similarly, some of the cooperative measures that are being put in place by offices to help them deal with workload problems may well end up creating a common platform on which they will have to compete. For example, under the PCT an international application has to be processed by an International Searching Authority (ISA), which is usually a national patent office that has been granted this status.[48] More than one ISA may be competent to do the work in relation to an international application that is received by a national patent office acting as a receiving office under the PCT system because the receiving office has agreed to more than one ISA being able to search and examine that international application. For example, US citizens and residents can elect to use the Korean Intellectual Property Office (KIPO) as an ISA for PCT applications filed in the USPTO. Given the backlog in the USPTO, this kind of cooperative arrangement makes sense, but it also shows that the PCT framework offers the basis for more direct competition amongst patent offices that are ISAs. Under present arrangements the ISAs fix and keep the search fee they charge for their search services under the PCT.[49] For 2009, the search fee ranged from around US$250 to about US$2,100.[50]

Worth noting at this point is that it is not only patent offices that make their living from administering the patent system. The PCT is administered by the International Bureau and under the PCT this means the International Bureau of WIPO.[51] Under the PCT fee system, the international filing fee goes to the International Bureau (1,330 Swiss Francs in 2009).[52] If one looks at WIPO's income from its various registration systems for 1998 to 2005 its PCT income accounts for about 70% of its total income.[53] WIPO is not just a crucial pro-patent ideological node in the international patent framework. It is also a wealthy node, one from which developing-country patent offices seek resources (see Chapter 10).

Market pressures on patent offices are only just beginning to emerge. A truly competitive system will emerge when all the world's major patent offices agree to the principle of mutual recognition when it comes to grant. This would mean that a granted patent in one office would be recognized

[48] Article 16 of the PCT.
[49] See paragraph 197 of the PCT Applicant's Guide available at www.wipo.int/pct/en/.
[50] See the PCT Fees Table at www.wipo.int/export/sites/www/pct/en/fees.pdf.
[51] See Article 2 of the PCT.
[52] See paragraph 197 of the PCT Applicant's Guide available at www.wipo.int/pct/en/.
[53] The annual reports for this period are available from WIPO at www.wipo.int/about-wipo/en/report.html.

by other offices in relation to applications for the same invention. Mutual recognition is a principle for which some European patent offices in particular have very little enthusiasm. The danger is that the principle might turn patent offices into re-registration offices, the substantive decision about grant being made offshore. For the time being, offices are focussed more on finding ways to exploit each other's work without binding themselves to the results of that work. The upshot is that state sovereignty continues to constrain the filing strategies of patent applicants. Some states for reasons of national security create special procedures around the filing abroad of applications on technologies that have been first invented in their territories or invented by their citizens.[54]

For the time being, patent offices do not operate as direct competitors in a market. The territorial nature of patent law and its procedural complexities create too many distortions to direct competition. Even if patent offices are not, at least for the time being, direct competitors, they are adopting a market rationality about their operations. The public service of all Western states has since the 1980s been the subject of seemingly endless cycles of reform by governments using the tools of 'privatization, marketization, managerialism, decentralization and agentification'.[55] One effect is that market rationalities are to be found everywhere in the public service of all Western states and increasingly non-Western states, including patent offices.[56] A market rationality was perhaps more likely to take hold in patent offices than in other parts of the public service as patent offices, since their emergence in the nineteenth century, have always provided a highly specialized service to a clearly identifiable group for a fee. The principle of fee for service has always been practised by states in the context of patents. The debates that have existed from time to time have been over the level of fees, who should keep the fees and the cross subsidies that should be met from those fees.

The ideological fashions of public service reform have left two linked cultural marks on patent offices in Western states. The first is that patent offices today, like many other parts of the public service, operate with a

---

[54] The US has a foreign filing license scheme with civil and criminal sanctions attached if applicants for foreign patents fail to obtain a license from the USPTO for an invention that was made in the US. See 35 U.S.C. 184. The USPTO generates foreign filing permission through its official receipt of filing system. India also has a foreign filing procedure. See section 39 of the Indian Patents Act.

[55] Tony Butcher, 'Modernizing civil services: an era of reform' in Tony Butcher and Andrew Massey (eds), *Modernizing Civil Services*, Edward Elgar, Cheltenham, UK, 2003, 1.

[56] See generally Donald F. Kettl, *The Global Public Management Revolution: A Report on the Transformation of Governance*, Brookings Institution Press, Washington, D.C. 2000.

client focus. Adopting a client focus has become one of the major features of public service professionalism in OECD countries over the last couple of decades.[57] Seeing applicants for patent monopolies as clients leads naturally to a focus on matters like the quality of the service to the client, the responsiveness of the service provider to the needs/demands of the client, the efficiency of the service and the price of the service. In order to improve service quality, governments have encouraged the transfer of private management technologies into the public sector.[58] Patent offices were always likely to be happy hunting grounds for the new public sector managerialists because the work of examiners in processing the stages of a patent application easily lends itself to measurement and quantification and therefore to quotas and targets. In all the major patent offices today performance measurement is a basic tool of management along with some performance reward schemes. Patent offices rush to adopt systems of performance management like the Balanced Scorecard system. As we will see, this private sector management ideology drives out of patent offices a sense of their public responsibilities under the patent social contract.

Along with the introduction of management techniques, patent offices have also followed another broad trend in public service reform in which governments have created semi-autonomous agencies to implement policy. During Thatcher's reign in the UK some bureaucracies were turned into agencies and allowed greater control over resources in exchange for agreeing to meet specified outputs.[59] In the US, the Clinton–Gore Administration created a long wave of reform of government administration through its National Performance Review of 1993, in which Gore promised government that 'works better and costs less'.[60] This, as the report made clear, meant becoming more like a business.

Over time the patent offices in many Western states as well as developing countries have assumed agency status with greater control over their own budgets. IP Australia, which has responsibility for patents, is an independent agency that reports directly to the Minister of the Department of Innovation, Industry, Science and Research. The USPTO is a federal agency within the Department of Commerce that since 1991 has been fully fee funded. In 2005 a report of the National Academy of

---

[57] David Shand and Morten Arnberg, 'Background Paper' in *Responsive Government: Service Quality Initiatives*, OECD, Paris, 1996, 15, 19.
[58] Butcher, 'Modernizing Civil Services: An Era of Reform'.
[59] Kettl, *The Global Public Management Revolution*, 13.
[60] See 'From Red Tape to Results: Creating a Government that Works Better and Costs Less', www.ibiblio.org/npr/npintro.html.

Public Administration, after observing that the USPTO must be able to function like a business, recommended that it be turned into a wholly owned government corporation.[61] The UK PO is an Executive Agency of the Department of Innovation, Universities and Skills. Financially, it operates as a trading fund and has to meet its future investments from its fee income. The quote from one of its annual reports below captures what is true of many patent offices in Western states – they have become businesses with a need to manage all the risks of business:

> As the Patent Office is entirely dependent on customers and stakeholder demand we cannot be complacent about our income and must continually look to add value for our customers.[62]

Patent offices, generally in Europe, are placing more emphasis on developing commercial services such as the low-cost fast-search service provided by the Austrian PO. The subcontracting of work by one PO to another, something we noted above, is also part of the patent office business in Europe. The Danish PO, for example, does work for the UK PO as well as for Iceland and Turkey.[63] Patent offices also seek the insignia of modern business enterprise, the most notable being certification to the standards of the International Standards Organization (ISO). Most of the developed-country offices that I visited either were, or were being, ISO certified.[64] The autonomous fee-dependent model of patent office administration is also being transferred to developing countries. Patent offices like the Indonesian PO would like more control over their budget (interview, Indonesian PO). They receive help from outside players like the WIPO and the EPO in building the case within their own countries for budgetary autonomy.

Summing up, patent offices have emerged out of decades of public sector reform as client-oriented, corporately managed and relatively autonomous agencies. In later chapters we will see that developing-country patent offices which have developed close ties with developed-country

---

[61] 'US Patent and Trademark Office: Transforming to Meet the Challenges of the 21st Century', Report of the National Academy of Public Administration, August 2005, xviii.

[62] UK Patent Office, 'Annual Report and Accounts 2005–2006', 12 www.ipo.gov.uk/about-anrep0506.pdf.

[63] See http://int.dkpto.dk/partnerships/contract-partnership/turkey.aspx.

[64] For examples of how patent offices advertise their ISO status see the Danish PO http://int.dkpto.dk/Business-policy/iso-certified.aspx and for the UK PO www.ipo.gov.uk/about/about-ourorg/about-awards/about-awards-iso.htm.

patent offices are also being encouraged to transform themselves into more business-like operations.

If one had to state the aim of all this reform in short form then the Gore slogan of 'government that works better and costs less' is one phrase. Essentially, it was about improving the efficiency and effectiveness of government. These are highly general goals and lead onto other more contextual questions for any public service organization concerning what kinds of efficiencies and effectiveness in what ways. In the case of the customer service statements of patent offices, the goals of patent offices revolve around the faster processing and grant of patents. The UK PO for instance for 2007–8 described its agency goals for patents in the following way:[65]

- Issue 90% of patent search reports within 4 months of request.
- Grant 90% of patents within 2½ years of request.
- Give good customer service in patent search and examination in 95% of quality assured cases.

For the UK PO a customer focus means improving the speed and quality of its service to patent applicants. Other POs take the same view. The Eurasian PO, the membership of which makes up the majority of the republics of the former USSR, has the same customer credo as the UK PO.[66] In fact one would struggle to find an office in either developed or developing countries that did not define the broad goals of contributing to economic improvement, efficiency and responsiveness in terms of granting patents to applicants as quickly as possible. Patent offices continue to set new targets promising their customers cheaper and faster patent examination, doing whatever is necessary to improve the productivity of their examiners.[67] The relative autonomy that they have gained has been used by a number of them to engage in services innovation with their corporate clients as the intended beneficiaries of those services.[68]

---

[65] www.ipo.gov.uk/about/about-ourperform/about-target.htm.
[66] See its 2007 'Annual Report', 4, available at www.eapo.org/eng/reports/.
[67] See, for example, the targets the Japanese PO promised in its 'Annual Report', 2006, 32–3.
[68] The literature on private sector service innovation helps to explain what is happening to patent offices. See Joe Tidd and Frank M. Hull (eds.), *Service Innovation: Organizational Responses to Technological Opportunities and Market Imperatives*, Imperial College Press, London, 2003.

The client credo that has swept through public administration has not been an end in itself, but along with other reforms has been an instrument to improve services to citizens. Citizens in the role of customers will be better off as citizens if agencies of the state treat them as customers. Initiatives like the UK Citizen's Charter programme in 1991 were aimed at giving citizens more control. Whether in fact things have worked out better for citizens in the role of citizens as customers is a complicated empirical and conceptual question with comparatively few studies searching for an answer.[69] Simple measurement approaches based on speed of response by an agency will not capture the public good dimensions of decision-making by agencies. When, for example, courts and tribunals hand down decisions in individual cases, those decisions have effects beyond the individual case and so the substantive quality of the decision itself becomes relevant to an assessment of an agency's performance. Assessing the quality of an agency's work is more difficult than measuring its response time. Simply measuring client satisfaction with decision-making may itself not necessarily point to a high level of substantive quality in decision-making. For example, tax tribunals that hand down decisions favourable to tax evaders may win a lot of acclaim from their clients, but will not be serving the interests of citizens in avoiding the degradation of the state's fiscal base.

Ultimately, an assessment of the quality of an agency's decision-making has to be linked to the distinctive public good mission for which that agency has responsibility. This in turn requires an understanding of the traditional public values by which the agency is meant to be guided and a contextual understanding of the way in which it delivers public goods. Governments may and do create new regulatory agencies, but those agencies for the most part are new organizations that serve to improve the operation of existing institutions and their guiding values. By way of example, contract is an old institution for which states have created new regulatory organizations such as consumer agencies. The rise of regulatory capitalism has been as much about a transformation and engineering of organizations to serve long-established institutions as it has been about new institutions and new values. When it comes to analysing the public good mission of patent offices the starting point is the patent social contract, an argument developed in the next two sections.

---

[69] For an exception see Eran Vigoda, 'Are You Being Served? The Responsiveness of Public Administration to Citizens' Demands: An Empirical Examination in Israel', 78 (2000) *Public Administration*, 165.

Disclosure and social value: two versions of the
patent social contract

Machlup and Penrose in an important article identified four nineteenth-century justifications for the creation of the patent institution.[70] These were the view that inventors had natural property rights in their inventive ideas, that the concept of justice required that inventors be awarded patents, that patents are a necessary incentive for invention and that the patent system is a social contract in which society induces the inventor to make public for the use of others what he might have otherwise have kept secret by offering him a monopoly for a limited period of time. All of these justifications, as Machlup and Penrose showed, had serious problems. Today's discussions of the justification for patent systems revolve around the same basic issues that Machlup and Penrose identified, except that we have more empirical work and evidence concerning the operation of national patent systems.

Four basic objections were put forward against the patent social contract justification. The collective nature of invention meant that even if one inventor did not disclose the invention the same invention would eventually be disclosed by others who were working in the same area in parallel. Merton's account of the phenomenon of double discovery in the history of science, in which many important scientific discoveries have been discovered by investigators working independently, provides some empirical substantiation for this argument.[71] A second counter-argument based itself on the likelihood of secrets not going on forever. Competitors in the marketplace would break down walls of secrecy surrounding an invention. It would eventually leak out (through employee mobility) or be found out. A third objection was that if secrecy was a genuine alternative form of protection (i.e. reverse engineering was not easy or was impossible) then the rational inventor would rely on secrecy since it could last longer than a patent. Why make public something that others were unlikely to find out? From the point of view of society, why offer monopolies for invention information when rational inventors would only disclose information that society would have eventually obtained anyway through processes such as reverse engineering? Finally, if disclosure was the aim, one would be better off without a patent system. In the absence

---

[70] Fritz Machlup and Edith Penrose, 'The Patent Controversy in the Nineteenth Century', 10 (1950) *Journal of Economic History*, 1.

[71] R. K. Merton, 'Singletons and Multiples in Scientific Discovery', 105 (1961) *Proceedings of the American Philosophical Society*, 470.

of patents more emphasis would be placed on status/reputational rewards that came from inventors disclosing their achievement to the world at large. The success of the open source movement in generating innovative software is an example that supports this line of reasoning.[72]

Essentially these nineteenth-century objections identified by Machlup and Penrose to the patent social contract justification remain valid today. Trade secrets are used by many companies in preference to patents, the disclosure that occurs through the patent system is limited in important ways and there is not much evidence that scientific communities read patents for their scientific value.[73] Of course this is not to say that the patent system could not be reformed to make it do a better job of disclosure and Chapters 11 and 12 make suggestions for recapturing the patent social contract. But this does raise a prior question of why we should use the patent social contract justification to develop a normative account of what society might expect from its patent office. Some writers have argued that the patent social contract is too indeterminate for the purposes of normative and empirical analysis.[74]

The answer to this question has a Burkean quality about it in that it pays attention to the traditional institutional practice of Anglo-American courts when it comes to interpreting and developing patent law. Of the four justifications that might be advanced for the patent system, the patent social contract justification has, within the Anglo-American tradition,

---

[72] For an account of how status and reputational norms help to generate innovation see Janet Hope, *Biobazaar: The Open Source Revolution and Biotechnology*, Harvard University Press, Cambridge, Mass., London, England, 2008.

[73] For a recent discussion of these problems see 'The Disclosure Function of the Patent System (or Lack Thereof)', 118 (2008) *Harvard Law Review*, 2007. For a discussion of surveys showing that many firms prefer to rely on first entry advantages and secrecy see David Encauoua, Dominque Guellec and Catalina Martinez, 'Patent Systems for Encouraging Innovation: Lessons from Economic Analysis', 35 (2006) *Research Policy*, 1423. In a survey of 1,478 R&D Labs in the US, Cohen, Nelson and Walsh found that secrecy, lead time and complementary capabilities were the major mechanisms of appropriation, with secrecy being a very important mechanism. Patents were seen as a less important mechanism. Wesley M. Cohen, Richard R. Nelson, and John P. Walsh, 'Protecting their Intellectual Assets: Appropriability Conditions and why U.S. Manufacturing Firms Patent (or not)', NBER Working Paper Series, Working Paper 7552, 2000.

[74] Shubha Gosh takes the view that the patent social contract is indeterminate and provides a poor basis for understanding the patent system. See, Shubha Ghosh, 'Patents and the Regulatory State: Rethinking the Patent Bargain Metaphor After Eldred', 19 (2004) *Berkeley Technology Law Journal*, 1315. Using the assurance game he argues that the role of the patent system is to generate trust and reciprocity. This is true, but it does not provide a justification for accepting the framework of obligations that the patent system creates and in relation to which trust and reciprocity are to evolve.

become over time the one to which the courts have most often turned.[75] In the modern version of this contract the emphasis is on a specific act of disclosure by the inventor in exchange for the grant of the patent monopoly. Disclosure is, the courts say, the 'consideration' or 'quid pro quo' for the grant.[76] The increasing use in the nineteenth century by the courts of the language of contract to describe the disclosure obligations of the patentee is readily understandable as this was also the century in which the rise and refinement of a classical contract law based on the doctrine of consideration took place.[77] The rise in influence of private contract law made it a natural resource for analogous reasoning when it came to considering the patent social contract. During the nineteenth century the courts in the UK and the US turned the patent application document into an increasingly complex legal document in which applicants used ever more sophisticated claiming language to settle the terms of the grant.[78] What might be termed the 'disclosure' conception of the patent social contract was clearly established by the beginning of the twentieth century. Today, TRIPS has globalized the disclosure obligation, making it mandatory for WTO members to require an applicant to disclose the invention.[79]

The rather narrow emphasis on disclosure in the modern patent social contract makes it easy to dismiss as a justification for the patent institution for all the reasons that Machlup and Penrose identify and subsequent work has confirmed. Disclosure rules, like so many parts of the patent system, have become the subject of relentless gaming by corporations. Consider what Justice Mayer (dissenting) said about the US standard of disclosure, a standard that is higher than found in other patent laws: 'With this case, the court blesses corporate shell games resulting from organizational gerrymandering and wilful ignorance by which one can secure the monopoly of patent while hiding the best modes of practicing the invention the law expects to be made public in return for its protection.'[80] Under the US disclosure standard there is a statutory obligation on the inventor to describe 'the best mode contemplated by the inventor of carrying out

[75] On the influence of the patent social contract idea in US law see ibid., 1315.

[76] See, for example, *British United Shoe Machinery Co. Ltd* v. *A. Fussel and Sons* (1908) 25 RPC 613, 649 and *LizardTech, Inc.* v. *Earth Res. Mapping, Inc.*, 433 F.3d 1373, 1375 (Fed. Cir. 2006).

[77] Hugh Collins, *The Law of Contract*, Weidenfeld and Nicolson, London, 1986, 25.

[78] For the history see Karl B. Lutz, 'Evolution of the Claims of U.S. Patents', 20 (1938) *Journal of the Patent Office Society*, 134 and David J. Brennan, 'The Evolution of English Patent Claims as Property Definers', [2005] (4) *Intellectual Property Quarterly*, 361.

[79] Article 29.1.

[80] See *Glaxo Inc.* v. *Novopharm Ltd*, 52 F.3d 1043,1053 (Fed. Cir. 1995).

his invention'.[81] (This 'best mode' element of disclosure is an option under TRIPS, but is not mandatory.) In this case the allegation was that Glaxo had deliberately isolated one of its employee inventors from knowledge about the use of a technique that considerably improved the flow properties of a new form of salt he had invented and that made it suitable for use in pharmaceutical compositions. Justice Mayer's argument is that in the corporate context where invention is a collective process it is possible for a corporation to compartmentalize the process so as to shield the employee inventor from knowledge about optimizing the performance of the invention. His solution of constructive knowledge in cases like this was not supported by the rest of the court. The best mode requirement has also been implicated in costly pre-trial discovery games since defendants have to obtain evidence of what the inventor might have known at the time of filing of the patent application, leading some to suggest that the US drop this element of its disclosure standard.[82]

A disclosure conception of the patent social contract has clear problems. But it does not follow that, because there are problems with a disclosure conception of the patent social contract, we should dismiss the patent social contract justification itself. Here I want to suggest that there is a simpler version of the patent social contract that one can defend and that does provide a coherent normative frame of reference for analysing the role of the patent office. In fact one of the problems with the disclosure conception of the patent social contract is its narrow focus on two institutional actors, the inventor and society, and its consequent neglect of the patent office as an actor. The simpler version of the patent social contract still draws on an exchange or bargain model of contract, but an act of disclosure is no longer the principal act of consideration. On the simple version of the contract, society offers a monopoly in exchange for the release of an invention of social value. The inventor receives a monopoly privilege because in Coke's words 'the inventor bringeth to and for the Commonwealth a new manufacture'.[83] The emphasis here is not on some legalistic act of disclosure in the patent specification, but rather on the patent applicant's obligation to provide something of social value in exchange for the monopoly privilege. This social value conception of the patent social contract offers a broader and more robust basis on which to

---

[81] 35 U.S.C. 112.

[82] See Stephen A. Merrill, Richard C. Levin and Mark B. Myers, (ed.), *A Patent System for the 21st Century*, National Academies Press, Washington, 2004, 120–1.

[83] Edward Coke, *The Third Part of the Institutes of the Laws of England* (1628), Garland Publishing, New York and London, 1979, 184.

assess the patent system and, more importantly for present purposes, to analyse the obligations of the patent office.

While it is not crucial for the present normative argument, it is worth pointing out that the disclosure conception of the patent contract developed well after the establishment of the patent institution and was pre-dated by the social value conception of the patent contract.[84] The disclosure requirement took a long time to evolve in English patent law. The use of specifications to describe the invention was rare in the seventeenth century, but by 1734 the law officers administering the system appear to have required the use of specifications as part of the enrolment process.[85] However, the obligation to provide a specification may not have become a fully fledged obligation imposed by the common law till 1778.[86] Clear also is that the idea of a patent as an exchange between the inventor and society in which the inventor provides something of social value was in place before the eighteenth century. Its clearest expression is to be found in the Statute of Monopolies of 1624 itself. The Statute defined the social value of invention in terms of seven conditions that had to be satisfied by the inventor before a monopoly privilege could be granted.[87]

The modern patent social contract justification assumes that disclosure is the essence of the bargain. It is not. What matters is that the patentee must deliver an invention of social value, or something that at least has potential social value. It is then up to society to find ways to realize the social value of the invention. Capturing the full social value of the invention information depends critically on policies aimed at the social diffusion of that information, something which the requirement of a mere

---

[84] Hulme, for example, argues that the essential consideration that supported the grant of a monopoly before and for some time after the Statute of Monopolies was the working of the patent. One can debate when the specification becomes the new consideration, but what cannot be debated is that it was not the consideration around the time of the Statute of Monopolies. See E. Wyndham Hulme, 'On the Consideration of the Patent Grant, Past and Present', 13 (1897) *Law Quarterly Review*, 313.

[85] Christine MacLeod, *Inventing The Industrial Revolution: The English Patent System, 1660–1800*, Cambridge University Press, Cambridge, 1988, 48–9 and H. I. Dutton, *The Patent System and Inventive Activity During the Industrial Revolution 1750–1852*, Manchester University Press, Manchester, 1984, 22.

[86] There is some debate amongst historians about when the use of specifications to disclose the invention was required. Some take the view that the turning point was the 1778 case of *Liardet* v. *Johnson*, but others disagree. For the debate and one view see John N. Adams and Gwen Averley, 'The Patent Specification: The Role of *Liardet* v. *Johnson*', 7 (1986) *Journal of Legal History*, 156.

[87] These were articulated by Sir Edward Coke, one of the architects of the Statute of Monopolies. See MacLeod, *Inventing The Industrial Revolution*, 18.

paper disclosure of the invention is unlikely to achieve and which in any case, as the history of the patent system to the present day shows, can be easily gamed by sophisticated users of the system. Medieval kingdoms imposed working requirements on inventors in order to capture the social benefits of invention. On a social value conception of the patent contract, it is the diffusion of invention information of social value that matters, not the legal ritual of disclosure.

Before considering the implications of the patent social contract for the patent office, it is worth pointing out that a more general advantage of this justification is that it brings long-standing traditions of social contract thinking and methodology to bear on the patent institution.[88] The simple privileges granted by the kings and queens of medieval Europe have in the twenty-first century become complex regulatory systems that have spread to most countries and are used by companies, very often multinational companies, as part of a private ordering strategy in technology markets that are themselves global. In 2006 there were more than 6 million patents, most of them in private hands, in force around the markets of the world.[89] This private ordering has efficiency and distributive effects, often, as in the case of access to patented medicines, large-scale effects. No institution that has such a global spread and global effects should escape the evaluative scrutiny of political philosophy.

The problem with the property-incentive perspective of patents is that it tends to place the weight of attention on the right holder's interest. It carries with it the danger that the interpretive playing field will be tilted too far in favour of protection of the right holder because the characterization of their interest as property invokes a long liberal rights tradition that has always defended property interests. A social contract perspective has the advantage that it places both parties to the contract firmly in view. The monopoly right of the patentee is the product of a bargain, not something that precedes it. In this bilateral context there is no reason to elevate one party's interests above the interests of the other and each party is seen as having obligations as well as rights. Contract is in this way a more neutral starting point than property when we come to think about the nature of patents.

---

[88] For an analysis of the advantages of construing patents as contracts from a legal perspective see Margaret Llewelyn, 'Schrodinger's Cat: An Observation on Modern Patent Law' in Peter Drahos (ed.), *Death of Patents*, Lawtext Publishing, London, 2005, 11, 56–9.

[89] *World Patent Report, 2008*, WIPO, Geneva, 8.

The duties of the patent office

Returning to the issue of the implications of the patent social contract for patent offices, we can start by observing that the contract is typically depicted as a contract between the inventor and society. Under the social value conception of the patent contract, this means that the inventor has to deliver an invention that has social value. In theory legislatures acting in the public interest specify this social value through criteria of patentability, along with other patent rules such as those relating to the duration of the patent that limit the private value that the inventor can extract from the invention by means of the monopoly. In practice legislatures have to deal with powerful rent-seeking interest groups such as the pharmaceutical lobby, groups that have proved successful in corrupting the patent social contract in their drive to extract greater private returns at the expense of social returns.

For practical purposes someone has to check that the patentee is delivering his side of the bargain. The criteria of patentability that help to define the social bargain are today largely the same in all patent systems. Roughly, they require the inventor to deliver something that is an invention (i.e. not a discovery), novel, inventive and that has some practical application that makes it part of the industrial arts. The invention must also be disclosed so that others can make use of it. Patent examiners in assessing applications have to report on these matters. Patent offices are agencies, increasingly independent agencies that have been created to do what citizens individually and collectively cannot do – to examine patent applications to determine whether the inventor has kept to their part of the bargain. For the purposes of the patent social contract, the patent office acts on society's behalf. In broad terms, its job is to ensure that the inventor delivers an invention of social value. Economists might fit this into a principal-agent model in which the patent office is an agent charged with looking after society's welfare.[90] Roughly speaking, in this type of modelling exercise one would ask about the incentives needed to ensure that the agent acted on the information that only the agent had in a way that was consistent with the principal's welfare.

The patent social contract prescribes an active administrative role for patent offices in ways that the other justifications for the patent system probably do not. In the nineteenth century no country had a patent office

---

[90] One could, however, set this up in a way that ignores the patent office, with the inventor in the role of agent.

doing substantive examination across the range of criteria that modern offices examine against (see Chapter 3). Registration-only systems were widely used in Europe. Only slowly did countries move towards examination. Of the major patenting powers, the French stayed with registration the longest and so the registration system has come to be linked with them.[91] A registration system probably best fits with a natural rights justification for patents. Under such a justification the right to a patent exists independently of the state. The state's role is to put others on notice of the existence of this right by providing a system of registration. Similarly, the incentive justification does not necessarily lead to a prescription for an active patent office in terms of examination since rigorous examination may reduce the number of patents granted thereby lowering the incentive effect of the patent system. Incentive theories of patents tend to focus on the attributes of the property right and to push the contractual aspects of the right and the role of patent offices into the background.

Apart from its duty to ensure the delivery of an invention of social value, a patent office has two other primary duties. One is a duty to help with the diffusion of the invention information that the inventor releases in the application process and the other is to ensure the highest degree of transparency of the patent system to those who may be affected by it. Patent offices have to assess whether the inventor has met his obligation to disclose the invention. The general rule is that patent offices have to publish a patent application 18 months after it has been filed. Publishing an inventor's application is only one of a multitude of processes of social diffusion that are required to capture the social value of invention information, and clearly patent offices are only one of very many actors that have a part to play in this process. Still, patent offices can do more than they currently do to ensure that the patent system works to diffuse information of social value, as opposed to simply disclosing information. This claim is illustrated later on in this section using the patenting of software as an example.

Patent offices are in a much stronger position to fulfil their duty to promote the transparency of the patent system. The requirement to disclose the invention to the public in the patent application is of little use to the public if the published patent itself cannot be readily found. Moreover, since patents are, in effect, private commands to competitors that are enforceable by the state, competitors have a need and right to know the

---

[91] On this point see Jan Vojacek, *A Survey of the Principal National Patent Systems*, Prentice-Hall, NY, 1936, 135.

details of this command. Since patent offices search, examine and grant patents they have a clear comparative advantage in being able to provide patent information to society at little cost to the public. As society's agent they have a responsibility to ensure that the patent information disclosed to them is in turn made easily accessible by them to members of the public. Amongst other things, this means that patent offices should be providing the public with search systems that are totally comprehensive and that make the task of finding relevant patents as easy as possible. In all developing-country interviews with generic companies and in some developed countries such as Australia, companies spoke about the difficulty of finding published patents. The public search systems in these countries were seen as inadequate. Of course, companies can and do pay for transparency by hiring commercial search services, but this means that the patent system in these countries is only privately transparent.

It is doubtful whether any office in fact fulfils its obligations to make the patent system transparent to the many publics and communities that have become affected by patents. A world in which in 2006 there were more than 6 million granted patents in force around the world and roughly another 1.7 million applications filed is also a very uncertain world.[92] My observation at the EPO that the system was generating uncertainty for smaller players drew the observation that 'even the biggest players do not know any more' (referring to the fact that even large players do not really know whether they are infringing patent rights). There is a lot of profit to be made from the kind of deep uncertainty that large-scale patenting brings and the attitude of most patent offices, especially those with commercial arms, was that they can (and do) offer search services to clients. Patent claims are claims over abstract objects and, like mist, abstract objects have no natural borders.[93] It is nonsense to suggest that patent claims function like fence posts. This is to draw an analogy with land that is false. In contrast to the real property system, the patent system generates massive uncertainty because of the inherent fuzziness of abstract objects.

It was striking through the interviews how little patent offices care about the social costs of the uncertainty that they are generating by granting so many patents. There are reflective individuals in patent offices who see the problems. At the EPO one individual nominated three areas where much

[92] See *World Patent Report, 2008*, 7–8.
[93] For an analysis of abstract objects in the context of intellectual property see P. Drahos, *A Philosophy of Intellectual Property*, Dartmouth, Aldershot, 1996.

more had to be done to combat the uncertainty that the patent system was generating: standard setting in information technology; technology transfer obligations under environmental treaties; and access to medicines. Behind the scenes a concerned patent office like the EPO might help an organization like Médecins Sans Frontières with a patent landscaping exercise for HIV medicines (interview, EPO). But this is a selective exercise and about managing the crises in which the patent system is deeply implicated. The many publics affected by patents have a right under the patent social contract to much greater levels of transparency than patent offices currently provide. But this is something patent offices do not want to talk about. Rather it is all about sharing in the profits that markets in uncertainty bring.

As we have already discussed, many states have let patent offices operate with much greater budgetary autonomy. Being allowed to keep the income one generates would lead, the economist would predict, to changes in organizational behaviour. Individuals in charge of bureaucracies like those in firms are assumed to engage in maximizing behaviour.[94] The danger of this kind of organizational transformation is that the incentives that patent offices have as business organizations will not necessarily line up with the obligations that they have under the patent social contract. The agent no longer truly serves the principal. Patent offices tend to invest in transparency and accountability mechanisms that meet the needs of their 'customers', especially those that are the biggest users of their systems. Customer needs overshadow the obligations that patent offices have to society under the patent social contract.

An example of patent offices having incentives to behave in a way that undermines their duties of diffusion and transparency, thereby reducing the social value of the patent contract, can be found in the field of software patenting. Computer software inventions have become one of the biggest areas of patenting activity.[95] The disclosure requirements in relation to software in both the US and European law do not require that the source code necessarily be disclosed by the inventor.[96] This is a matter

---

[94] William A. Niskanen, Jr., *Bureaucracy and Public Economics*, Edward Elgar, UK, 1994, 37.

[95] WIPO reports that in 2005 computer technology was one of three areas where there were large filings across the world. See *World Patent Report, 2008*, WIPO, Geneva, 8.

[96] For a discussion of the position in the US see Kenneth Caufield, 'The Disclosure of Source Code in Software Patents: Should Software Patents be Open Source?', 7 (2006) *Columbia Science and Technology Review*, available at www.stlr.org/cite.cgi?volume=7&article=6. On disclosure in the EU see 'Guidelines for Examination in the European Patent Office', Ch. II 4.11.

for the patent applicant. Typically many companies will not disclose the source code, preferring to rely on trade secret protection.[97] Yet, as the Free Software Foundation makes clear, the freedom to study and adapt a program requires access to the source code.[98] Much of the social value of software innovation depends on access to the source code. It is clear that many software programmers do not see patent specifications as a useful source of technical information.[99] Disclosure through patent law has to meet legal standards of disclosure rather than standards of technical intelligibility and usefulness to other users.

Patent offices could, of course, be much more active in terms of pushing for standards of disclosure or interpreting existing standards in ways that would make patent specifications more valuable sources of information for the community of programmers, but one likely consequence is that many companies might choose not to patent. This might actually be an efficient result, if, as some have argued, software innovation is sequential innovation and that sequential innovation is better served when there are fewer stronger patents to prevent successive generations of innovators from standing on each others' shoulders.[100] It is also an efficient result in that fewer patents would mean more scope for independent discovery in computer software, since trade secret protection does not prohibit independent discovery. And it may also be more efficient in that in the absence of easy patent protection more companies might be encouraged to experiment with open source forms of innovation in software.

But the deterrence effect of a high disclosure standard would most likely mean that an important source of worldwide patenting might rapidly dry up for patent offices. The incentive then is for patent offices to accept standards of passive legal disclosure that produce little information of use to programmers, but are of strategic value to companies. Patent offices are complicit in a process in which companies are allowed to go through

---

[97] There are many issues raised by keeping such basic information as source code out of the public domain of an information society that relies on digital machines in almost endless ways. For one interesting example see Charles Short, 'Guilt by Machine: The Problem of Source Code Discovery in Florida DUI Prosecutions', 61 (2009) *Florida Law Review*, 177.

[98] www.gnu.org/philosophy/free-sw.html.

[99] See 'The Patentability of Computer Programs: Discussion of European-level Legislation in the Field of Patents for Software', European Parliament, Directorate-General for Research, Working Paper, Legal Affairs Series, JURI 107 EN, April 2002, 21.

[100] See James E. Bessen and Eric S. Maskin, 'Sequential Innovation Patents, and Imitation' (January 2000). MIT Dept. of Economics Working Paper No. 00–01. Available at SSRN: http://ssrn.com/abstract=206189.

a ritual of disclosure that meets legal requirements but robs society of the social value of the invention.

It was striking that, with a little over 140 patent officials interviewed, the patent social contract was mentioned twice: once by an examiner from the Indian PO and once in the interview at the German PO. Instead patent officials from developed-country offices talked about the looming world of competition amongst offices for work and the 'business opportunities' and threats that this presented. A business culture in these offices seemed to be well and truly flourishing. Most developing-country offices, with some obvious exceptions such as Brazil and India, realized that they would not be players in the patent office business, but that nevertheless they could make their situation more comfortable by gaining control over their fee income and cooperating with large developed-country offices to gain more resources.

Summarizing, a patent social contract justification forms a natural starting point for developing a normative account of the public good mission of patent offices. A contract perspective encourages a deeper look at what both sides are entitled to under the patent bargain and the role that a patent office should serve in securing society's entitlements under that bargain. Patent offices have three primary duties: they have to check that the inventor is delivering an invention of social value; they have to focus on ways to improve the social diffusion of invention information; and they have to ensure that the system is maximally transparent. The public sector reforms that have transformed patent offices into business agencies have created a set of incentives for patent offices to view patent applicants as their main clients. The danger is that they will administer the patent system in ways that enhance the private value of patents for these clients and reduce the social value of invention information.

The fieldwork trail and some findings

Patent offices produce a lot of measurable outputs: most obviously the number of patent applications they receive and the number of patents that they grant, along with lots of data about time taken to process applications, number of applications from residents compared to the number from foreigners, which fields of technology are the subject of heaviest patenting and so on. This kind of output data stretches back to the nineteenth century and in some cases even further for some of today's developed-country offices and has been the subject of an economic literature that is too big to document. As Griliches observes '[p]atents and patent statistics have fascinated economists for a long time'.[101] The increasing complexity and globalization of patent law has added to the difficulty of interpreting patent statistics.[102]

While this study drew on this output data, its focus was on gathering qualitative data about the extent of cooperation amongst patent offices. Cooperation amongst patent offices is not especially well documented. The annual reports of many patent offices will usually contain a brief section on international cooperation. Typically, this will provide the barest detail of visits by the heads of other offices, exchanges of personnel and the signing of some kind of cooperation agreement between the offices. The websites of patent offices will also sometimes provide additional information on cooperation activities. As one might expect, the literature that looks at the operation of patent offices tends to focus on the USPTO or the EPO, often looking at the operation of the office in the context of patent quality.[103] The study of patent offices as opposed to patent law or the economics of patent law or patents and innovation is not common. Boehm and Silbertson's wonderful study of the British patent system, which was published in 1967, is a rare example of two scholars looking in detail at the workings of a national patent office.[104] Relations amongst patent offices tend not to be studied. Little is known about developing-country patent offices.[105]

The aim of the fieldwork was to find out about patent office cooperation and integration, the extent of that cooperation and integration and the factors driving it. Evidence of cooperation and integration amongst

[101] Zvi Griliches, 'Patent Statistics as Economic Indicators: A Survey', 28 (1990) *Journal of Economic Literature*, 1661.

[102] For how economists should respond to these changes see Hariolf Grupp and Ulrich Schmoch, 'Patent Statistics in the Age of Globalisation: New Legal Procedures, New Analytical Methods, New Economic Interpretation', 28 (1999) *Research Policy*, 377.

[103] See, for example, the papers on patent quality and the USPTO in Wesley M. Cohen and Stephen A. Merrill (eds.), *Patents in the Knowledge-Based Economy*, National Academies Press, Washington DC, 2003. For a study of the EPO see Philip Leith, *Harmonisation of Intellectual Property in Europe: A Case Study of Patent Procedure*, Sweet and Maxwell, London, 1998.

[104] Klaus Boehm with Aubrey Silbertson, *The British Patent System, Volume 1*, Cambridge University Press, Cambridge, 1967.

[105] The UK Commission on Intellectual Property Rights commissioned some work in this area and this work noted the absence of literature on the operation of institutional arrangements for intellectual property in developing countries. See Mart Leesti and Tom Pengelly, 'Institutional Issues for Developing Countries in Intellectual Property Policymaking, Administration & Enforcement', Study Paper 9, 2002, Commission on Intellectual Property Rights.

patent offices includes formal recognition of another office's examination results (rare), informal recognition of those results (common), examiner exchanges, document exchange systems, information technology integration or access (for example, one office making its search system available to another office), work-sharing arrangements in which office A outsources work to office B or allows a patent applicant to nominate office B to do work that office A might have done, and benchmarking projects. Since the initial hypothesis linked this cooperation to an emerging system of global governance of knowledge, the fieldwork had to target the most significant offices as measured by application and grants, offices that were insignificant in terms of applications and grants, and some offices that were somewhere along that spectrum of significance. In other words, I was looking for evidence of integration between an office that might receive around 400,000 applications per year and an office that might only receive three or four.

The interviews aimed to capture the diversity of patent offices around the world, starting with the obvious criterion of the size of the office as measured by patent filings. According to WIPO's patent data the top five offices in terms of number of patent filings are those from Japan, US, China, Korea and the European Patent Office.[106] All these offices were interviewed (including the Hong Kong Office which has a separate patent jurisdiction). The USPTO, Japanese Patent Office (JPO) and the EPO are known as the 'Trilateral Offices' and have formal arrangements for cooperation dating back to the early 1980s (see Chapter 6). During the interviews people referred to the Asian Trilaterals as an important entity – JPO, the Korean Intellectual Property Office (KIPO) and the State Intellectual Property Office (SIPO) of China. The POs in Brazil and India were interviewed because these countries have been important developing-country leaders on international patent issues. They are also offices that are growing in size.

We will see that within Europe a more networked approach to patent office administration is developing. The national European offices interviewed were a mixture of large and small players: Germany and the UK (ranked sixth and tenth in terms of total number of filings[107]), along with three smaller players, Austria, Denmark and the Netherlands. Austria and Denmark are involved in doing outsourced work for other offices,

---

[106] Based on 2005 filings. See *WIPO Patent Report, 2007*, WIPO, Geneva, 12. The order changed slightly based on 2006 filings with the USPTO and JPO swapping places. See *World Patent Report, 2008*, WIPO, Geneva, 14.

[107] *WIPO Patent Report, 2007*, 12.

while the Netherlands is an interesting example of a once large examining office that has shrunk in size because of the emergence of the EPO. Other developed-country patent offices that were part of the fieldwork were Australia, Brunei, Canada, New Zealand and Singapore. Australia and Canada are both in the top ten in terms of patent filings.[108] New Zealand is an example of a small developed-country patent office that has had to meet the cost of running an examination system and has a history of regulatory cooperation with Australia. Singapore is a developed country that has made high-standard patent protection a priority and is using outsourcing to meet its examination needs. Brunei is an example of a small developed country using a re-registration system.

Other developing-country offices that were interviewed included Indonesia, Laos, Malaysia, Philippines, Thailand and Vietnam. Amongst other things, this meant that I was able to interview countries that were part of a regional association, the Association of Southeast Asian Nations (ASEAN), which did not have a regional patent office, but where the possibility of creating such an office had been expressly raised (Myanmar was the only country from which officials were not interviewed). During the course of the project I had the opportunity to attend international meetings involving representatives from patent offices. The Australian PO, for example, facilitated my attendance in 2005 as an observer on the Australian delegation at an Asia-Pacific Economic Cooperation (APEC) meeting of the Intellectual Property Rights Experts Group. Similarly, I attended as an observer at a WIPO-organized meeting of Asia-Pacific Heads of Intellectual Property Offices in Singapore in 2007. Prior to that, in 2006, I was invited to a Pacific Regional High Level Consultation on HIV and Law, Ethics and Human Rights organized by UNAIDS and United Nations Development Programme. Attending were legal officials with responsibility for patent administration from fifteen Pacific Islands. At these and other meetings I took the opportunity to have follow-up discussions with officials from patent offices I had already interviewed (for example, SIPO, the Indian PO, KIPO) or I interviewed patent officials from countries that I had not previously interviewed. In the latter category I discussed patent office cooperation with officials from Bhutan, Cambodia, Iran, Nepal and Pakistan, as well as with a large group of Pacific Island countries – the Cook Islands, Federated States of Micronesia, Fiji, Kiribati, Marshall Islands, Nauru, Niue, Palau, Papua New Guinea, Samoa, Solomon Islands, Tokelau, Tonga, Tuvalu and Vanuatu. Having patent officials congregated

[108] Ibid.

in one spot enabled me to gather information about a large number of offices quickly and efficiently. In the case of the Pacific Island countries in particular it turned out that there was no fully fledged patent office but rather a system for registering patents that had been granted elsewhere. Patenting activity was almost non-existent with, for example, three or four patents per year being re-registered in Samoa and a similar number in Kiribati. Where possible, I cross-checked this information from other sources. Generally it is difficult to obtain information about patenting levels in smaller developing countries. One WIPO official explained that many developing countries do not regularly provide WIPO with national data. In the case of Pacific Island countries, a report for the Pacific Island Forum revealed very low levels of patent activity and in my discussions with the Australian PO the very low number of patents appearing in Pacific Island countries was also confirmed.[109] But as I have already suggested the surprising fact is that there are any patents registered in what are some of the smallest and poorest countries in the world.

With each office I raised the same set of issues for discussion. Where the office was an examining office we discussed examiner training, recruitment of examiners, pressures on examiners and quality control issues, access to databases, approach to examination, and outsourcing of searching and/or examination. A standard question for every office was the relationship between the fees it collected and its budget. On the subject of international cooperation I began by asking whether the office cooperated with other offices and the nature of that cooperation. Two key questions here were 'Which offices' work do you trust?' and 'What causes trust between offices to develop?' On the first question there is no doubt that the EPO emerged as the office most trusted by developing countries. The one qualification here is that the EPO is more trusted outside of Europe than it is by some of the national European offices that operate within the European Patent Network. Within Europe it is clear that the German PO is also a highly respected office. The perception of the USPTO was that of an office where the quality of work varied. JPO was also mentioned for its quality, but like the quiet studious student in class it did not get the attention that the EPO or USPTO received when I asked this question.

---

[109] Susan Farquhar, 'A Regional International Property Rights Office for the South Pacific: Cost-Benefit Analysis', An Asian Development Bank-Commonwealth Secretariat Joint Report to the Pacific Islands Forum Secretariat, Pacific Studies Series, Volume 3: Working Papers, Working Paper No. 16 (2005) available at www.adb.org/Documents/Reports/Pacific-Regionalism/vol3/default.asp.

On the second question, the single most important trust-building factor turned out to be examiner exchanges over a period of years. This was true in the case of exchanges between developed- and developing-country offices and between developed-country offices. Some offices reported the use of buddy systems in which examiners from different offices would be paired together. The pattern is that of a personal relational trust growing amongst examiners from different offices based on examiner exchanges or examiner training exercises, a relational trust that eventually spreads and changes into a technocratic trust by one organization of another organization's system (see Chapter 4). Personal trust changes into systems trust. Systems trust is particularly important in integrating developing-country offices into the patent office governance network. It is clear that systems trust takes time to build. Whatever one thinks of the patent system, it is clear that patent offices from the developed world, the EPO in particular, know how to build organizational capacity in developing countries, something that development agencies could certainly learn from. Developing-country offices that received very short training bursts were more frustrated than helped by them. They were looking for longer-term training commitments.

Trust also follows the path of 'like-mindedness'. One office will see another as like-minded and begin a dialogue that might lead to an exchange of patent applications for the purposes of assessing each other's systems. Seeing how one office deals with another office's applications is an important trust-building device. As trust grows between like-minded offices more formal cooperation programmes are established to deal with issues such as the mutual exploitation of results or outsourcing arrangements. Since it is patent office representatives that participate in crucial patent treaty negotiations, trust-building provides a foundation for coalition building in such negotiations. Trust-building exercises cost and so offices have to make choices about which relations with other offices they will deepen. So, for example, while it is important to integrate the Nigerian patent office into the international patent framework, it only needs minimal training in order to participate in the increasingly automated processes of the international patent framework. Many offices will not make it a priority to foster relations with the Nigerian office.

I also asked offices for their views on the work of the patent attorney profession. One clear finding was that in developing countries genuine patent attorney expertise is very scarce. One problem that was often mentioned was the lack of local experts to draft patent claims, meaning that local inventors essentially had no way of entering the system. In those developing countries where I was able to speak to local generic companies those companies reported problems in accessing patent attorney expertise. The pattern in India, Malaysia and Philippines was one where there were a few local experts, but who tended to work for the subsidiaries of pharmaceutical multinationals. Another striking finding was that developing-country patent offices were critical, often highly so, of the expertise of local attorneys, whereas developed-country offices all described the work of attorneys as being of good quality. This almost certainly comes down to the high degree of professionalization of patent attorneys in developed countries compared to developing countries. Dutton, for example, points out that in the UK by 1851 patent agents were established actors in the patent system, handling about 90% of granted patents.[110] Many developing countries did not have a patent law in the first half of the nineteenth century. At the time of my interview at the Indonesian PO in 2005, I was told that there were some forty registered patent attorneys. Knowing how to 'work' a sophisticated rule intensive system like the patent system requires a profession that has high levels of technical expertise and experiential knowledge. Patent attorneys are long-established players in developed countries and an important interest group in their own right, but in developing countries the profession is only just beginning to emerge. This lack in developing countries of professional expertise in the critical art of patent claim drafting (on its importance see Chapter 2) means that local companies or research institutes either do not apply for patents or have much difficulty in getting their applications through their national patent office. A number of developing-country patent offices reported in the interviews that applications from residents were more likely to be rejected. The lesson here is that if one is to buy the patent rent-seeking machine one needs a patent attorney profession to drive it.

The fieldwork revealed a lot of diversity amongst offices. Some offices ran re-registration systems acquired during colonial times; others had modernized their patent laws and were building examination capacity with an eye to having more global influence as patent offices (e.g. Brazil and India); others seemed to be treading water (e.g. Malaysia, Indonesia); some were re-organizing their patent system as part of a broader economic strategy (e.g. Singapore); and yet others were offices of ambition, keenly looking for work outside of their borders in order to retain and

---

[110] H. I. Dutton, *The Patent System and Inventive Activity During the Industrial Revolution 1750–1852*, Manchester University Press, Manchester, 1984, 86.

increase their influence in the international framework (e.g. Australian PO, Austrian PO, KIPO).

From 2004 to 2008, a little over 140 officials from 45 patent offices were interviewed.

The interviews generally continued for no less than an hour and a half and in many cases I had up to half a day, sometimes longer. In India, for example, after some one-on-one interviews, I was given the opportunity to meet in a round-table format all the patent examiners working in the Mumbai Office. In addition to interviewing patent officials, I was able to interview thirty members of generic pharmaceutical companies or representatives from a generic pharmaceutical association in Australia, Canada, Malaysia, the Philippines, Vietnam and Thailand. Local generic companies in a country form a useful litmus test for some issues relating to patent office administration. Generic companies tend to be on the receiving end of the patent system in that they have to find their way through the patent maze built by brand companies. By targeting generic companies one learns something about the user friendliness of a patent office's search systems, the kind of legal expertise companies can draw on in order to find (or fight) their way through the maze, the extent of pharmaceutical patenting and the kinds of practical problems that generic companies face with a country's patent system.

The offices from which officials were interviewed are listed below in groups, the basis of the grouping explained in parenthesis:

1. USPTO, EPO, JPO (the Trilaterals – in 2006 they received about 70% of applications).[111]
2. JPO, SIPO, KIPO (Asian Trilaterals which together with the Trilaterals in 2005 accounted for 77% of all patents filed).[112]
3. German PO, UK PO, Austrian PO, Danish PO and the Netherlands PO (offices from small and large European countries that are part of the EPO's network).
4. Australian PO, Canadian PO (offices of middle power countries).
5. Singapore PO, Brunei PO, Hong Kong PO and New Zealand PO (offices of smaller developed economies).
6. Indian PO, Brazilian PO (offices of developing countries that have been leaders on intellectual property and development issues).

---

[111] See *Trilateral Statistical Report 2007*, EPO, JPO, USPTO, 21.
[112] *WIPO Patent Report, 2007*, 12.

7. Cambodia, Indonesia, Malaysia, Philippines, Thailand, Vietnam (developing countries that are members of the ASEAN group, this group having raised the possibility of a regional patent office).
8. Bhutan, Iran, Pakistan (other developing countries).
9. Cook Islands, Federated States of Micronesia, Fiji, Marshall Islands, Nauru, Niue, Palau, PNG, Tokelau, Tonga, Vanuatu (Pacific Island group of developing countries, a regional grouping that represents countries on the periphery of international patenting strategies).
10. Laos, Kiribati, Nepal, Samoa, Solomon Islands, Tuvalu, Vanuatu (offices from countries that appear on the UN list of least-developed countries and that are also on the periphery of international patenting strategies).

We will see that various forms of cooperation connect these offices. Not every office cooperates with every other office. The USPTO does not have much to do with Pacific Island countries. The Australian PO is more active in this region. Overall the fieldwork evidence provides strong inductive support for the hypothesis that patent offices are cooperating and integrating, thereby helping to form a system for the global governance of knowledge.

A finding of the fieldwork is that this global patent governance system is emerging as a hierarchical network that is automating the process of decision-making about patent applications. The network of patent offices is not a flat structure of equals. Rather it is a tiered structure dominated by a core of large offices made up of the EPO, JPO and the USPTO with KIPO and SIPO now also forming part of this networked core. Within the core, the relationship is much more one of network equality in which convergence upon standards and practice is the product of dialogue and cooperation. The patent offices outside of the core forge relationships with those in the core in different ways, but as we will see it is the core that leads when it comes to developing a global system of patent administration. Patent offices are networked in two distinct ways. First, they are networked by means of the operation of treaties that enable an application that is first filed in office A to be then filed in office B. Patent offices are networked, in other words, by means of filing routes. The second way in which patent offices are networked is through cooperative arrangements that can be formal or informal. In some rare cases a decision to grant a patent in one office will lead another office to grant a patent for the same application (the principle of mutual recognition). Much more common are cases where one patent office has come to trust the work of another office and so as a matter of practice follows the examining decisions of that office. The

EPO has, as we will see, been able to engender in developing countries this kind of technocratic trust in its systems. The network leaders of the patent office network are working in various ways to take advantage of each other's examination output and systems in order to reduce their workloads. The principle that governs relations amongst core offices is one of mutual exploitation.

Developing-country offices, on the other hand, are being encouraged to accept the standards and decisions of the core offices. Progressively an automation of decision-making is taking place in which independent examination by many offices will be replaced by an examination by a very few and a mechanical acceptance by the many. One consequence of this is that a high degree of dependency is being built into patent governance. Developing-country patent bureaucracies may be formally autonomous entities within the civil service structures of their countries, but in network governance terms they are integrated entities, deeply affected by decision-making processes elsewhere in the network. Most developing-country patent offices actively seek integration because the global patent governance system contains wealthy agents (for example, WIPO and the Trilaterals) from which they are able to obtain resources. Whether developing countries should be allowing this kind of regulatory automation of their systems and what the alternatives to it might be are issues discussed in Chapters 11 and 12.

Some offices like the EPO and KIPO (and perhaps SIPO) are, through technical assistance, investing heavily in the creation of technocratic trust. Other offices are less concerned with this and are simply competing for outsourced work. Chapter 6 argues that the cooperation of today amongst the large offices is also creating the possibility of a greater competition amongst them. Those offices that have had technocratic trust extended to them by many other offices will be in the strongest position to exercise networked leadership in this competitive world.

'Invisible' patent harmonization and why patent offices matter

In order to understand the importance of patent offices to patent harmonization one needs to distinguish four levels of norms at which harmonization may occur. These levels are principles, rules, administration and interpretation. At the level of principle, the treaty mechanism has proved to be successful in first triggering a process of convergence and then harmonization of the core principles of patent law. This convergence process at the level of principle can be said to have started with the

Paris Convention in 1883, which established 'a Union for the protection of industrial property'.[113] The Paris Convention introduced some general principles such as the principle of national treatment and the principle of the independence of patents obtained for the same invention in different countries. The Convention remains thin on substantive rules, its most important contribution being a set of rules that govern the priority rights of applicants in other Union countries once they have filed a patent application in one Union country. Other rules relate to the forfeiture of patents and their compulsory licensing.

TRIPS provides another example of an international agreement that has been important at the level of the harmonization of principle. It requires its members to make patents available 'for any inventions, whether products or processes, in all fields of technology, provided that they are new, involve an inventive step and are capable of industrial application'.[114] Despite more than a hundred years of treaty-making on patents, differences of principle amongst national patent systems remain.[115] The US, for example, continues to operate on the basis of first to invent while other countries operate on the basis of first to file. Similarly there is a wide variety of practice around the principle of a grace period. Under the principle of a grace period, a patent applicant is allowed a set time during which the disclosure of the invention by the applicant by any means to the public prior to the making of the patent application will not count as prior art that will defeat the application. Some states have a small number of narrow exceptions that allow the inventor to disclose the invention without the immediate loss of novelty (for example, exhibiting the invention at a trade fair), whereas others, the US being an example, allow much broader scope for an inventor to make a public disclosure that will not defeat a subsequent patent application. The debates here revolve around the length of a grace period and its scope. The interviews in Europe confirmed what is well known, namely that some European companies do not like the uncertainty of a grace period.

One of the features of the treaties that operate in the patent harmonization field is that they require states to adhere to a minimum set of standards and allow states to move beyond those minimum standards providing that any new standards do not compromise the prevailing

---

[113] See Article 1.1 of the Paris Convention.
[114] Article 27.1.
[115] On harmonization issues see Harold C. Wegner, *Patent Harmonization*, Sweet and Maxwell, London, 1993.

minimum standards. For states that can make trade gains from higher standards one option is to keep on raising the minimum standards of harmonization by setting new standards of protection and then persuading other states to agree to those new standards.[116]

When it comes to the harmonization of patent rules there is a long road to travel. The patent law of most developed states goes back to the nineteenth century and so the bare principles of their patent law systems have experienced a long organic accretion of rules and doctrine. The result has been that the principles have been operationalized in different ways. For example, the patent systems of all countries apply the principle of novelty to inventions. The novelty of an invention is determined by reference to the prior art base. The basic issue is whether the invention is new when compared to the information that is already available to the public as at the priority date of the application. This in turn raises definitional issues. What is meant by available to the public? Does it mean that a member of the public needs to have accessed the information? Is it enough that the document was available to a single member of the public? What types of information will be admitted into the prior art base and what types will not? Will oral disclosures of the invention form part of the prior art base and, if so, will oral disclosures anywhere in the world count? A survey by WIPO in 2001 of forty-nine countries revealed that different countries have different rules for the definition of the prior art base.[117] Under the EPC, novelty is linked to a prior art base made up of oral and written disclosures anywhere in the world whereas in the US knowledge or use of the invention by others outside of the US do not count for the purposes of assessing novelty.[118]

At the level of the harmonization of procedural and substantive rules, WIPO remains the principal forum of negotiation for states. On some types of procedural rules there has been some modest progress in the shape of the Patent Law Treaty of 2000 (PLT). The PLT aims to harmonize aspects of patent procedure in ways that are favourable to applicants.[119] Under the PLT, states can make things easier for an applicant, but they cannot impose more requirements than are stipulated by the Treaty. The

[116] Peter Drahos, 'BITS and BIPS: Bilateralism in Intellectual Property', 4 (2001) *Journal of World Intellectual Property*, 791.

[117] See 'Information Provided by Members of the Standing Committee on the Law of Patents (SCP) Concerning the Definition of Prior Art Brief Summary', SCP/6/INF/2, 2 November 2001.

[118] See Article 54(2) of the EPC and 35 U.S.C. 102(a).

[119] Article 2(1).

PLT imposes maximum requirements on matters such as obtaining a filing date, the form and content of an application, and the effects of non-compliance with formal requirements.

In the case of the harmonization of the substantive rules of patent law, the rule intensiveness of national patent systems have functioned like swamps, engulfing negotiators and slowing their progress to a crawl. Preparatory work on the harmonization of substantive patent law rules started in WIPO in 1983 and led to an unsuccessful Diplomatic Conference at the Hague in 1991.[120] US support for the draft treaty was not great and it put more of its energy into TRIPS, which was also being negotiated at that time. WIPO's Standing Committee on the Law of Patents began working on patent law harmonization in 2000, targeting in particular the rules around prior art, novelty, inventive step/non-obviousness, industrial applicability/utility, the drafting and interpretation of claims, and sufficiency of disclosure. In 2001, WIPO launched the 'WIPO Patent Agenda', its aims being to assist in the ratification of the PLT, the reform of the PCT and further work on a Substantive Patent Law Treaty.[121] A major theme of this agenda is the need to address the duplication of work by patent offices in separately examining national applications for the same invention.[122]

Progress within WIPO on a Substantive Patent Law Treaty has been slow.[123] In 2004, WIPO received a submission from the US, Japan and the EPO noting that complexity and political sensitivities (a reference to disagreements amongst developed countries as well as between developed- and developing-country groups) were standing in the way of a sweeping agreement and so it might be better to focus on a smaller set of issues – the definition of prior art, grace period, novelty and non-obviousness/inventive step.[124] This has not, however, speeded matters up. The rule-intensive nature of patent systems means that most states have something to defend because some domestic lobby or another has won the political fight for that rule or set of rules and has said to its country's negotiators that it will die in a ditch defending those rules. Patent harmonization negotiations

---

[120] A. Bogsch, *Brief History of the First 25 Years of the World Intellectual Property Organization*, WIPO, Geneva, 1992, 37.

[121] See WIPO, Agenda for Development of the International Patent System, A/36/14, 6 August 2001.

[122] See WIPO, Agenda for Development of the International Patent System, A/36/14, 6 August 2001, 5.

[123] See Heinz Bardehle, 'Patent Harmonization: Quo Vadis?', 88 (2006) *Journal of Patent and Trademark Office Society*, 644.

[124] WIPO, Proposal from the United States of America, Japan and the European Patent Office Regarding the Substantive Patent Law Treaty (SPLT), SCP/10/9, 22 April 2004.

become like a circus act in which the clowns go through a fixed routine while pretending spontaneity. The US holds first to file as a bargaining chip against all countries. Parts of European industry do not want a grace period. Developing countries raise the development implications of patent harmonization.[125] Given the level of integration of their patent offices into the system this seems a little late in the day. Developing countries also argue for an obligation on patent applicants to disclose the source of biological materials and any traditional knowledge linked to those materials. US industry swoons with horror and announces the end of civilization. Patent harmonization talks are a circus, but without the laughs, and so those wanting real action rather than spectacle have shifted their attention to patent offices.

When it comes to harmonizing patent systems at the level of principles and substantive rules, officials from national patent offices can represent states in a negotiation, but it is states that must pass the required laws to bring principles and rules into alignment. Patent offices have much more capacity for independent action at the level of administration and interpretation. National offices will generally have some form of delegated rule-making power (although not the power to make substantive rules of patent law).[126] They also have the capacity to issue guidelines about how they will approach the interpretation of principles such as inventive step. Courts have de jure power over the interpretation of principles, but this de jure power is exercised through written formulations and re-formulations of the law, formulations that themselves have to be interpreted. Patent offices have a tremendous de facto power over the interpretation of patent standards because they have to establish practicable routines for the day-to-day application of these standards.

The relative autonomy that patent offices have over aspects of their administrative systems and interpretive practices means that they can

---

[125] For a discussion of harmonization as it affects developing countries see Jerome H. Reichman and Rochelle Cooper Dreyfuss, 'Harmonization without Consensus: Critical Reflections on Drafting a Substantive Patent Law Treaty', 57 (2007) *Duke Law Journal*, 85.

[126] A good example is the USPTO. See *Merck and Co. v. Kessler* 80 F.3d 1543, 1550 (Fed. Cir. 1996). The EPO is in a different position since it is established under the EPC. Generally it is a more autonomous body than a national patent office. There is an appeal structure that is part of the EPO that hears appeals against decisions of the EPO (see Article 15 of the EPC). The Enlarged Board of Appeal is the final appeal body (Article 22 of the EPC). The President of the EPO has a number of powers including the power to place proposals for general regulations under the EPC to the Administrative Council. See Article 10(2)(c) of the EPC.

have important effects on the harmonization of principles and rules. For example, two states may have harmonized at the level of principles and rules, but their respective patent offices may be coming to different results in respect of applications for the same invention because they interpret the same principles differently. The Trilateral Offices are well aware of this possibility and have carried out projects in order to ascertain the extent to which their examiners will arrive at the same results applying the same standards. One exercise in which the three offices examined some hypothetical cases involving the patentability of DNA fragments showed the offices getting to roughly similar results but for different reasons.[127] Another study which looked at actual results for non-PCT applications for 1990–5 that had been granted in the US and submitted to JPO and the EPO found 'significant disharmony' of outcomes across the offices.[128] JPO in particular had rejected 7,024 patents that had been granted by the USPTO and EPO. The study was not able to explain what accounted for these differences of outcome but it suggests that even where patent offices converge on the same standards there is no guarantee that a common interpretation of the standards will follow.

Just as interpretive practice may defeat a harmonization of principles and rules, so it may overcome a lack of harmonization of rules. For example, a particular patent system may contain a prohibition on the patenting of X. Patent attorneys may draft claims, which define the invention, that in effect cover X and a patent office may be prepared to accept that form of claim (Chapter 6 discusses such a case in relation to methods of human treatment). The prohibition on the patenting of X is circumvented and the national system in terms of effects (but not rules) aligns with those systems that do not have the prohibition.

Patent offices are important members of the patent interpretive community and can do much to hamper or promote patent harmonization.[129]

---

[127] See Trilateral Project B3b, Comparative study on biotechnology patent practices. Theme: Patentability of DNA fragments. For an analysis of the results see Melanie J. Howlett and Andrew F. Christie, 'An Analysis of the Approach of the European, Japanese and United States Patent Offices to Patenting Partial DNA Sequences (ESTS)', Working Paper No. 5/03, Intellectual Property Research Institute of Australia, Victoria, Australia, 2003.

[128] Paul H. Jensen, Alfons Palagkaraya and Elizabeth M. Webster, 'Patent Application Outcomes across the Trilateral Patent Offices', Melbourne Institute Working Paper No. 5/05, 2005.

[129] For the argument that the direction of interpretation is given by membership of an interpretive community see Stanley Fish, 'Don't Know Much About the Middle Ages: Posner on Law and Literature', 97 (1988) Yale Law Journal, 777.

Much of the training that the Trilaterals provide for examiners in developing-country patent offices is aimed at building a borderless interpretive community when it comes to the application of now largely globalized patent law principles. This is the main reason why, for example, the USPTO is prepared to train Indian examiners in the examination of pharmaceutical products (see Chapter 7). It is also clear that patent offices are directing their harmonization efforts at the administrative level, the level over which they have much more command and which is less transparent to outsiders. In the words of one patent office in Europe, 'Administrative cooperation is a form of harmonization working on a nearly invisible level, but nevertheless very efficient.' The same interviewee then went on to describe the progress that had been made in Europe on software patenting, a progress he attributed directly to increased cooperation amongst patent offices. 'The same people in the same fora' were able through regular meetings to take a much closer look at the software patenting issue, do studies and gradually bring their approaches into a closer alignment.

Turning all the world's patent offices into one interpretive community is a not an insignificant task. The fieldwork data suggests that this is evolving in the following way. As we saw above, patent office integration is taking the form of a hierarchical network. At the top horizontal level in this network the major patent offices are building trust in each other's systems and developing administrative means to exploit each other's examination results. All offices at this horizontal level favour arrangements that allow one office to exploit the work of another, but some offices (for example, the EPO and the German PO) for the time being are against mutual recognition agreements that would oblige one office to recognize the work of another. At the vertical levels within this hierarchical network enough training is done to foster technocratic trust so that developing-country examiners will follow the decisions of the major players at the top of the system. The goal is to promote a regulatory automation of decision-making in which the uncertainty generated by interpretive autonomy is taken out of the system. Patent offices of developing countries that are also major markets can expect long-term training commitments (most obviously, Brazil, China and India) because they are potential players at the top horizontal level of the hierarchy. China is already at this horizontal level and the Brazilian and Indian patent offices aspire to this level. Patent offices of other developing countries can expect enough training for them to be integrated into the vertical, automated lines of decision-making in the system. The PO of Pakistan, for example, has trouble in getting long-term training commitments from the large patent offices. Two- or three-day seminars do not have much impact according to the Director General of Pakistan's PO. China, as we will see, has had no problem in getting such long-term training commitments.

2

Labyrinths and catacombs

Patent office procedure

Welcome to the maze

As we saw in our discussion of patent law harmonization, while convergence in patent law is taking place at the level of principles, there is a long way to go at the level of rules. When it comes to the procedural rules relevant to the patent application process there is an enormous diversity of very detailed rules. For example, in the US the Consolidated Patent Rules amount to about 350 pages and a few thousand rules. This does not count the notices, guidelines and amendments that the USPTO issues in any one year relevant to its rules. The USPTO is not alone in administering a system of great rule complexity. In Australia, the Patent Regulations take up more than 490 pages.

The comparative advantage of patent attorneys lies not in their knowledge of patent law, but in their knowledge of many hundreds of rules and guidelines that make up patent procedure and the drafting of the claims that define an invention.[1] A key part of their work is keeping track of the many deadlines that exist for the submission of documentation that accompanies the application process, deadlines which if not kept to will result in extra fees or in some cases the loss of the applicant's rights.[2] The tedium of precise time and document management over what may be many years in relation to a single application, which may end up being withdrawn or rejected, is the price patent attorneys pay for their lucrative practices. Like tax attorneys, they help their corporate clients

---

[1] For a description of the work of the patent attorney in the European context see Philip Leith, *Harmonisation of Intellectual Property in Europe: A Case Study of Patent Procedure*, Sweet and Maxwell, London, 1998, Ch. 4.

[2] For example, if an applicant is relying on the priority of a first filing in an office of second filing, the second office will require documentation showing the first filing. For an example of the timelines and options related to this situation, including how the right might be lost, see Rule 52 of the Implementing Regulations to the Convention on the Grant of European Patents.

navigate their way through these rules, delaying, speeding up, splitting or redrafting the application as needs be. The difference is that patent attorneys help their clients collect private taxes, while tax attorneys help companies to avoid public taxes.

The description of patent office procedure that follows focuses on the principal steps that a patent office will go through in processing a patent application. This description is minimal and does not describe the work of any one office in detail. Its purpose is simply to help the reader understand some of the arguments developed in other parts of the book.

Filing routes

The act of filing an application in a patent office is crucial since it establishes a priority date for the application. (However, in a first-to-invent system the date of invention is determinative of priority.) The priority date of the application is used, especially by multinationals, to ground an international patenting strategy that is made possible by treaties that recognize a right of priority that flows from the first act of filing. Understanding the relationships amongst applications is often difficult because the combination of treaties and national rules provide time frames that allow for applications to be split, the claims of applications to be redrafted, new claims to be added, as well as other variations.

Patent applications can arrive in a patent office through different routes. The simplest case is where a national patent office receives an application that has not been filed anywhere else. First national filings can also serve as the basis for other filing options that have been created by treaties. As was noted in Chapter 1, patent offices are part of a filing route network that has been created by two treaties in particular – the Paris Convention for the Protection of Industrial Property, 1883 (Paris Convention) and the Patent Cooperation Treaty, 1970 (PCT). The Paris Convention has been of profound importance in creating a network of filing route options for applicants. Under the Paris Convention the filing of a patent application in one state that is a member of the Convention gives rise to a right of priority, which lasts for 12 months, for filing an application in the other member states.[3] Figure 2.1 depicts the Paris Convention filing route.

Importantly, the Paris Convention stipulates that its members can make special agreements for the protection of industrial property providing that those agreements do not reduce the standards of the Paris

---

[3] Article 4.

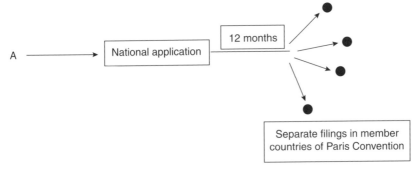

Figure 2.1   Paris Convention route

Convention.[4] Subsequent treaties have made use of the Paris Convention, including the priority rights it creates. From the point of view of facilitating simpler procedures for filing in multiple countries the PCT has been the key treaty (discussed further in Chapter 6). Membership of the PCT is open to members of the Paris Convention.[5] Under its procedures an applicant can file a single international application. This single international application can eventually be transmitted to as many national offices of PCT members as the applicant chooses. Under the Paris Convention the applicant starts with one national application and then has to follow up by making other national applications in Paris Convention countries. For an applicant pursuing an international patenting strategy the PCT offers a low-cost way of beginning such a strategy. Basically, the applicant pays a single set of fees to cover the cost of filing, searching and transmitting the international application.[6] In contrast, a Paris-filing strategy requires an applicant to deal with and pay the fees of each national office that is part of the strategy. The PCT through its single set of fees generates a low-cost option for an applicant to patent in all PCT states, whereas the Paris route requires an applicant to begin paying the national fees of patent offices in order to generate the same option.[7] The PCT is fundamental to the

[4] Article 19.
[5] See Article 62(1) of the PCT.
[6] The international filing fee in 2009 was set at 1,330 Swiss Francs. There is also a small transmittal fee and a search fee. The search fee varies depending on the office doing the work. For example, the Austrian office charges US$257 and the Canadian office US$1,309. For a table of fees for 2009 see www.wipo.int/export/sites/www/pct/en/fees.pdf.
[7] Some sense of the cost advantage of the PCT can be gained by looking at fee schedules of national offices. For example in the USPTO there are fees for filing ($330), searching ($540) and examining ($220), along with other possible fees such as those for excess independent claims ($220). See the USPTO's Fee Schedule for 2009 at www.uspto.gov/web/offices/ac/qs/ope/fee2009january01_2009may01.htm.

process of regulatory automation of the patent system that was mentioned in Chapter 1.

Another advantage the PCT gives an applicant is the chance to stretch out the application process. An applicant can first file a national application in a Paris Convention country and then up to 12 months later claim the priority of that application when making an international application under the PCT. After the PCT international application, the applicant has another 18 months in which to delay entry into the national offices the applicant has chosen. Essentially under this extended PCT filing route, the applicant has 30 months from the first national filing before the PCT application has to start being processed by national offices. Once the applicant enters this national phase the fees of each national office have to be paid. The advantage of the PCT is that the applicant can delay this national phase in order to better work out which states are to be part of the applicant's patenting strategy. This national phase may itself take several years, depending on, amongst other things, the backlog of the national office in question. An applicant can simply begin with the international application under the PCT, but this shortens the application process, something which companies may not want if they need more time to find commercial partners, assess or refine the invention and so on.

Other treaties have also built on the Paris Convention and the PCT thereby increasing filing route options for applicants. The Preamble to the European Patent Convention (EPC) expressly states that it is a regional treaty for the purposes of the PCT and a special agreement within the meaning of the Paris Convention. Under the EPC an applicant with a prior filing in a Paris Convention country enjoys a 12-month priority right for the purposes of filing an application under the EPC.[8] The fact that the EPC is a regional patent treaty for PCT purposes creates further filing route options for applicants. Using an international application filed under the PCT, an applicant can apply for a European patent that is granted by the European Patent Office (EPO) or it can bypass the EPO and use the PCT to apply directly to national European offices (although some European offices we will see later have closed this particular PCT route). The former route known as the Euro-PCT route has proved popular. Typically this route starts with a national filing. Figure 2.2 describes this more popular route.

Obviously the availability of filing routes to applicants will depend on their country of residence and the treaties to which that country is party.

[8] Article 87.1 of the EPC.

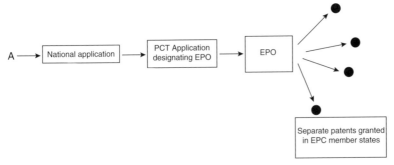

Figure 2.2   Euro–PCT route

Both the Paris Convention and the PCT have a large membership (more than 170 for the former and more than 130 for the latter). The important point here is that many of the world's patent offices and all the major offices in terms of filings are networked by means of treaties. An applicant can choose to enter the network using a particular office and then using that first application embark on a filing route that will see other related applications end up before other offices in the network. Applications that are related through a priority lineage are referred to as a 'patent family'. 'Family' is right, since the applications end up resembling each other rather than being identical. Different substantive patent rules and procedural rules, along with different approaches to searching and examination by patent offices as well as different claiming formats, mean that applications end up differing in some respects but not all. The rise in the number of patent families, especially Trilateral families (a first filing under the EPC, in the Japanese Patent Office (JPO) or the USPTO that creates a priority for subsequent filings in the other two offices) has been occurring for several decades.[9]

More and more patent families have swept through the world's patent filing routes overwhelming them and giving offices a reason to cooperate on sharing the work and exploiting work that has already been done by one office. At the same time the treaty networks and administrative solutions that patent offices devise also lay the basis for competition amongst them. The coordination of today is building the platform for the competition of tomorrow. Applicants today can choose to enter the PCT network at a number of points (see Figure 2.3). Offices that want to remain

---

[9]   By way of example see the Trilateral Statistical Report, 1992 at p.19 which reports figures on Trilateral patent families for 1988.

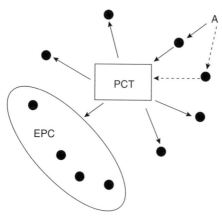

Figure 2.3   Entering the network

relevant in the system have to find ways in which to remain important filing destinations. One finding of the study is that patent offices themselves have only a limited understanding of the 'incredibly sophisticated strategies' that companies now employ (interview, UK PO). The offices that are important in filing strategies want to stay that way and so work hard to make themselves as customer friendly as possible. We will also see in Chapter 6 that one office can allow another office to do its PCT work. When one office extends technocratic trust to another it can also decide to let that office assist it with PCT examination (this becomes an applicant's choice). It follows that offices that wish to become or remain leaders in the system have strong incentives to invest in the creation of technocratic trust. The fieldwork suggested that some offices understood this better than others.

A procedure, another procedure and yet more procedures

Different filing routes give rise to different procedures for patent offices. Each major patent office will have a number of procedures that it administers. For example, there will be a procedure for a national filing that is not linked to a treaty process. Where the national patent office is party to a regional patent agreement it will have other procedures in place that link it to the regional office which does the examination and grant work. Membership of the PCT also means that a patent office will need to have yet other procedures for dealing with PCT applications. For example, the PCT distinguishes between patent offices that are receiving offices, designated offices, elected offices and offices that have been specially appointed as International Searching Authorities (ISAs) and International Preliminary Examining Authorities (IPEAs).[10]

PCT procedures can be broadly divided into an international phase, which is linked to the international application, and the national phase, which is linked to an international application that now has to be processed as a national application by a national (or regional) patent office. The PCT makes matters easier for applicants with its one international application, but it has created interlocking procedural complexities for patent offices. For example, an applicant might start the PCT process in the USPTO with the USPTO acting as a receiving office. The applicant might nominate the Korean Intellectual Property Office (KIPO) as the ISA because it is able to process the application faster than the USPTO. The applicant may choose the Euro-PCT route for countries in Europe, meaning that the EPO will examine the application in the national phase and national European offices will have to validate the grant of the European patent for their jurisdictions. Alternatively the applicant might decide not to use the EPO, preferring instead to designate national offices to do the examining. Patent offices, then, do not administer just one procedure but a number of them, and in the case of patent families will find themselves part of different filing routes for which they have to have different procedures.

The extent to which one office can make use of the work of another office in this procedural chain will depend on a range of factors including the extent to which the patent offices apply the same criteria of patentability and the extent to which they have common grant procedures and therefore common time flows of work. For example, all examining offices have to examine for novelty. Novelty is assessed against the prior art, which, as we have seen, can include in some patent systems oral descriptions of the invention anywhere in the world (sometimes referred to as absolute novelty). An office that operates under a standard of absolute novelty will get maximum benefit out of the work of an office that searches the prior art using the same standard. If both offices use the same search system then this may increase the confidence in each

---

[10] The definitions of these offices are to be found in Article 2 of the PCT. In simple terms receiving offices can receive PCT applications, designated offices and elected offices are named by the applicant in a PCT application (the difference being that they relate to different PCT procedures) and ISAs/IPEAs carry out search and examination work under the PCT (see Articles 16 and 32).

other's results. The EPO, for example, is making its EPOQUE search system (containing more than a hundred databases) available to an increasing number of patent offices outside of Europe, a system thought by many I interviewed to be the best in the world. In a world where patent offices were in competition one might expect that the EPO might be reluctant to make EPOQUE available to other offices. The interview at the EPO revealed a different way of thinking. The EPO sees itself as a leader and promoter of patent quality: 'we would like to bring offices to high-quality standards' (interview, EPO). Distributing EPOQUE is one way of improving the quality of work of other offices. Since the EPO is often an office of second filing, distributing EPOQUE to other offices means that EPO examiners will get the benefit of searches done by first filing offices using the system and as one interviewee observed, 'they have more trust in the search if it is EPOQUE-based'. Under the contracts that the EPO signs concerning EPOQUE, it also ensures that the receiving office makes its patent documentation available to the EPO, thereby increasing the comprehensiveness of the system.[11] In this way EPOQUE becomes a 'gold standard' (EPO official) that helps the EPO to form strategic partnerships with key developing-country players like China, Brazil and India, thereby creating a network that operates with the EPO's conception of patent quality. In the words of one interviewee: 'same legislation, same tools, the Chinese [patent office] will develop in the same way as the EPO'.

As my interview at the EPO suggested, a great deal can be achieved between two offices based on those offices sharing technology and agreeing to cooperate. But the different grant procedures of offices do set limits on the extent to which offices can cooperate. Historically, there have been major divergences in grant procedures that meant that offices would end up doing searching and examining at different times. Major differences in grant procedure remain. For example, Japan ran a deferred examination system (the Dutch having developed this system) in which an applicant had up to seven years in which to request a search and examination, but applications were published after 18 months from the priority date whether or not they had been examined. In the USPTO there is no deferred examination with applications being automatically searched and examined. But it used to be the case that applications were not published until the decision to issue the patent had been made (this position still holds where the

---

[11] For example, under its arrangement with China, databases are updated on a weekly basis. See www.epo.org/about-us/office/international-relations/projects/china.html.

applicant is only seeking protection in the US). As we shall see in Chapter 5, applicants could stretch out the application process for years, meaning that the USPTO had to keep the application in confidence for years. The EPO splits search and examination with a search report being mandatory and the applicant having to request an examination. Like the JPO, the EPO adheres to the 18-month publication rule.

Different procedures for the timing of search and examination can make it difficult for offices to share their results in ways that are mutually beneficial. Under the Japanese system applications could linger for a long time without being searched and examined, even though the application had been published. In the US, applications were automatically searched and examined, but had to be kept in confidence by the USPTO until they were issued. Slowly, there have been changes to patent laws that are increasing the possibility of the major offices being able to exploit each other's search and examination results. The US has adopted the 18-month publication rule and Japan has reduced the deferral period to 3 years (discussed in Chapter 5).

Changing grant procedures through legislation attracts complicated interest-group politics in the three major jurisdictions and so, for the time being, the Trilaterals have looked to ways to devise programmes of administrative cooperation that will allow the three offices to exploit each other's results so that they can speed up the processing of applications within the context of their existing grant procedures. The superhighway arrangement, which allows an applicant to fast-track an application in a second office after the first office has examined, is one example, and another is the Triway Pilot Program launched in 2008 by the Trilaterals.[12] Under this programme the office of first filing will produce a search report that is available to the second office of filing when it does its search. The office of third filing will have both search reports when it does its search and examination, the examination report then being available for the office of first filing. Yet another example of the way administrative cooperation is moving ahead of treaty and national law is the way in which the rules around filing requirements are being harmonized by the Trilaterals through the establishment of a technical working group on the formal aspects of patent applications. Aspects of this are dealt with by the Patent Law Treaty, but it does not yet apply to the Trilaterals. The

---

[12] Details of the Triway Pilot Program are to be found on the websites of the Trilateral Offices. The JPO has a clear statement of the program. See www.jpo.go.jp/torikumi_e/t_torikumi_e/triway_e.htm.

technical working group devised a common format application that the Trilaterals adopted in 2007 and will implement by 2009.[13]

Grant procedure

In terms of search and examination procedure the less detail that one uncovers the greater the similarities seem to be between the offices, and the more detail that one uncovers the greater the differences seem to be. What follows is a basic description of the major phases of the grant procedure based on the Trilateral Offices. After an application is filed with an office it will go through a formalities check, including making sure that the relevant filing fees have been paid. During this stage a date of filing will be established for the application which becomes crucial for determining issues around prior art and novelty.

Some offices permit an application to be filed in one of a number of languages. For example, the EPO works with three official languages, English, French and German. Filing in other languages is permitted, but this leads to extra translation obligations for the applicant. Translations generally are one source of expense in patenting and so there are initiatives to reduce translation obligations on applicants or to satisfy those obligations through automated translation. It is worth noting in passing that translation is consistent with the diffusion function of patents and, while patenting becomes cheaper if translation obligations are reduced, this does cut across the diffusion function of the patent system.

As the discussion above has shown, search and examination take place within the context of a patent system whether that system is national, regional or part of the international application process under the PCT. These systems have basic principles in common, meaning that offices examine applications using those principles. Trilateral reports over the years, for example, have pointed out that the three offices have to examine an application for novelty, inventive step (non-obviousness) and industrial applicability (usefulness). The PCT also stipulates that the purpose of the international preliminary examination is to formulate an opinion about an application using these three principles.[14] While these principles are certainly core to an examiner's work, the examiner looks at other things such as the relationship between the claims and the description of the invention.

---

[13] Details of the common application format can be found on the Trilateral website. See www.trilateral.net/news/20080425/index.php.

[14] See Article 33 of the PCT.

Examiners in the Trilateral Offices work with similar substantive principles of patentability that have different rule specifications. Under the EPC there has to be an invention that is new, involves an inventive step and is susceptible of industrial application.[15] The EPC excludes some things from the meaning of invention (for example, mathematical methods and computer programs),[16] some inventions from patentability (for example, biological processes)[17] and deems some inventions not to have industrial applicability.[18]

The US patent statute does not contain the list of exceptions and qualifications to patentability that is to be found in the EPC. But as was argued earlier, such exceptions to patentable subject matter do not necessarily stop POs from granting patents that cover the subject matter. In Chapter 4 we will see that the exception in the EPC relating to the patentability of software has not stopped the EPO from granting patents on software. Both the EPO and JPO work with absolute novelty. As pointed out earlier the US has a relative novelty standard excluding, from a loss of novelty, knowledge or uses of the invention outside of the US. EPO examiners, however, do not tour the world in an anthropological search for oral prior art. Instead, much like their US counterparts, they search databases consisting of patented and non-patented literature. The actual practice of searching is deeply driven by highly technical patent classification systems developed for the patent literature. The interviews suggest that a patent office's classification system becomes for examiners something of a mental map of the prior art. This in turn means that the search for novelty is at its most robust for technology areas where the patent literature is the thickest and at its weakest for prior art that exists in some non-written form of social practice.

All three offices have to decide whether the gap between the prior art and the invention is sufficient to take an invention out of the category of being obvious to the person skilled in the art. A lot of patent case law clusters around issues of how to formulate and apply a measure of this gap. Obvious inventions do not deserve monopoly protection. Non-obvious ones do. Where the line falls depends on how much capacity one invests in 'the person having ordinary skill in the art'. Investing this notional person with a level of skill is an artificial exercise, especially when an

15   Article 52.1 of the EPC.
16   See Article 52.2 of the EPC.
17   See Article 53 (b) of the EPC.
18   See Article 52.4 of the EPC.

individual examiner is dealing with an invention that is the product of a team or network of scientists. Patent offices have developed guidelines for dealing with the inventive-step requirement.[19]

All three offices have to consider whether the invention has industrial applicability, a principle which in US law is referred to as the requirement of utility. Inventions cannot be ethereal, but must have a concrete context in which they deliver a practical benefit. Finally, all three offices have to consider whether the applicant has sufficiently disclosed the invention to a person skilled in the art so that person can make and use the invention.[20] In the US this disclosure obligation goes beyond the mere enablement of the invention to include a specific obligation of disclosing the best mode of carrying out the invention.[21] US law, in other words, imposes a higher set of disclosure obligations on the patent applicant.

One can see from this very brief discussion that the Trilaterals share the core principles of patentability. My interviews at the Trilaterals suggested that the three offices believe that much of the further harmonization of these principles in terms of common outcomes can be achieved through various forms of administrative cooperation such as examiner exchanges. All three offices are searching for ways to move the patent harmonization agenda outside of the interminable dialogue of patent treaty negotiation.

Returning to the grant procedure, under the EPC a search report is mandatory.[22] Once drawn up it is sent to the applicant. Amongst other things, it contains an assessment of whether the application complies with the unity of invention requirement and a list of the prior art that the search examiner has concluded is relevant to the issues of novelty and

---

[19] The Guidelines for Examination in the EPO prescribe 'the problem and solution approach' in which the examiner determines the closest prior art, establishes the technical problem to be solved and then considers whether the claimed invention would have been obvious to the skilled person. See Part C, Ch.IV, 11.7 (2007 version). The USPTO's guidelines take into account the recent decision of the US Supreme Court in *KSR International Co.* v. *Teleflex Inc.* (KSR) 82 USPQ. 2d 1385 (2007) and place more emphasis on taking a fluid fact-finding approach to determining obviousness. See *Manual of Patent Examining Procedure* (July 2008 version), 2141. The JPO's guidelines require the examiner to engage in a careful comparison of the claimed invention and cited inventions and then to see if it is possible to establish a chain of reasoning that leads to the conclusion that the 'invention could easily have been made' (Section 29(2) of the Japanese Patent Law) by a person with ordinary skill in the art. See Part II, Chapter 2.2 of the *Examination Guidelines for Patent and Utility Model* (English version 2005).

[20] See 35 U.S.C. 112, Article 83 of the EPC and Article 36(4) of Japan's Patent Act, 1959.

[21] 35 U.S.C. 112.

[22] Article 92.1 of the EPC.

inventive step.[23] Over recent years the EPO has blurred the separation of the searching and examination stages. In addition to a search report, the search examiner also writes a non-binding opinion outlining whether the application and invention comply with the substantive principles and rules of the EPC.[24] The search report, if it is available, is published along with the application but not the search opinion.[25]

In the JPO and the USPTO, search and examination take place together in one stage rather than being formally divided in the way it is in the EPO. In the case of the JPO this does not mean that the same person carries out search and examination. The JPO for many years has outsourced the search function. Under the JPO's grant procedure examination must be requested within three years of filing, whereas in the USPTO filing automatically puts an application on the path to examination.[26] Under the EPO's procedures the applicant has to request examination (within 6 months of the mention of publication of the search report).[27]

All three offices adhere to the basic 18-month publication rule for applications, meaning that applications are published 18 months after the filing date. There are some exceptions to this 18-month rule in the case of the US. Applicants can certify that they will not be seeking protection for the invention abroad or using a multilateral procedure that applies the 18-month publication rule.[28] In these cases the USPTO has to keep these applications confidential until they are withdrawn or granted. One of the complaints about US patent procedure prior to its adoption of the 18-month rule was the problem of 'submarine' applications that might surface years later after winding their way in secret through the USPTO's corridors. In the eyes of some European POs this problem has not entirely gone away because of the exceptions that the US permits to the 18-month publication rule.

The EPO's procedure for examination is different to the other two offices in that the EPC establishes a three-person examining division for applications, with one examiner having primary custody of the application.[29] For

---

[23] See Rule 61.1 and Rule 64 of the EPC Implementing Regulations and Chapter II.2 of the Examination Manual.

[24] Referred to as the Extended European Search Report. See Rule 62 of the EPC Implementing Regulations.

[25] See Rule 62.2 and Rule 68.1.

[26] See Articles 48.2 and 48.3 of Japan's Patent Act, 1959.

[27] See Article 94 of the EPC and Rule 70 of the Implementing Regulations.

[28] See 35 U.S.C. 122(b)(2)(B)(i).

[29] Article 18 of the EPC.

all three offices it is true, however, that a single examiner does the lion's share of the work in relation to an application. During the examination stage the applicant's attorney will respond to the examiner's objections to the application and file amendments to the application. In the US especially, an application that is granted first off without any changes is grounds for nervousness by a patent attorney since it perhaps means that the attorney has not been ambitious enough in drafting the claims. Moreover, the attorney may be representing a client who may have reasons for wanting to drag out the application process. If every applicant wanted a patent quickly then they would take advantage of the accelerated examination procedures possessed by each of the Trilaterals.[30] The JPO, apparently wishing to be the fastest draw in the West and East, has introduced a super-accelerated procedure with a patent application being granted under it in 17 days.[31] Many applicants, however, do not want speedy processing.

The first action by an examiner will more often than not identify problems with the application based on the examiner's prior art search. Typically the examiner will point to problems around novelty and obviousness. The process of substantive examination is regulated by various rules about permissible amendments and the introduction of new material, as well as appeal options if the examiner decides to reject the application after it has been amended. One of the features of the US procedure, which has been criticized, is that it is difficult for an examiner to reject finally an application because an applicant can restart the prosecution process with new arguments or amendments by filing a Request for Continued Examination.[32] At the USPTO interview, the US patent procedure was described as being flexible and patent attorneys were said 'to take maximum advantage of this flexibility'.

One important issue that affects the dynamic between examiners and attorneys is whether patent offices sufficiently recognize in their measures of an examiner's productivity an examiner's action that involves maintaining a rejection in the face of various procedural strategies that attorneys will employ to get that rejection overturned. Individuals, as a general rule, will not consistently increase their workload if they are not recognized for doing so in some way. The cost, for example, to a USPTO examiner of rejecting an application might be the threat of an appeal to

[30] An example is the EPO's PACE program. For the USPTO's accelerated examination programme see www.uspto.gov/web/patents/accelerated/.

[31] See www.jpo.go.jp/torikumi_e/hiroba_e/first_patent_granted.htm.

[32] Mark A. Lemley and Kimberly A. Moore, 'Ending Abuse of Patent Continuations', 84 (2004) *Boston University Law Review*, 63.

the Board of Patent Appeals and Interferences, involving the examiner in, amongst other things, a conference with the examiner's supervisors. Apart from the procedural gamesmanship of attorneys, there is the fact that some areas of technology are more complicated than others. Biotechnology applications were regularly mentioned by offices for being time-consuming to manage. All the major offices were aware of the fact that in measuring the productivity of their examiners they had to take account of the complexities that faced their examiners, something that had not been done sufficiently well in the past. Productivity measures had to weigh properly the costs to an examiner of justifying the rejection of an application.

Following the grant of the patent, the EPO provides a post-grant opposition procedure in which any person may file an opposition to the patent.[33] This is heard by the Opposition Division of the EPO and if successful will result in the revocation of the patent. At one time Japanese patent procedure allowed for pre-grant opposition, but this was replaced by a post-grant procedure which itself has been dropped with an invalidation trial system taking its place.[34] The USPTO does not have a pre-grant or post-grant opposition procedure. It does have re-examination procedures for granted patents, but these are not often used. For example, the USPTO in a report to Congress noted that from 2000 to 2004 it had received some 1.6 million patent applications and issued almost 900,000 patents, but only 53 requests for inter partes re-examination had been filed.[35]

Patent quality

Patent quality and the quality of invention are two different things. A patent is a legal instrument that is granted for an invention. Within a capitalist system a patent office does not judge the quality of an invention independently of the criteria of patentability. Judgements about the quality of invention are left to markets or to the inventor's relevant peer groups. In later chapters we will see that in China and Russia some attempts were made to determine the quality of an invention by linking the size of the reward that the state gave to an inventor to the savings in the cost of production that resulted from the invention. In market systems patent offices

[33] Article 99 of the EPC.
[34] Article 123 of Patent Act 1959 (Japan).
[35] See USPTO, 'Report to Congress on Inter Partes Reexamination', available at www.uspto. gov/web/offices/dcom/olia/reports/reexam_report.htm.

assess an invention in order to ensure that it meets the prevailing legal standard of inventiveness or non-obviousness. Once a patent examiner decides that the invention satisfies the standard there is no further inquiry into the quality of the invention.

When it comes to analysing patent quality the starting point is the fact that a patent is a legal product – a personal property right that may be assigned or licensed. This legal product is the outcome of an examination process in which, if the standards of patentability are applied correctly, the applicant will be granted a valid patent. Patent quality then can be defined in terms of the correct application of the standards of patentability by a patent office. High quality patents (correctly issued patents) do not necessarily mean high invention quality. If the prevailing standard of non-obviousness is set low then the patent office may correctly grant patents over inventions in which the inventive step is a slight shuffle as opposed to a giant leap. It follows that patent quality and invention quality are only contingently related. One can have quality patents issued for insignificant inventions.

Patent quality should not be confused with issues about the scope of patentable subject matter. Patent systems set few restrictions on patentable subject matter. One consequence of this is that patent offices issue patents over inventions such as packaged crustless peanut butter and jelly sandwiches and methods of swinging a swing, inventions that perhaps do not need the support of a patent system.[36] There is quite a lot of insignificant invention about. IBM, which likes to portray itself as a leader in patent quality, applied for and was granted a patent on a method of queuing to use the toilet.[37] It subsequently disclaimed the patent claims. In patent systems with few restrictions on patentable subject matter and a pro-patent culture, patent offices will have to contend with applications on all manner of inventions. Such patents may turn out to be correctly granted, depending on the prevailing standards of patentability, especially for inventive step.

The interviews revealed that patent offices take the view that patent quality is linked to the correct application of standards of patentability. As one interviewee put it, the issue of quality for a patent office consists in asking whether the steps in the process of patenting have been followed. Drawing an analogy with the production of Sarah Lee cakes, he went

[36] See US Patent No. 6,004,596 and US Patent No. 6,368,277.
[37] US Patent No. 6,329,919. The patent was the subject of a Director Initiated Order for Reexamination on the basis that not all the relevant prior art areas had been searched. A copy of the order is available through the US Public PAIR system.

on to observe that it was not possible to test the quality of every cake so instead one had to check that the steps in the production process were being followed correctly and if they were one could assume the quality of the product. The National Academy of Public Administration in its study of the USPTO found that the USPTO officials 'believe that discussions regarding patent quality should focus on whether a particular patent meets the statutory criteria'.[38] In short, patent offices take the view that a quality patent is one that has been correctly granted. This raises the question of how one knows whether a patent office is correctly applying the criteria of patentability.

One possibility is to use court decisions concerning the validity of granted patents in order to gain some sort of insight into the quality of work of a patent office. There are some problems with using court decisions to assess the quality of a patent office's work. Even in the US, where the patent litigation market is large, only a small percentage of patents are litigated and the vast majority are settled by the parties (see the discussion in Chapter 1 concerning litigation rates). In other countries there is little patent litigation. For example in Australia, Rotstein and Weatherall report that of the 277 patent actions filed from 1995 to 2002 only 42 proceeded to a judgement by the court.[39] The number of cases may not be significant and since they are examples of a patent office's work that have been selected on the basis of litigation alone there is the problem of selection bias. It is not clear that a court's decision itself is necessarily a reliable guide to the correctness of the patent office's work. Farrell and Merges, for instance, argue that there are strong links between a party's chances of winning and how much it spends, spending itself being affected by the party's incentive and capacity.[40] The point behind their analysis is captured by the old saying of 'better a weak patent in strong hands than a strong patent in weak hands'.

One can also look at other kinds of proceedings that test the work of a patent office such as pre-grant or post-grant opposition proceedings, but the same problem of small numbers occurs here as well. Also the use or lack of use of these procedures may well reveal more about the

[38] *US Patent and Trademark Office: Transforming to Meet the Challenges of the 21st Century*, Report of the National Academy of Public Administration, August 2005, 62.

[39] Fiona Rotstein and Kimberlee Weatherall, 'Filing and Settlement of Patent Disputes in the Federal Court, 1995–2005', Intellectual Property Research Institute of Australia, Working Paper No. 17.06, 10.

[40] Joseph Farrell and Robert Merges, 'Incentives to Challenge and Defend Patents: Why Litigation Won't Reliably Fix Patent Office Errors and Why Administrative Patent Review Might Help', 19 (2004) *Berkeley Technology Law Journal*, 943.

strategic behaviour of the users than the quality of a patent office's work. A company, for example, with some prior art information about a patent may choose not to use it in a pre-grant opposition, preferring instead to wait to see if it gets sued and then use that information in a private bargaining process.

Patent offices are well aware of the fact that they make mistakes. The patent law of some countries states that the grant of a patent is no guarantee of its validity.[41] These days all the large developed-country patent offices have internal quality control procedures in place. (A finding of the interviews was that smaller and mid-size developing-country offices have virtually none.) The USPTO, for example, carries out annual quality reviews sampling somewhere between 2% and 3% of the patents that it allows with error rates of between 4% and 6% being reported.[42] Internal quality audit procedures are certainly part of an approach to assessing and improving patent quality, but they may also be compromised by things such as budget cuts. Independent reviews of the USPTO's quality procedures in 1990 and 1997 found serious problems with it.[43] This suggests the need to complement or bolster internal quality procedures with external audit mechanisms of some kind, a point that is developed in Chapter 11.

Aside from external and internal reviews of patent office procedures that might be used to test patent quality, there are also indicators that might be used either individually or in aggregate to measure or assess patent quality. From the moment a patent application hits a patent office it begins to generate information that can potentially be used in an assessment of its quality (for example, searches, examinations reports, rejections, amendments, appeals, and pre-grant or post-grant review). No one measure will be determinative of quality but one possibility is to aggregate this kind of information into an overall patent quality index.[44]

One indicator that was mentioned during the course of the interviews was the use of prior art information that is cited in a patent application. For example, in areas of technology such as Internet business methods where there is only a small patent literature but a large non-patent literature, one would expect the applicant and the examiner to cite more non-patent

[41] See, for example, s.20 of the Patents Act 1990 (Australia).
[42] *US Patent and Trademark Office: Transforming to Meet the Challenges of the 21st Century*, 64.
[43] Stephen A. Merrill, Richard C. Levin, and Mark B. Myers, (eds.), *A Patent System for the 21st Century*, National Academies Press, Washington, 2004, 50.
[44] For an example of a project to develop a patent quality index see www.law.upenn.edu/blogs/polk/pqi/index.html.

literature than patent literature. This type of approach to assessing quality is likely to be rough since each indicator will be rooted in the context of a specific patent system and affected by other factors such as the conventions and strategies that patent attorneys have developed in that jurisdiction. For example, citation in the US patent system is affected by the fact that there are specific rules that create an obligation to disclose prior art to the USPTO.[45] Long lists of citations do not necessarily correlate with quality since there is always a question about the degree of relevance of any individual citation. Dumping large amounts of prior art references on busy examiners may be a way of complying with the disclosure obligation while hiding an individual instance of prior art that threatens an application. Many attorneys will not try to game the system in this way, but it is worth noting that in 2006 the USPTO suggested that information disclosure requirements were not screening out irrelevant information and were compromising the quality of examination.[46] The citation of prior art in a jurisdiction may also be affected by the approach that an office takes to examining claims. Some offices may place more emphasis on examining the independent claim rather than the dependent claims, in which case one would expect dependent claims to achieve less attention in terms of citation. In short, there are complicated micro-dynamics around each possible indicator of patent quality that set limits on the reliability of a patent quality index.

The factor affecting patent quality that patent offices most often mentioned was the experience of examiners – 'you don't get good examination quality until you have years of experience' and 'examiners have to be long stay' are examples of comments on the importance of experience to quality. One reason, it emerged during the interviews, for why the USPTO was not seen to be able to produce quality with the same consistency as the EPO was because the USPTO has a high staff turnover compared to the EPO. Other factors that were mentioned were time for examination and metrics of productivity that recognized the degree of difficulty of examining particular areas of technology. The effect of not recognizing that more time is needed for some technologies is that examiners faced by crudely devised production quotas will 'cut corners' (interview, Canadian PO).

---

[45] For the basic rule see 37 C.F.R. 1.56 and for the rules governing Information Disclosure Statements see 37 C.F.R. 1.97 and 1.98.

[46] For the USPTO's concerns see 'Changes to Information Disclosure Statement Requirements and Other Related Matters', *Federal Register*, 71(131), 10 July 2006, 38,808.

When it came to perceptions of quality in examination, the EPO was often mentioned in the interviews at developing-country offices as doing quality work. This may have a lot to do with the time that the EPO has invested in building capacity in those offices (see Chapter 4). Developed-country patent offices tended to see the EPO as being more consistent in terms of quality than the USPTO. It was thought that the USPTO had a very high grant rate compared to the EPO (one study suggesting that the USPTO grant rate between 1993 and 1998 was as high as 97%).[47] This kind of grant rate can be used to attack the quality standards of an office, especially if it is receiving around 200,000 applications per year as the USPTO was receiving in the mid 1990s. But as the literature has developed it has become clear that calculating the real grant rate is not straightforward and inferences about quality from grant rates even less so. Another study, for example, suggests while the USPTO's grant rate increased during the 1990s it only reached 76% by 1998.[48] One would predict that, given the Trilaterals have much the same business model (see Chapter 1), and given their increasing coordination on examination quality issues, their grant rates would start to come closer together. There is some evidence of a convergence of grant rates. In 2007 the EPO reported a grant rate of about 51%, compared to about 49% from both the JPO and the USPTO.[49] It is worth keeping in mind that this grant rate still translates into a large number of patents being granted because of the number of applications being received. Collectively in 2007 the Trilaterals received a little over 993,000 applications.[50]

The interviews found that time spent on the examination of an application generally falls into a range of 10 to 20 hours. In developing countries it might be significantly less than 10 hours if, as is often the case, the examiner is able to rely on a PCT report generated by an ISA. In such a situation, the developing-country examiner might, at best, carry out some minimal extra searching. In cases where the developing-country examiner does not have a PCT report to access (for example, a first application by a local) then a full examination can take up to 16 to 20 hours. Many developing-country offices do not have access to the extensive electronic databases that examiners in

---

[47] For a discussion of some of the studies see Merrill, Levin and Myers (eds.), *A Patent System for the 21st Century*, 52–5.

[48] See Ron D. Katznelson, 'Bad Science in Search of "Bad" Patents', 17 (2007) *Federal Circuit Bar Journal*, 1.

[49] See *Trilateral Statistical Report, 2007 Edition*, EPO, JPO, USPTO, Munich, 2008, 47.

[50] See ibid., 36.

developed countries do and so there is a greater manual component in their examination process.

The interviews revealed, not surprisingly, that in the trade-off between quality and meeting production targets those in management positions spoke about the overriding importance of meeting production targets. Examiners wanted more time to do searches and examination. Managers, even if they had been examiners, tended to see this request for time as falling into the trap of diminishing returns. This raises two issues, the first being whether the search for prior art can be likened to a simple input-output model governed by the law of diminishing returns. The second is that even if diminishing returns apply, is it true that 20 hours in total for processing an application is close to the point where additional hours of processing will do little to improve patent quality? On the second issue King, using US data, suggests that there is a statistical relationship between increased examination hours and a reduction in patent litigation such that even a one hour increase in examination for all patent applications would bring about significant net savings from the reduction in litigation costs.[51] As he goes on to point out, one would want to target technological areas where the cost-to-benefit ratio of increasing the cost of examination but gaining savings on patent litigation was high. Patents on tennis racquets that, for example, claim increased frame width in order to increase resistance to twisting of the frame, probably do not need the intense focus that patents on pharmaceuticals do.[52]

Another argument that is used to support a minimalist approach to patent quality by a patent office is to claim that since few patents are used in litigation or licensing it is better to invest more in patent litigation as a means of quality control than in patent offices.[53] This argument rests on the assumption that litigation is likely to lead to the correct decision. As we saw earlier, some have suggested that there are serious problems with this assumption. Patent litigation is also a quality filter that cannot be relied on in developing countries where there is not a tradition of litigation, there are low levels of local patent litigation expertise and, in some countries, problems relating to the integrity of the judicial system.

---

[51] John L. King, 'Patent Examination Procedures and Patent Quality' in Wesley M. Cohen and Stephen A. Merrill (eds.), *Patents in the Knowledge-Based Economy*, National Academies Press, Washington DC, 2003, 54.

[52] See, for example, US Patent 6,383,099.

[53] Mark A. Lemley, 'Rational Ignorance at The Patent Office', 95 (2001) *Northwestern University Law Review*, 1495.

The argument for patent office minimalism also assumes that it is safe to tolerate wrongly granted patents because when one looks at many of these patents individually they are unlikely to be licensed or used. This assumption commits the fallacy of composition. What is true about the individual effects of a patent is not necessarily true when it is part of a patent portfolio, in much the same way that what is true of a single rocket is not true of an arsenal of rockets. It is the 'arsenal' effects of patent portfolios that we need to understand before we conclude it is safe to allow the patent office to become a night watchman.

Patent office managers are somewhat schizophrenic about patent quality. They see its importance, readily concede that examiners are under time pressures and that this impacts on quality, but they keep coming back to measures of productive efficiency and ways to improve service to their corporate clients. As mentioned earlier, one of the findings of the interviews is that patent offices no longer have a sense of their duties under the patent social contract. This has all sorts of repercussions for their operations, including the way in which they approach patent quality. The patent social contract and the obligations that a patent office has under it to the public it ostensibly serves were, with the exception of management in the German PO, not mentioned by PO managers. Patent quality is seen by most offices solely as a means to attract business and to compete with other patent offices in doing so. This in turn translates into more time pressures on examiners. The performance of examiners is constantly monitored and measured in the large patent offices, giving rise to a wealth of data that is used in an attempt to assess and improve patent quality.[54] For the purpose of assessing the performance and productivity of examiners some patent offices such as the USPTO and EPO will award points for particular actions. There is an obvious danger to patent quality if the particular scheme does not recognize the extra work involved for examiners in rejecting an application.[55] The interview in the EPO suggested the points scheme had, from an examiner's perspective, improved on this front. Amidst all the statistics and measurement there is one elusive intangible that seems important to patent quality and this is whether

[54] For an example see US Department of Commerce, Office of Inspector General, 'USPTO should Reassess how Examiner Goals, Performance Appraisal Plans, and the Award System Stimulate and Reward Examiner Production', Final Inspection Report No. IPE-15722 September 2004, available at www.oig.doc.gov/oig/reports/2004/USPTO-IPE-15722-09-04.pdf.

[55] See Adam B. Jaffe and Josh Lerner, *Innovation and its Discontents*, Princeton University Press, Princeton, 2004, 136.

examiners in an office have an *esprit de corps*, something difficult to instil by means of performance incentives and bonus payments.

Much of the patent quality debate is about outsiders criticizing patent offices for issuing too many patents. But patent offices themselves have insider views as to which offices do quality work. Compared to 30 or 40 years ago there are many more search tools and databases that can be used by one office to check the search results of other offices. Middle-size offices such as the Canadian PO have a much greater capacity to generate their own searches than they once did (interview, Canadian PO). This gives them a greater window of transparency on the work of other offices, especially the major offices, and allows them to form views about where quality work is really done. Most developing-country patent offices are in a weaker position to check the work of other patent offices because they have poor access to databases and have to rely on freely available search systems meant for general public use, like the EPO's esp@cenet. In the words of one examiner from a developed country: 'You get what you pay for. At least it allows developing-country examiners to have a go, but you still need training in its use.' The speed and power of electronically generated transparency will probably lead to a much greater exposure of the problems of the patent system than its supporters would like. Once all the world's databases, including those on traditional knowledge, are connected like so many brain cells it will not just be apparent that there is nothing new under the Sun, but that it is also all part of the prior art.

Within Europe, the EPO and the German PO see themselves as leaders in maintaining high standards of examination. It is also true that other offices perceive them as having high standards. However, whether this commitment to quality meets the duties of a patent office to maintain the social value of patenting is doubtful. The commitment of these offices to patent quality is part of a broader defensive strategy that has the support of European companies and industries, especially those in Germany that fear the costs of a flood of low-quality patents from the US. Moreover, the patent quality debate becomes bound up with the sector specific concerns of large industrial enterprises that use national patent offices to advance their own agendas in the patent quality debate. So, for example, the Netherlands PO will have regular meetings with key stakeholders such as Philips, Shell and Unilever, all of which will make 'very helpful' suggestions about patent quality that the Netherlands PO can take to meetings of the Administrative Council of the European Patent Organization (interview, Netherlands PO). The same is true of the German PO, the UK PO and other offices. Large industrial enterprises view patent quality through the prism of their business models. What a pharmaceutical company sees as important to patent quality is not necessarily what a telecoms company will see as important. In the hands of multinationals, the patent quality debate often turns into a debate about the usefulness of particular grant procedures to their individual business operations.

An approach to patent quality that is informed by the patent social contract would reverse the current emphasis of patent offices. The reforms of patent office procedure would be driven by the goal of improving the quality of invention. The patent social contract is not a contract aimed at the grant of more and more patents, but rather at the diffusion of more and more significant inventions. Under the patent social contract, society cannot be taken to be contracting for obvious inventions since by definition these are already available to society in the storehouse of skills of the workers skilled in the relevant arts. Instead society is contracting for the delivery of non-obvious inventions. Lachlan James in an extensive examination of the neuropsychological foundations of creativity and its links to patent law's criterion of non-obviousness argues, on the basis of a neuropsychological model of creativity, that non-obviousness is the search for a set of 'novel associations between previously disparate concepts'.[56] On this account the prior art base functions like a network of concepts that the ordinary worker could have connected to solve the invention problem. If this network could not have been used by the ordinary worker to solve the problem and instead what was required was a novel association of disparate concepts, then one can say that the criterion of non-obviousness has been satisfied. To think creatively, then, is to think outside of the network of conventional associations.

Patent offices carefully steer away from the kind of rigorous analysis of the link between invention and prior art that Lachlan James' approach would require because they would not be able to grant the millions of patents that they do grant. Courts for the most part engage in wordplay around the concepts of inventive step or non-obviousness without any evidence-based understanding of the neuropsychological foundations of creativity. Some courts on occasions are honest enough to admit that lawyer's words do not constitute an evidence-based approach to the nature of invention.[57]

[56] Lachlan James, 'A Neuropsychological Analysis of the Law of Obviousness' in Peter Drahos (ed.), *Death of Patents*, Lawtext Publishing, London, 2005, 67, 82.
[57] For a list of citations see James, 'A Neuropsychological Analysis of the Law of Obviousness', 70–1.

The patent quality issue has to be linked back to the patent social contract. One does not need abstract Rawlsian methods of the original position and the veil of ignorance to assume that citizens acting rationally would only want to grant monopoly rewards to inventions that were genuinely creative and that the relevant understanding of creativity should have some basis in psychological evidence rather than lawyers' word games. It is high-quality inventions that society wants, not high-quality patents which can only be a means to an end and never an end in themselves. The focus on measures of patent quality represents a grotesque reification process, in which multinationals like IBM have persuaded policy makers that it is more important to care about the quality of monopoly rights than the more fundamental question of whether the patent system is generating invention information of a quality for which society would want to contract.

Patent quality is not just about the correct application of the standards of patentability. More fundamentally, it requires those who administer the patent system to operate with an evidence-based understanding of creativity that drives the patent system's test of non-obviousness. On this approach, improving patent quality is very much about improving the quality of invention that the patent system serves to disclose to the public. Confining patent quality to the correct application of patent standards may serve patent offices and their multinational customers but it does not serve the public. The primary benefit to the public of the patent system comes if the patent system is responsible for the disclosure of genuinely creative inventions that in the post-patent period become the subject of price competition. At least some offices appear to be arriving at this conclusion. The German, Danish and Dutch offices in a note to the Administrative Council of the European Patent Organization suggested that 'patent protection can only be provided for inventions that are truly innovative, the disclosure of which will enrich the present state of the art far beyond the obvious'.[58]

The dark heart of complexity: patent claims

The monopoly heart of the patent system lies in the claims that are applied for and granted. When a patent application is lodged it consists of a description of the invention and one or more claims. The function of

---

[58] See 'Notes on the patenting situation in Europe', CA/92/05 Munich 18.05.2005, 1.

claims, to borrow the words of the PCT, is 'to define the matter for which protection is sought'.[59] In Chapter 1, we saw that the patent system is a system of private taxation. Through claims the drafter determines the products and activities that are to be the subject of this power of taxation.

It is in the drafting of patent claims that so much of the relentless gaming of the patent system is to be found. Through the art of claim drafting, attorneys circumvent the patent social contract and patent offices, by accepting these claims and granting the patents, participate in that circumvention. One finding of this study is that developed-country patent offices extend that process of circumvention by training developing-country examiners in the recognition of different types and styles of drafting, so that claims drafted in developed countries gain smooth passage through developing-country offices because the examiners have been taught to recognize and accept these types and styles of claims. So, for example, the patenting of naturally occurring biological materials can be achieved if a claim format that distinguishes the natural from the isolated or purified material is accepted by an office. 'An isolated Y comprising sequence X' is one example of this kind of patent drafting magic. Large developed-country offices probably help their industries by investing in training developing-country examiners. Malaysian examiners explained to me that they had more trouble with applications in which the claims had been drafted in the US than those from Europe because 'we don't have training from US patent office, we are less familiar with their patents' (interview, Malaysian PO).

The main purpose of this section is to illustrate how the patent office and the attorneys responsible for the drafting of patent claims co-evolve the patent system in directions favoured by large industrial users of the system. In Chapter 1, a co-evolutionary relationship was defined as one in which two actors confer advantages on each other that assist them in their competitive struggles with others. We will see in a moment that, by accepting different types of claims, patent offices expand the operation of the patent system and in some cases circumvent restrictions on patentability. During the course of the fieldwork more than one attorney suggested that through the art of claiming much could be done to avoid restrictions on patentability and improve protection for clients. This is almost certainly no idle boast. Much of the practical impact of any national patent system lies not in what the patent statute says is or is not patentable, but rather

---

[59] Article 6 of the PCT.

in what types of claims the patent office recognizes. Granted claims lie at the core of daily commerce in patented technologies. Granted claims give their owners the right to exclude others from the use of the resources to which the claims relate (for example, the use of a chemical compound). Patent attorneys in drafting claims and in inventing new types of claims that are accepted by patent offices are changing the selection pressures that operate on firms in a given industry. In terms of evolutionary theory, patent agents in devising and promoting new claiming formats are important sources of variation. Borrowing Darwin's language, variation 'if it be in any degree profitable to an individual of any species ... will tend to the preservation of that individual'.[60] Clearly, the patent claims that confer advantages upon firms are not randomly generated but are the subject of deliberate design.

An example of the practical power of claiming formats can be given using European patent law as a source. Assume for a moment that a polity decides to prohibit the patenting of plants and animals, a prohibition that takes the form of an exclusion from patentability of 'plant and animal varieties'. TRIPS allows its members to exclude plants and animals from patentability.[61] One way around such a prohibition is to use a claiming format that does not operate at the level of an animal variety. So, for example, a claim format of the kind 'animal X of sub-species Y having characteristic Z' would run into problems because it operates at the level of a variety. A patent office might be prepared to accept a claim format that read 'animal X having characteristic Z' because it does not claim a variety. The European Biotechnology Directive expressly contemplates this kind of possibility since it allows for the patentability of plants and animals 'if the technical feasibility of the invention is not confined to a particular plant or animal variety'.[62]

Patent claims can be categorized by reference to the type of subject matter they define or the style in which they are drafted. Running through both categories is a basic distinction between independent claims or dependent claims. Independent claims stand on their own whereas dependent claims refer back to other claims. The most basic subject matter categorization is into product or process claims. Claims can also be distinguished by reference to a particular format. For example, in the

---

[60] Charles Darwin, *On the Origin of Species (1859)*, Oxford University Press, Oxford, 2008, 50.
[61] See Article 27(3)(b).
[62] See Article 4(2) of Directive 98/44/EC on the legal protection of biotechnology invention.

chemical field applicants will sometimes claim a large class of compounds using a product claim in the form of a Markush claim (discussed below). Another distinct claiming format is the Swiss claim, a format that was first accepted by the Swiss patent office to overcome the unpatentability of the second use of a known compound in a method of treatment under the EPC (discussed in Chapter 6). Claiming formats need not be confined to a particular technology. For example, use claims for products or functional claims in which the invention is defined in terms of its effects and actions can be drafted for a range of technological areas.

According to the PCT, patent claims are meant to be 'clear and concise'.[63] In later chapters we will see that in fact one of the problems facing offices is an increase in the complexity of claims that makes meaningful examination very difficult. The complexity of patent claims is an old problem. Consider, for example, a complaint from a member of the US Patent Bar in 1952 about the patent claims being allowed by the USPTO in the electronics field. Referring to an issued patent, he points out that the first claim, which relates to a wave filter, contains twelve mathematical formulae that in turn rely on other formulae so that there is a 'pyramiding of complexity which even the most skilled mathematician would have difficulty unravelling'.[64] Working out what does and does not constitute infringement of the patent would be beyond even the most skilled electronics specialist.

Chemical patenting has generated styles of claims that circumvent the patent social contract in various ways. One of the most well known of these is the Markush claim. This takes the form of a claim for a compound that has an abstract formula of the kind A-X-B in which X can have many complex chemical substituents each of which may involve further selections from a chemical class. Essentially, instead of referring to a particular material, one can refer to a material that has to be selected from a specified group of materials. It follows that Markush claims are not a claim to a single compound but a class of compounds that may number in the millions or even billions. This type of claim was allowed by the USPTO Commissioner in 1925, when the applicant Markush presented a draft claim which in part read 'material selected from the group consisting of aniline, homologues of aniline and halogen substitution products

[63] Article 6 of the PCT.
[64] Frederick Breitenfeld, 'Complex Terminology in Patent Claims', 34 (1952) *Journal of the Patent Office Society*, 904. The US Patent No. is 2,591,838.

of aniline'.[65] The Commissioner, in recognizing Markush claims through administrative fiat, created a class of claims that have become a very significant part of chemical patenting practice.

Not surprisingly, the patent attorney profession very quickly saw the potential in making broad claims using the Markush style and so over the succeeding decades and not for the first time the USPTO found itself embroiled in a technical rule-intensive game of attempting to set limits on the use of Markush claims.[66] One problem that was rapidly identified was the problem of disclosure. The Commissioner, in a 1934 decision, pointed out that in 'the mass of verbiage presented by the claims, the invention is effectively concealed rather than clearly pointed out'.[67] If Rumplestilskin had decided to hide his name amongst the many millions of possible members of a Markush claim there would have been little chance of it being discovered by the princess's many searchers. The use of Markush claims has been refined, but over the decades concerns about the format have persisted.[68]

Markush claims present a good example of the way in which patent offices and industry co-evolve. Once the Commissioner had recognized this style of claim the attorney profession was able to use it to allow firms in the chemical industry to make more expansive claims than would otherwise have been possible. The new claim format is a favourable variation that becomes preserved and transmitted by means of law.[69] The patent office is the key agent in this legal process of preservation and transmission. Claims form the proprietary rule base of the patent system. Once the patent office recognizes a particular claiming format, attorneys not surprisingly begin to use it to obtain as strong and broad a protection as they can for their clients. The patent office, faced by many more such claims that probe in various ways the edges of allowable protection, generally responds by issuing guidelines for their appropriate use. The use

---

[65] See Manuel C. Rosa, 'Outline of Practice Relative to "Markush" Claims', 34 (1952) *Journal of the Patent Office Society*, 324.

[66] For the history until the 1970s see Edward C. Walterscheid, 'Markush Practice Revisited', 61 (1979) *Journal of Patent Office Society*, 270.

[67] Ex Parte Dahlen, 21 U.S.P.Q. (Com'r. Dec. 1934) 397, 398, cited in Walterscheid, 'Markush Practice Revisited', 270, 272, fn.10.

[68] See G.W.A. Milne, 'Very Broad Markush Claims: A Solution or a Problem? Proceedings of a Round Table Discussion Held on August 29, 1990', 31 (1991) *Journal of Chemical Information and Computing Science*, 9.

[69] 'This preservation of favourable variations and the rejection of injurious variations, I call Natural Selection.' See Darwin, *On the Origin of Species (1859)*, 63.

of the format becomes routinized in two principal ways.[70] Patent offices develop routines for searching and examining the new formats and patent attorneys come to use the claiming format as a matter of routine. The system expands in the sense that a method of claiming something that previously could not be claimed has been allowed, thereby enlarging the ways in which invention can be defined under the patent system.

By recognizing the new format, the patent office encourages the use of it in applications and therefore creates an area of examination work for itself that did not exist before. Patent offices would not be the size they are today if they had not accepted new claiming formats. The claim format begins as an innovation that eventually becomes part of a patent office's organizational routine. This can be a lengthy process in which the format is the subject of incremental innovation, as in the case of Markush claims, the structure of which became more expansive because subgenus claims were permitted.[71] The effect on the industry of the new format is an empirical matter, but clearly the new format changes the selection pressures that now operate on firms. Allowing product claims in pharmaceuticals, for example, changes the selection pressure on the generic industry (see Chapter 7 for further discussion). Firms have a new tool that they can use in the process of competition with other firms. Patent offices by allowing new claiming formats change the selection pressures that act on industries for which the format is relevant. These selection pressures, because of the globalization of the patent system and the fact that a claim format innovation in one office diffuses to other offices (Markush claims being an example), can be brought to bear in many countries, impacting on the firms in those countries. We noted earlier in this section that developing-country examiners are taught acceptable drafting formats and in Chapter 10 we will see that these formats are built into the regulations that implement the Convention that establishes the African Regional Intellectual Property Organization. Figure 2.4 illustrates this co-evolutionary partnership between patent offices and industry.

New areas of technology will sometimes generate new claiming formats in order to avoid patentable subject matter problems. For example, patent

[70] On the importance of routines in an evolutionary model of technological change see Henk van den Belt and Arie Rip, 'The Nelson-Winter-Dosi Model and Synthetic Dye Chemistry' in W.E. Byker, T.P. Hughes and T. J. Pinch (eds.), *The Social Construction of Technological Systems: New Directions in the Sociology and History of Technology*, MIT Press, Cambridge Mass. and London, 1987, 135.

[71] Lucille J. Brown, 'The Markush Challenge', 31 (1991) *Journal of Chemical Information and Computing Science*, 2.

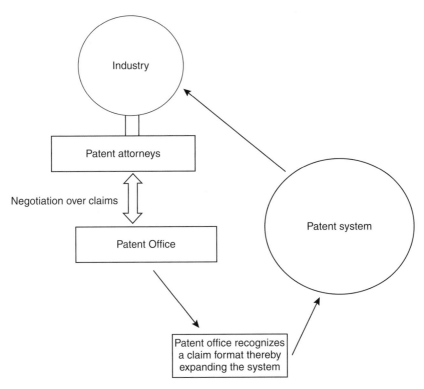

Figure 2.4 Patent offices, patent attorneys and industry – co-evolving the patent system

systems exclude from patentability laws of nature and abstract ideas.[72] This exclusion of abstract ideas can potentially defeat the patentability of computer software, the essence of which consists of a mathematical idea in the form of an algorithm. As a result, the computer software field has seen the emergence of claiming formats that steer around potential patentable subject matter exceptions, an example being the 'Beauregard' claim. This is a form of claim over a computer program stored in a tangible medium of some kind. This format was accepted after the US Commissioner for Patents agreed in an appeal by Beauregard that the printed matter doctrine did not apply to defeat product computer claims of this kind.[73]

---

[72] The language of exclusion varies. For example, Article 52(2)(a) of the EPC excludes discoveries, scientific theories and mathematical methods. A law of nature is an example of a discovery.
[73] See *In re* Beauregard 53 F.3d 1583 (Fed. Cir. 1995).

Another example of a claiming format that steers its way past potential patentable subject matter objections is the signal claim. In this type of claim electrical, optical or acoustic signals using a medium such as wire, air or fibre optics are claimed.[74] Originating in the US, one of the sung praises of the signal claim is that it offers the patent owner a means of protecting computer software sent in signal form.

It will be evident from what has been said so far that claiming formats have their origins in particular national patent systems. The requirement that is standard today in patent statutes, namely that the patent application contains claims, made its first appearance in statutory form in the UK in 1883.[75] In the US, the patent statute of 1836 codified a prior practice of claiming that had become customary.[76] In both the UK and the US, one factor that contributed to the evolution of patent claiming in the nineteenth century was the role of judges in interpreting claims in infringement actions, creating a need for claims that would stand up to judicial scrutiny.[77] Patent laws then as now moved within broader national legal traditions and philosophies and so, not surprisingly, different national traditions of claiming developed. Potts in an early discussion of different methods of claims drafting distinguished between the central method of defining the invention, which he suggested characterized the German approach, and the peripheral method, a method favoured in the US.[78]

The central method involved the drafter in isolating the key characteristics of the invention and produced narrower claims in which courts bore more of a burden in deciding the scope of the claim. Under the peripheral method, the drafter focussed more on defining the outer limits of what the inventor might conceivably say was his invention. This approach produced broad claims that were more likely to be read down by a court. One can see from this example that styles of claiming were linked to a national jurisprudence of claims interpretation. National styles of claiming are one example of the persistence and resistance of local legal traditions to global

---

[74] Stephen G. Kunin and Bradley D. Lytle, 'Patent Eligibility of Signal Claims', 87 (2005) *Journal of Patent and Trademark Office Society*, 991.

[75] See Sub-Section 5(5) of the Patents, Designs and Trade Marks Act of 1883. A practice of claiming existed before then. For a detailed history see David J. Brennan, 'The Evolution of English Patent Claims as Property Definers', 4 (2005) *Intellectual Property Quarterly*, 361.

[76] See Karl B. Lutz, 'Evolution of the Claims of U.S. Patents', 20 (1938) *Journal of the Patent Office Society*, 134, 143.

[77] For the history see ibid., 134 and David J. Brennan, 'The Evolution of English Patent Claims as Property Definers', 4 (2005) *Intellectual Property Quarterly*, 361.

[78] H.W.E. Potts, 'British Claims', 6 (1923–4) *Journal of the Patent Office Society*, 218.

forces of convergence and harmonization. Differences in national styles of claiming were something that the drafters of the EPC had to address in the context of the interpretation of claims.[79]

National patent statutes contain few standards concerning the drafting of patent claims, meaning that patent attorneys have considerable leeway in terms of developing new claiming formats.[80] The more detailed rules that affect claims are to be found in delegated legislation or patent office guidelines, regulatory tools over which patent offices exert some control or influence. Patent systems, in other words, remain open to innovation in claiming formats. This openness has produced a variety of formats including Beauregard claims, function claims, Jepson claims, Lowry claims, Markush claims, means plus function claims, method claims, omnibus claims, product-by-process claims, signal claims, Swiss claims and use claims. What is available in terms of a claim-drafting strategy for any given invention will be affected by the technological area of invention, the guidelines that the patent office has developed for various claim formats and the court jurisprudence that has developed around the interpretation of claims. Patent attorneys develop nuanced understandings of the strengths and weaknesses of particular claiming formats, an understanding that is situated in the context of a national or regional system in which they practice. Thomas, for example, points out that many US attorneys do not favour the Jepson format.[81] This format involves the drafting of a preamble in which the prior art is described, the preamble being followed by an identification of the improvement that the inventor has made. The danger lies in the preamble being used to ground an argument that the description of the prior art shows that the invention fails the test of non-obviousness. In Japan, patent attorneys do not recommend the use of the Jepson format for new chemical products.[82] Functional claiming formats

[79] See Article 69(1) of the EPC and Protocol on the Interpretation of Article 69 of the Convention, adopted at the Munich Diplomatic Conference for the setting up of a European System for the Grant of Patents on 5 October 1973. The Protocol attempts to create a third way of interpreting patent claims based on a combination of fairness to the patentee and certainty for third parties.

[80] By way of example, Article 84 of the EPC simply requires that claims be clear and concise. Rule 29 of the Implementing Regulations contains much more detail concerning the drafting of claims. In the US, 35 U.S.C. 112 contains some standards for the drafting of claims.

[81] John R. Thomas, 'The Responsibility of the Rulemaker: Comparative Approaches to Patent Administration Reform', 17 (2002) *Berkeley Technology Law Journal*, 727, 756.

[82] M. Watanabe and IP Study Group of Tsukuni & Associates, 'How to Read and Write Japanese Patent Specifications in Chemistry and Biotechnology', *Maruzen Planet Co. Ltd*, Tokyo, 2007, 55.

in which the invention is defined in terms of effects and actions offer broader protection, but also carry greater risks of invalidity. The use of independent and dependent claims allows for a multi-layered form of protection in which the invalidity of one independent claim may still leave the inventor with other independent claims upon which to rely. Crafting layers of protection will depend on the way that the patent office itself treats independent and dependent claims. In the EPO, the use of many independent claims may lead the examiner to conclude there is more than one invention being applied for, whereas in the US multiple independent claims are recommended as a way of minimizing prosecution history estoppel.[83]

For large corporate users of patent systems, the fact that claims-drafting strategies have to be tailored to the context of a national system is a factor that raises the costs of patenting. So far there is not a standardized claiming language that can be used in all the world's major offices. This also complicates the use of the PCT system because the applicant drafts one international application that will eventually end up as a series of national applications before as many national offices as the applicant chooses. If patent offices insisted on very different claim formats and at the same time restricted the capacity of applicants to amend patent applications, this would undermine the utility of the PCT system. The solution that has emerged to this problem is that patent offices have over time recognized claim formats that have their origins in other offices. The widespread acceptance of the Jepson and Markush claim formats, both of which were first recognized in the US, is one example. This process of mutual recognition of claim formats was underway before the advent of the PCT process, but the creation of the PCT system has heightened the incentive for offices to accept different claim formats. Once an office recognizes a claim format it can potentially take advantage of another office's search and examination work in relation to applications with that format. The PCT system itself has seen the production of a set of guidelines for the examination of claims to be used by all those offices that are examining authorities under the PCT.[84]

Another explanation for why patent offices are prepared to accept claiming formats lies in the combination of beliefs that patent offices might hold

---

[83] For a discussion of this and related issues see John D. Collins, 'Drafting an International Patent Application', IP and Technology Programme, 04/06, 13.

[84] See 'PCT International Search and Preliminary Examination Guidelines', PCT/GL/ISPE/1, March 11, 2004, available at www.wipo.int/export/sites/www/pct/en/texts/pdf/ispe.pdf.

about the patent system and the competitive pressures that these beliefs generate. Whatever they think privately, publicly patent office officials will say that the patent system is needed to generate innovation and/or foreign direct investment. It would be surprising if they said anything to contradict this. As discussed earlier, the claiming formats allow applicants to steer around restrictions on patentability. So, for example, claiming formats such as Beauregard, Lowry and signal claims allow for much greater patentability of computer software applications. Swiss claims allow applicants to overcome restrictions on method of treatment claims. A patent office that believed that patents offer an incentive to innovation or foreign direct investment would have a rational reason for allowing such claiming formats, especially if other patent offices were doing so. Not to allow those formats would be to disadvantage one's domestic industries and economy. Not to do so might also mean that the office becomes less important in terms of patent applications and grants, and this in turn would have repercussions for it in terms of status, influence and budget.

Incentives around work sharing and competitive pressures are not the reasons why most developing-country patent offices accept a variety of claiming formats. Developing-country offices look to developed-country patent offices for assistance in setting up their offices and the training of patent examiners. So, for instance, the EPO as part of its assistance may draft a patent examination manual for a developing-country office and that manual will contain examples of the kinds of formats that an examiner should or should not allow. For example, the Philippines patent examination manual, a copy of which the Philippines PO gave me in 2004, had been drafted by an EPO official as part of the EC-ASEAN Patents Programme.[85] Amongst other things, it includes examples of valid Markush claims and use claims for pharmaceutical products.[86] At the interview at the Indonesian PO it was a similar story, with the EPO being involved in the drafting of the Indonesian patent examination manual. Thus claiming formats that begin as innovations in developed-country patent offices over time become part of office routines that are adopted by other offices. Patent offices function as a mechanism of transmission for claim formats that, in terms of evolutionary theory, are favourable variations for multinational firms in particular. In the case of developing-

---

[85] See Acknowledgements, Bureau of Patents, 'Manual of Substantive Examination Practice', Republic of Philippines, Office of the President, Intellectual Property Office (undated).

[86] See ibid., 138 and 144.

country offices, claiming formats arrive as part of turnkey administrative systems delivered as part of a capacity-building programme. Particularly if developed-country offices follow up with some training in the use of the format, developing-country examiners will respond correctly to the incantation of words in the format.

Summing up, understanding the actual operational effects of the patent system depends just as much on an analysis of claiming formats as it does on knowing the substantive rules of patentability, and perhaps more so. New claiming formats devised by attorneys expand the operation of the patent system and add to the selection pressures that the patent system exerts on firms. Developed-country patent offices are key players in the recognition of new formats and have strong incentives to participate in a process of mutual recognition of claiming formats. These formats are transmitted to developing-country patent offices through technical training programmes in which examiners from these offices are trained to accept these formats.

3

The rise of patent offices

Patent statutes

We know much more about the history of patent law than we do about the history of its administration. The emergence of patent law in statutory form is generally said to be 1474 when the Venetian Republic passed a short decree that gave ten years of protection to any person who built 'any new and ingenious device in this City'.[1] The other early major statutory landmark is the English Statute of Monopolies of 1624.[2] This statute crystallized the pronouncements of the common law courts concerning the use by the English Crown of its prerogative power to grant monopolies in business. Monopolies in general were declared to be void, but an exception was made for patents and grants of privilege for 'any manner of new manufactures within this realm'.[3]

The spread through Europe of a patent institution based on legislation that gave inventors rights under law as opposed to having to depend on the exercise of prerogative was a slow process. In France public rights of inventorship are linked to laws adopted by the National Assembly in 1790 and enacted in 1791.[4] After this there is something of a take-off in Europe of patent statutes: Austria 1810, Russia 1812, Prussia 1815, Belgium and the

---

[1] See Giulio Mandich, 'Venetian Patents (1450–1550)', 30 (1948) *Journal of the Patent Office Society*, 166. Mandich also draws attention to a law of 1453 that is not a patent law, but that does reward innovation. See Giulio Mandich, 'Venetian Origins of Inventors' Rights', 42 (1960) *Journal of the Patent Office Society*, 378, 380.

[2] An official version of the statute can be found at www.statutelaw.gov.uk/content. aspx?activeTextDocId=1518308 and this gives the citation as 1623. Boehm and Silbertson explain why the correct citation should be 1624. See Klaus Boehm with Aubrey Silbertson, *The British Patent System*, volume 1, Cambridge University Press, Cambridge, 1967, 16, fn.4.

[3] See Section 6 of the Statute of Monopolies.

[4] Statutes relating to patents had been passed earlier in France, but the 1790 Act was the clearest statement of a general public right of an inventor to a property right. See Frank D. Prager, 'A History of Intellectual Property From 1545 to 1787', 26 (1944) *Journal of the Patent Office Society*, 711, 734.

Netherlands 1817, Spain 1820, Bavaria 1825, Sweden 1834, Wurtemburg 1836, Portugal 1837, Saxonia, 1843.[5]

Outside of Europe, the First Congress of the United States passed a patent statute in 1790. Prior to that patents had been granted in US colonies, but for the most part these were private grants made in response to petitions by individuals for patent protection.[6] In South America, Brazil passed patent legislation in 1830, Chile in 1840 and Argentina in 1864.[7] Japan's first patent law was enacted in 1871, but suspended the following year because of operational difficulties.[8] This was followed by the Patent Monopoly Act of 1885.

We shall see in this chapter that the slow diffusion of patent statutes was accompanied by an even slower evolution of patent offices. For example, in the UK modern patent administration is said to emerge only with the Patent Act of 1883.[9] The following two sections briefly discuss the origins of the patent system and its accompanying procedures. The history of patents in the Anglo-American context has been extensively researched and so is only briefly sketched, mainly in order to illustrate the deep territorial origins of the patent system and its use by states to attract and enclose resources of innovation.[10] This territorial and protectionist history would not have led one to predict the high level of cooperation that, as we shall see in later chapters, is taking place amongst today's major patent offices.

Monopoly privileges

The creation of privileges in the sale or importation of goods and in the crafts more generally was a well-established practice in both the ancient and medieval world.[11] Privileges could be used to create a monopoly for a guild over a particular area of trade or to create a non-exclusive form of

---

[5] See Fritz Machlup, 'An Economic Review of the Patent System', Study of the Subcommittee on Patents, Trademarks and Copyright of the Committee on the Judiciary, US Senate, 85th Congress, 2d Session, *US Government Printing Office*, Washington, 1958, 3–4.

[6] Bruce W. Bugbee, *Genesis of American Patent and Copyright Law*, Public Affairs Press, Washington, DC, 1967, Ch. 3.

[7] Stephen P. Ladas, *Patents, Trademarks, and Related Rights: National and International Protection*, Harvard University Press, Cambridge Mass., 1975, 7, fn. 27.

[8] A brief description is available at www.jpo.go.jp/seido_e/rekishi_e/rekisie.htm.

[9] Boehm with Silbertson, *The British Patent System*, volume 1, 30.

[10] For example, A. Gomme, *Patents of Invention: Origin and Growth of the Patent System in Britain*, Longmans, London, 1946; H. G. Fox, *Monopolies and Patents: A Study of the History and Future of the Patent Monopoly*, Toronto, University of Toronto Press, 1947; Bugbee, *Genesis of American Patent and Copyright Law*, 1967.

[11] See Fox, *Monopolies and Patents*, chs. 3 and 4.

reward such as a tax exemption or bonus payment. Venice, for example, used special funds or special positions to reward those who were skilled in the making of canons.[12] During the course of the Middle Ages the privilege system was adapted by sovereigns to create monopoly privileges for those who were willing to bring new processes and techniques to the sovereign's territory. So, for example, Fox relates the example of the Letter of Protection that was granted in 1331 to John Kempe, a Fleming, in order to encourage him to bring the technology of cloth weaving to England.[13] Privileges became a means by which sovereigns could grant exemptions to foreign artisans from local guild control. Local guilds, of course, had a strong interest in being able to control competition from foreigners. From the point of view of patents for invention, the critical institutional innovation was the use of the privilege system to create an exclusive right over the practice of a technique thought by the sovereign to be of benefit to the realm.[14]

Monopoly privileges were used by sovereigns to entice and keep valuable and mobile human resources within their borders. Training others in the working of the invention was usually an important part of the grant of the privilege. Sovereigns wanted economically or militarily useful techniques and products to be worked within their realms. The medieval system of privileges was very much about rewarding those who first offered to work an invention within a territory than it was about rewarding those who first invented it. Granting privileges was not just a monarchical enterprise. The City Republics of Florence and Venice used such grants of exclusivity to entice skilled individuals to settle within their borders. Mandich cites examples of what he calls 'true patents' (a period of manufacturing exclusivity in exchange for the working of the device in the territory) being granted to individuals by the City of Venice during the 1400s for things such as machines to improve fabrics.[15] Prager gives the example of Guerinus de Mera, a Milanese who defected to a guild in Florence to establish an improved process for wool manufacture in exchange for a monopoly privilege.[16] The pattern of monopoly

---

[12] Giulio Mandich, 'Venetian Origins of Inventors' Rights', 42 (1960) *Journal of the Patent Office Society*, 378, 380.

[13] Fox, *Monopolies and Patents*, 43.

[14] On this point see Frank D. Prager, 'Brunelleschi's Patent', 28 (1946) *Journal of the Patent Office Society*, 109, 127–8.

[15] Mandich, 'Venetian Origins of Inventors' Rights', 378, 379.

[16] Prager, 'Brunelleschi's Patent', 109, 127.

privileges for inventions evolving out of a system of general privileges also occurred in France.[17]

The use of monopoly privileges to reward purveyors of invention was an endogenous response of sovereigns to Europe's broader disorders. Europe experienced a general economic decline from roughly the end of the thirteenth century to the mid-fifteenth century.[18] There was widespread warfare between the powers of Europe of which the Hundred Years' War between England and France was but one example. Natural disasters such as the Black Death and crop failures were other sources of instability. Sovereigns found themselves having to compete for skilled artisans who could bring commercially and militarily important goods and techniques to their lands. To some extent the comparative advantage of nations and city states was locked up by them in the guilds that formed around all important technologies such as mining, the making of sail cloth, machines for milling, weaving and so on. Local guilds could not, however, provide all the innovation that any one emerging state of the time needed. Using the privilege system to encourage foreign workers to defect from their guilds and relocate to another territory was a natural step for sovereigns to take. It was a way of building comparative advantage and perhaps robbing others of theirs. For this reason many monopoly privileges of the Middle Ages went to foreigners.

Procedures for the grant of monopoly privileges

In the case of the grant of patents for invention in Venice, the procedure prior to the law of 1474 was by way of petition from individuals to the Senate. The terms of the granted petition varied according to the circumstances of the applicant and what was being asked for by the applicant. In effect, the Venetian Republic was issuing individualized contracts for invention. There does appear to have been, at least in some cases, an investigation or a test of the invention by officials of the General Welfare Board.[19] After the patent law of 1474, applications for patents proceeded

---

[17] Frank D. Prager, 'A History of Intellectual Property From 1545 to 1787', 26 (1944) *Journal of the Patent Office Society*, 711.

[18] For an overview of the debate about causes see W.C. Robinson, 'Money, Population and Economic Change in Late Medieval Europe', 12 (1959) *Economic History Review (New Series)*, 63.

[19] Giulio Mandich, 'Venetian Patents (1450–1550)', 30 (1948) *Journal of the Patent Office Society*, 166, 173.

by way of supplications addressed to the Duke. Foreigners and citizens alike were allowed to apply. The potential usefulness of the invention to the city state of Venice was apparently stressed by applicants.[20] The final decision rested with the Senate but in the divided political and administrative machinery of Venice other agencies such as the General Welfare Board or the Water Committee were involved in the process of grant. In cases where the invention had not been fully realized by the inventor, officials could order an examination of the invention after its grant to ensure that it had been successfully used.[21]

The French state had devised an intricate 'system of multiple monopolies' in the belief that this was the best road to power in Europe.[22] Privileges were used to regulate manufacturing, including the relationship between French guilds and those who wished to import goods and techniques that threatened the commercial interests of those guilds. Driving the grant of privileges for invention was a mercantilist thinking that wanted to establish new industries in France and break foreign monopolies such as England's monopoly in the manufacture of flint glass, thereby reducing the need to pay for imports.[23] This mercantilist approach began to be reassessed in the second half of the eighteenth century as France began to worry about the competitiveness of its industries.

Privileges were applied for at the French royal court. Letters conferring these privileges did not automatically take effect, but had to go before the local parliament of Paris. The Paris parliament turned out to be an important forum for contesting the grant and modifying its terms, a kind of pre-grant opposition procedure.[24] One French institutional innovation was the creation of a system of examination. Based on a royal decree of 1699, the French Royal Academy of Science on order of the King had to examine an invention and certify its novelty and usefulness.[25] This examination system lasted until it was abolished by the 1791 patent law. As in Venice, the French state had the power to use the invention if it so needed. A statute of 1762 limited the patent term to 15 years and rendered void privileges that had not been successfully put into 'actual practice' or

[20] Ibid. 166, 183.
[21] Ibid. 166, 189.
[22] Warren C. Scoville, 'State Policy and the French Glass Industry, 1640–1789', 56 (1942) *Quarterly Journal of Economics*, 430, 437.
[23] Ibid. 430, 438.
[24] Prager, 'A History of Intellectual Property From 1545 to 1787', 711, 724–5.
[25] Jan Vojacek, *A Survey of the Principal National Patent Systems*, Prentice-Hall, NY, 1936, 136.

which had never been used by the grantee.[26] As in other nation states, the aim was to put the onus on the inventor to work the invention so that its benefits could be materialized.

The French patent law of 1791 linked the rights of inventors to the 'Rights of Man', but the real agenda, as in other European states, was a mercantilism of technology based on enclosing the production of inventions within France's borders.[27] The first importer of an invention was by legal fiction treated as the inventor and inventors who obtained foreign patents had their French patents declared void. The 'natural rights' of inventors, in other words, were only respected to the extent that they brought the French state useful inventions. Inventors also lost their patents if they did not work their inventions within 2 years of grant. Applications had to contain a description of the invention. There was no substantive examination of the invention. From this time the French system began to evolve as a registration-only system and over time came to exemplify it. Section 15 of the statute required the description to be made public on the basis that once the patent had expired the invention belonged to society. The statute in substance implemented a social contract approach to patents.

The patent statute of 1844 continued the registration-only approach.[28] It also maintained the policy of high fees (100 francs per year) that had been a feature of the 1791 statute. Applications, which had to be in French, were by way of letter to the Minister of Agriculture and Commerce and were required to contain a description of the invention. Descriptions were to be published, but in practice this appears not to have happened and in fact getting access to patent documentation was difficult.[29]

After the Statute of Monopolies of 1624 in England there was very little activity in terms of statutory law. Patent legislation was passed in 1835, but major reform did not occur until 1883. Patent law was thus left in the hands of the law officers that administered the grant of the privilege and of the courts for more than 200 years. The Statute of Monopolies did not in

---

[26] The text of the statute is available in Prager, 'A History of Intellectual Property From 1545 to 1787', 711, 753.

[27] The following discussion of the 1791 Act is based on the English translation, ibid. 711, 756–7.

[28] An English translation of the 1844 law is available in Alfred Carpmael and Edward Carpmael, *The Patent Laws of the World, Collected, Edited and Indexed*, 2nd edn., William Clowes and Sons, London, 1889, 170.

[29] B. Zorina Khan, 'Intellectual Property and Economic Development: Lessons from American and European History', Study Paper 1a, Commission on Intellectual Property Rights, 2002, 17, available at www.iprcommission.org/papers/pdfs/study_papers/sp1a_khan_study.pdf.

practical terms sweep away the personal exercise of prerogative power by British sovereigns when it came to creating monopolies in trade. Charles I continued to grant monopoly privileges to corporations, something the Statute had not abolished. Moreover, the Statute did not touch the procedure for obtaining the grant of privilege, something that had been laid down by statute in 1535. Applicants had to go through a ten-stage process of paying high fees to various Crown officials who provided services such as turning a Patent Bill into a Signet Bill so that the Lord Privy Seal could prepare a Writ of Privy Seal.[30] If the applicant wanted patent protection in Ireland and Scotland separate applications had to be made. This procedure stayed more or less the same until the 1852 Patents Act when, amongst other things, Commissioners of Patents were appointed to administer the system and a patent office was established.[31]

The English system at this time was 'one of simple registration' and for the most part it seems to have operated in this way.[32] Interested parties could file a caveat with the law officers for the purposes of being notified of a patent application that might affect their interests, thereby giving them the chance to stop the grant of the patent.[33] It was the courts that became the most important regulators in the patent system. Proceedings for the revocation of a patent were based on a writ of *scire facias*.[34] Under this procedure any person prepared to pay a bond to cover the costs of a losing an action could allege the invalidity of the patent and require the patentee to come to court to defend the patent. The courts saw the patent in terms of a social bargain and progressively developed the disclosure conception of the patent social contract (see Chapter 1). Emblematic of this disclosure conception was Lord Mansfield's conclusion in *Liardet* v. *Johnson* (1778) that the 'fullest and most sufficient description' of the invention is the 'price the patentee should pay to the public for his monopoly'.[35] But it is also clear that specifications did not function to disclose the invention,

---

[30] Christine MacLeod, *Inventing the Industrial Revolution: The English Patent System, 1660–1800*, Cambridge University Press, Cambridge, 1988, 41.

[31] Boehm with Silbertson, *The British Patent System*, volume 1, 28–9.

[32] MacLeod, *Inventing the Industrial Revolution*, 41.

[33] Ibid. 43–4.

[34] See Lord Reid in American Cyanamid Company (Dann's) Patent, [1971] R.P.C., 425 at 435.

[35] Hayward's Patent Cases (1600–1883), vol. 1, 195,198. Hulme argues that Mansfield in fact is responsible for the disclosure conception of the patent social contract. E. Wyndham Hulme, 'On the History of Patent Law in the Seventeenth and Eighteenth Centuries', 18 (1902) *Law Quarterly Review*, 280.

especially in the chemical area where deliberate obscurity seems to have been the practice.[36]

Beginning in the 1850s and for several decades after an intense debate took place over whether the UK should continue with a patent system.[37] In fact debates over the future of the patent system took place in many European countries.[38] It was not just an academic debate. Holland discontinued the granting of patents in 1869.[39] The architect of modern Germany, Bismarck, suggested eliminating all monopoly privileges rather than pursuing the task of patent reform.[40] Patent administration reform in the UK slowly continued. The Patents Act of 1835 allowed a patentee to correct errors in an enrolled specification. The Patents Act of 1852 made the most significant changes to that point. A patent office run by Commissioners of Patents was established. One patent would now cover the UK and the initial cost of obtaining that patent fell from about £300 to £25, with protection for the full term of 14 years costing £180.[41] There was no substantive examination of the patent application. Specifications had to accompany applications and they could be inspected by the public. An index system was required to be established for this purpose. The Act also excluded British colonies from its operation. British-based sugar refiners, who had to contend with process patents, were unhappy that their competitors in the colonies would not have this burden, but their attempts to change this failed.[42]

The Patents Act of 1883 modernized patent administration in the UK. A Comptroller-General replaced the Commissioners of Patents. The Comptroller operated under the overall supervision of the Board of Trade. For the first time, patent examiners were appointed. Provisional or complete specifications had to be lodged with a patent application. Complete specifications had to end with claims defining the invention. The Comptroller had to refer applications to examiners. Upon acceptance of the application it and the complete specification became open to public inspection. Reports of examiners were not open to public inspection.

---

[36] MacLeod, *Inventing the Industrial Revolution*, 50–1.

[37] For a detailed analysis see Moureen Coulter, *Property in Ideas: The Patent Question in Mid-Victorian Britain*, Thomas Jefferson University Press, Kirksville, Missouri, 1991.

[38] See Fritz Machlup and Edith Penrose, 'The Patent Controversy in the Nineteenth Century', 10 (1950) *Journal of Economic History*, 1.

[39] For the history leading up to the Act of 1869 see G. Doorman, 'Patent Law in the Netherlands, Part I', 30 (1948) *Journal of the Patent Office Society*, 225.

[40] Ibid. 225, 238.

[41] Boehm with Silbertson, *The British Patent System*, volume 1, 29.

[42] Coulter, *Property in Ideas*, 66–7.

Section 11 of the Act created a pre-grant opposition procedure to be heard in the first instance by the Comptroller-General and with an appeal to a Law Officer rather than a court. This was a much cheaper process than a court trial. Under Section 22 compulsory licences could be applied for before the Board of Trade on the grounds that the patent was not being worked in the UK, that the reasonable requirements of the public were not being met or that a person holding an invention was being prevented from using it to best advantage. The 1883 Act made the patent grant binding on the Crown and required some sort of terms to be settled between the patent owner and Crown for any use by the Crown. One of the most important changes that the 1883 Act brought for inventors was a dramatic reduction in patent fees. An application and complete specification attracted a fee of £4. Fees for renewal were higher and could be done on an annual basis or in blocks. The policy behind fees was to make entry into the system cheap and to recover the cost of administration over the term of the patent.[43] The 1883 Act created the basic structure for the administration of UK patent law. The patent statutes that followed built on or refined the operation of this structure.

The US Patent Act of 1790, the first patent statute to be passed by Congress, reflected in its language the idea that the patent represented an exchange between the inventor and society. Section 2 of the Act required the patentee to 'deliver to the Secretary of State a specification in writing, containing a description, accompanied with drafts or models' so that the invention could be distinguished from previous things 'known and used' and so that a person skilled in the art could make or use the invention so that 'the public may have the full benefit' of the invention in the post-patent period. The Secretary of State was under a duty to make copies of specifications available to any person requesting a copy. Section 6 of the Act was also aimed at ensuring that the public received the benefit of the invention. Under the section defendants could gain a verdict in their favour if they could show that the inventor had filed a specification that 'does not contain the whole of the truth concerning his invention or discovery; or that it contains more than is necessary', this omission or addition being intended to or having the effect of actually misleading the public.

A board consisting of the Secretary of State (at that time Thomas Jefferson), the Secretary for the Department of War and the US Attorney General received petitions and under Section 1 of the Act any two of them could decide to grant the petition, if they deemed 'the invention

---

[43] Boehm with Silbertson, *The British Patent System*, volume 1, 31.

or discovery sufficiently useful and important'. The grant of the patent was therefore a matter of administrative discretion in the hands of three members of the US Executive. Although the Act did not expressly specify an examination procedure, the three members of the board did examine applications, apparently with considerable rigour (only fifty-seven patents were issued under the Act).[44] Patent fees were low compared to those prevailing in England, a point we shall come back to later in this chapter. Section 7 set the fee for making out the patent at $2 and for affixing the great seal at $1.

The 1790 Act had a brief life. It was replaced in 1793 by an Act that operated on the basis of a formal registration procedure. The patent board under the 1790 Act was replaced by a procedure in which the Secretary of State had to make out letters patent to a US citizen (non-citizens gained the right under an amendment in 1800) for an invention 'not known or used before the application'.[45] However, the application was not examined for novelty. Instead the Attorney General granted the patent if the application on the face of it conformed to the requirements of the Act. The novelty of an invention could be tested in the courts by a defendant in an infringement proceeding.

Under Section 11 of the 1793 Act, the inventor had to pay $30 into the Treasury before presenting his petition to the Secretary of State. The combination of a registration-only system and comparatively low fees saw about 10,000 patents issued between 1793 and 1836.[46] Accompanying this rise in patent numbers were complaints that too many worthless and fraudulent patents were being issued. A Senator from Maine, John Ruggles, became a key advocate for reform, arguing that the 1793 law had turned patenting into a wasteful and speculative business.[47] Not for the last time the Congress was confronted by the issue of patent quality. After a Senate committee reported in April of 1836 the Congress passed a new patent law in July of 1836.

The Patent Act of 1836 established a Patent Office that was attached to the Department of State. A Commissioner of Patents was charged with

---

[44] A good account of the work of the Patent Board under the 1790 Act and Jefferson's influence is to be found in P. J. Federico, 'Operation of the Patent Act of 1790', 18 (1936) *Journal of the Patent Office Society*, 237.

[45] See Section 1 of the 1793 Act.

[46] This number was obtained from the USPTO's website which provides data on US granted patents from 1790. See www.uspto.gov/go/taf/h_counts.pdf.

[47] See Lawrence C. Kingsland, 'The United States Patent Office', 13 (1948) *Law and Contemporary Problems*, 354, 359.

examining inventions and all applications had to be examined.[48] To assist
the Commissioner, the Act provided for other staff including a Chief Clerk,
an examining clerk, a competent draughtsman and a machinist. From
this small beginning was to grow a large bureaucracy that would come
to influence the course of patent administration globally (See Chapter 5).
The 1836 statute is not the first example of an examination system (grants
of monopoly privileges were examined in France and the Netherlands
in earlier centuries),[49] but it is the first example of the establishment of a
recognizably modern patent office with extensive examination duties, an
example that other European states followed much later in the century
and in some cases not till the twentieth century.[50]

An examination had to satisfy the Commissioner that the invention
had not been invented by any other person in the country prior to when
the applicant had claimed to invent it, that it had not been patented or
described in a printed publication in the US or any other country and that
it had not been publicly used or put on sale with the applicant's consent
prior to the making of the application.[51] Examination seems to have been
taken seriously if we assume a high rejection rate correlates with serious
examination. In his 1843 report the Commissioner of Patents points out
that about half the applications are rejected and others are reduced by a
third.[52] Robert Post in an analysis of the examining staff of the USPTO
during 1837 to 1861 has shown that a significant number of examiners
were appointed who were properly trained in science, resulting in a higher
rejection rate of applications as from 1842.[53] Patent agents mobilized 'to
induce key politicians and administrators to weed out' these scientific
types with the result that the success rate of applications began to climb
from lows of 30% to more than 60% in 1859.[54]

Disagreements between the Commissioner and the applicant over the
specification and claims, as well as decisions concerning applications
that appeared to cover the same invention were to be appealed to a Board
of Examiners. The 1836 Act also continued the conception of the patent

[48] See Section 7.
[49] MacLeod, *Inventing the Industrial Revolution*, 41.
[50] Jan Vojacek, *A Survey of the Principal National Patent Systems*, Prentice-Hall, NY, 1936,
       116.
[51] See Section 7.
[52] Report is available at www.ipmall.fplc.edu/hosted_resources/PatentHistory/poar1843.
       htm.
[53] Robert C. Post, '"Liberalizers" versus "Scientific Men" in the Antebellum Patent Office',
       17 (1976) *Technology and Culture*, 24.
[54] Ibid. 24, 26, 50.

as a social contract. Section 6 required inventors to provide a written description of their invention or discovery in sufficiently exact terms so as to enable a person skilled in the relevant art or science 'to make, construct, compound and use the same'. Drawings, specimens of ingredients ('sufficient in quantity for the purpose of experiment') or models also had to be lodged if they were appropriate to the invention. Fees continued to be low for US citizens and for residents intending to be citizens ($30), but for UK citizens it was $500. Other foreigners were charged $300. Fees went into a special patent fund set up to cover the running of the office.

There were many changes to US patent law following the 1836 Act, but it was this Act that laid down the modern core of US patent administration. Through it the US closed the door on its experiment with a registration-only system and embraced a system of compulsory examination. The application was examined for novelty under rules that required, amongst other things, absolute novelty for printed materials. The emphasis on the patent being granted to the 'original and first inventor' of the invention is to be found in various sections of the 1836 Act, including in Section 6 which required an applicant to make an oath or affirmation to that effect. Section 7 for the purposes of examination for novelty required that at the time of the applicant's act of invention there had been no prior invention of it by another person. An application could be rejected by the Commissioner under Section 7 if the examination showed that the applicant was not the 'original and first inventor' or the description of the invention was 'defective and insufficient'. Full disclosure by the inventor as part of the patent bargain was clearly established by the 1836 Act. Section 8 of the Act also specified a procedure for dealing with patent applications that interfered with each other, interference proceedings being one distinctive feature of US patent law today. Finally, the 1836 Act was also important for what it left out. It did not have a pre-grant or post-grant opposition system, a general procedure for revocation of the patent (however, the patent could be invalidated as part of infringement proceedings) or a system of compulsory licensing.

In Europe, Germany also chose to go down the path of patent examination. There is some suggestion that the German princes of the Middle Ages used privileges based on some sort of examination to reward innovation.[55] Prior to the unification of Germany in 1871, some

---

[55] Fritz Machlup, 'An Economic Review of the Patent System', Study of the Subcommittee on Patents, Trademarks and Copyright of the Committee on the Judiciary, US Senate, 85th Congress, 2d Session, US Government Printing Office, Washington, 1958, 2.

of the various monarchies and cities that were to make up the German Empire had adopted patent laws. Prussia had a system in which experts were required to examine the application for novelty and report to the Minister on the scope and duration of the patent.[56] Patents could be granted for as short a time as 6 months. Evidence gathered by a UK Commission on the work of the Prussian examination board showed that from 1860 to 1862 only 11% of patent applications made it to grant.[57]

Arguments for a strengthening of patent law (and therefore investing in patent administration) by the states that made up the German customs union of 1834 faced counter-arguments from a strong patent abolition movement made up of industrialists, trade associations and economists who favoured free trade.[58] Like other patent abolition movements in Europe at that time, the German one did not prevail. Following unification, Germany passed a patent statute in 1877.[59] Novelty of the invention was required (absolute for printed publications, but prior use was confined to Germany).[60] The law also established the German Patent Office and set up a system in which a division consisting of at least three members (at least two of these had to be 'expert in some branch of technical science') was responsible for the grant of a patent.[61] At first examiners were appointed for a period of 5 years, but in 1891 they became permanent employees of the PO.[62] Fees were also set high to discourage trivial or speculative patenting.[63] Another important feature was that it provided for a pre-grant opposition procedure that was run by the PO.[64] Patent applications were also published prior to grant. One important examination practice that separated the German PO from the USPTO was that the German office did not grant patents for slight improvements over

---

[56] *Report of the Commissioners Appointed to Inquire into the Working of the Law Relating to Letters Patent for Inventions*, Her Majesty's Stationery Office, London, 1865, 154.

[57] *Report of the Commissioners Appointed to Inquire into the Working of the Law Relating to Letters Patent for Inventions*, Her Majesty's Stationery Office, London, 1865, 154.

[58] Machlup and Penrose, *The Patent Controversy in the Nineteenth Century*, 1, 4.

[59] An English translation of this law is available in Carpmael and Carpmael, *The Patent Laws of the World*, 187.

[60] See Section 2.

[61] See Sections 13 and 14.

[62] See Section 13 of the 1877 Act and Khan, 'Intellectual Property and Economic Development'.

[63] Ibid.

[64] See Section 24.

fundamental technologies, while the USPTO did.[65] The combination of pre-grant opposition and examination as to novelty in the 1877 law laid the foundation for the German model of patent administration, a model that eventually spread to other countries, including Holland, Denmark, Sweden, Austria, Great Britain and Japan.[66]

Worth noting is that the 1877 law came to be heavily used by the German chemical industry.[67] In a process of co-evolution it helped German chemical companies achieve commercial success and over time those companies also came to exercise an important influence on the law itself.[68] Rival companies learned to use it to lodge process patents in order to block the capacity of their competitors to make compounds (patents were only available for chemical processes). This patenting along with the litigation saw German companies acquire great experience in the strategic use of patents, experience that allowed them to build some of the most dominant international cartels of the first half of the twentieth century.

Finally, in the Netherlands and Switzerland, patent administration evolved even more slowly. The Netherlands suspended the operation of its patent law of 1817 in 1869 with the result that no new patents could be granted. The 1817 law operated on the basis of examination and there was also the option for the King in deciding whether to grant the privilege to seek the views of members of the Royal Academy of Science or the Royal Netherlands Institute.[69] Eventually the Netherlands passed a new patent law in 1910 that came into operation in 1912. The Netherlands was able to get a modern patent office going with the help of the German and UK patent offices, both of which allowed Dutch examiners to spend time in their offices.[70] One Dutch company in particular stood out as benefiting from the reintroduction of the patent system – N. V. Philips'

---

[65] This was the conclusion of two USPTO examiners who visited the German PO in the summer of 1914. See John Boyle and Titus Ulke, 'The German, Austrian and Hungarian Patent Offices' in Patent Office Papers prepared by Chas W. Mortimer (undated) and available at www.ipmall.info/hosted_resources/ip_antique_library/Patent/USPO_1917_v1_a.pdf.

[66] Vojacek, *A Survey of the Principal National Patent Systems*, 28.

[67] Georg Meyer-Thurow, 'The Industrialization of Invention: A Case Study From the German Chemical Industry', 73 (1982) *Isis*, 363, 368.

[68] For an account see J. P. Murmann, *Knowledge and Competitive Advantage: The Coevolution of Firms, Technology, and National Institutions*, Cambridge University Press, Cambridge, 2003.

[69] G. Doorman, 'Patent Law in the Netherlands', Part I, 30 (1948) *Journal of the Patent Office Society*, 225, 228.

[70] G. Doorman, 'Patent Law in the Netherlands', Part III, 30 (1948) *Journal of the Patent Office Society*, 347.

Gloeilampenfabrieken. Doorman, a former Dutch patent office employee writing in 1948, pointed out that Philips had filed 10,000 patent applications of which 1,650 at the time of writing had been granted.[71] This is in the context where between 1911 and 1946 the Dutch PO processed 107,710 applications and granted 58,845.

Switzerland, one of TRIPS greatest supporters, resisted introducing a patent law until 1888. Eric Schiff in a study of Switzerland's patentless era of industrialization describes it as 'probably the most incomplete and selective patent law ever enacted in modern times'.[72] Amongst other things, it required the deposit of a model of the invention with the Swiss PO, a requirement that was more or less impossible to meet in the chemical sector for processes, thereby allowing the Swiss chemical industry freedom from foreign patenting in this sector. Pressure, both internal and external, to reform the 1888 law led to another patent law in 1907. The Swiss PO did not examine for novelty, carrying out instead what at times some thought to be an excessively formal examination of the application.[73]

The gap between patent law and patent administration

Patent law in statutory form emerge in the Middle Ages beginning in Venice and then slowly spread to other parts of Europe. The US can probably claim credit for the first recognizably modern patent office. Admittedly its staff of less than ten people was a small beginning, but it is still a recognition that a professional specialized bureaucracy would have to be created to implement the patent social contract. This approach was very different to the approach that had grown up in the UK in which Crown officials, who were not specialized in technology, took fees from the inventor more or less as a perquisite of office. It was not until 1883 that the UK had a patent office staff that carried out examination beyond that of a mere formalities check. Germany appoints examining staff to its patent offices under its 1877 law. France invests less in patent office administration because it goes down the path of a registration-only system. Under its 1844 law, applicants followed a procedure to obtain the registration of the

---

[71] Ibid. 347, 363.

[72] Eric Schiff, *Industrialization without National Patents*, Princeton University Press, Princeton, 1971, 93.

[73] On this point see Vojacek, *A Survey of the Principal National Patent Systems*, 28. It remains true that the Swiss PO does not examine applications for novelty and inventive step. See the Swiss PO website www.ige.ch/e/patent/p11.shtm.

patent that was not examined and delivered to them 'at the risk and peril of the applicants'.[74] This registration system did not change much for the remainder of the century.[75]

Patent offices in modern regulatory form emerged in most European countries in the second half of the nineteenth century and in some cases (for example, the Netherlands and Switzerland) in the beginning of the twentieth century. There is a significant period between countries passing a patent statute and then investing in the creation of a patent office with professional staff. Fully developed patent systems emerge well after patent law. Table 3.1 below shows the gap for countries that could be described as the patenting powers of the nineteenth and twentieth centuries.

The effect on innovation of this gap between the development of patent law and patent offices has not yet been investigated. It may be important. Economists generally take the view that clearly defined, secure, enforceable property rights are key to economic growth. Ultimately what matters from the point of view of the dynamic efficiency effects of patent law is not whether a country has a law on the books, but whether that law changes behaviour. Whether book law produces behavioural changes will itself depend on a range of factors including whether it is enforced and whether or not there is an administrative agency that deals with issues of implementation. For example, if a state passes a patent law but does not create a patent office to grant patents one could safely predict that the effect of the patent law on behaviour would be minimal (this was more or less the position in Indonesia for a time – see Chapter 10). Given the late emergence in Europe of patent offices staffed by professionals, the contribution of these offices to a well-defined property rights system in the nineteenth century might not be great. In fact one might argue that nineteenth-century patent offices in issuing pieces of paper that purported to enclose some complex area of knowledge for private purposes were in fact issuing invitations to private contests over the ownership of those knowledge resources. On this view the patent office was a generator of widespread uncertainty, leaving the future of socially valuable knowledge resources to be determined by the negotiations and battles of private players.[76]

---

[74] Section 11 of the 1844 Act available in Carpmael and Carpmael, *The Patent Laws of the World*, 173.

[75] Vojacek, *A Survey of the Principal National Patent Systems*, 138.

[76] For a theory of property rights that emphasizes contestation and uncertainty see Daniel Fitzpatrick, 'Evolution and Chaos in Property Rights Systems: The Third World Tragedy of Contested Access', 115 (2006) *Yale Law Journal*, 996.

Table 3.1. *The gap between patent offices and patent law*

Country	Date of national patent law	Date of modernized patent office
United Kingdom	1624	1883
USA	1790	1836
France	1791	1844
Prussia	1815	1877 (as part of a unified Germany)
Netherlands	1817	1912
Germany	1877	1877
Switzerland	1888	1907 (or some time after)

This leaves courts as the other institutional actor in shaping the real incentive effects of the patent system in various countries. The role of the judiciary in creating real incentive effects is a matter of historical analysis of national patent systems. For example, Christine MacCleod, in looking at the work of the English courts for the period 1660–1750 concludes that '[p]atentees dreaded the law courts: financial costs were ruinous, while the outcomes seemed random'.[77]

Patent office fees may also be an important variable in explaining the incentive effects of a patent system. Boehm and Silbertson suggest that the first 82 years of the nineteenth century were 'the age of patentless invention'.[78] Their data shows that the key variable in explaining the rise of patenting in the UK was the reduction in fees in 1852 and then again in 1883. They may have a point about fees. As we have seen, from 1793 to 1836, the US ran a registration-only system with a fee of $30 for the issue of a patent prevailing for most of that time. This represented a substantial cost in real terms.[79] But it was much less than the fee prevailing for a patent in the UK during this time.

---

[77] MacLeod, *Inventing the Industrial Revolution*, 73.

[78] Boehm with Silbertson, *The British Patent System*, volume 1, 37.

[79] On this point see Kenneth L. Sokoloff, 'Inventive Activity in Early Industrial America: Evidence From Patent Records, 1790–1846', 48 (1988) *Journal of Economic History*, 813, 818.

The number of patents issued in the US for the period 1793–1836 was 10,088.[80] In England for the same period, the number is 5,339.[81] During this period, which falls within the Industrial Revolution, England could claim to be the world's leading industrial power. Therefore one might have expected it to outstrip the US economy in terms of granted patents. The US was still primarily an agricultural economy and had not that long ago achieved independence by revolution. In fact the number of English patents is about half that of the US number. What accounts for the difference?

The scope of patentable invention in both countries at this time in history is basically the same. Importantly, both countries are running registration-only systems for the period of 1793–1836, meaning that inventors in both countries face only a formalities examination. England allows the first importer of an invention to be granted a patent and the US does not. The US progressively opened its patent system to foreigners.[82] Under the 1793 Act only US citizens could obtain patents. In 1800 foreigners who had been resident in the US for 2 years could apply for a patent and in 1832 all resident foreigners could obtain patents if they declared their intention to become US citizens. The difference in numbers of granted patents between the US and the UK cannot be explained in terms of the treatment of the patenting rights of foreigners. The key difference is the level of fees. The official fee for obtaining a patent in England has been estimated at £100 and for the rest of the UK £200.[83] On any method of calculating the present-day value of a fee of £100 in 1830 that fee was extraordinarily high, amounting to more than £7,000.[84] In the US, a fee of $30 in 1830 is almost $700 in present day values. Patent fees in the US for the period 1793–1836 are much lower than in the UK.

The simple message from this nineteenth-century UK and US experience is that patent office fees were a big determinant of patent filing and

---

[80] This number was obtained from the USPTO's website which provides data on US granted patents from 1790. See www.uspto.gov/go/taf/h_counts.pdf. This number seems to be in line with the data provided by Sokoloff in 'Inventive Activity in Early Industrial America', 813, 820.

[81] This number was derived from the Table on English patents 1617–1852 provided by Boehm with Silberston, *The British Patent System*, volume 1, 22–3.

[82] For a summary see Vojacek, *A Survey of the Principal National Patent Systems*, 123.

[83] Boehm with Silberston, *The British Patent System*, volume 1, 20.

[84] This figure and the other comparisons in this paragraph come from the calculators available at MeasuringWorth.com.

grant. As patent fees came down in the UK more inventors sought patents. Cheaper fees had the effect of integrating more and more inventors into the patent system. In the UK, the use of very high patent fees to control the demand for patents was a deliberate policy.[85] It also appears that the US patent system in the first half of the nineteenth century was more afford-able than in most European countries.[86] We shall see in later chapters that today the use of super-large fees by states to control the demand for patents is not considered to be a policy option. The relationship between fees and demand for patents has, not surprisingly, remained robust over time.[87] The long-run historical trend from the nineteenth to the twentieth century is for the cost of patent office fees to come down.[88] For example, today the fee to have a patent application processed in the UK PO is about £200.[89]

Once patent office fees came down other variables would have driven patenting behaviour, including the missionary behaviour of the patent profession.[90] Cheaper patents would have given them more reason to sing about the virtues of the patent system. The behaviour of patent attorneys and companies can be analogized to an arms race in which patent offices and patent attorneys together play the role of arms merchants. In an arms race one party tries to stay ahead of the other through stockpiling more arms in order to maintain superiority. The other party does precisely the same. As the US and the USSR discovered this leads to very large, expen-sive stockpiles. If some companies begin obtaining monopoly privileges their competitors are likely to follow suit. Naturally the attorneys and patent offices will encourage the purchase of more arms. If the costs of patenting are cheap one would expect patenting to go up. This of course means that patent offices will become flooded with patent applications.

---

[85] Christine MacLeod, Jennifer Tan, James Andrew and Jeremy Stein, 'Evaluating Inventive Activity: The Cost of Nineteenth-century UK Patents and the Fallibility of Renewal Data', 3 (2003) *Economic History Review*, 537, 540.

[86] Khan, 'Intellectual Property and Economic Development', 22.

[87] For a paper that shows that changes in the EPO's fee structure had a major effect on pat-enting see Jonathan Eaton, Samuel Kortum and Josh Lerner, 'International Patenting and the European Patent Office: A Quantitative Assessment', August 2003, available at www.nber.org/CRIW/papers/eaton.pdf.

[88] Sullivan suggests that patent fees in Britain were more expensive by a factor of 18.5 in 1865 than in 1965. See Richard J. Sullivan, 'Estimates of the value of Patent Rights in Great Britain and Ireland, 1852–1876', 61 (1994) *Economica*, 37, 38.

[89] See www.ipo.gov.uk/types/patent/p-applying/p-cost.htm.

[90] On the role of US patent agents in liberalizing standards of patent examination in the USPTO in the nineteenth century see Robert C. Post, ' "Liberalizers" versus "Scientific Men" in the Antebellum Patent Office', 17 (1976) *Technology and Culture*, 24.

This, as we shall see, is precisely what happens to the major patent offices early on in the twentieth century, forcing them to take steps to deal with the flood of patent applications.

The rise and spread of patent administration

By the end of the nineteenth century it had become clear that states had decided to stick with the patent system. The outsiders, the Netherlands and Switzerland, were on their way back to joining the patent club. In the UK those who had opposed the patent system on free-trade grounds somewhat paradoxically threw their support behind the initiatives being proposed for international cooperation on patent law. They had not changed their minds about the dangers of patent monopolies. Rather the leaders in the movement like Robert Macfie concluded that if the UK was to suffer the disadvantage of the patent system so should all its major competitors. He and other patent critics began to lobby the Gladstone government 'to assimilate the patent laws of all nations'.[91]

The failure of the patent abolitionist movement in the nineteenth century was, Machlup and Penrose suggest, attributable to the remarkable propaganda techniques of the pro-patent movement combined with the broader move away from free trade in the 1870s.[92] Other factors, perhaps more prosaic, are to be found in Herbert Simon's explanation of the persistence of a given course of administrative behaviour.[93] Administrative behaviour often continues because once the initial decision is made to invest in that administrative approach actors are reluctant to incur the new costs of a radical change in direction. By beginning the process of investing in patent administration states triggered the influence of sunk costs. The administrative solution itself constitutes a paradigm, full of internal problems that subsequent generations of actors work to solve. Actors working within the administrative system become largely impervious to considering radical alternatives and instead focus their attention on solving narrow technical problems within the system. In the case of the patent system this meant looking at issues such as the cost of patenting, the merits of an examination system, what kind of examination, the role of opposition proceedings and many other issues of eye-glazing technicality.

---

[91] Moureen Coulter, *Property in Ideas: The Patent Question in Mid-Victorian Britain*, Thomas Jefferson University Press, Kirksville, Missouri, 1991, 174.

[92] Machlup and Penrose, 'The Patent Controversy in the Nineteenth Century', 1, 5–6.

[93] Herbert A. Simon, *Administrative Behavior*, Macmillan Company, New York, 1951, 95–6.

Patent officials took carriage of these issues. The Paris Convention of 1883 created a forum for officials from the major patent powers of the time (US, UK and Germany) to begin the detailed, technical discussions that would characterize the evolution of international cooperation on patent law in the twentieth century.

The growth of patent offices in the second part of the nineteenth century was itself a contributing factor to the growth of the patent system. Patent offices became part of a process of co-evolution with firms such as those from the chemical sector that made a heavy use of their services.[94] National patent offices become resources for some national firms that enable these firms to grow. The political elites of the lead patenting states have, by the beginning of the twentieth century, very little reason to question the growth of the patent system. They see that their economic and military power depends on their capacity to compete in the heavy industries of coal, iron and steel as well the new industrial technologies based on chemicals and electricity. If the firms in these sectors that matter to state power support the patent system there is no reason to oppose it.[95]

The period of growth for the patent offices of today's developed states is roughly from the 1850s to the 1920s. States settle on a model of patent procedure (for example, choosing between a registration-only or examination system) and then begin to refine it. Variety is one of the chief features of these procedures. By 1930, Ladas in his monumental survey of international intellectual property was able to identify seven different models of patent office administration (with Mexico counting as one unique model).[96] Writing a few years later, Vojacek puts forward a typology of five main procedures: pure registration (the French system), formal examination with opposition, examination as to novelty but no opposition (the US), rigorous formal examination (Switzerland) and examination as to novelty and pre-grant opposition (Germany, UK and Japan).[97]

The procedures adopted by lead industrial states (the UK, the US, Germany, France) also end up taking hold in other countries. One explanation for this lies in the mechanism of diffusion based on learning

---

[94] For one detailed account of the role of patent law in co-evolution in the context of the synthetic dye industry see Murmann, *Knowledge and Competitive Advantage*, 2003.

[95] For example, the only manufacturing group to call for the abolition of the patent system in the UK was the sugar refiners from NW England and Scotland. See Coulter, *Property in Ideas*, 184.

[96] Stephen P. Ladas, *The International Protection of Industrial Property*, Harvard University Press, Cambridge Mass., 1930, 231–4.

[97] Vojacek, *A Survey of the Principal National Patent Systems*, 27–8.

in which actors are drawn to external models to solve a problem that confronts them.[98] National regulatory actors of countries do not choose to learn from other countries in a random way, but make choices based on factors like geographical proximity, language, religion and in the case of patent systems the broader type of legal system (civil versus common law). So, for example, the French registration system of patent procedure spreads to Belgium, Italy, Greece, Spain and Portugal.[99] Diffusion based on learning is probably the most important mechanism to explain the spread of patent procedures amongst European states in the nineteenth and early part of the twentieth century, but there are probably other types of diffusion at work also. Diffusion mechanisms based on tipping points or threshold points in which an increasing number of actors adopt a course of action making it more probable that others will also become adopters might help to explain why Switzerland facing mounting moral pressure reformed its grant procedure to remove the model requirement for chemical processes.[100]

Diffusion mechanisms are not the only means by which models of patent procedure were spread. Between 1870 and 1900 the European powers and the US acquired new territories. The scale of this expansion was huge.[101] The UK, for instance, increased its territory by half. Germany and France took control of 1 million and 3.5 million square miles respectively. Belgium, Portugal, Russia and the US also gained colonies. One consequence of this period of imperialism is that Western states, which had developed patent laws to suit their own economic circumstances, applied these laws to their colonies. Similarly, the administration of these laws was usually dependent upon a model of administration that was designed by the imperial power. Taking the French registration-only system as an example, it had spread from France to other European countries such as Spain, Portugal and Belgium via diffusion by learning and these European countries, which either were or became colonizing powers, transplanted patent laws and procedures to their colonies. In this way the French

---

[98] For a discussion see Zachary Elkins and Beth Simmons, 'On Waves, Clusters, and Diffusion: A Conceptual Framework', 598 (2005) *The Annals of the American Academy of Political and Social Science*, 33.

[99] Ladas, *Patents, Trademarks, and Related Rights*, 344.

[100] See Schiff's analysis about the moral pressure that began to mount against Switzerland's position on the patentability of chemical processes. Eric Schiff, *Industrialization without National Patents*, Princeton University Press, Princeton, 1971, 88–90.

[101] The figures that follow are taken from J.M. Roberts, *Europe: 1880–1945*, Longman, London and New York, 105.

registration system spread to countries in Africa and South America.[102] Models of patent office procedure thus arrived in developing countries through the operation of a sequence of mechanisms of diffusion, military and economic coercion.

In the decolonization movement that took place after the Second World War many newly independent states found themselves with patent laws and systems of administration not of their own design. Imperialism spread the patent institution much faster than might have occurred naturally in developing countries. Moreover, there is no reason to believe that the models of patent law that developing countries acquired through this process would have in the absence of imperialism evolved endogenously. The diversity of patent law and administration amongst European states of the nineteenth century suggests precisely the reverse.

---

[102] For the list of countries see Ladas, *Patents, Trademarks, and Related Rights*, 344.

4

The Sun and its planets

The European Patent Office and national offices

Europe's national patent offices

In Europe, the early decades of the twentieth century were a period of consolidation and growth of national patent offices. European offices developed their own approaches to the regulation of the patent grant. A proposal put to a UK Parliamentary Committee of 1931 that examiners should more deeply investigate the invention before grant, including its practicability, was rejected by that committee on the basis that it was better to have a scheme that ensured that patents were granted cheaply so as to favour the 'poor inventor'.[1] The higher standard approach to patent examination in Germany and the Netherlands in which patent examiners had the power to demand evidence of the invention's practicability was rejected. The same UK Committee also considered whether the UK should follow the US and Germany down the path of increasing the scope of the search of the prior art when it came to assessing novelty. Under UK law, the examiner essentially had to search only published British patent specifications. In Germany and the US, foreign specifications and other sources of published technical information formed part of the prior art base that examiners had to search. Investing heavily in extending the searches by examiners was rejected by the UK committee on the basis of its expense. The Committee took the view that the UK patent office should make some return to state revenues rather than reinvesting surpluses for the purpose of improving its service.

By the 1930s the UK Patent Office was facing a problem that would continue to grow for patent offices in important technology markets, a problem that would grow to huge proportions for the European, Japanese and US patent offices (the Trilateral Offices). From 1920 to 1930 the number of applications containing complete specifications grew steadily (from

---

[1] *Report of the Department Committee on the Patents and Designs Acts and Practice of the Patent Office*, His Majesty's Stationery Office, London, 1931, 8.

36,681 to 39,367) as had the number of examining staff (from 231 to 303).[2] The work of examining those applications was becoming much more difficult. From 1905 onwards examiners had to examine a patent specification for novelty. If an applicant decided to go all the way to grant, a complete specification had to be lodged (the alternative was to begin the process with a provisional specification). This complete specification had to contain a full description of the invention along with a description of the manner in which it was to be performed.[3] Examining complete specifications formed the time-consuming core of an examining office's work. The more specifications that were published each year meant that there was more material for an examiner to search.

Examiners did not simply face quantitative problems. The UK patent attorney profession, as in the US, was turning the drafting of patent specifications into a specialist technique. This technique delivered anything but the clear and certain boundaries for inventions that most economists would say was a pre-requisite for efficient property rights in general. The UK committee of 1931 found that it had become common practice for patent attorneys to include far-reaching claims of 'very doubtful validity' in specifications.[4] The technique of claims drafting was a 'technique of obscurity'.[5] The increased complexity left examiners struggling to distinguish inventions from those that had gone before. Patent attorneys were happy to chance their arm with such broad claims because the invalidity of one claim did not affect the validity of the patent as a whole, a principle that had been introduced into UK patent law in 1919.[6] This principle, in effect, reduced the cost of making broad claims with the predictable result that broad claims became a serious problem for the UK Patent Office. The advantage to patent attorneys and their clients was that such claims could be used to 'terrorise' subsequent inventors.[7] By 1930 the UK office had a backlog of some 11,000 complete specifications to be examined and a 9-month wait to issue the report.[8] This was thought to be a serious problem at the time, but nothing like the problems that would face the Trilateral Offices some 70 years later. In 2006 the time between filing and examination in the USPTO was 22.6 months.[9]

---

[2] Ibid. 103.   [3] See Sub-section 2(2) Patents and Designs Act, 1907.
[4] *Report of the Department Committee*, 34.   [5] Ibid. 35.
[6] See Section 32A, Patents and Designs Act, 1919.
[7] *Report of the Department Committee*, 34.
[8] Ibid. 104.
[9] Patent Public Advisory Committee, 'Annual Report', 30 November 2006, 8.

The most important difference amongst patent offices in Europe was whether or not they ran an examination system and, if they did, the resources they devoted to the examination. As we saw in Chapter 3, the French had committed themselves to a registration-only system as did many other European countries. This meant that patent offices in these countries were small since only a formalities examination was undertaken. In the mid-1930s for example, the French PO was reported to have had only three examiners.[10] Fewer countries examined, the main ones being Germany, the United Kingdom and the Netherlands. Germany decided that substantive examination was the key to patent quality. This is still a position that the German Patent Office holds today. In the eyes of some, granted German patents were of the highest quality in Europe.[11] Prior to the Second World War, the German PO (*Reichspatentamt*) had 1,600 employees. It had a wealth of experience in the examination and granting of patents because the German pharmaceutical industry was a sophisticated user of the system. The office functioned as the first port of call in Europe for many patentees, those patentees reasoning that if they were successful in Germany they would be successful in other parts of Europe. Many companies today continue with this strategy. The Second World War changed its location. Relocated to the potash mines of Bavaria from Berlin to avoid the bombs, the office was closed by the Allies for a number of years. The head of the office, Dr Klauer, facing trial (the office had enforced decrees stripping Jewish inventors and patent attorneys of their rights), committed suicide in 1948. The German PO, however, survived. It left the potash mines and re-opened for business in Munich in 1949.

The principal feature of national patent administration in Europe in the first half of the twentieth century was its diversity. European states operated under conditions where they had sovereign discretion over patent law standards, the interpretation of those standards and their administration. The upshot was a variety of systems and patent offices. The French registration system represented one model. Other states such as Germany and the Netherlands took the view that maintaining a high-quality examination system was an important part of ensuring that the patent system served to strengthen national industries. These two states probably had the strongest commitment to examination quality. States

[10] Anson R. Tracy, 'Visit to the British, French, and German Patent Offices', 18 (1936) *Journal of the Patent Office Society*, 208, 211.

[11] Richard Spencer, 'The German Patent Office', 31 (1949) *Journal of the Patent Office Society*, 79. But others took a very different view. See H. Marans, 'German Patent System', 32 (1950) *Journal of the Patent Office Society*, 468.

took different views as to how much of the prior art they should examine. The UK approach was based on examination, but it restricted the search for prior art in order to determine novelty to UK patent specifications. Size did not necessarily affect the commitment to running an examination system. The Danish PO, which by the 1940s had an examination corps of some 40–50, examined on the basis of a novelty requirement that took in publications anywhere in the world.[12] Around 57% of applications made it through to grant. The Danish commitment to quality examination was helped by the fact that patent applications averaged three to four thousand per year.

The birth of the European patent system

In the International Congress of 1878 the vision of a unified patent law was described by one delegate as a 'utopia' that would be impossible to achieve because the existing differences in patent law were themselves rooted in generically different legal systems and cultures.[13] Surrounded by the ruins that the Second World War had brought, European states began to work towards an ideal of a cooperative Europe, one that through shared law and economic integration would, forever, bring peace to Europe. In the decades following the war, patent administration and law became part of the broader currents that gathered around this European ideal of peace through integration, currents that carried Europe to the signing of the Treaty of Rome in 1957 and beyond.

In 1973, twenty-one states met in Munich beginning on 10 September to conclude the negotiations to set up a European system for the grant of patents. The final meeting of the conference took place on 4–5 October 1973. The French delegation thanked Dr Gerhard Jahn, the German Minister of Justice, who had been elected the President of the Diplomatic Conference, for all his work and for showing that Germany was 'now in the forefront of the architects of this peaceable Europe we desire to bequeath to our children'.[14] The President himself had observed that

---

[12] A brief history of the office is to be found in Host-Madsen, 'Danish Patent System', 30 (1948) *Journal of the Patent Office Society*, 160.

[13] S.P. Ladas, *Patents, Trademarks, and Related Rights: National and International Protection*, Harvard University Press, Cambridge, Mass., 1975, 61.

[14] Minutes of the Munich Diplomatic Conference for the Setting up of a European System for the Grant of Patents (Munich, 10 September to 5 October, 1973), published by the Government of the Federal Republic of Germany, 209.

with its emphasis on European cooperation, the Munich conference had been 'eminently political'.[15] The European Patent Convention (EPC) was opened for signature. The Convention established the European Patent Organization, the organs of which are the European Patent Office (EPO) and the Administrative Council. It entered into force in 1977.

Bearing in mind the use of patent law by states for their own protectionist purposes and the fact that two world wars had been fought on European soil, the creation of the EPO was and remains a remarkable achievement. If one had to choose an area of law to be the standard bearer of political integration ideals, patent law with all its national diversity and entrenched interests is not an obvious candidate. The fact that patent law was chosen says something about the perceptions of its importance, perceptions readily understandable in the light of America's dominant presence in Western Europe after the Second World War. US companies had the advantage of having to go to only one office to obtain protection in their large domestic market. Those who believed in the power of the patent system thought that European companies should also be able to go to one patent office and register a patent that applied across the borders of European states. The French delegation outlined Europe's offensive and defensive interests in creating the EPC. The existence of a European patent would help to harmonize the patent laws of European states, a necessary step towards a 'genuinely technological Europe' and the EPC system would help to protect states from having their economies 'swamped by patents of dubious and unreliable value', especially those states like France that did not run high-quality examination systems.[16]

The French Senator Longchambon had triggered a discussion of the possibilities for a European patent by submitting a plan in 1949 to the Consultative Assembly of the Council of Europe.[17] Following work by the Council, three conventions were signed (1953, 1954 and 1963) that kept the process of convergence upon a European patent system moving.[18] The convention of 1954, the European Convention on the International Classification of Patents for Invention, which provided for a uniform patent classification system, had a successful evolution. In order to open up membership of the convention beyond that of the European Council,

[15] Ibid.   [16] Ibid. 201–2.
[17] M. Van Empel, *The Granting of European Patents*, A.W. Sijthoff, Leyden, 1975, 10–11.
[18] These were: European Convention Relating to the Formalities required for Patent Applications, 11 December 1953; European Convention on the International Classification of Patents for Invention, 19 December 1954; Convention on the Unification of Certain Points of Substantive Law on Patents for Invention, 27 November 1963.

the model was incorporated into the Strasbourg Agreement Concerning the International Patent Classification of 1971 and its administration handed over to the World Intellectual Property Organization (WIPO). It was a generous act, but it also opened the way for the European system to become a world system.

The Convention of 1963, the Convention on the Unification of Certain Points of Substantive Law on Patents for Invention (sometimes referred to as the Strasbourg Patent Convention) did not come into operation until 1980, but its articulation of substantive principles of patent law on what constituted a patentable invention and what might be excluded by states from patentability was a crucial step in promoting the unification of patent law at the level of principle amongst European states and beyond. For example, in Article 2(b) it provides that states shall not be bound to grant patents for 'plant or animal varieties or essentially biological processes for the production of plants or animals; this provision does not apply to micro-biological processes and the products thereof'. A more refined version of the principle can be found in Article 27(3)(b) of the Agreement on Trade-Related Aspects of Intellectual Property Rights, 1994 (TRIPS).

There were other important steps. Belgium, France, Luxembourg and the Netherlands in 1947 agreed to establish the International Patent Institute at the Hague.[19] The International Institute was not a patent office. Instead it offered a search and advisory service as to novelty of an invention. The grant and application process remained in the hands of national offices. The 1947 agreement was revised in 1961 and signed by Belgium, France, Luxembourg, Monaco, the Netherlands, Switzerland and Turkey. These countries supported the creation of an international organization that would provide them with a number of services, including expert analysis of the novelty of an invention, services that they could incorporate into their national processes for registering patents.[20] For them, committing to a centralized European patent granting procedure was less of a step.

After the creation of the European Economic Community (EEC) through the Treaty of Rome of 1957, the EEC began to work on a European community patent. If the EEC was to achieve full market integration it was thought that it should be possible to lodge one patent application that

---

[19] Agreement Concerning the Establishment of an International Patents Bureau, The Hague, 6 June 1947.

[20] For a full description of the work of the Institute see J. W. Baxter, *World Patent Law and Practice*, 2nd edn., Sweet and Maxwell, London, 1973, 202–8.

would result in the grant of a patent that covered all the territories of the member countries of the EEC. A draft convention was produced in 1962, but the broader European politics of that year in the form of the French refusal to allow Britain to enter the Community saw work on it come to an end. If President de Gaulle's veto of Britain's EEC membership brought an end to one draft patent convention, the resulting crisis of relations between the EEC and other European countries saw another European group choose patent law to be the vehicle of integrative values. In May 1965 the Ministerial Council of the European Free Trade Association established a working party to study the draft EEC patent convention of 1962.[21] This working party produced a draft in which a European patent office would make one grant of a bundle of national patents. Membership of this system would be open to non-EEC countries. The draft also provided for an EEC patent. A memorandum issued by EEC countries in 1969 invited interested countries from the Council of Europe and the European Free Trade Association that had been working on patent unification to participate in drafting a convention that would create a patent system for European countries as well as allow for the development of a community patent for members of the EEC. Crucially, membership of a European Patent Convention would be open to non-EEC members. This meant that the final convention would have in it the tectonic plates of EEC members and non-EEC members. Twenty-one states in 1969 entered the intergovernmental process that produced a draft European Patent Convention for signing in 1973.

At the Munich conference, the French delegation speaking on behalf of the EEC stated that the states of the EEC intended to ratify the EPC in a way that would make a second draft patent convention also binding on them.[22] The French were referring to the draft Convention for the European Patent for the Common Market (the Community Patent Convention). This second convention provided for the creation of a single patent that would have 'unitary and autonomous effects' in all members of the EEC. The Community Patent Convention was signed by all EEC members in Luxembourg in 1975. This second pillar of the European patent system did not, however, enter into operation. In 1989, Luxembourg was the site of another attempt to bring the Community Patent Convention to life. The then twelve members of the European

---

[21] Dennis Thompson, 'The Draft Convention for a European Patent', 22 (1973) *International and Comparative Law Quarterly*, 52, 54.

[22] Minutes of The Munich Diplomatic Conference, 200.

Communities signed the Agreement Relating to Community Patents, but because they did not all ratify the Agreement it once again failed to come into operation. The sources of the failure to achieve complete ratification included concerns about the workability of the scheme for centralized patent litigation, the distribution of fee income from patents and the obligations surrounding translation of patents into the various languages of the EEC.[23] With this failure, the strategy of using an international convention to bring a community patent into existence had run its course.

During the 1990s, the European Commission pushed the cause of a community patent.[24] The Commission had come to the view that harmonization of the patent laws of the members of the EU was not enough to promote innovation. The basic logic was simple. The EU was in competition with the US and Japan. Success in this competition depended on innovation. Patents were a crucial factor, perhaps even the crucial factor in promoting innovation. Both Japan and the US had one set of patent laws and administrative institutions for regulating the role of patents in innovation. This unitary patent system reduced costs and complexity and increased enforceability and certainty. It followed that the EU should move to a unitary system. The Commission embarked on a strategy of implementing a community patent using a Community Regulation rather than an international convention. In 2000, the Commission issued a Proposal for a Council Regulation on the Community Patent.[25] Debates amongst members over the extent to which they would have to translate patent claims into various languages continued to dog the feasibility of the Community Patent. Influential business organizations like the International Chamber of Commerce (ICC), which were in principle supportive of the idea of a community patent, came out against the Commission's version.[26] Included in the ICC's complaints was the view that the cost of obtaining and maintaining patents would not be low enough. Meetings of the Competitiveness Council of Ministers in

[23] For further comment and references see Hanns Ullrich, 'Patent Protection in Europe: Integrating Europe into the Community or the Community into Europe?', 8 (2002) *European Law Journal*, 433, 439.

[24] See Green Paper on the Community patent and the patent system in Europe, COM(97) 314 Final, Brussels, 24.06.97 and Promoting innovation through patents: the follow-up to the Green Paper on the Community patent and the patent system in Europe, COM(1999) 42 Final, Brussels, 05.02.1999.

[25] See OJEC 2000 C E 337, 278.

[26] See the ICC's paper criticizing the Community patent at www.iccwbo.org/id544/index.html.

2004 were unable to make progress on the issues and so the Community Regulation for the time being remains a draft.[27]

The European Patent Convention

The EPC came into force on 7 October 1977. There were seven members – Belgium, France, Germany, Luxembourg, the Netherlands, Switzerland and the United Kingdom. Membership has climbed to thirty-five states.[28] The EPO has also been able to extend its territorial reach by concluding bilateral agreements with states that are not members of the EPC. These agreements allow for the extension of European patents to non-members: 'the logic of extension agreements is that the country will join the EPO' (interview, EPO).

The long title of the EPC accurately describes its nature. It is a European patent system for the grant of patents, but not for their administration or enforcement. Membership is open to European states.[29] The European patent system is a partial supra-national system in that a supra-national patent-granting body has to work with the many national patent systems of its member states. This hybrid of the supra-national and national makes for complexity, both legal and political. In terms of EPC membership states can, as we have noted, be divided into those which are members of the European Union and those which are not. Within the EU issues of patent harmonization and patenting in new areas such as biotechnology have attracted growing levels of political activity, with the European Parliament especially becoming a more important forum for patent politics than one might have predicted. All twenty-seven members of the EU are members of the EPC. The EU and the European Patent Organization (the organization set up by the EPC) are, like Siamese twins, closely linked.

The EPC is one means through which applicants can file for patents in European states. There are, however, different routes that an application might travel before it arrives at the EPO. Applicants may file for a patent in the EPO's offices using one of the three official languages (English,

---

[27] See Results of the Competitiveness Council of Ministers, 11 March 2004, available at http://europa.eu/rapid/pressReleasesAction.do?reference=MEMO/04/58&format=HTML&aged=0&language=EN&guiLanguage=en. The draft text of a 2004 proposal for a Council Regulation on the Community Patent is available at http://register.consilium.eu.int/pdf/en/04/st07/st07119.en04.pdf.

[28] www.epo.org/about-us/epo/member-states.html#contracting.

[29] See Article 166 of the EPC.

French or German).[30] Alternatively they may file the European patent
application with a national office that can act as a receiving office for
the EPO.[31] More typically applicants choose a route in which the EPO
ends up being an office of second rather than first filing. For example,
an applicant may first file an application in a national office and then
relying on a right of priority that is created by that filing under Article 4
of the Paris Convention for the Protection of Industrial Property (Paris
Convention) file within 12 months in the EPO. An applicant may also
begin the application process outside of the EPO, but use the procedure under the Patent Cooperation Treaty (PCT) to arrive at the EPO.
However the application ends up before the EPO, it is a single application in which applicants designate those members of the EPC in which
they would like a patent to take effect. Under the EPC the application
is made equivalent to a national filing in the designated contracting
states.[32] Similarly, the EPC makes clear that the European patents
granted by the EPO shall have the effect of national patents and be
subject to the same conditions as those granted by the national offices
of EPC members.[33] As we saw in Chapter 2, a granted patent may be
opposed within 9 months of the date of grant. After registration in the
national patent office, the patent is administered nationally and issues
of infringement and enforcement are decided by national courts. States
may also require that the granted patent be translated into their official
language.

Requiring the translation of the patent specification into a national language of a state is one way to assist disclosure and more importantly the
diffusion of patented knowledge in that state. Diffusion obligations are
part of the patent social contract (see Chapter 1). Yet the social contract
ideal has not been invoked by the EPO to justify the cost of translation
in the EPC system. Instead the EPO sees in translation obligations a cost
obstacle to patenting.[34] The EPO realized in the mid-1990s that the rising
cost of translation and the increased numbers of states joining the EPC

---

[30] Article 14.1 of the EPC. Filing in other languages is permitted, but a translation into one
of the official languages must follow.

[31] Article 75(1)(b) provides that a European patent application filed at a national office will
have the same effect as if it had been filed on the same date in the EPO.

[32] See Article 66.   [33] See Article 2.2.

[34] In its 1996 Annual Report at p. 51 the EPO observed that translation costs amounted to
about 40% of the cost of a European patent.

would see translation costs for patent grants reach very high levels.[35] As a result it has supported initiatives like the London Agreement of 2000, an agreement that has the express objective of reducing translation costs for patent owners.[36] States do worry about the diffusion costs of reducing translation obligations. The Netherlands Parliament, for example, took advantage of its right under the London Agreement to have claims translated into its official national language because it wanted to maximize the chances of that information being accessible to its small to medium enterprise sector.[37]

One of the important changes that the EPC brought to Europe was a centralized examination system. At the time of the EPC negotiations only nine of the twenty-one participating states ran a patent examination system.[38] The EPC divided the task of search and examination by creating a search division and an examination division.[39] Under this division of labour a prior art search was carried out by a search division located in the Hague and substantive examination by an examining division located in Munich. During the 1990s the EPO embarked on a strategy of bringing search and examination together (the BEST programme).[40] The EPO's own assessment is that by training staff in both search and examination skills it has improved its efficiency in dealing with applications.[41] The gain comes from removing the double handling of files by searchers and then examiners. Improving productivity was the main motive for training individuals in both search and examination.

Funding and fees at the EPO

At the time of the negotiation of the EPC it was estimated that the EPO would receive in the vicinity of 40,000 applications per year. A working party on financing the EPO, which included the three likely biggest users

---

[35] These translation costs had gone from DM 8,000 to 22,000 from 1985 to 1995. See EPO, *Annual Report 1996*, 51.

[36] Article 65 of the EPC imposes obligations of translation. Under the Agreement on the application of Article 65 of the Convention on the Grant of European Patents (known as the London Agreement) states have to dispense with some of these obligations. The Agreement came into operation in May of 2008. Essentially those countries having one of the EPO's official languages as an official national language will waive the need for translation and other states not in this position may require the translation of the patent claims into their official language.

[37] Netherlands Patent Office, *Annual Report 2007*, 32.

[38] Minutes of The Munich Diplomatic Conference, 11.   [39] See Articles 17 and 18.

[40] See Leith, *Harmonisation of Intellectual Property in Europe*, 40–2.

[41] See 'Mastering the Workload' CA/132/02, Munich, 08.10.2002, 20.

of it (France, Germany and the UK) agreed that the running of the EPO should be paid for by the users of the system.[42] Roughly speaking, patent offices derive most of their income from the application process and after the grant of the patent from renewal fees. Renewal fee income is a vital long-term source of income for patent offices. The EPO like other patent offices follows a model in which the initial search and examination fees do not cover the actual costs of providing these services (the shortfall is in the order of 70% – interview, EPO).

Each granted patent, in effect, sets up a stream of fee income that lasts until the patent term expires (a 20-year term is the international standard) or the patent owner decides not to renew the patent. Many patents are not renewed, but lucrative patents (for example, a patent on a blockbuster drug) do run to term and may be the subject of patent term extension in countries that permit term extension for pharmaceuticals. Under the EPC, patents are granted by the EPO, but administered as national patents, thereby potentially depriving the EPO of a source of income. Rather than allowing national patent offices to keep all the renewal income it was agreed that national patent offices and the EPO would share this income.[43] Under the current arrangement the EPO receives 50% of the renewal fee that is charged by a national patent office.[44] By way of example in 2007 the Netherlands PO returned to the EPO some €23 million of the €53 million it received in fees.[45] The arrangement has proved lucrative for the EPO by virtue of the designation rates for EPC applications. During the 1980s and 1990s applicants were designating an average of 7–8 states meaning that for one examination that led to grant, the EPO was potentially gaining 50% of the renewal income from 8 national patent offices.[46] For national patent offices in Europe this financial arrangement provides a possible constraint on their fee income (and therefore capacity to expand) to the extent that European patents replace national patents (patents that are filed directly with the national office). As against this, however, the EPC system makes it easier to pursue patenting in Europe. The increase in the number of patents registered in a national patent office as a result of the EPC could be said to offset the loss that is incurred through the sharing of renewal income.

[42] Dennis Thompson, 'The Draft Convention for a European Patent', 22 (1973) *International and Comparative Law Quarterly*, 52, 61.
[43] The obligation of states to refund part of the renewal fee is contained in Article 39 of the EPC.
[44] Decided by the Administrative Council in 1984. See OJ EPO 1984, 296.
[45] Netherlands Patent Office, *Annual Report 2007*, 28.
[46] For example, in 1990 the designation rate was 7.5 and in 1996 it was 7.8. See EPO, *Annual Report 1990*, 54 and EPO, *Annual Report 1996*, 31.

It is also worth noting that the fee income generated by the EPO is part of a bigger market in patent fee income in which a number of actors make their living from the handling and processing of patent information. We saw in Chapter 3 that the English patent system prior to its reform had become riddled with rent-seekers and sinecures. This history may be the object of chortling, but, in some respects, the situation is not all that much different today. Companies playing the patent game in Europe support through their fees a very large patent service industry comprised of the EPO, national patent offices, patent attorneys specializing in EPO work, patent attorneys specializing in national work, patent searchers and analysts, patent database firms, translators, drafters of technical drawings, software programmers, litigators and others (see Figure 4.1 below). All these players have, of course, strong incentives to sing the praises of the patent system.

The EPO also provides an example of the argument in Chapter 3 that the reduction in fees charged by patent offices is a key variable in explaining the rise in patenting. In one of the comparatively few studies of the costs of patenting during the 1990s Joachim Beier, using survey data obtained from twenty-six patent attorney offices from fifteen countries, showed that the EPO's fees for obtaining the grant of patent were 3.5 times

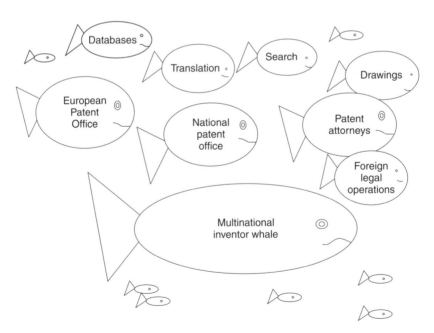

Figure 4.1   The multinational inventor whale and its sucker fish

higher than the USPTO and six times higher than the Japanese Patent Office (JPO).[47] Patent attorney fees were in the same range across the three offices.

The purpose of Beier's study was to show that the EPC could do much more to reduce the high costs of patenting in Europe and that these high costs were not the fault of the patent attorney profession. However, if one compares the cost of using the EPO to the cost of using national patent offices in Europe to obtain the same coverage, the EPO had clearly brought down the cost. Prior to the EPO an applicant had to pursue patents in European countries using the Paris route. Beier's study suggested if a patent applicant wanted to file in more than four member countries it would be cheaper to take the EPO route. Since most large businesses, especially multinational businesses, would want coverage of Europe's most important markets and there are more than four of these, it follows that most would end up filing in the EPO.[48] The fact that the USPTO or JPO were cheaper in terms of fees at the time of survey is neither here nor there since neither of those offices could grant patents for European countries. The EPO had to deliver a cheaper alternative compared to the combined costs of obtaining grants from a number of national offices and this it had done. Nevertheless the study showed that the EPO could, if it wished, reduce its fees further. There was a considerable amount of fat built into its fee structure. Clearly one reason for doing so would be to attract more and more applications, thereby making it the supreme focal point for entry into Europe. In 1997 the EPO did reduce its fees and this, on its account, probably contributed to the growth in patent filings.[49] An independent study suggested that some 40% of the 70% increase in European patenting in the 1990s was due to changes in the EPO's fee structure.[50] Reducing the costs of patenting continues to be part of the EPO's agenda.[51]

---

[47] See Joachim Beier, 'Actual Costs of Patenting in European and National Procedure – Results of a FICPI Study', 26 (1995), *International Review of Industrial Property and Copyright Law*, 213.

[48] By way of example, the EPO's 1990 Annual report showed that the most designated states were Germany, Great Britain, France, Italy, the Netherlands and Switzerland and that the average number of designations was 7.5. In 1997 the average number of designations went up to 14 because of fee reforms. See EPO, *Annual Report 1997*, 19.

[49] Ibid.

[50] Jonathan Eaton, Samuel Kortum and Josh Lerner, 'International Patenting and the European Patent Office: A Quantitative Assessment', August 2003, 19, available at www.nber.org/CRIW/papers/eaton.pdf.

[51] See for example, 19.12.2005 Decision of the Administrative Council of 15 December 2005 adjusting the decision of 10 June 2005 (CA/D 3/05 as formulated in CA/D 6/05 of

Surf's up: PCT waves

During the negotiations over the PCT, a key objective for European states was to allow for the diversion of national PCT applications to the EPO.[52] Some European states did not want to deal with the volume of international work that the PCT might generate for their patent offices.

Closing off the PCT national route is an option under the PCT. In such a case the international application under the PCT goes to the EPO rather than the national patent office of the country.[53] Even in those cases where the PCT national route has not been closed an applicant under the PCT can choose whether to go via the EPO (known as the Euro-PCT route) or straight to a national patent office. Over time the Euro-PCT route has turned into a large pipeline carrying many applications. During the late 1980s, the EPO was reporting sharp increases in Euro-PCT applications and by 1996 the number of Euro-PCT applications accounted for more than 52% of all European applications.[54] By 2006 Euro-PCT applications had more than doubled direct European filings.[55]

It is not just the number of Euro-PCT applications that is generating work for the EPO, but the number of claims in these applications. Applications travelling the PCT route average twenty-five claims (fifteen claims being the average for Euro-direct applications).[56] Applications with more claims raise the processing costs for a patent office. The explanation for this increase is said to be 'the transmission to Europe of habits developed by applicants in the US patent system'.[57] Probably, companies in the US both large and small, especially in sectors such as information technology and biotechnology, are being advised by patent attorneys to develop a global

---

27 October 2005) reducing the fee for the supplementary European search where the international search report was drawn up by the Austrian Patent Office, by the National Board of Patents and Registration of Finland, by the Spanish Patent and Trademark Office or by the Swedish Patent and Registration Office CA/D 15/05, available at www. epo.org/patents/law/legal-texts/decisions/archive/19122005.html.

[52] Dennis Thompson, 'The Draft Convention for a European Patent', 22 (1973) *International and Comparative Law Quarterly*, 52, 67.

[53] Examples of countries that have closed the national route are Belgium, Cyprus, France, Greece, Ireland, Italy, Latvia, Malta, Netherlands and Slovenia. See *PCT and Newsletter*, April 2007, No. 04/2007, 20.

[54] EPO, *Annual Report 1996*, 28.   [55] EPO, *Annual Report 2006*, 15.

[56] See 'The increased voluminosity of patent applications received by the EPO and its impact on the European Patent System', CA/73/05, Munich, 30.05.2005, 5.

[57] Ibid.

patenting strategy in key markets using the PCT system. This would be consistent with the evidence that small to medium-sized firms in a number of countries are moving more rapidly into internationalization of their activities.[58] The increased number of claims has the goal of getting a better coverage of the various dimensions of the invention. It may also be the product of a simple negotiating strategy in which some doubtful claims are put in to help the rest achieve safe passage. Aside from increasing the volume of applications the PCT has also added to the procedural complexity that the EPO has to manage. Included in the eight procedures the EPO has to administer are PCT procedures. In a fine-grained analysis of its workload problems in 2002, the EPO concluded that administering these PCT procedures had been one reason why there had been growing delays in the substantive examination of European patent applications.[59] The response of the EPO to its workload problems has been to hire more examiners, squeeze more productivity out of examiners (for example, through the BEST programme), invest in better information technology systems and look to cooperate with other patent offices both inside and outside of Europe.

The PCT procedure is a good example of the long-run trend in the international patent framework to increase the number of filing options and strategies for applicants. Filing options are generally not taken away from applicants, the closing of the national PCT route in some European countries being one rare example. Instead the combination of national patent systems, the Paris Convention and the PCT, along with regional patent systems gives applicants lots of choices. Coinciding with the greater filing choice for applicants has been the reduction in the costs of filing. The EPO system is part of that longer historical trend that we saw in Chapter 3 in which the cost of patenting has continued to decline since the nineteenth century. Aside from being cheaper to use, the patent system has also become easier to use for companies. Predictably, giving online filing options to applicants has seen more applicants file online (50% of PCT applications at the EPO were filed online, as were 32% of direct European filings).[60]

The PCT is thus part of a broader international patent framework that has maximized the strategic freedoms of applicants (patent offices have had to absorb the costs of those freedoms by maintaining multiple grant

---

[58] See Jorge Rodriguez, 'The Internationalization of the Small and Medium-Sized Firm', 25 (2007) *Prometheus*, 305.

[59] 'Mastering the workload' CA/132/02, 08.10.2002, 33.

[60] See EPO, *Annual Report 2006*, 17.

procedures) and made patenting cheaper and easier. If the arms-race model of the patent system described in Chapter 3 is correct then patent offices will continue to face increasing volumes of patenting. Cooperation amongst them will, for a while at least, become an imperative. In the next section we will see how the EPO and national patent offices have moved towards greater networked cooperation, a cooperation that contains within it the seeds of competition.

The EPO and national patent offices: from centralization to cooperation and competition

Policy planning does not always work out. The purpose of states agreeing to the EPC was to create 'a single procedure for the grant of patents'.[61] The EPC administers multiple procedures. At the time of the negotiation of the EPC it was thought that the EPO would have to deal with some 40,000 applications per year. In 2006 there were 208,500 filings.[62] One view was that Europe's national patent offices would eventually close their doors. Some national patent offices have been transformed, some are full of plans and ambitions, but none have closed their doors.

The Netherlands PO has probably undergone the greatest transformation. In the first half of the twentieth century it along with the German PO led the way in terms of standards of patent searching. Its patent databases were a 'goldmine' of information, this perhaps explaining why the search divisions of the EPO were located in the Hague (interview, Netherlands PO). Faced by a decline in the number of direct national applications to its patent office (13,000 in 1978 to a little over 2,000 in 1993), the Netherlands in 1995 switched to a registration-only system.[63] The Netherlands PO still retains some search and examination competency ('you need a certain strategic minimum' – interview, Netherlands PO). Its examiners do some work for the UK PO. It sees its role now to be one of promoting awareness of the patent system, helping the small to medium enterprises (SMEs) in the Netherlands by providing advice and searches and acting as a stepping stone into the patent system.

We saw in Chapter 3 that the German PO was the dominant national PO in the first half of the twentieth century in Europe. It has retained that dominance. After the establishment of the EPO, the German PO experienced a decline in patent applications, but at the interview the patent situation was

---

[61] See the Preamble to the EPC.   [62] EPO, *Annual Report 2006*, 15.
[63] See the description of the Netherlands patent office at http://sct.wipo.int/patent/agenda/en/meetings/2002/program/index.html.

described as being 'stable' (it receives around 60,000 patent applications per year). It has a strong commitment to developing the best possible search systems and databases. This also gives it great capacity to check the work of other offices. As one UK examiner wryly observed of the German PO, 'if it moves they scan it'. The German PO remains an important office in terms of first filing.[64] Its commitment to quality in examination, which is something of a long tradition (see Chapter 3) is one factor and the other is the size of the German market. Applicants seeking patent protection via the EPO will ninety-nine times out of a hundred designate Germany for the purposes of obtaining a national patent.[65] Over the years the Netherlands has attracted a lower rate of designation at the EPO than Germany. So, by way of example, in 1990 it was 61.5% for the Netherlands and 97% for Germany and in 1995 it was 54.5% and 97% respectively.[66] One would expect the German PO to remain an important office precisely because it can offer patent applicants an examination service and it is a key market. Once an office gives up most of its examination expertise, companies in search of patent quality are not likely to use it as an entry point into the system and the office itself will lose the technical expertise upon which the capacity of a patent office to influence other patent offices is based. It will not, for example, have the expertise to produce examination guidelines for new areas of technology.

Patent offices that have small domestic markets clearly face a challenge in maintaining an examination capability. The Danish office has embarked on a strategy of doing examination work for other offices such as the Singapore PO, the UK PO and the USPTO. The Austrian PO has also taken on outside work. The Danish and Austrian POs which operate with around seventy and a hundred examiners respectively are examples of competitively-minded offices. They actively seek work beyond their borders. The UK PO, which is a much bigger office and the only one to rival the German PO, has the same competitive outlook. The business model approach that we described in Chapter 1 is very much alive in these offices.

The national patent offices of Europe were a diverse group in the first part of the twentieth century and they remain so at the beginning of the twenty-first century. It is a diversity that, as one interviewee remarked, makes

---

[64] Hanns Ullrich has pointed out that applicants use the German Patent Office as a first filter of the application process. See Ullrich, 'Patent Protection in Europe', 433, 448, fn. 74. Under the EPC a priority date that is obtained under the Paris Convention by means of a national filing gives rise to a right of priority under the EPC. See Article 87(1).

[65] In the EPO's *Annual Report 2005*, the percentage of applications designating Germany is stated to be 99.6%. See page 77.

[66] See *EPO, Annual Report 1990*, 54 and *EPO Annual Report 1995*, 73.

cooperation difficult. National offices also have very different views of the EPO. Some, like the Netherlands PO, see the EPO as part of a bigger integrative European dynamic: 'We believe in the European dream' (interview, Netherlands PO). Whatever dream the UK PO believes in, it does not include the EPO. To my question 'Do you trust the EPO?', the answer was a blunt no. In part an office's view of the EPO is coloured by how competitively inclined it is and its views about which areas the EPO should stay out of and leave for national offices (for example, bidding on large technical assistance projects). One interviewee suggested that some offices were distinctly less Europe-oriented and had a much greater focus on national interests (the UK, Spain, Greece and Portugal being offered as examples). The Eastern European states joining the EPC are also contributing to a new dynamic. And there is also the fact that there are a number of offices in Europe that have the status of being International Searching Authorities (ISAs) under the PCT (Austria, Spain, Finland, Russia, Sweden and the Nordic Patent Institute). The EPO in other words has competitors for PCT work. As one interviewee put it: 'The EPO is not the only central office in Europe'.

Far from disappearing, the national patent offices of Europe remain vociferously and vigorously present in Europe's patent landscape. In 2002 the EPO concluded that national patent offices could play a much greater 'filtering' role when it came to helping the EPO deal with its workload problems.[67] Beginning in 2004, the Administrative Council of the EPO led a debate in which the EPO and national patent offices discussed strategies for the future of the European patent system based on the idea that the EPO and the national patent offices would begin to operate much more as an integrated network.[68] This led in 2006 to the formation of the European Patent Network. The principles governing the network are free choice by applicants, no compulsory outsourcing by the EPO, no automatic utilization by the EPO of the work of national patent offices, equal treatment of all member states and a commitment to a set of quality standards for the network.[69] Amongst other things, this network will focus on the utilization by the EPO of the work done by national patent offices on patent applications. As the EPO's annual reports over the years have noted, most patent applications have been filed with a national office

---

[67] 'Mastering the workload' CA/132/02, 08.10.2002, 44.

[68] The documentation relating to this debate is to be found at www.epo.org/about-us/epo/consultation-processes/strategy-debate/documentation.html.

[69] The expression of this network philosophy is to be found in 'Joint Statement on the European Patent Network' CA/94/05 Munich 31.05.2005.

first and then filed at the EPO. While there is a trend towards direct filing at the EPO such direct filings represented only 14% of the total European applications in 2007.[70] This means that the EPO remains an office of second filing, with about half its applications coming from residents of member states.[71] It follows that national patent offices within Europe are producing search and examination information that is potentially useful to the EPO.

On the face of it network thinking has well and truly arrived at the EPO. Whether the European Patent Network, however, turns out to be a network of cooperation in which the EPO is the important coordinator or instead the basis of a platform for competition in which the EPO becomes a much less important office is an open question. Cooperation amongst patent offices depends critically on trust, and this, for the time being at least, is not part of the network in the quantities that are needed. The increase in membership of the European Patent Organization, which in the eyes of one interviewee makes it increasingly 'ungovernable', does run the risk that a combination of the cultural underpinnings of trust and economic self-interest will work to divide Europe's patent offices into smaller coalitions that will war with each other over work and the principles that govern the network. The two most critical principles here are the principles of mutual exploitation versus mutual recognition. For the EPO, for the time being, the principle of mutual recognition is unacceptable, just as it is to the German PO: 'The de jure recognition of examination work by other offices would be the end of examination capacities in Europe' (interview, EPO).

It is not clear that it would be the end of examination capacities in Europe because a European network in which a number of patent offices were able to operate to quality standards agreed by the network would mean that an examination by say the Danish PO or Austrian PO would have to be recognized by the EPO.[72] It would mean however that the EPO would no longer be the central route to a European patent. Companies could choose the office in the network that offered the fastest or cheapest service knowing that the EPO would under the principle of mutual recognition have to recognize the work of their chosen office. Once a set of quality standards are agreed by the EPO and national patent offices, the European Patent Network becomes open to the transformative effects of mutual recognition. Some offices like the EPO and German PO fear this and others like the UK PO are less concerned.

[70] EPO, *Annual Report 2007*, 18.   [71] Ibid. 17.
[72] A quality project is one of the pillars of the European Patent Network. See www.epo.org/about-us/european-patent-network.html.

Technical assistance and technocratic trust

In the first two decades of its operation the EPO concentrated on building its own resources so that it could deliver the search, examination and opposition services that were required under the EPC. Technical assistance formed a relatively small part of its work. So, for example, in 1989 its technical assistance activities consisted of training sixty-six nationals from developing countries at the EPO and sending twenty-eight experts on technical assistance missions covering various aspects of how to build and administer a patent system.[73] Gradually it began investing more in technical assistance. So, for example, in 1996 it funded the Tacis programme (national assistance for Ukraine and Uzbekistan), the Regional Industrial Property Programme (covering thirteen states) and the ECAP programme for the Association of Southeast Asian Nations (ASEAN) countries as well as cooperation projects with national patent offices from Argentina, China, Mexico, Malaysia and the Philippines.[74]

The fact that the EPO has a reasonably predictable income stream over which it has autonomy means that it can plan and fund long-term technical assistance programmes. It has been and remains a long-term player in technical assistance activities. Its annual reports show that it has worked with developing-country patent offices over many years.[75] This in turn has allowed it to build relationships of trust between itself and other offices. In the fieldwork a standard question of an office was which other offices did it trust? Almost all the developing-country offices would always mention the EPO as a highly trusted office. The pay-off for the EPO of many years of delivering technical assistance to developing-country patent offices is that those offices have come to trust the EPO.

In the case of patent offices, organizational trust has the effect of leading the trust-giving office to depend on and use the work of the trusted office. So, for example, after cooperation projects with the EPO, Argentina, Mexico, Malaysia, the Philippines and Thailand decided to use the EPO's search results to speed up their granting procedures.[76]

The fieldwork data suggest that the steady drip-drip of technical assistance over a period of years has led to the formation of trust between the EPO and developing-country offices. Trust in institutional and

---

[73] EPO, *Annual Report 1989*, 45   [74] EPO, *Annual Report 1996*, 55–6.

[75] By way of example the EPO, *Annual Report 1997*, at 41 describes activities with the African Regional Intellectual Property Office and the Brazilian Patent Office. The EPO, *Annual Report 2006*, at 46 also describes technical support activities with these offices.

[76] EPO, *Annual Report 1996*, 56.

organizational contexts is a difficult concept to unpack. Trust between individuals involves the person who trusts another believing that the entrusted person has an interest to act in a way that takes into account the interests of the trust-giver.[77] This account of trust works well in the context of smaller group face-to-face interactions, but seems less applicable when one is dealing with relations between large organizations and individuals or between large organizations. In large organizational contexts the sheer numbers and consequent facelessness act against individuals outside of the organization from giving their trust to it. Trust between patent offices from different countries faces the additional hurdle that the patent institution has been and continues to be used by countries as an instrument of economic competition.[78] This would work against rather than for the evolution of trust between offices.

How then are we to make sense of the apparent fact that trust has evolved between the EPO and some developing-country offices? The trust that is being referred to here is of a limited kind that targets systems rather than individuals. Over the years the EPO has spent hundreds of millions of dollars on automating and then digitising its systems of searching and examination.[79] The EPO, JPO and USPTO have had to develop systems for managing patent documentation that are of a scale that dwarfs anything in developing-country patent offices. By way of example, in 1996 the EPO reported that its search files had reached 24.5 million patent documents and 2.5 million scientific or technological documents.[80] In that year it added a further 1.1 million documents bringing its total holdings to 28.1 million. Developing-country examiners making the exciting journey to the patent metropoles of Europe (Munich, the Hague, Berlin, Vienna) for training during the 1980s and 1990s would have been exposed to these systems. Their own systems and offices would not have looked good by comparison. When, for example, I visited the Philippines Patent Office in 2004 patent searching was based on a manual system. A Philippines generic company described the process as a time-consuming one in which files had to be obtained on one floor and taken for photocopying

---

[77] For more details see Russell Hardin, 'Trust in Government' in Valerie Braithwaite and Margaret Levi (eds.), *Trust and Governance*, Russell Sage Foundation, New York, 1998, 9, 12–13.

[78] The European Commission takes this view of the patent institution. See Green Paper on the community patent and the patent system in europe, COM(97) 314 Final, Brussels, 24.06.97 (1997).

[79] The importance of automating its systems is a regular item in the EPO's annual reports. See, for example, EPO, *Annual Report 1989*, 26 and EPO, *Annual Report 1997*, 25.

[80] EPO, *Annual Report 1997*, 37.

to another.[81] In Laos at the time of my visit the four people in the Laotian Patent Office were waiting for the arrival of some personal computers from WIPO so that they could get the office up and running.[82] At the time of the visit to the Indonesian Patent Office in 2005 patent examiners had only just each gained their own computer.[83] Before then it had been a question of sharing – five examiners to one machine. Things will have almost certainly improved since my visits to these offices. But it is interesting to compare this state of affairs in these developing countries with the EPO's systems as they stood in 1996, systems that included bibliographic data in respect of all patent documents published since 1968 and facsimile images of all documents published since 1920 in the USA, Japan and the members states of the EPO and WIPO. Access to these data and images was through various databases including 13 full-text patent databases holding some 60 million searchable records.[84] A patent examiner from a developing country visiting the Hague in 1989 might have been given a tour of the corridors that at that time held 17 kilometres of shelving used to store the patent documents needed for patent searches.[85]

The issue here is not how objectively efficient the EPO's systems were at this time, but how they would have *appeared* to outsiders coming from developing countries. The key here is the projection of technological superiority and efficiency. It is this projection of technological image that leads visitors into the process of comparison and the generation of beliefs and impressions about the adequacy or inadequacy of their own systems and the superiority of the systems in which they are being instructed. The EPO's technical assistance programmes during the 1980s and 1990s would have created in developing-country examiners a sense of confidence in the EPO's systems. The limitation of their own search and examination systems would be all too apparent, systems housed in run-down buildings that lacked a sufficient number of computers or computers at all. At the time of my visits to developing-country patent offices such as those in Indonesia and Malaysia, patent examiners were relying on free, publicly available search systems from the EPO and other major developed-country offices. Yet, no developed-country

---

[81] Interview with the Philippine Chamber of Pharmaceutical Industry, Manila (6 May 2004).

[82] Interview at the Department of Intellectual Property, Vientiane, Laos, (12 May 2004).

[83] Interview in the Sub-Directorate of Patent Administration and Technical Services, Jakarta, Indonesia, (24 January 2006).

[84] EPO, *Annual Report 1996*, 10.

[85] For those who believe that seeing is believing a photo of some of this shelving appears in the EPO, *Annual Report 1989*, 40–1.

examiner working in, for example, pharmaceuticals, works without access to private commercial databases. One cannot complete a proper patent search without access to subscription databases. Making the technocratic judgement that the EPO's systems could be trusted to generate reliable results would be a natural step for developing-country examiners to take once they had been through the process of training in the EPO's systems.

The trust that develops between patent offices is a narrow technocratic trust based on a confidence in the reliable performance of a system rather than individuals, a confidence that technical training builds over time. Technocratic trust is the trust that individuals within systems place in the technical output of other systems. This trust has its foundations in a personal or relational trust. When I asked patent offices of both developed and developing countries to identify the factors that affect trust, the one factor that all offices identified as crucial was the exchange of examiners. The longer-term systematic exchange of examiners between two offices or the training of examiners from one office creates relational trust that eventually becomes the basis for a trust in the technical output of the systems of an office. Once the confidence based on relational trust generalizes into technocratic trust, a creeping lock-in of systems begins to grow in the developing-country patent office, involving access to some of the EPO's databases and new software systems and ultimately a reliance on the EPO's searches and granting decisions. In this way technocratic trust becomes the basis of regulatory automation. Those receiving the assistance assume the reliability of the system and become drawn into the interpretive community that the EPO represents. Technical assistance of this kind is clearly integrative. It allows the EPO to build and lead a community of patent examiners that stretches around the globe.

An example of this leadership based on technocratic trust came from fieldwork in Vietnam, where over the years the EPO has been active.[86] When examiners in the Vietnamese PO come to consider say a patent application in the pharmaceutical field they begin by looking at how the EPO has decided the application and what it has said in its search report either as the EPO or in its capacity as an authority under the PCT system.[87] They do not confine themselves to the EPO as the examiner's decision tree in Figure 4.2 makes clear.[88] They may also look at the way in which the

---

[86] A description of the EPO's activities in Vietnam is available in the EPO, *Annual Report 1997*, 56 and EPO, *Annual Report 1998*, 41.

[87] Interview at National Office of Industrial Property of Vietnam, Hanoi (3 June 2004).

[88] This decision tree was explained to the author during the course of the interview.

USPTO and JPO have treated the application. This decision tree is typical of the developing-country offices that were interviewed. Out of the Trilaterals, it was clearly the EPO that developing-country offices looked to first when making their own examination decisions. Some offices also mentioned that they might look at the examination decisions of the Korean Intellectual Property Office (KIPO) and the State Intellectual Property Office of China (SIPO). The picture of examination leadership is probably a fluctuating one and would be affected by the investments that the major offices make in examiner exchange and training programmes. The decision tree below is the product of years of EPO technical assistance, which includes training visits to beautiful Munich with its designed gardens and wonderful restaurants. It is the story of quiet and steady cultural integration in which examiners from patent offices of the periphery journey to the patent kingdoms of the West to be instructed in systems of apparent technological superiority to their own, systems that continue to influence them once they return home.

The effects of technocratic trust

It is through technocratic trust and the regulatory automation that it grounds that the patent system comes to have practical operational effects in developing countries. Over the years the steady drip-drip of technical assistance leads to the formation of a strong belief in developing-country patent offices that the EPO's systems produce quality results and that

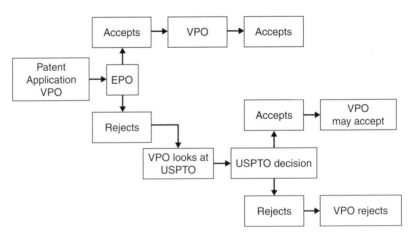

Figure 4.2   Leadership in examination. (VPO = Vietnamese Patent Office).

belief in turn forms the basis of decision-making by patent examiners in under-resourced developing-country patent offices. Technocratic trust thus fosters a circle of decision-making in which the EPO trains developing-country examiners to make decisions in their own countries using the EPO's systems and decisions.

In the case of personal trust, the trust-giver assumes that the trust-receiver will take proper account of the trust-giver's interest. Technocratic trust is an impersonal form of trust in which the trust-giver comes to have an expectation about the performance of the system. The system designer has an interest in ensuring the reliability of the system since otherwise there is no possibility of an expectation about its reliability. Beyond that the system designer may not necessarily have the interests of the trust-giver in mind.

During the EPO interview, officials stressed that the EPO's philosophy of technical assistance was to try and make the patent system work for that particular country: 'We give them technical solutions for their real needs.' These technical solutions involve giving some offices access to EPOQUE, examiner training, sharing documentation and various information technology solutions so that 'there is something left behind in the country, something tangible'.

At one level the EPO's technical assistance work is an example of how technical assistance should be done. Much technical assistance ends up having little positive development impact.[89] The EPO has been involved with many developing countries on a long-term basis and patent offices in these countries have gained superior information technology systems, better-trained examiners and probably represent in many developing countries examples of stable functioning bureaucracies with a well-defined mission and skilled personnel being paid a reasonable salary. But there are two deeper problems here. The first is that the EPO (along with JPO and the USPTO which also do technical assistance) is transferring software and skills aimed at producing a purring efficiency in a patent system that itself has arrived in a developing country via a complex historical sequence involving mechanisms of colonization and economic or military coercion. Rarely have patent systems evolved in developing countries in the way that they evolved in nineteenth-century Europe

---

[89] For a review of the reasons see Ashok Chakravarti, *Aid, Institutions and Development*, Edward Elgar, Cheltenham, UK, 2005, 56–70.

(see Chapter 3). It is not at all clear that patent systems in their present form as foreign transplants have development benefits.[90]

The other problem is that to the extent that the EPO's technical assistance work promotes regulatory automation of decision-making in developing-country patent offices, it undermines the administrative autonomy of developing countries to adjust the patent system to meet the conditions that exist in the various sectors of their economies. EPO officials emphasized that 'we don't want them (developing countries) to be externally dependent on us'. But this does not really square with the reality that developing-country patent offices are administering patent systems that are foreign transplants, that the EPO has drafted examination manuals for developing-country patent offices, trained examiners in their use and set up information technology systems that enable examiners to track the decisions of EPO examiners (working either as the EPO or a PCT authority). Perhaps there is not a simple external economic dependence on the EPO, but the systems that the EPO leaves behind do automate the decision-making processes of developing-country patent offices in ways that integrate their countries more deeply into the global system of patent governance that is being administered by the world's major offices. The EPO also has European economic interests in mind when it fosters technocratic trust through technical assistance. In 1995 it pointed out that in the case of patent filings in ASEAN countries 95% had originated outside of these countries, with 40% coming from Europe.[91] Moreover patent filings in ASEAN countries were growing at the rate of 20% per year.[92] This growing backlog in ASEAN patent offices resulted in a programme of technical assistance that included,

> further-training courses for employees, *incorporating search and examination results from other offices into grant procedures* and the automation of patent and trade mark administration. In addition four ASEAN patent offices were supplied with CD-ROM workstations and facilities to access the EPO's INPADOC databases [emphasis added].[93]

One important effect of technocratic trust and regulatory automation in patent offices is that it opens the way to the transfer of economic rents to

---

[90] For an overview of the issues see Keith E. Maskus and Jerome H. Reichman, 'Globalization of Private Knowledge goods and the Privatization of Global Public Goods', in Keith E. Maskus and Jerome H. Reichman (eds.), *International Public Goods and Transfer of Technology Under a Globalized Intellectual Property Regime*, Cambridge University Press, Cambridge, 2005, 3.

[91] This figure excludes Vietnam. See EPO, *Annual Report 1995*, 62.   [92] Ibid.

[93] Ibid.

European patent owners.[94] Patent examiners in developing-country offices spend most of their time granting patents to foreign firms from Europe, Japan and the US. Another important effect of technical assistance is its effect on the capacity of developing-country patent offices to become players in national policy networks. Policy networks have become an important variable in explaining the evolution of economic planning and performance of states.[95] The fieldwork evidence suggests that patent offices in developing countries play a role in the policy networks of a country. So, for example, when a developing country has a trade negotiation with a developed country, often it is the patent office that provides the patent negotiating expertise when it comes to the intellectual property chapter. Amongst other things, these negotiations cover patent standards that deal with matters such as scope of patentable subject matter, patent term extension, patent and drug registration linkage, protection of test data for pharmaceuticals and scope of compulsory licensing, matters that can impact in major ways on the local companies and sectors in a developing country, especially the pharmaceutical sector.[96] Similarly patent offices have an input into innovation policy because of the assumption that patents are integral to innovation. Patent offices do not behave as simple land title registries. Instead they participate in processes of interpreting, advising and negotiating standards of patent protection. As players in national policy networks developing-country patent offices have the following features. First, by virtue of the long-running technical assistance programmes, they are integrated into one or more of the Trilateral Offices. Second, they receive resources from these offices, often on a long-term basis, and they have the capacity to generate income from the grant of patents. This means that in comparison to other national bureaucracies in developing countries they are often better resourced. Third, the fee income they generate comes largely from a foreign clientele, especially multinational companies with global patenting strategies. Fourth, because of the technological and jurisprudential complexity of patent work the operation of patent offices remains opaque to other policy areas of the developing-country's

[94] On the rent transfer from developing to developed countries as a result of TRIPS see J. Michael Finger, 'The Doha Agenda and Development: A View from the Uruguay Round', Asian Development Bank, ERD Working Paper Series No. 21, Sept 2002, 13.

[95] For an overview see Michael M. Atkinson and William D. Coleman, 'Strong States and Weak States: Sectoral Policy Networks in Advanced Capitalist Economies', 19 (1989) *British Journal of Political Science*, 47.

[96] See Frederick M. Abbott, 'The WTO Medicines Decision: World Pharmaceutical Trade and the Protection of Public Health', 99 (2005) *American Journal of International Law*, 317, 349–54.

civil service. Developing-country patent offices are thus unusual players in national policy networks because they are disposed to be pro-patent, are integrated into international patent policy networks from which they draw resources and serve a clientele that is predominantly foreign. From the perspective of innovation policy, patent offices are likely to close off or circumscribe policy initiatives that question the role of patents in innovation. Technical assistance that builds the capability of patent offices to be players in policy networks is essentially building a capability that is pro-patent in disposition. This in short is technical assistance that tilts the policy playing field in a particular direction.

The echoes of empire

Finally it is worth observing that international patent structures that were created during colonization have been recreated under the EPC. During the national phase of patent office building by Western countries in the first half of the twentieth century some developing countries were quietly integrated into an emerging system of international patent governance. Probably the largest scale example of this integration was the development of the re-registration system that was adopted by colonies of the British Empire. The idea of an Empire patent had been discussed at various points, but what resulted was not one patent for the Empire, but rather the right of the UK patent holder to register that UK patent in a colony or protectorate of the British Empire that had adopted a law allowing for re-registration. Table 4.1 shows the extent of the re-registration system.[97] In the case of the UK, the re-registration system that was created in its Empire days seems to have been recreated under the EPO. In a number of UK territories and Commonwealth countries (for example, Fiji, Gambia and Uganda) the owner of the UK European patent has 3 years within which to apply for the re-registration of that patent in those territories and countries.[98]

---

[97] *Report of the Department Committee on the Patents and Designs Acts and Practice of the Patent Office*, His Majesty's Stationery Office, London, 1931, 71.
[98] For the full list see *Official Journal* EPO 4/2004, 179.

Table 4.1. *The British Empire patent re-registration system*

Bermuda	Mauritius
British Guiana	Nigeria
British Honduras	Northern Rhodesia
Brunei	Palestine
Cyprus	St Helena
Falkland Islands	St Lucia
Federated Malay States	St Vincent
Fiji	Seychelles
Gambia	Sierra Leone
Gibraltar	Solomon Islands
Gilbert and Ellice Islands	Somaliland
Gold Coast	Straits Settlements
Grenada	Tanganyika Territory
Hong Kong	Trinidad and Tobago
Kenya	Uganda
Leeward Islands	Zanzibar

5

The USPTO and JPO

The USPTO

The USPTO is the oldest examining office in the world. As we saw in Chapter 3 the US committed itself to substantive examination in 1790 and has stayed with it, aside from its experiment with a registration-only system from 1793 to 1836. It has, therefore, the longest experience of the problems of an examination system. An examiner travelling in time from the nineteenth century to the USPTO building in twenty-first century Alexandria, Virginia would see, once he had gotten over the marvel of computers and automatically flushing toilets, the same basic problems that confronted the office in the nineteenth century. These problems include finding and classifying prior art, retaining a sufficient number of trained examiners, dealing with a backlog of applications and coping with the gaming behaviour of the users of the system. These problems have proved to be remarkably persistent.

The US patent system in the blink of an eye

The US patent system has deeper constitutional roots than other patent systems. Article I, Section 8, Clause 8 of the US Constitution states: 'To promote the Progress of Science and Useful Arts, by securing for limited Times to Authors and Inventors the exclusive Right to their respective Writings and Discoveries.' As one US Supreme Court decision has put it, by 'constitutional command' the patent system must serve the progress of useful arts.[1] The clause is also consistent with the social value conception of the patent contract that was argued for in Chapter 1. Exclusive rights are not an end in themselves, but are created in order to promote progress. They are to be exclusive for a limited time, meaning that an inventor's discovery must eventually be open to inclusive use. Congress cannot

---

[1] *Graham v. John Deere Co.* 383 U.S. 1, 6 (1966).

authorise the grant of patents that have the effect of removing knowledge from the public domain or restricting access to such knowledge.[2] US patent law like other patent law systems has gone down the path of creating disclosure obligations for patent applicants, obligations that are stronger than in other patent systems. As we noted in Chapter 1, inventors have a duty to disclose the best mode of operation of the invention, an obligation not to be found in other patent systems. At the same time the US patent system undercuts the diffusion of patent information by allowing for the award of treble damages in cases where wilful patent infringement has been found, something that discourages the reading and use of published patent information.[3] US patent law also imposes a duty of candour on the inventor to bring relevant prior art to the attention of the patent office, but the duty is seen to have little practical value in its present form.[4]

When it comes to patentable subject matter, US patent law does not contain the kind of list of exceptions to patentability that one sees in other patent statutes. Instead US courts have been left to work out the scope of patentable subject matter. In one of its most famous patent decisions, the US Supreme Court in *Diamond* v. *Chakrabarty* referred to court decisions that excluded laws of nature, physical phenomena and abstract ideas from patentability.[5] But it also drew attention to a fundamental interpretive axiom that has been crucial to the expansion of patentable subject matter in the US – that the words of the patent statute had to be broadly construed.

Aside from patentable subject matter, the other criteria of patentability are novelty (35 U.S.C. 102), utility (35 U.S.C. 101), non-obviousness (35 U.S.C. 103) and adequate disclosure of the invention (35 U.S.C. 112). As in other legal systems there are also well-established exceptions to the patent owner's exclusive rights, including mechanisms that allow for the unauthorized use of a patent (these mechanisms include compulsory licensing remedies and government use procedures),[6] experimental use,[7]

---

[2] Ibid.

[3] See 35 U.S.C. 284. For a discussion of the problems of treble damages see Federal Trade Commission 'To Promote Innovation: The Proper Balance of Competition and Patent Law and Policy' (October 2003), Ch. 5, 28–31, available at www.ftc.gov/opa/2003/10/cpreport.htm.

[4] 37 C.F.R. 1.56. See 'Federal Trade Commission, To Promote Innovation', 9.

[5] *Diamond* v. *Chakrabarty* 447 U.S. 303, 309 (1980).

[6] Unlike other patent statutes the US patent statute does not contain a general compulsory licensing provision. However, a compulsory licence may be ordered by a court in the context of an antitrust proceeding. The law of the US also allows for government use of a patent without the permission of the patent owner (the UK equivalent of a Crown use provision). See 28 U.S.C. 1498.

[7] For a discussion see *Madey* v. *Duke University* 307 F.3d 1351 (Fed. Cir. 2002).

a specific exception for the use of patented inventions needed to generate information required for submission processes under Federal drug laws[8] and a limited defence for infringement of patents on methods where the alleged infringer can show he was the first to practice the subject matter of the patent.[9]

The US runs a first-to-invent system rather than a first-to-file system.[10] As the phrase 'first to invent' suggests the inventor who first invents is entitled to be awarded the patent, not the person who first files for the patent. It is the act of invention and not the first act of filing that determines priority. Disputes over priority are settled by reference to a procedure known as an 'interference proceeding'.[11] The fact that the US is now the only patent jurisdiction to run a first-to-invent system has been one of the key issues in patent harmonization talks over the decades. A US patent law reform committee pointed out in 1992 that in more than 99.9% of patent applications there was no dispute over the true first inventor.[12]

Once an application has been lodged with the USPTO there are detailed procedures to be followed for examination, examination of the application being obligatory. There is a Manual of Patent Examining Procedure. At more than 40 megabytes there is no shortage of detail. In essence the examiner has to decide whether the invention being claimed by the inventor is novel, whether it satisfies the test of non-obviousness (the US version of the inventive-step requirement), whether it has utility and whether it has been so fully described in the specification that a person skilled in the art can make and use the invention. The examiner has to carry out a prior art search of the patent and non-patent literature that forms the basis upon which judgements about novelty and non-obviousness are made. For the purposes of the prior art search the US works with 'relative novelty' (unlike the standard of absolute novelty to be found in the European Patent Convention (EPC)). Inventions that have been patented or described in a publication in any country can destroy novelty, but when it comes to the invention being known or used by others, that knowledge or use must have taken place in the US before it can cause a person to lose their right to a patent.[13] The effect of the

---

[8] See 35 U.S.C. 271(e)(1).   [9] See 35 U.S.C. 273.
[10] See 35 U.S.C. 102 (g).   [11] See 35 U.S.C. 135.
[12] See 'The Advisory Commission on Patent Law Reform: A Report to the Secretary of Commerce', 1992, 44.
[13] 35 U.S.C. 102(a).

rules around prior art in relation to US patent applications that have an earlier foreign filing date are another source of disagreement in patent harmonization talks.[14]

In the case of US law ascertaining inventiveness is a matter of working out the difference or gap between the invention being applied for and the prior art. If the step to making the invention was obvious 'to a person having ordinary skill in the art' a patent cannot be granted.[15] Amongst other things, this requires an examiner to keep up with technological developments in his or her field so that they have some sense of the prevailing ordinary level of skill. In fast-moving areas of technology like computer software keeping up is a non-trivial endeavour. Increasing numbers of commentators take the view that when it comes to the non-obviousness test, US patent law has come to operate with a lower standard, allowing a small inventive step to render the invention non-obvious.[16] Examiners also have to evaluate the patent claims, the basic idea being that these claims must not extend beyond the invention being disclosed to the public. Under the patent social contract, the public contracts to provide protection for what the inventor has actually invented and not more than that. Patent attorneys seeking to maximize protection for their client will generally draft broad claims to begin with knowing that at worst they may have to redraft them if the examiner objects. There is everything to gain by beginning with broad claims and little to lose.

An examiner will typically find some problems with the application and so reject all or some part of it by means of a letter to the applicant called a 'First Office Action'. Rejections offer applicants various negotiating and procedural options. The simplest scenario is one in which the applicant amends the application and the examiner approves it. Examiners and applicants may not be able to agree in which case the examiner has the option of issuing a Second Office Action to decide finally the matter. Finality, however, is not really a feature of the US application process as applicants can restart the process by filing a Request for Continued Examination or if they have new subject matter to add a Continuation in Part application. The use of continuations to create a loop in which

---

[14] For a discussion see 'The Advisory Commission on Patent Law Reform', 65–6.

[15] 35 U.S.C. 103.

[16] For examples see the citations given by Stephen A. Merrill, Richard C. Levin and Mark B. Myers (eds.), *A Patent System for the 21st Century*, The National Academies Press, Washington, DC, 2004, (a report of the National Research Council of the National Academies), 61. The Federal Trade Commission has recommended a tightening of the test. See Federal Trade Commission, 'To Promote Innovation', 10–12.

the same application is recycled through the USPTO's procedures at the applicant's discretion adds to the USPTO's workload problems.[17] There is also the possibility of appealing the examiner's decision with the Board of Patent Appeals and Interferences and from there to the Court of Appeals for the Federal Circuit. Applications are for one invention, but where it turns out that there is more than one invention the applicant has the option of filing a divisional application in relation to the second invention. The use of continuations and divisionals can create complex patent application trails in relation to a given invention. Issued patents are presumed to be valid.[18]

The US introduced a patent term of 20 years in order to meet its obligations under the Agreement on Trade-Related Aspects of Intellectual Property Rights (TRIPS).[19] Before then the term had been 17 years calculated from the date of the patent issuing. In 1999 the US introduced a pre-grant publication system. Patent applications are now published 18 months after the filing date, although if an applicant decides to apply for patent protection only in the US the applicant may request that the application not be published.[20] Linked to its first-to-invent system the US statute bars a person from obtaining a patent if they have under certain circumstances released the invention (for example, publishing the invention in the US or abroad) and that release takes place more than 12 months prior to the date of their application to the USPTO.[21]

The US does not have a pre-grant opposition system that enables third parties to challenge the issue of a patent prior to its grant and nor does it have a post-grant opposition system. It has been a strong critic of the former arguing that it leads to delays in the grant of patents.[22] Other countries have taken a different view of a pre-grant opposition system. The German and British models of patent administration, which proved to be so influential in the twentieth century, both had pre-grant opposition and some countries such as Australia and India retain it as part of their system. At the interview in the German PO, pre-grant opposition was said to be a very important tool of patent quality.

[17] See Mark A. Lemley and Kimberly A. Moore, 'Ending Abuse of Patent Continuations', 82 (2004) *B.U. L. Rev.*, 63.
[18] 35 U.S.C. 282.
[19] See Uruguay Round Agreement Act 1994, 35 U.S.C. 154(a)(2).
[20] For the general 18-month rule and the exceptions to it see 35 U.S.C. 122.
[21] 35 U.S.C. 102(b).
[22] Even progressive groups on patent reform in the US come out against pre-grant opposition. See Merrill, Levin and Myers (eds.), *A Patent System for the 21st Century*, 96, fn.35.

Concerns about patent quality in the US have led to proposals for the adoption of a post-grant system.[23] Currently the US does have a re-examination system that allows the patentee, a third party or the Director of the USPTO to have a granted patent re-examined.[24] In its present form the re-examination procedure is not seen as having a radical impact on quality.[25] Early on in the history of the re-examination procedure the rights of third parties to appeal decisions made during the process were limited and this naturally enough discouraged its use. There have been changes to the procedure allowing third parties more scope to partici-pate in or appeal a decision made during the re-examination procedure, but the procedure itself has a narrow range of operation being triggered only by prior art issues.[26] For the time being at least most players which have prior art information capable of invalidating patent claims have con-cluded that it is better to wait for the open warfare of litigation rather than risk a narrow administrative procedure.

The lack of use of the re-examination procedure is a good example of a more general problem that recurs in US patent reform. A proposal that looks promising in terms of efficiency is put forward, but efficiency turns out not to be the determining criterion. Instead proposals have to satisfy the test of politics. Under this test a proposal that undermines the 'nat-ural' right of a major patent owner to amass patents or engage in gam-ing behaviour using those patents is subjected to relentless Congressional politicking, a process in which schools of piranha-like lobbyists tear draft proposals apart. Patent law reform is made up of the bits and pieces that float to the surface from these murky Congressional depths.

The problems in 1845

Nine years after the shift to a registration system in 1836, the Commissioner for Patents in his annual report for 1845 stated that the PO had received 1,246 applications and issued 502 patents.[27] The office had two examiners each with one assistant. There were delays in dealing with applications for which the office was being criticized. The solution

---

[23] Federal Trade Commission, 'To Promote Innovation', 21.
[24] Known as 'ex parte re-examination'. There is also inter partes re-examination that allows for third-party participation.
[25] See Federal Trade Commission, 'To Promote Innovation', Ch. 5, 16.
[26] Merrill, Levin and Myers (eds.), *A Patent System for the 21st Century*, 96.
[27] A copy of the 1845 Annual Report is available at www.ipmall.fplc.edu/hosted_resources/ PatentHistory/poar1845.htm.

lay in hiring more examiners. Here one had to find Renaissance men who were happy to work for next to nothing, as the following quote from the report makes clear:

> An examiner should be a living encyclopedia of science, if the expression may be used. His multifarious duties require an intimate and thorough knowledge of the whole circle of science and art, together with a knowledge of modern languages – particularly of the French and German – and the most attentive and incessant mental labor. Yet, for all these high qualifications, and for labors scarcely second in intensity to those required by any officer in the government, the principal examiner is allowed only a salary of $1,500 per annum, and his assistant but $1,250.

In 1848 another two examiners and two assistants were hired. By 1853 the number of applications had climbed to 2,673 and more examiners had been hired to deal with them. But as of December 1853 there were 582 undisposed of cases. Also out in the open were a set of problems that were to afflict the USPTO to its present day.

On the increasing complexity of examination:[28]

> The labor and expense of making examinations is every year increasing as the field for examinations is constantly and rapidly widening.

On the need to search more material for prior art purposes:

> [I]t may be stated that there are now in the Office very nearly 25,000 models, and about the same number of drawings in the portfolios. The number received within the last nine years is a little upwards of 17,000, and the number filed within the past year nearly 3,000. The number of volumes in our library at this time is about 5,750; in 1847 it was only 1,850. There have been 1,550 added during the past year; most of these are works which require to be frequently referred to by the examiners in the course of the year.

On the problem of retaining examiners and the need to pay them more:

> These vacancies not unfrequently result from resignations, caused by the fact that a person well qualified for an examiner finds a more profitable employment elsewhere than in the Patent Office. One remedy for this would be to increase the compensation of the examiners.

These themes were repeated in subsequent annual reports. By 1893 the office was just keeping its head above water. It had 199 examiners and was

---

[28] The following quotes are all taken from the 1853 Annual Report available at www.ipmall. fplc.edu/hosted_resources/PatentHistory/poar1853.htm.

receiving around 40,000 applications per year. On 1 January 1893 it had 9,011 applications awaiting attention, about 100 more than on 1 July 1891.[29] Keeping the backlog to this number, the Commissioner warned, had only been made possible because examiners had worked overtime.

The backlog problems never went away. Instead throughout the twentieth century they got worse.[30] The number of patents applied for grew very fast. In its first 46 years (1790 to 1836), the US patent system produced roughly 10,000 patents, a number that it reached again in only 17 years and by the early 1920s it was granting that many every 3 months.[31] No matter how the big the office grew, the backlog grew bigger. Some blamed it on a shortage of examiners, claiming that the US government did not appropriate enough money to run an efficient USPTO.[32] Examiners working in patent offices knew that a good patent search required knowledge of the technology and the literature as well as a reliable patent classification system. In the case of the latter the problem was that while the USPTO had established a classification division in 1898, that division did not have enough resources to improve the classification system.[33] The pressure of dealing with the backlog of applications meant not enough resources were devoted to this task. In any case the more pigeon holes of classification that were added to the system, the more likely it would be that classifiers would diverge when it came to classifying given inventions. Patent attorneys drew attention to this danger of classification work and with some justification pointed to the difficulty of doing reliable searches.[34] By the 1950s the classification system had evolved to a point where even patent savants might make mistakes either in classifying a patent or searching for one. Around 2.5 million patents had been placed into 350 classes which in turn were further sub-divided into 45,000 subclasses, those subclasses being further divided.[35] Those

---

[29] www.ipmall.fplc.edu/hosted_resources/PatentHistory/poar1892.htm.

[30] See, for example, 'Patent Office Report for 1951', 34 (1952) *Journal of the Patent Office Society*, 163.

[31] Karl Fenning, 'Growth of American Patents', 52 (1925–26) *Journal of the Patent Office Society*, 52, 54.

[32] See Chas H. Keel, 'Patent Office Backlog', 30 (1948) *Journal of the Patent Office Society*, 73–5.

[33] Manuel C. Rosa, 'Patent Office Organization, Viewpoint and Classification' 31 (1949) *Journal of the Patent Office Society*, 414, 437.

[34] See, for example, the short treatise by the patent attorney, Richard B. Owen, *Patents, Trademarks, Copyrights, Departmental Practice*, Washington, New York, 1925, 11.

[35] On the complexity and problems see Manuel C. Rosa, 'Patent Office Organization, Viewpoint and Classification', 31 (1949) *Journal of the Patent Office Society*, 414; B.E. Lanham, 'Chemical Patent Searches,' 34 (1952) *Journal of the Patent Office Society*, 315, 315–16.

doing the classification had to be careful not to 'bury' the patent through inappropriate classification.[36] Once buried its existence would likely only be known to the patent holder. For companies a buried patent was only a problem if it was not their own patent.

Examiners who had perfected their skills of searching were often lured to the greener fields of private practice. The patent attorney profession thus built search expertise while the USPTO was left with having to make up for deficits in searching skills. Examiners in the USPTO drew attention to this continual loss of expertise, pointing out that it affected the reliability of the office's searches and suggesting solutions.[37] A Patent Committee set up in 1917 reported to the National Research Council that in the previous 3 years 25% of examiners had resigned.[38] It also pointed out that salaries, which in 1848 had matched that of Congressional representatives, had only gone up 10% since that time. Other parts of the US government paid their scientifically trained people much more. Increasing the salaries of examiners, the Committee concluded, was crucial to raising the quality of examination and patents.

The problems today

The USPTO is the patent gateway to the world's most important high-technology market. The fee-paying users of its services include multinationals that operate in globally important sectors such as biotechnology, chemicals and semiconductors. Few government offices have to face such a tough crowd. As a result the USPTO's problems have over the last few years received a considerable public airing.

These problems are a good example of history repeating itself. The rising number of patent applications in the nineteenth century has become the king of king tides. We saw in the previous section that in the early 1890s the USPTO was receiving approximately 40,000 patent applications per year with a backlog of about 9,000. In its 2006 report, the USPTO reported that it had received more than 417, 000 patent applications and over 52,000 PCT applications.[39] The number of pending applications for

---

[36] Rosa, 'Patent Office Organization, Viewpoint and Classification', 414, 441.

[37] See W. L. Thurber (Examiner), 'A Suggestion for Improving Patent Office Searches', 1 (1918–19) *Journal of the Patent Office Society*, 167–8.

[38] See 'Report of the Patent Committee to the National Research Council', 1 (1918–19) *Journal of the Patent Office Society*, 341, 348. See also Wm. I. Wyman, 'Examiners' Salaries', 1 (1918–19) *Journal of the Patent Office Society*, 392–5.

[39] See www.uspto.gov/web/offices/com/annual/2006/3020100_patentperfrm.html.

fiscal year 2006 was more than one million.[40] The scale of the backlog problem that the USPTO faces is significantly different to what it faced in the nineteenth century.

In order to deal with the number of applications the USPTO hired 1,218 examiners in 2006 and announced plans to hire another 1,200 every financial year to 2012.[41] But here it faces another problem that has plagued it since the nineteenth century. Its human resources problem lies not so much in not being able to recruit sufficient numbers of examiners as in retaining them. A report by US National Academy of Public Administration in 2005 on the USPTO concluded that the USPTO did not have enough experienced examiners.[42] It pointed out that for ten of the years between 1992 and 2004 for every ten examiners that joined five left.[43] The upshot was a comparatively inexperienced workforce. Only 45% of its workforce had more than 5 years experience. Training examiners is not cheap. The same report pointed out that $22 million had been spent on training junior patent examiners in financial year 2000.[44]

There is a limit to what a government agency can do when it comes to improving pay and conditions when it has to compete in high technology markets for graduates. When a particular area of technology becomes high demand, such as computer and electrical technologies during the late 1990s, many patent examiners in that area will join the private sector. The magnetic lure of private sector salaries in a boom phase is hard for individuals to resist. The USPTO's pending patent applications do not grow evenly across all sectors of technology, but are affected by boom–bust technology cycles in the marketplace.[45] This problem is not confined to the USPTO. In an interview in the UK PO the same problem was described, one examiner pointing out that during the 1990s it was impossible to get telecoms engineering expertise for 'love or money'. To some extent the USPTO will always be in the situation of having to react to and manage the loss of staff. It will be able to recruit examiners in the

---

[40] The fiscal year in the US ends 30 September. The pendency number is available at www.uspto.gov/web/offices/com/annual/2006/50305_table5.html. It includes plant and reissue applications.

[41] See www.uspto.gov/web/offices/com/annual/2006/3020100_patentperfrm.html.

[42] *US Patent and Trademark Office: Transforming to Meet the Challenges of the 21st Century*, National Academy of Public Administration, USA, 2005, xviii.

[43] Ibid. 80.   [44] Ibid. 81.

[45] On the strong variations in pendency and workload in the different technology centres of the USPTO, See *US Patent and Trademark Office: Transforming to Meet the Challenges of the 21st Century*, 36.

bust phase of a technological cycle, but by then there will be a backlog of applications awaiting action by examiners and training examiners to process the backlog takes time. Many of the offices interviewed stated that it takes about 2 years to train an examiner to a good level of competency. This was also the USPTO's view. It has attempted to speed up the process of training through group intensive methods rather than using a one-on-one mentoring system. In the German PO, the one-on-one method is seen as an important part of examiner training (interview, German PO). The USPTO's ability to fight fires is thus hampered by the fact that when a fire breaks out many of its best fire fighters leave to help fuel the blaze and those left to do the fighting often lack experience.

One possible solution is to outsource work. The USPTO is carrying out some outsourcing of PCT search reports using private companies and some other patent offices (for example, the Australian PO), leaving the USPTO to concentrate on national applications (interviews, USPTO and Australian PO). But outsourcing to private firms brings with it the costs of managing for quality and ensuring that the use of private firms does not result in a loss of confidence in the integrity of the system. There is also the issue of whether the separation of search and examination improves or worsens the quality of patent examination. Proposals to outsource the search function have drawn opposition from many USPTO examiners, including in the form of a petition to Congress.[46] Many examiners argue that the process of searching helps an examiner to do a better examination. We shall see later in this chapter that the Japanese Patent Office (JPO) does outsource searching but brings searching and examination back together by bringing searchers and examiners face-to-face to discuss the results of the search. Another objection to outsourcing that involves using foreign offices is that it involves a loss of sovereignty.[47]

So far we have seen that the USPTO is flooded by applications and faces difficulties in keeping an experienced workforce to process those applications. Added to this is the fact that the number of claims to be found in applications has gone up. In 2004 the average number was 23.6 whereas in 1998 it was 18.4.[48] Claims involve examiners in potentially time-consuming interpretive exercises in which they have to judge the validity of claims using the law that surrounds claims in general as well as the specific prior art that relates to the claims in question. Computer

---

[46] For a description of this opposition see the Patent Office Professional Association's newsletter, *POPANEWS*, August 2002, v.02, No. 5, p.1.

[47] *POPANEWS*, August 2002, v.02, No. 5, 2.

[48] *US Patent and Trademark Office: Transforming to Meet the Challenges of the 21st Century*, 39.

technology can speed up the gathering of information, but ultimately an examiner still has to interpret that information. One study has suggested that once an application contains more than 12 claims, each claim above that requires an extra 1.67 days of work.[49]

Examiners faced with this increase in complexity argue that they are not being given the time they need to do quality examination work. For some, the patent examiner's cubicle has become a lonely pressure cooker in which production quotas, constant reviews and high levels of firings lead to an organizational culture that is not healthy.[50] Patent examiners better than most understand the kind of gaming behaviour that lies behind complicated patent claims that they have to examine. They understand firsthand, what other government bodies have now also concluded, that there are problems with the quality of patents being issued.[51] They are almost certainly right to say that some increase in their time would result in an improvement in patent quality. But they also live in a world of production targets, where senior management lives and manages by numbers – the backlog number, the first action pendency number, the number of patents granted, performance numbers and so on.

USPTO management has recognized these kinds of problems. My interviewees at the USPTO pointed to improvements that had been made in the working conditions of examiners, improvements that included greater pay and more flexible working conditions.[52] These improvements have probably narrowed the gap that used to exist in favour of the EPO in terms of conditions (interview, EPO). My interviewees were not convinced that USPTO examiners could be brow-beaten by experienced attorneys into accepting an application. The system in the USPTO, including the count system for tracking examiner productivity, was more sophisticated than that. In a large organization like the USPTO one would perhaps find different views. The real problem seems to lie in the backlog. It forces managers into trade-offs between productive efficiency and patent quality.

Gaming behaviour

We saw in the previous section that the USPTO has to process more complex applications than at any time in its history and faces a structural

---

[49] Ibid.

[50] For a good description of these problems from the perspective of examiners see *POPANEWS* 2005, v. 05, No. 6.

[51] See Federal Trade Commission, 'To Promote Innovation' Ch. 5, 16.

[52] For a statement of benefits see http://usptocareers.gov/Pages/PEPositions/Benefits.aspx.

problem in keeping enough experienced staff to do so. An outsider to the patent system might assume that patent applicants themselves would do what they could to ensure the smooth passage of their application. This assumption does not hold for all patent applicants. The reason goes back to the fundamental nature of the patent monopoly itself. Over time patent owners have developed many patent-based strategies to hinder or obstruct their competitors. The patent application process itself has become a target of this strategic behaviour. Once again this is a historical feature of the US patent system. Writing in 1925, Donald Sweet pointed out that many applicants before the USPTO did not want a patent to issue quickly because a delay meant that the patent monopoly would end at a later date (at this time the patent term ran from date of issue) and the products of competitors brought out while the application was pending could be studied and claims redrafted in the light of that study.[53] Sweet's solutions included having a patent term of 20 years fixed to the date of application and requiring that patent applications be published at the end of 3 years. Some 70 years later the US adopted a 20-year patent term and required the publication of patent applications that would also be filed abroad. It had taken a long time to react to abuses of the system that had been present for many decades.

An example of strategic behaviour within the context of the application process that has received attention over the last few years has been the use of continuations. Continuations are applications for inventions that have already been claimed in earlier applications. They are a way of keeping the application process going. For example, in 2002 the US Court of Appeals had to decide whether an application that claimed the priority date of another application filed on 14 June 1978 had been rightly rejected by the USPTO. During the prosecution process the applicant Bogese had filed 12 continuation applications in 8 years. The court pointed out that the aim of this gaming behaviour was to delay the issuance of the patent until the industry and technology had matured to the point where it made sense to surface with the patent and begin to exploit it.[54] In this particular

---

[53] Donald H. Sweet, 'On Delay in the Issuance of Patents', 7 (1924–5) *Journal of the Patent Office Society*, 535.

[54] *In re* Bogese, 303 F.3d 1362, 1366 (Fed. Cir. 2002). The incentive for this type of behaviour was enhanced by the fact that at the time of Bogese's continuation applications the US patent term was 17 years from the date that the patent was issued from the USPTO. In 1995 the US changed the way its patent term was calculated because of its obligations under TRIPS. The term is now 20 years calculated from the date of filing. Using continuations to link back to an earlier filing date shortens the effective patent term.

case the examiner, the Board of Patent Appeals and Interferences and the Court of Appeals all drew on the patent social contract at various stages to point out that it required the inventor to move towards the disclosure of the invention rather than to use the application process to keep it secret for an unreasonable length of time.

The purpose behind allowing continuations was to give applicants the opportunity to craft a better final application after having received an examiner's response.[55] Continuations are used most heavily in the biotechnology and chemical fields. The lack of restrictions on their use means that examiners have to devote time to reworking applications already examined, time that could be used to deal with new applications.[56]

The rules that create the opportunities for gaming behaviour can, of course, be changed. In the case of continuations the USPTO did issue practice rules placing limits on their use.[57] These rules also set limits on the number of claims that would be examined in an application. Rule changes in the US patent system have to be steered past big and sophisticated users of the system. In the case of continuations some corporations, such as Intel, have a patent strategy based on filing for many patents and obtaining them as quickly as possible. Rules that allow an applicant to play for delay hold no advantage for them and in fact hurt their patent strategy because continuations divert scarce examination resources to applications with the earlier priority dates (applications forming part of a continuation chain get the benefit of earlier priority dates). Intel thus supported the USPTO rule change.[58] Members of the biotechnology industry on the other hand file early and then use the continuation process to refine their original application.[59] GlaxoSmithKline was part of a group of plaintiffs that were successful in temporarily stopping the USPTO from implementing the rules on 1 November 2007. Corporations can, like the Clashing Rocks, wreck proposals for improving the efficiency of the patent system.

---

[55] See 71 Fed. Reg. 48, (January 3 2006).

[56] See the USPTO's comments on the effect of continuations on its workload, ibid. 48–9.

[57] See Changes to Practice for Continued Examination Filings, Patent Applications Containing Patentably Indistinct Claims, and Examination of Claims in Patent Applications, 72 Fed. Reg. 46716, (21 August 2007) (Claims and Continuations Final Rule).

[58] See Intel's comments in support at www.uspto.gov/web/offices/pac/dapp/opla/comments/fpp_continuation/continuation_comments.html.

[59] The comments of the Biotechnology Industry Organization in favour of continuations can be found at www.uspto.gov/web/offices/pac/dapp/opla/comments/fpp_continuation/continuation_comments.html.

Patent fees

We saw in the previous chapter that the European Patent Office (EPO) has been in the position of being able to fund its various activities because of its fee income. Like other offices the USPTO charges fees for filing a patent application and then maintaining the patent on its books. At various points in its history the USPTO has drawn attention to the fact that its costs have exceeded the budget that it has been given by Congress.[60] Complaints about insufficient funds occurred in the nineteenth century and a special Patent Office Fund was tried, but eventually failed.[61]

In 1990 the USPTO became a self-funding federal agency. The volume of patent applications should in theory have given it a river of riches. Instead it found that the river was being diverted by politicians for other purposes. Fee diversion began in 1992 under the first Bush administration and was continued by Clinton and the second Bush administration.[62] Complaints from patent owners about fee diversion led to the passage of the Patent and Trademark Authorization Act of 2002 that, amongst other things, allowed the USPTO to keep its fees for the following 5 years. In financial year 2005, the President's budget submission left the USPTO with all its projected fee earnings – $1.53 billion.[63] Then, at least in the eyes of some US industries and patent practitioners, the USPTO did something unfair. Under its Twenty-first Century Strategic Plan, the USPTO proposed to split filing and examination fees and to increase both. Much more threatening to some companies was its proposal to use fees to regulate the volume and complexity of patent applications. Exponential fees were to cut in once, for example, the applicant went past three independent claims starting with a base of US$160, moving then to $320, $640 etc.

In proposing this exponential model the USPTO was being entirely rational since, as we saw in Chapter 3, the level of patent fees has been a critical determinant of patenting activity. The US biotech industry, which tends to lodge longer and more complex patent applications than other industries, objected to the USPTO's plan arguing that fee increases had to

---

[60] See, for example, 'Patent Office Report for 1953', 34 (1954) *Journal of the Patent Office Society*, 555.

[61] Under the 1836 patent statute the money the patent office received went into the patent fund. This fund was abolished in 1868. For a discussion see William R. Ballard, 'Money for the Patent Office', 37 (1955) *Journal of the Patent Office Society*, 435.

[62] See Peter L. Giunta, 'Quid Pro Whoa!: An Exponential Fee Structure for Patent Applications', 25 (2004) *Cardozo L. Rev.*, 2317, 2337–8.

[63] www.uspto.gov/web/offices/com/speeches/04–03.htm.

be 'reasonable and proportionate'.[64] Listening to a chorus of complaints about the discriminatory effects of the exponential model on companies and the impecunious inventor, the USPTO revised its Strategic Plan by shifting to a linear model.[65] It expressed its gratitude to the following business organizations for their help with its Strategic Plan[66] – American Intellectual Property Law Association, the Intellectual Property Owners Association, the American Bar Association's Section of Intellectual Property Law, the Biotechnology Industry Organization, the International Trademark Association, the Patent Public Advisory Committee and the Trademark Public Advisory Committee.

Industries within the US can live with modest fee increases, providing that those fees are then used to improve the quality of the service that they can purchase from the USPTO. Quality like beauty is in the eye of the beholder. There will always be disagreements amongst US industries about the details of how the USPTO can provide a better quality service. What there is no disagreement about is that the USPTO is there to serve them. The industries that came out against fee diversion have sent the US government the message that industry will react if government raids the patent fee pot. The USPTO has been granted its wish of more money to cover its operations. At the same time it has learnt that it cannot use fees in radical ways to deal with problems of volume and patent complexity. A powerful policy lever has been taken from its hands. The USPTO also knows that as a self-funding agency it has a fee-dependent future. When in the nineteenth century the USPTO operated by means of an independent patent fund a slump in business in the early 1860s led to redundancies and a rescue package from Congress.[67] An organization that operates on a fee-for-service basis is likely to see the person paying the fee as its customer. But as the analysis of the patent social contract in Chapter 1 made clear this belief is simply wrong in the case of a patent office. Its real client is the public.

In whom do we trust?

Chapter 1 suggested that because patent systems were embedded in different national economic systems one would predict that cooperation

---

[64] See www.bio.org/ip/domestic/.
[65] For a table comparing the USPTO's original proposal with what was eventually agreed to by it as part of its Strategic Plan see www.uspto.gov/web/offices/com/strat21/feeproposalcomparison.htm.
[66] See http://www1.uspto.gov/go/com/strat21/index.htm.
[67] Ballard, 'Money for the Patent Office', 435, 438.

and integration amongst patent offices would not be high because each office would in the final instance be serving to administer rules that advantaged that national system. This is not to say, however, that patent offices would not study each other's systems in order to learn from them. As we shall see in the next chapter, cooperation amongst the USPTO, EPO and JPO began to intensify in the early 1980s and has reached high levels. Before then there were some initiatives that explored whether offices could work together to reduce their respective backlogs. For example, in 1966 the USPTO and the German PO exchanged search results for 1,000 cases where applications had ended up being filed in both countries (at this stage the USPTO had a backlog of over 200,000 patent applications).[68] But progress was slow and it is only after 2000 that more serious work-sharing arrangements began emerging in the form of bilateral patent prosecution highway arrangements between offices.

Today the USPTO like the other major offices is building trust with other offices. Examiner exchange is foundational to this process, as is personal contact amongst the heads of patent offices (interview, USPTO). Pilot projects between two offices build confidence in each other's systems, allowing offices to achieve a 'good comfort level with each other's work' and this in turn leads to work-sharing arrangements between the USPTO and other offices such as, for example, the Australian PO (interview, USPTO). One aim for the USPTO is get other offices to do its PCT work, leaving it more time for national applications.

The world's major patent offices are faced by backlogs that make work-sharing an imperative. But work-sharing depends on trust and this takes time to build. For the time being the US prefers to work with a small number of offices that include its Trilateral partners, China and Korea. These are offices where there are high levels of cross-filing of applications (US companies will file in Europe and European companies in the US and so on) and so there are workflows that it makes sense to try and exploit. In its own region it sees Canada and Mexico as partners. Like the EPO, the USPTO provides technical assistance to developing countries, but it is not clear that it has been as systematically engaged over as long a period as the EPO has been on this front. This may be one reason why in this study developing-country patent offices reported that the EPO was the office they trusted the most. The USPTO is scaling up its efforts in the technical

---

[68]   Edward J. Brenner, 'Patent Office Activities during Fiscal year 1966 – Outlook for Fiscal Year 1967', 48 (1966) *Journal of the Patent Office Society*, 475, 478.

assistance field. For example, it formed the Global Intellectual Property Academy in 2006 and through it in 2008 delivered training on intellectual property issues to 4,100 officials from 127 countries.[69] Some of the technical assistance that the USPTO has provided, such as its training of Brazilian examiners in pharmaceutical examination, has attracted criticism (interview, USPTO).

A concrete way in which work-sharing is being enhanced is through the bilateral patent prosecution highway arrangements that the USPTO has entered into, beginning with the JPO (discussed in more detail in Chapter 6). The basic idea is that whenever an office carries out a first search and examination a second office will be able to utilize the results to speed up the processing of the same application in its office. But as USPTO officials pointed out in the interview a lot depends on the degree of reliability of the first search. Examiner exchanges and pilot projects help shape beliefs about this reliability.

Examiner exchanges and pilot projects create the trust that is necessary to enter into a prosecution highway arrangement and these arrangements in turn 'lay the foundation for mutual recognition' (interview, USPTO). These patent prosecution highway arrangements also serve to keep patent offices engaged in the process of aligning and integrating their administrative systems. Mutual recognition by offices of another office's results is a way off. Some offices such as the German PO do not want to implement a principle that could cause them to lose control over national examination. But it is a principle that a group of trusted offices could work their way towards and use in their network. This network of trusted offices could end up doing most of the world's examining. The USPTO by virtue of size would obviously remain a key player in this network. To some extent it is through prosecution highway agreements that smaller offices like the Danish PO and the Australian PO are integrated into its systems. This potentially creates a dependency of these offices upon US work that will allow the USPTO to be the most important voice on the standards of patent quality of the network as a whole. The offices of countries that were outside the network could recognize the decisions of the network. Countries that were not part of a regional patent arrangement could enter into one, an option that the USPTO favours since it would reduce the number of patent offices that companies would have to deal with. Ultimately the patent systems of all the world's countries could be managed by a small network of large integrated offices.

---

[69] See www.uspto.gov/go/dcom/olia/training_history.htm.

The Japanese patent system: from diffusion to monopoly rights

The Japanese patent system for much of the twentieth century placed less emphasis on strengthening the scope and rights of the patent monopoly and more on the diffusion of technological information.[70] Certainly patent infringers were not harshly treated. Until 1998 a patent infringer was allowed to pay a normal licensing fee of around 3%.[71] Patent protection for chemical substances *per se*, an area of patenting that affects materials manufacture of all kinds, was not included till 1975.[72] In that same year a multiple patent claiming system, which makes it easier for the patent applicant to define a zone of protection for an invention, was introduced. Patentable subject matter expanded slowly with the patentability of micro-organisms accepted in 1979 and the 1980s seeing patents on genetically engineered products and animals accepted.[73] Patent term extension was introduced in 1987. Pre-grant opposition, which we noted earlier was part of the German model, was replaced by a system of post-grant opposition in 1995. In 1999 more reforms were introduced simplifying the patent application process and making it easier for patent owners to prove damages in patent infringement cases.

Japan's moves to strengthen the rights of patent owners came comparatively late. For most of the twentieth century, patent law and administration were part of a catch-up strategy that helped Japanese firms gain access to foreign technology through the publication of patent applications and rules that encouraged licensing deals and limited the capacity of foreign patent owners to interfere with the domestic adoption of foreign technology.

By the 1980s 'catch up' had become 'caught up' and possibly 'overtaking' as Japanese firms came to be seen as technological leaders in various fields. Japanese models of innovation and marketing came to be widely studied and discussed. The large trade surplus that Japan enjoyed with the US led

---

[70] Janusz A. Ordover, 'A Patent System for Both Diffusion and Exclusion', 5 (1991) *Journal of Economic Perspectives*, 43.

[71] Hisamitsu Arai, 'Intellectual Property Policies for the Twenty-First Century: The Japanese Experience in Wealth Creation', 3 (2000) *Journal of World Intellectual Property*, 423, 425.

[72] M. Wantanabe and IP Study Group of Tsukuni & Associates, *How to Read and Write Japanese Patent Specifications in Chemistry and Biotechnology*, Maruzen Planet Co. Ltd, Tokyo, 2007, 4.

[73] Christopher Heath, 'Industrial Policy and Intellectual Property in Japan and Beyond' in Christoph Antons (ed.), *Law and Development in East and Southeast Asia*, Routledge Curzon, London and New York, 2003, 197, 199–200.

to accusations that Japan was using its patent system as a protectionist tool.[74] Some US business representatives argued that the Japanese system was run in a way that stripped US companies of their patent rights or the benefits of those rights.[75] But as Bob Dylan once pointed out 'the times they are a-changin'' and so it has proved with innovation times in Japan. The Japanese innovation system has fallen from its pedestal with scholars now focussing on its problems and why patent reform appears not to have helped much.[76] The Japanese patent system has for the most part lost its reputation as the protectionist hard-man of the Japanese market.

Important changes have taken place in Japanese patent administration. These changes come out of a broader shift in Japanese government policy on intellectual property rights in general. In 2002, the then Prime Minister Junichiro Koizumi elevated the policy importance of intellectual property.[77] In 2003 in a speech to the Japanese Diet he said that patent examination would be speeded up as part of a plan to make Japan 'a nation built on the platform of intellectual property'.[78] Flowing out of these policy ideas was the development of a new policy framework for intellectual property that included the passage of legislation and the setting up of the Intellectual Property Strategy Headquarters (the Headquarters).[79] The Headquarters is home to various taskforces such as the Task Force on Intellectual Property Enforcement and the Task Force on Patent Protection for Medical Activities. These task forces have developed the strategic programmes needed to implement Japan's goal of being a nation built on intellectual property.[80] Intellectual property has made it into the inner court of Japan's policy priorities. Policy on intellectual property is steered by a ministerial council comprised of all ministers, ten outside private sector experts and chaired by the Prime Minister. The major shift in direction has been the development of regulatory strategies that serve the goal of the early patenting of technologies both in Japan and abroad.

---

[74] For a detailed discussion see Robert J. Girouard, 'U.S. Trade Policy and the Japanese Patent System', BRIE Working Paper Series, Working Paper 89, August 1996.

[75] On the Japanese response see Ove Granstrand, *The Economics and Management of Intellectual Property*, Edward Elgar, UK, 1999, 140.

[76] See Lee G. Branstetter, 'Do Stronger Patents Induce More Local Innovation?' in Keith E. Maskus and Jerome H. Reichman (eds.), *International Public Goods and Transfer of Technology Under a Globalized Intellectual Property Regime*, Cambridge University Press, Cambridge, 2005, 309.

[77] JPO, *Annual Report 2006*, 26.

[78] www.kantei.go.jp/foreign/koizumispeech/2003/01/31siseI_e.html.

[79] Basic Law on Intellectual Property (Law No. 122 of 2002).

[80] For a description of the programs see JPO, *Annual Report 2006*, 27.

The faster issue of stronger patents is seen by the government as being the key to Japan's success in global competition over innovation. In terms of structure the Japanese PO is an agency within the Ministry of Economy, Trade and Industry. In order to see the extent to which Japan has changed direction on patent administration, the next section briefly describes the history of Japan's approach to patent administration.

Joining the club

Like other nations, Japan entered the international patent system keeping a watchful eye on the fact that it was an industrializing country and therefore had the most to gain from a system that kept down the cost of invention information. It was not an early entrant into intellectual property law. A law passed by the Tokugawa military regime in 1721 actually prohibited technical innovation.[81] The Meiji period that began in 1868 brought a different approach emphasizing, amongst other things, the search for knowledge of all kinds. A patent law was passed in 1871 only to be removed a year later. A second patent law was passed in 1885 and a patent office was also established in that year.[82] Under the 1885 law, foreigners were excluded from obtaining patents and chemical products, food and medicines were not patentable. Japan joined the Paris Convention for the Protection of Industrial Property in 1899 meaning that it had to treat foreigners on the same basis that it treated its own citizens.[83] In that same year it passed a law extending patent rights to foreigners.[84]

The first Commissioner of Patents, Korekiyo Takahashi, had visited the US Patent Office for study purposes and had been much impressed by the US patent system.[85] Japan's 1885 law shared things in common with the US system. It was a first-to-invent system and the patent term was calculated from the date of issue. Over time it lost these US characteristics. Pre-grant

---

[81] Christopher Heath, 'Industrial Policy and Intellectual Property in Japan and Beyond', 197.

[82] See Granstrand, *The Economics and Management of Intellectual Property*, 138. A brief history of Japanese patent administration is also to be found in 'Views from across the Pacific: JPOS (Japanese Patent Office Society) Talks', 72 (1990) *Journal of the Patent and Trademark Office Society*, 1025, 1033–8.

[83] See WIPO website for membership of treaties at www.wipo.int/treaties/en/Remarks.jsp?cnty_id=254C.

[84] Takahiko Kondo, 'Roles of Intellectual Property Rights Systems in Economic Development in the Light of Japanese Economy', 25 (2000) *AIPPI*, 28, 30.

[85] 'Views from across the Pacific: JPOS (Japanese Patent Office Society) Talks', 72 (1990) *Journal of the Patent and Trademark Office Society*, 1025, 1033.

opposition, it is worth reminding ourselves, was seen then and is still seen today as an important tool of patent quality. Following German patent law, Japan in 1921 went to a first-to-file system as well as providing for the publication of the examined application and pre-grant opposition. In 1960, an inventive-step requirement was made part of the statute, the patent term was fixed to be no more than 20 years from the filing date and publications overseas were allowed to defeat novelty.[86] Two other reforms adopted by West Germany in 1967 were adopted by Japan in 1970; patent applications were published within 18 months of filing (and essentially prior to grant) and patent applicants had 7 years from the date of filing in which to request examination of their application.

During the first half of the twentieth century, especially in the first 25 years, Japanese industry was small scale and applied for few patents. When Japanese nationals did apply for patents their success rate was not as high as that of foreigners who were responsible for most of the patenting in Japan.[87] What was true of Japan then is true of many developing countries today. My interview in the Indonesian PO, for example, revealed that local inventors had a lower success rate in obtaining patents than foreigners. After the Second World War, Japanese companies began to use the patent system more and more. Ove Granstrand in his analysis of the patenting practices of Japanese companies concludes that they have 'an outstanding post-war record of patent growth'.[88]

We will see later in this chapter and the next that the relationship between the USPTO and JPO is one of deepening cooperation. Cooperation between the two offices had to survive the patent wars of the 1980s.[89] During this decade one of the principal differences between the two systems was the secrecy surrounding the examination process. Under the US system, applications were examined in secret while Japanese applications were published after 18 months. The complaint on the US side was that automatic publication in the Japanese system allowed competitors to study the invention and start to file their own patents on variations of the original invention. In some cases the original invention might be surrounded by hundreds of other patent applications, a tactic known as 'patent flooding'. The aim of patent flooding was to encourage the holder of the original patent into some sort of cross-licensing arrangement – 'I'll give you a license under my ten narrow patents for a license under your

---

[86] Ibid. 1025, 1035.   [87] Ibid. 1025, 1034.
[88] Granstrand, *The Economics and Management of Intellectual Property*, 162.
[89] Ibid. 140.

one broad patent'.[90] This tactic was made more effective in the Japanese patent system because the applicant could defer examination of the patent for 7 years, leaving the target of the flood in a state of uncertainty about the status of the applications.

Under the US system patent flooding was less of a problem. But it generated another kind of gaming behaviour in the form of 'submarine patents' (discussed below). In part the sheer number of patent applications in a given technological area under the Japanese system was for a long time due to the fact that the JPO only allowed one independent claim per application, whereas the USPTO allowed for more than one. The JPO also took an approach to patent claims that encouraged the drafting of claims of narrow scope making it easier for competitors to find permissible alternatives to the original invention.[91] These problems have faded as Japan has adopted a more liberal approach to claiming.[92]

There were other complaints from the US about the Japanese system, all rooted in the basic complaint that Japanese firms were apparently using the system to their own advantage. The following quote from the US State Department's 1994 country report on Japan captures the gist of US woes:[93]

> Many Japanese firms use the patent filing system as a tool of corporate strategy, filing many applications to cover slight variations in technology. Public access to applications and compulsory licensing provisions for dependent patents facilitate this practice. The rights of U.S. filers in Japan are often circumscribed by prior filings of applications for similar inventions or processes. The need to respond individually to multiple oppositions slows the process and makes it more costly. Japanese patent examiners and courts interpret patent applications narrowly and adjudicate cases slowly. Japanese patent law lacks a doctrine of equivalence and civil procedure lacks a discovery procedure to seek evidence of infringement.

Until the 1970s Japan's administration of its patent system was designed to encourage innovation for a country that was a technological borrower and

---

[90] Frederick M. Ritchie, 'So, You Want A Commercially Important Patent in Japan!', 74 (1992) *Journal of the Patent and Trademark Office Society*, 186, 188.

[91] See, for example, Michael Todd Helfand, 'How Valid Are U.S. Criticisms of the Japanese Patent System?', 15 (1992) *Hastings Communications and Environmental Law Journal*, 123, 150; Ordover, 'A Patent System for both Diffusion and Exclusion', 43, 48.

[92] On drafting claims today for JPO with a comparison to the EPO and USPTO see John D. Collins, 'Drafting an International Patent Application', 04/06 *IP & Technology Programme*, 13.

[93] Available at http://dosfan.lib.uic.edu/ERC/economics/trade_reports/1994/Japan.html.

which focussed on incremental innovation.[94] In broad terms this meant tempering the private rights of the patent monopoly owner with rules and incentives aimed at the public diffusion and use of invention information (for example, the early publication of the patent application, a restrictive approach to the use of patent claims, keeping the costs of patent infringement low, encouraging the granting of patent licences through pre-grant opposition). The 1980s and 1990s were a transition period in which Japan began to refine its system of patent administration to suit the fact that it was now the world's second largest economy with some of the world's largest technology companies. The next section looks at this period in a little more detail.

On being a senior member of the club

During the 1980s and 1990s Japanese companies filed more patents in the US than companies from any other country.[95] The biggest complaint of Japanese companies, shared with companies from other countries, was the problem of submarine patents. US patent applications were examined in secret and the applicant could drag out the examination process for years, surfacing with the granted patent at the most commercially convenient moment in time. This was by no means the only complaint. Others included the discriminatory effects of the first-to-invent system, complicated interference proceedings and the uncertain and expensive patent litigation environment.[96]

During the 1980s the US and Japan had bilateral trade dialogues covering a range of issues including intellectual property under initiatives like the Structural Impediments Initiative. The Clinton Administration kept on with these bilateral talks, announcing in 1993 the US–Japan Framework for a New Economics Partnership. This bilateral venue offered the possibility of quiet discussions between officials from the two patent offices on some of the technical issues of patent harmonization relating the two countries' systems. The JPO agreed to allow foreign nationals to file first in English and then to provide translations and in

---

[94] For an excellent analysis along these lines see Girouard, 'U.S. Trade Policy and the Japanese Patent System'.

[95] For the period 1981–98 Japan led the world in terms of number of patents filed in the US. See Jean-Christophe Dore, Christian Dutheuil, Jean-Francois Miquel, 'Multidimensional analysis of trends in patent activity', 47 (2000) *Scientometrics*, 475, 486.

[96] For the complete list of concerns see Girouard, 'U.S. Trade Policy and the Japanese Patent System', 6, fn 9.

exchange the US agreed to shift from its 17-year patent term from the date of issue to 20 years from the date of filing of the application.[97] The incentive to keep the US application process going under this rule was considerably diminished. Another agreement in 1994, which took the form of an exchange of letters, saw Japan undertake to introduce legislation eliminating pre-grant opposition, introduce a simplified post-grant opposition procedure, further speed up accelerated examination and restrict the granting of dependent patent compulsory licences; the US in turn promised to adopt the 18-month publication rule for applications and to revise its re-examination procedure to allow for more grounds for re-examination and better opportunities for third-party participation.[98] The agreements in 1994 were part of a process of building a partnership between the USPTO and the JPO, a process which today lets the JPO bring a big initiative like the Patent Prosecution Highway to the USPTO with the expectation that it will get serious attention. As Table 5.1 shows the 1990s proved a busy period for the reform of Japan's patent law.

Like other offices the JPO found that its backlog of applications was increasing. It decided in 1970 to adopt a system in which the applicant had to request examination.[99] Known as deferred examination this system was one way of dealing with the rise in patent applications. Unlike in the US, applications were not examined automatically. In the Japanese system the applicant had 7 years from the filing date in which to request examination. One estimate was that in the late 1980s about 50% of applications in a given year resulted in a request for examination.[100] With the number of filings in Japan in 1988 running at 344,000 there was a considerable short-term saving in examination resources. The alternative to deferring examination was to hire more examiners. The US with its system of automatic patent examination had to have a bigger examination workforce (at the end of the 1980s the USPTO's patent examination workforce was roughly double that of Japan's workforce).[101] Over time the JPO came to the view that deferring examination was simply deferring the problem. Beginning in 1989 it hired more examiners. It also introduced a system

---

[97] See 'Mutual Understanding between the Japanese Patent Office and the United States Patent and Trademark Office', 20 January 1994 in 33 I.L.M. 313 (1994).

[98] See Exchange of Letters Containing Patent Systems Agreement, 16 August 1994, in 34 I.L.M. 121 (1995).

[99] 'Views from across the Pacific', 1025, 1036.   [100] Ibid., 1025, 1027.

[101] Helfand, 'How Valid Are U.S. Criticisms of the Japanese Patent System?', 123, 133.

Table 5.1. *Revisions to Japanese Patent Law 1990–2002*

Date	Effective date	Revision
1990	*1 December 1990*	Introduction of an electronic filing system
1993	*1 January 1994*	Introduction of a bar to the addition of new matter to a specification and procedures regarding improper amendment of a specification
		Abolition of an appeal against examiner's decision to dismiss amendment and of a trial for invalidation of a correction
		Revision of the Utility Model Law
1994	*1 July 1995*	Review of the requirements of a description
		Introduction of a system for filing an application with a foreign language specification
		Modification of the patent term extension system
		Consideration by the examiner of the content of the detailed description of the invention when interpreting a claim
		Recovery or reinstitution of a patent right
		Official announcement of operation guidelines for examination
1994	*1 January 1996*	Adoption of the post-grant opposition system and introduction of the demand for correction system
1996	*1 April 1996*	Adjustment of the provisions in the Patent Law in accordance with the revision of the Code of Civil Procedure and simplification of the proceedings in the prosecution of a patent application
1998	*1 January 1999*	Review of the system for assessing damages as a consequence of patent infringement, the infringement system and the status of earlier-filed applications
1999	*1 January 2000*	Adoption of statutory bar events ('known or used in Japan or foreign countries')
		Relaxation of restrictions (conditions) for applying the relief provisions under Article 30 of the Patent Law ('exception to loss of novelty of invention')

Table 5.1. (*cont.*)

Date	Effective date	Revision
		Introduction of a system for early laid-open (Kokai) publication upon request by the applicant
		Simplification of the procedures for a converted or a divisional application
		Expansion of court order to produce documents
		Introduction of a system for providing an expert opinion on the calculation of the amount of damages in IP litigation
		Easing of the proof required for the amount of damages (the amount of lost profits incurred by a patentee) in a court
		Strengthening of the HANTEI system (advisory opinion on the technical scope of a patented invention)
		Introduction of heavy penalties for corporate bodies committing fraudulent actions and false marketing of goods
		Expansion of the patent term extension system
		Improvement of the function of notarization in trial proceedings (with respect to the record of the oral proceedings in the trial prepared or changed by the trial clerk)
1999	*1 October 2001*	Shortening of the term for filing a request for examination

Source: M. Watanabe and IP Study Group of Tsukuni & Associates (2007), *How to Read and Write Japanese Patent Specifications in Chemistry and Biotechnology*, Maruzen Planet Co Ltd: Tokyo.

of accelerated examination in 1986 and a system of preferential examination to deal with cases where an invention in a published but unexamined patent application was being worked by a third-party without permission. The period for deferring examination was reduced from 7 to 3 years for applications filed after October 2001. In 1989 it moved to the outsourcing of patent searching, something it had been experimenting with since 1985.[102]

Today the JPO, like the EPO and the USPTO, is confronted by a rising sea of applications – 2005 brought more than 420,000 national applications.[103] In addition the JPO also received 24,290 international applications under the PCT system. Despite hiring more examiners and increasing its outsourcing capabilities, first action pendency in 2005 was 26 months, up from 22 months in 2001, although some of this can be attributed to the transition to a 3-year period of deferral of examination.[104] The rate of requests for examination has also climbed from roughly 50% in the early 1990s to 66%. Like the other two Trilateral Offices, the JPO is facing more complex patent applications from companies and having to service the needs of an increasing number of users of the PCT system and like those offices it is betting that hiring more examiners will help it to solve its pendency problem. Hiring more examiners remains key to its goal of an 11-month first action pendency by 2013.[105] In 2008 it had a workforce of almost 1,700 patent examiners, a workforce that on its analysis processed three times the number of applications that the USPTO did and five times the number of the EPO.[106] Competition along with cooperation amongst the major offices is well on its way.

Becoming an IP nation

An agenda for economic growth based on an expansion of patenting requires that domestic firms obtain patents in key markets around the world. Here there is something of problem in Japan. Japanese companies file many patent applications in Japan (around 370,00), but only about 25% end in patents and only 10% end up with an equivalent patent granted in an overseas jurisdiction.[107] The Japanese government wants a much more aggressive patent strategy being adopted abroad by Japanese firms.

Japan's national patent expansionist agenda has seen the JPO progressively changing its systems to make sure that patents enter the market as quickly as possible. During the interview at JPO, officials suggested that the early examination and release of patents onto the market would help make patent rights 'stable' and 'to promote innovation means to increase

---

[102] *US Patent and Trademark Office: Transforming to Meet the Challenges of the 21st Century*, 239.
[103] JPO, *Annual Report 2006*, 6.   [104] Ibid. 10.   [105] Ibid. 31.
[106] JPO, *Annual Report 2008*, 43.   [107] JPO, *Annual Report 2006*, 42.

the stability of IPRs' (interview, JPO). Shortening the period of time in which the patent applicant had to request an examination was one means by which to encourage the early entry of the patent right onto the market. Similarly, Japan eliminated its pre-grant opposition system because it was 'not good for the stable protection of IP' (interview, JPO). The delays in finalizing pre-grant oppositions were creating too much uncertainty. This combined with pressure from the US led Japan to drop pre-grant opposition, but as we saw in the previous section in the 1994 agreements the JPO received concessions from the USPTO in return. Dropping pre-grant opposition was part of a move towards more cooperation with the USPTO on patent harmonization issues (interview, JPO).

Increasing cooperation with its two Trilateral counterparts, especially the USPTO, has become important to the JPO's implementation of Japan's patent expansionist agenda. A good example of this increasing cooperation that also meets the goal of helping Japanese companies to gain patents abroad is the Patent Prosecution Highway (PPH) programme between the JPO and the USPTO. From the JPO's perspective, the PPH will 'help Japanese applicants to make foreign applications' (interview, JPO). The JPO approached the USPTO first with the idea of a PPH because the US market remains the most important market for Japanese companies. The PPH is an example of a reciprocity mechanism in which both parties (the parties being the offices) potentially gain. First trialled in 2006, the basic aim is to allow one office to utilize the search and examination work of another office. Once one office examines an application the results of that examination can be utilized by a second patent office that has in its system a corresponding patent application. This kind of arrangement avoids the sovereignty issues that arise under the principle of mutual recognition. One office can exploit the work of another without being formally bound to defer to the examination of that other office. For the PPH to help Japanese companies the JPO has to, as the office of first filing, provide the results of its examination in time for a second foreign office to be able to use them. To this end it has devised a fast-release strategy.[109] Lying behind the cooperation of the PPH system is the kind of national agenda that the patent system has always served – encouraging domestic firms to obtain monopolies abroad.

Both JPO and USPTO officials see merit in the patent superhighway approach, but it is equally clear that superhighway arrangements will only be put in place between patent offices that can be trusted to

[108] See JPO, *Annual Report 2008*, 52.

do a reliable first search and examination, the method and results of which are transparent to the first office (interview, JPO and interview, USPTO). The use to date by applicants of the PPH system between the USPTO and JPO, which has moved to full implementation, has been very low.[110]

Another example of an initiative in which the JPO is seeking the support of other major patent offices is its 'New Route' proposal. Currently companies wishing to apply for patents in more than one country can use either the Paris Route or the PCT route. The PCT route offers much greater administrative convenience than the Paris Route because it can be started by just one application. JPO officials have concerns about the cost effectiveness of the PCT route when an applicant is seeking patents in only a few countries. Formally revising the PCT to accommodate this need is in their view too difficult and so they have devised a proposal for a third route that bypasses the need to revise the PCT, a proposal put forward by the JPO at the Trilateral Conference held in 2005.[111] The New Route idea starts by deeming one filing date for both the first and second office of filing. One of its consequences would be to eliminate the discriminatory effects of the prior art rules in the US (the so-called 'Hilmer doctrine').[112] It is yet another example of how the major offices are working out issues at the level of administration that have not been worked out in the context of treaty harmonization negotiations. The JPO and the USPTO are conducting a pilot of the New Route idea.[113]

Cooperating with the patent offices of big markets like the US and EU makes obvious sense, but the JPO has a more sweeping cooperation strategy that takes in smaller offices. By way of example it has set up the Asian Industrial Property Network (AIPN).[114] Relying on machine-translated English, the AIPN provides information about the fate of applications first filed in Japan, most of which are from Japanese companies (companies tend to start the patent application process in the country in which they are headquartered). The AIPN helps other offices in the network to exploit the JPO's work. Its aim therefore is to help Japanese companies obtain patents more quickly in the twenty-eight countries that participate in the

---

[109] There have been 343 requests to the USPTO and 239 to the JPO. See JPO, *Annual Report 2008*.

[110] For a description see Hiroki Kitamura and Yuki Shimizu, 'Outline of the Proposed New Route for Patent Applications Abroad', 31 (2006) *AIPPI Journal*, 55.

[111] Ibid. 55, 57.   [112] See JPO, *Annual Report 2008*, 53.

[113] See www.jpo.go.jp/cgi/linke.cgi?url=/torikumI_e/kokusaI_e/kokusaI_e_list.htm.

network, countries that include Indonesia, Malaysia, the Philippines and Vietnam.

In order to improve patent examination, the Headquarters for Expeditious and Efficient Patent Examinations was established in December 2005. Headed by the Minister of Economy, Trade and Industry it has taken a number of initiatives, including increasing the number of fixed-term examiners by approximately 100 per year for 5 years beginning in 2004. If a fixed-term examiner stays with the JPO for 10 years he or she will qualify for a patent attorney licence (interview, JPO). Losing newly trained examiners is less of a problem for the JPO than it is for the USPTO. Aside from increasing the number of patent examiners the JPO has increased the number of organizations to which it can outsource patent searching (interview, JPO). As a result of reforms in 2004 aimed at placing patent searching on a more commercial basis private companies can become registered search organizations. More private companies are becoming part of JPO's search network.[115] Before then searches had been outsourced to the Intellectual Property Cooperation Centre, a non-profit organization. Now the system is open to any company, provided that it meets the JPO's quality standards. One of the features of this formal split between searching and examination is that it is informally unified through face-to-face meetings between searchers and examiners because 'it improves understanding and examination' (interview, JPO). This 'dialogue type' of search reporting improves patent quality in the JPO's eyes.

Other initiatives for increasing the efficiency of examination have included the creation of a high-level dialogue with companies and industrial associations making them aware of the JPO's improvements and asking the private sector to engage in some internal level of screening of their applications to ensure they are truly wanted for examination.[116]

Trust and automation

The JPO carries on a programme of examiner exchange with the other major offices.[117] It is active in its region, sending examiners on a longer-term basis to Indonesia, the Philippines, Vietnam and Thailand.[118] Examiner exchange programmes really do matter. They build trust

---

[114] For a list see JPO, *Annual Report 2008*, 45.

[115] See JPO, *Annual Report 2006*, 41.   [116] See JPO, *Annual Report 2008*, 53–4.

[117] See www.jpo.go.jp/cgi/linke.cgi?url=/torikumI_e/kokusaI_e/kokusaI_e_list.htm.

amongst examiners, trust that translates into a trust by one office of another office's systems. Personal interaction between examiners was the factor that patent offices kept coming back to in the interviews when asked about trust.

Aside from personal interaction, the JPO also gives a lot of weight to the impersonal in the form of information technology. It began working on the computerization of patent applications in 1964 and embarked on the total computerization of the patent process through the Paperless Project in 1984. It was the first office in the world to accept electronic applications.[119] Perhaps more than the USPTO and the EPO it sees 'IT liberation for patent offices' (interview, JPO). The officials interviewed suggested that the idea of the one centralized office was built around paper technology requiring large paper-holding capacity. IT, they pointed out, 'allows for easy access to other offices' work, to patent databases'. This in turn makes possible the construction of a networked decentralized model of patent office administration in which patent offices will compete for work. Better quality patents, they suggested, would be the result of this competition.

It is clear the JPO is part of a general national strategy on intellectual property that in the case of patents is shifting the emphasis away from the diffusion of invention information through markets to the creation of strong enforceable patent rights in markets. The JPO's goal is to ensure the rapid transit of patent applications through its systems. Placing outsourcing on a commercial basis, eliminating pre-grant opposition and reducing the period of deferral of examination are all part of this rapid transit strategy. Another goal is to help Japanese companies obtain patents in foreign countries by implementing administrative models such as the PPH that enable a group of trusted offices to exploit the search and examination results of other offices in the group. Outside of the reform of patent administration, other systemic changes are taking place in Japan that will encourage the supply of patents to the market, most notably the deregulation of the legal services market in Japan (interview, JPO). Amongst other things, this should see more patent attorneys competing for work in Japan.

The trust that arises between offices through examiner exchanges grounds the formation of a technocratic trust in office systems that leads to a process of further integration of those systems. The personal trust enables the construction of a networked architecture of patent offices

---

[118] 1990 – see www.jpo.go.jp/seido_E/index.htm.

that through a combination of IT and rules will become a more and more automated system. Electronic files will travel through an integrated network of offices with the acceptance of one office's work on those files being largely a mechanical process. Personal trust will have provided the foundation for a system of impersonal regulatory automation. Built into the system will be a standardized view of inventiveness. Competition will rule the network. The office with the fastest examiners and systems will be the entry point that patent applicants choose. This is one possible world of patent office administration.

6

The age of Trilaterals and the spirit of cooperation

Trilateral cooperation

In the last quarter of the twentieth century three patent offices, often referred to as the Trilateral Offices, received the bulk of patent applications and issued most of the world's patents: the United States Patent and Trademark Office (USPTO), the European Patent Office (EPO) and the Japanese Patent Office (JPO). Of the 5.5 million patents in force at the end of 2004, 83% were in force in the US, Japan and the member countries of the European Patent Convention (EPC).[1] Two other offices have because of their large number of filings joined this first tier of patent offices – the Korean Intellectual Property Office (KIPO) and the State Intellectual Property Office (SIPO) of China.[2]

The Trilateral story is one of informal cooperation that becomes grounded in a bilateral memorandum of understanding between the USPTO and the EPO in June 1982 and another between the USPTO and the JPO in 1983, followed by a memorandum amongst all three in 1983.[3] What accounts for this deepening of international cooperation given, as we saw in Chapter 3, that the patent institution has been important to the trade and protectionist policies of states? The explanation hinges on two factors – the role of transnational corporations (TNCs) in the system as demanders of patent office cooperation and the workload problems facing the Trilaterals.

TNCs, the biggest users of the patent system, want a world in which at a moment of their choosing they can obtain high-quality patents at low

---

[1] See the 'Trilateral Statistical Report, 2005 edition', p.5, available at www.trilateral.net/tsr/tsr_2005/.

[2] In 2006 SIPO received more than 200,000 and KIPO more than 160,000. See *World Patent Report: A Statistical Review*, WIPO, Geneva, 2008, 15.

[3] On the origins of the Trilaterals, see Louise Davies, 'Technical Cooperation and the International Coordination of Patentability of Biotechnological Inventions', 29 (2002) *Journal of Law and Society*, 137, 151.

cost. The diversity of patent law and administration stands in the way of this kind of world. It means drafting different patent applications for different jurisdictions, going through different procedures, meeting the costs of translation, using the services of local patent attorneys etc. TNCs acting either individually or through business organizations have become important forces for change in the international patent regime.[4] Industry has its own version of the Trilaterals. Formed in 2003 and with representatives from Europe, Japan and the US, the Industry Trilateral Group seeks the harmonization of patent administration and ultimately patent law:[5]

> As a first step toward harmonization and enhanced efficiency, patent offices should adopt a common patent application format for a global patent application so that conforming applications (i) can be filed, preferably electronically, in any patent office without the need for any change in the submitted application to accommodate national/regional rules, and (ii) aid in facilitating machine translation of the applications.

TNCs ultimately seek a harmonization of the world's patent systems in terms of outcomes and effects. A harmonization of effects and outcomes means that when patent offices around the world examine an application using discretionary standards such as inventive step and utility, the outcome in each office should be the same and the effects of the law in terms of patentable subject matter, exclusive rights and enforcement should also be the same. We saw in Chapter 1 that there are four different levels of a patent system relevant to achieving a harmonization of outcomes and effects – principles, rules, administration and interpretation. The cause of harmonization is most advanced at the level of principles, particularly since the Agreement on Trade-Related Aspects of Intellectual Property Rights (TRIPS) came into force on 1 January 1995. All WTO members under TRIPS have to make patents available for inventions (products or processes) provided that they are new, have an inventive step (are non-obvious) and are capable of industrial application (useful).

When it comes to the other three levels of harmonization – rules, administration and interpretation – one can, at best, speak of convergence rather than harmonization. So, for example, the rules that determine the operation of even foundational principles, like the principle of novelty, vary amongst countries. The EPC, as we saw in Chapter 2, operates on the

---

[4] On their role in shaping TRIPS see P. Drahos with J. Braithwaite, *Information Feudalism*, Earthscan, London, 2000.
[5] See 'Industry Trilateral Report: Global Patent Application', 14 November 2006, available at www.ipo.org.

basis of absolute novelty. The US does not. The US rules on disclosure of the invention by the inventor impose a higher standard on inventors than is to be found in other jurisdictions. There are enough differences amongst national systems at the level of rules and their interpretation to keep comparative scholars going for a long time.

Patent offices can through administrative practice in some cases circumvent the operation of a rule that prevents a patent from being granted. For instance, the EPC excludes from the category of invention programs for computers.[6] The demand for patents on computer software protection led the EPO in 1985 to publish 'revised guidelines for examination with a view to enabling appropriate protection to be made available for software technology'.[7] By 1994 it had granted over 11,000 software patents.[8] While probably millions of words have been written, mostly by patent attorney mystics bent on justifying this on behalf of their clients, nothing changes the fact that the EPO has through administrative practice achieved an outcome that the Convention prohibits. Similarly, the EPC did not allow for a patent on the second medical use of a product that had a known first medical use.[9] The Swiss PO had devised a claim-drafting solution to this problem and this solution was adopted by the EPO (referred to as a 'Swiss claim').[10] The claim had to be directed to the use of the product for the manufacture of a medicament rather than to the use of the product for human treatment. By using the magic formula patent attorneys could push through patents on second medical uses of known products.[11] The amendment of the EPC in 2000 has placed claims for second pharmaceutical uses on a more secure basis. Something that began as a patent office practice has produced a change in treaty language. This example also illustrates the co-evolutionary process described in Chapter 2 in which new claim formats change the selection pressures that act on companies.

These two examples show that patent offices can through guidelines and administrative practice overcome rule exclusions to patentability in

---

[6] See Article 52(2)(c) of the EPC.

[7] EPO, *Annual Report 1994*, 12.   [8] Ibid.

[9] A patent on the first medical use of a known product was permitted by virtue of the operation of Articles 52(4) and Article 54(5) of the EPC. Other uses were ruled out because of novelty problems. There was no novelty problem with the first medical use because of the specific exception in Article 54(5).

[10] See the EPO's Enlarged Board of Appeal in G5/83 EISAI/second medical indication *OJ EPO* 1985, 64.

[11] The words that produce the magical effect are '*Use of compound X in the manufacture of a medicament for the treatment of disorder Y*'.

ways that help some software and pharmaceutical companies. In doing this the EPO through administrative practice achieved greater convergence with the US patent system which did not expressly exclude methods of human treatment and computer programs from patentability. The bigger lesson is that patent offices can sometimes through their practices achieve a convergence or harmonization of outcomes even if on the face of it a rule divergence exists between two systems.

The patent rules that surround the patenting of animal life, computer software and pharmaceuticals has attracted the critical attention of civil society groups, meaning most probably that patent reform has never been more closely scrutinized or more contested.[12] One consequence of this greater political contestation of patent rules is that it is harder to achieve a harmonization at the level of rules. Since the costs of change at this level have become higher one would predict that the actors interested in harmonization would look more to the less transparent level of administrative cooperation to achieve their goals. The interviews in the USPTO and JPO suggest that these offices see administrative cooperation as fundamental to achieving patent harmonization. US officials suggested that a 'critical mass of harmonization' had been achieved amongst developed countries and this laid the basis for much greater administrative cooperation on the key issues of workload and quality (interview, USPTO). Officials at the JPO spoke of the difficulty of patent treaty reform, something that had led them to develop the New Route proposal that was discussed in Chapter 5 (interview, JPO). Keeping in mind that the World Intellectual Property Organization (WIPO) began preparatory work on a patent harmonization treaty in 1983 and that negotiations on such a treaty more than 20 years later still break down along developed- and developing-country lines, the resort by the Trilateral Offices to more covert administrative techniques is not surprising.[13] Nor is it surprising that the TNC users of the system would through bodies like the Industry Trilateral demand higher levels of cooperation amongst the lead patent offices.

Overwork

The other factor in explaining cooperation, the workload problem, has, as we have seen in previous chapters, faced the world's major patent offices

---

[12] For an account see Amy Kapczynski, 'The Access to Knowledge Mobilization and the New Politics of Intellectual Property', 117 (2008) *Yale Law Journal*, 804.

[13] On the stresses and strains of patent harmonization talks see *Intellectual Property Watch*, 2(1), March 2005, 1.

for much of the twentieth century, but it has taken on exponential qualities by virtue of the increasing use of the Patent Cooperation Treaty (PCT) (1970). The scale of the problem that the increasing use of the PCT brings was well and truly in evidence by 1994. WIPO reported that for that year the 34,104 PCT applications had the effect of 1,321,216 national applications.[14] The duplication of work by the major patent offices of the world was a problem prior to the creation of the PCT system and was one of the reasons it was created in the first place. But the PCT increased the workload problems of the world's major patent offices beyond what might have been imagined at the time of its negotiation. At the same time the labour saving potential of the PCT had not been sufficiently harnessed by patent offices.[15]

The Trilateral Offices were at first reluctant to exchange detailed information about their backlogs. Following 'lengthy and difficult negotiations' at the 7th Trilateral conference in 1989, a project on 'long-term methods of coping with the increasing number of patent applications' was established.[16] Essentially the Trilaterals concluded that they were in the same lifeboat when it came to storms in the patent ocean. These storms have their origin in the PCT. It is the PCT that has made cooperation amongst the Trilaterals more urgent and it is also the treaty that in practical terms is most directly responsible for the integration of developing-country patent offices into the patent regime.

The spirit of cooperation: the Patent Cooperation Treaty

On Monday 25 May 1970 in Washington, the then Director of the Bureaux Internationaux Réunis pour la Protection de la Propriété Intellectuelle (BIRPI), Mr Bodenhausen declared the Conference on the Patent Cooperation Treaty open.[17] Later that day the UK delegate described the draft treaty as the 'biggest breakthrough in patents since 1883'.[18] The US and UK delegates along with other European delegates in their opening remarks praised the spirit of cooperation that the treaty represented. The

---

[14] 'The Patent Cooperation Treaty (PCT) in 1994', WIPO Press Release PCT/89, 31 January 1995.

[15] See generally WIPO's discussion paper prepared for a meeting of international authorities under the PCT, PCT/MIA/15/2, 3 March 2008.

[16] EPO, *Annual Report 1988*, 36.

[17] BIRPI was WIPO's predecessor organization.

[18] Records of the Washington Diplomatic Conference on the PCT, 1970, Verbatim and Summary Minutes, 565, available at www.wipo.int/pct/en/texts/washington.html.

US and UK had been involved in its drafting. The origins of the treaty lay in a proposal by the US in September of 1966 to the Executive Committee of the Paris Union for the Protection of Industrial Property that the Director of BIRPI study possible solutions to the problem of duplication of work facing national patent offices and patent applicants. The first Director General of WIPO, Arpad Bogsch, claimed the PCT as his idea, adding that the encouragement of the then US Commissioner of Patents, Edward J. Brenner, was crucial along with engagement of the then West Germany, the UK and France.[19] Nations with a lot to gain from the globalization of the patent system were responsible for bringing the PCT system into existence. They also brought into existence a funding model for WIPO that would turn it into a wealthy servant of their interests in expanding the system on their terms. The International Bureau of WIPO assumed responsibility for administering the PCT, receiving for its services the international filing fee that is charged for each PCT application. Today its income from the PCT is in the hundreds of millions.[20]

Other country delegates attending the meeting looked beyond the spirit of cooperation and to the effects of the treaty. The Australian delegate pointed out that the treaty was a treaty between exporters of inventions and importers of inventions. Exporters had clear interests in 'simplification and uniformity of procedures and cheaper patents'.[21] The delegate from Brazil pointed to 'a world market for technology where there is a striking discrepancy between the purchasing and bargaining powers of developed and developing countries, where the former are usually the sellers and the latter tend to be the buyers'.[22] Brazil's worry about the PCT was that it would increase the monopoly strength of patents without much thought being given to development objectives. The Algerian delegate was even more direct pointing out that at most there were about fifteen countries in the room contributing to inventive activity and the rest were 'clients of the major inventor countries'.[23] He finished on a note of displeasure, pointing to a micro-truth that bespoke of a macro-truth. The Steering Committee of the Conference, he noted, was dominated by 'big powers, industrialized countries' creating the impression that 'this Conference is in fact reserved for some fifteen countries' (seventy-seven

[19] Arpad Bogsch, *Brief History of the First 25 Years of the World Intellectual Property Organization*, WIPO, Geneva, 1992, 24.
[20] Its PCT income for the 2006–7 biennium amounted to 451 million Swiss Francs. See its financial report available at www.wipo.int/about-wipo/en/report.html.
[21] Records of the Washington Diplomatic Conference on the PCT, 562.
[22] Ibid. 572.   [23] Ibid. 574.

states attended the Conference).[24] More than 30 years later developed and developing countries are having similar conversations in places like WIPO.

More than 30 years after the PCT was signed at Washington, from where do most PCT applications originate? In 2006, the countries that produced the most applications were the USA (50,089), Japan (26,906), Germany (16,866), France (6,109) and the Republic of Korea (5,935).[25] Applicants from Brazil filed 328 and from Algeria there were 4 applications.

The spirit of cooperation: companies and the PCT

The purpose of the PCT was probably best summed up in a single sentence by the US delegate at the Washington Conference: 'It is a Treaty designed to assist applicants who seek patent protection in many nations.'[26] The emphasis here should be placed on the many. An inventor who seeks protection in just his own country or perhaps his own and another has no need of the PCT. Much above this and the convenience of the PCT comes into play. Multinationals with global patenting strategies clearly see it as an important route to obtaining a national patent. So, for example, the top ten PCT applicants for 2006 were all multinational companies from the US, Japan and Europe.[27] More generally, the usage of the PCT has grown. When it came into operation in 1978 the number of PCT applications in that year reached 459.[28] In 2004, WIPO, which administers the PCT, announced that the total number of applications under the PCT had reached one million.

From the perspective of companies with international patenting strategies we can identify four core principles by which to evaluate the PCT. Obviously a treaty that covers only a few countries will not help companies that want the option of extensive coverage. Many companies only seek patents in the US, Europe and Japan, but others will want them in Korea, China, India and Brazil, and yet other companies will have an even broader spread of countries that they wish to cover. The principle of coverage is important to users of the PCT. The second principle is control over the speed of the application process. Some companies will want to stretch out the application process while they explore the commercial

---

[24] Ibid.
[25] See *The International Patent System in 2006: PCT Yearly Review*, WIPO, Geneva, 3.
[26] Records of the Washington Diplomatic Conference on the PCT, 568.
[27] *The International Patent System in 2006*, 4.
[28] The Patent Cooperation Treaty (PCT) in 1994, 3.

dimensions of the technology and others will want to move quickly to national grant (the principle of time control). The third principle is the capacity to amend applications to make the granted patent stronger (the principle of amendment) and the last is the cost of the process. High costs will defeat the principle of extensive coverage. As we will see in a moment the PCT is evolving in the direction of these four principles.

The PCT is essentially a procedural treaty. It allows an applicant to make one international application that can be used to designate countries that are members of the treaty for a national application in that country. As from January 2004 the designation of all states under the PCT in an application became automatic.[29] The applicant has the option of withdrawing states from designation. The PCT process leads to national patents in the designated countries (not one international patent). Membership of the PCT stands at more than 138 countries, so one international application can reach many national offices and all the world's most important economies.[30] The principle of coverage is thus being met. One way in which smaller countries are being integrated into the PCT system is through free trade agreements. A standard provision of a free trade agreement with the US, for example, is an obligation for both parties to ratify the PCT. The Central America-Dominican Republic-United States Free Trade Agreement, which was signed on 5 August 2004, for example, contains an obligation that the parties ratify the PCT by 1 January 2006.[31] The US was already a member of the PCT, as were Costa Rica and Nicaragua, but El Salvador, Guatemala and Honduras became members in 2006 and the Dominican Republic in 2007.

Under the PCT, an international application has to be the subject of an international search.[32] The applicant is provided with an international search report. The international search report lists prior art relevant to the patentability of the applicant's invention and is carried out by a patent office that has been appointed as an International Searching Authority (ISA) under the PCT.[33] We will see in the next section that only a few

---

[29] See Rule 4.9(a) of the Regulations Under the Patent Cooperation Treaty.

[30] Membership information is available at www.wipo.int/treaties/en/ShowResults. jsp?lang=en&treaty_id=6.

[31] See Article 15.1.3 of the agreement.

[32] Article 15.1 of the PCT.

[33] ISAs have to meet certain standards in order to become ISAs and report to WIPO on steps they take to maintain and improve quality. These reports to WIPO are available at www.wipo.int/pct/en/quality/authorities.html. For the purpose of carrying out a search an ISA has to search a prescribed minimum of documentation. See Rule 34 of the Regulations Under the Patent Cooperation Treaty.

offices have this status. Along with the search report the ISA also provides a preliminary written opinion on the patentability of the invention.[34] The search report (along with the written opinion) should be finalized by the ISA within 3 months of having received a copy of the international application, but the large number of applications under the PCT has meant that ISAs have not always been able to comply with the prescribed time limits.[35]

Most applicants with global patenting strategies will begin the process by establishing a priority date in a national office of a PCT contracting state by filing a national application (for example, US companies will file nationally in the USPTO, Japanese companies in JPO, German companies in the German PO and so on) and then move to the PCT. The national filing will give them a period of 12 months under the Paris Convention for the Protection of Industrial Property (Paris Convention) in which to file a PCT application and from that filing applicants have about 18 months before the international application turns into a bundle of national applications.[36] Essentially applicants can defer national entry for up to 30 months. Deferral of national entry is a common goal of PCT applicants.[37] We have seen that companies from some industries like the pharmaceutical industry find advantage in delay while those in the information technology field may prefer to move quickly to grant. Both options are possible under the PCT.[38] A company can maximize the time under the PCT and minimize its disclosure obligation by starting at the national level with a provisional patent application. Alternatively, if it wants to speed up matters it can bypass the national phase and start with a PCT application. We can see that the PCT supports the principle of time control favoured by users of the patent system. The opportunity to delay the timing of the application process allows companies to gather more information about

---

[34] See Rule 43bis.1 of the Regulations Under the Patent Cooperation Treaty. The written opinion relates to novelty, inventiveness and industrial applicability.

[35] Rule 42.1 of Regulations Under the Patent Cooperation Treaty requires that the search report has to be established within 3 months of the ISA receiving the search copy or 9 months from the priority date, whichever is the later. The former time limit deals with the case where the applicant is using the Paris Convention and the latter where the PCT filing is the first filing. WIPO's data indicates that a little less than half of the search reports being issued are not meeting the time limits. See *The International Patent System in 2006: PCT Yearly Review*, WIPO, Geneva, 11.

[36] On the use of Paris Convention priority under the PCT see Article 8(1).

[37] The US made this point to the PCT Assembly in 2000 on the topic of PCT Reform. See WIPO document PCT/R/1/2, 23 March 2001, 5.

[38] On faster entry into the national phase see Article 23(2) of the Patent Cooperation Treaty.

the commercial desirability of moving to the national phase of the patent process. The ability to delay the national application process means that the costs of that process can also be delayed (for example, costs of filing, translating and using local attorneys). Obviously those costs can be avoided if the international application is withdrawn. The main costs to an applicant of filing an international application are a filing fee, a search fee and a transmittal fee.[39] There are discounts available for electronic filing and this may help to explain why electronic filing now exceeds paper filing in the PCT system.[40] The PCT system has lowered the costs of a global patenting strategy and is part of that historical process that was identified in Chapter 3 in which the costs of patenting have declined.

The PCT also supports the principle of amendment. There is scope for amending the international application once the international search report has been done and the written opinion can be the subject of informal comments provided to the International Bureau of WIPO.[41] If the applicant demands an international preliminary examination (available under Chapter II of the PCT) there is also a right to amend claims and to respond to the written opinion of the International Preliminary Examining Authority (IPEA).[42] The IPEA produces a report that is transmitted to the national or regional offices that the applicant has chosen. This report can be used by a national or regional patent office as a guide and reduce the need for that office to do a full independent examination. An applicant may choose not to request an international preliminary examination in which case it is the written opinion on patentability done by the ISA under Chapter I of the PCT that ends up before the national office (called an international preliminary report on patentability). This written opinion can help save the national office time in examining the application.

Developing countries that enter the PCT system generally do so with few resources to carry out substantive examination. Their offices will be presented with a pre-packaged analysis of patentability under the PCT system. Often their examiners will have been trained by one of the Trilateral Offices, meaning that the developing-country office extends technocratic trust to the judgement of the systems of the relevant

---

[39] The filing fee is fixed (currently 1,330 Swiss Francs), but search fees vary amongst offices. See the table of fees published by WIPO at www.wipo.int/pct/en/fees/index.html.

[40] See, *The International Patent System in 2006: PCT Yearly Review*, WIPO, Geneva, 2.

[41] See Article 19.1 of the PCT. On the opportunity to make informal comments, which seems to exist as a matter of custom, see PCT Newsletter-No.12/2003, 14.

[42] See Article 34(2) of the PCT.

Trilateral Office when, operating as an ISA or IPEA, that office generates a report on patentability. This in turn results in the kind of decision tree that we saw in Chapter 4 in which developing-country examiners largely follow the decision of the relevant major office when it is acting as an ISA or IPEA. In many developing countries the patent system is the subject of a high degree of regulatory automation. Developing-country patent offices electronically track and largely follow the decisions of the major offices.

Broadly then we can see that the PCT is evolving in the direction of the four principles that users of the PCT favour. But this is not meant to imply that users, especially multinational users, are happy with the PCT system. The US reform proposals of 2000 signalled a much more radical agenda in which, for example, there would be fewer PCT searching and examining authorities doing the work and their examination results would be binding on the contracting states of the PCT.[43] The US proposal accurately describes this more radical revision of the PCT as a 'longer-term undertaking'. Within the PCT Reform Committee process the US, Japan and the EPO have made it clear that the reforms made to the international search and preliminary examination system of the PCT, which began operating in 2004, are simply the first stage.[44] Users of the PCT continue to monitor this reform process very closely arguing, for example, that the 2004 reforms do not pay sufficient heed to the needs of users when it comes to having a right of dialogue with examiners when an international preliminary examination has been demanded under Chapter II of the PCT.[45] Being able to engage an examiner in dialogue over an application is important to getting a favourable examination report that in turn will favourably affect the chances of obtaining the patent at the national level. The problem for patent offices acting as PCT examining authorities is that the right of dialogue means more work.

---

[43] See United States Proposal for Reform of the Patent Cooperation Treaty, PCT/A/29/3, 18 August 2000, available at www.wipo.int/edocs/mdocs/govbody/en/pct_a_29/pct_a_29_3.pdf.

[44] Committee on Reform of the PCT, PCT/R/2/9, 5 July 2002, 3.

[45] See the summary of the comments by users of the PCT in Committee on Reform of the PCT, PCT/R/2/9, 5 July 2002, 6. The basic complaint of users is that under Rule 66.1bis of the PCT Regulations the written opinion of the ISA becomes the written opinion of the IPEA. A negative first opinion can result in a negative international preliminary examination report, something applicants want to avoid.

On being an international authority

Most national patent offices are part of the PCT system in that they function as receiving offices for PCT applications. However, only a few offices have ISA-IPEA status – Austrian PO, Australian PO, Canadian PO, SIPO, EPO, Spanish PO, Finish PO, JPO, KIPO, Russian PO, Swedish PO, USPTO and the Nordic Patent Institute. India and Brazil have recently been recommended for ISA-IPEA status.[46] Essentially such offices have to meet certain manpower and documentation standards.[47] Developing-country representation on the list is confined to Brazil, China and India and these countries, we will see in later chapters, increasingly see themselves as having different interests in the patent system to other smaller developing countries. For most developing-country patent offices there is little prospect of gaining ISA-IPEA status. They act as mailboxes in the PCT system, mechanically following the decisions of the large players in the system. The PCT system generates fees for participating offices. If an office acts as a receiving office it is entitled to a transmittal fee and ISAs, as we saw in Chapter 1, charge search fees for their services.

We have seen that the PCT has become a focal point of reform activity because its procedures allow companies to implement global patenting strategies at comparatively low cost. The longer-term US agenda of reform for the PCT is a much simpler system in which patenting costs play 'little or no role' in business decisions.[48] Presumably the cost of patenting would have to drop much further for it not to be a factor in business decision-making. The system would have to be a highly automated one in which there were only a few offices. In a reformed PCT world where the use of the PCT was even higher than it is today those offices that survived the reform process to remain as ISAs (meaning also IPEAs) would be in an even greater position of dominance than they are today. This dominance would be stronger if, for example, the examination decisions of these offices were binding on the patent offices of other countries, a suggestion that has been floated by the US.

Becoming an ISA is thus one way in which the national patent office of a country can ensure that it remains part of the lead pack of patent offices

---

[46] See PCT Committee for Technical Cooperation PCT/CTC/23/5, 12 November 2007.
[47] See Articles 16(3)(c) and 32(3) of the PCT.
[48] United States Proposal for Reform of the Patent Cooperation Treaty, PCT/A/29/3, 18 August 2000, Annex, 2, available at www.wipo.int/edocs/mdocs/govbody/en/pct_a_29/pct_a_29_3.pdf.

in terms of attracting work and having influence in the patent regime. The Canadian Patent Office (CPO), for instance, decided several years ago that 'we were not going to be irrelevant' and as part of its expansion plans managed to become in 2002 an ISA (interview, CPO). The decision to become an ISA 'added a lot of stress' to the CPO because, amongst other things, it meant recruiting many more examiners (at the time of interview the CPO in 2005 had gone from about 100 to 300 examiners). But it was also clear from the interview that the CPO saw that being an ISA was crucial to its long-term survival strategy and important to preserving a degree of Canadian sovereignty over an increasingly globalized patent system. Examiners from the UK Patent Office, which is not an ISA, also believe that that the ISA badge is a more important indicator of the quality of a patent office's work than, for example, certification under an International Standards Organization (ISO) standard (interview, UK PO). The interviews in India and Brazil also revealed that achieving ISA status was a critical priority for both offices. In India ISA status is seen as having both offensive and defensive dimensions. As an ISA an office has the potential to influence other patent offices and at the same time it has the technical capacity to steer independently of the influence of other offices.

The Trilateral hub

Following their first annual conference in 1983, the Trilaterals have continued to sign annual memoranda of understanding.[49] These three offices have become a global hub of cooperation and convergence in patent administration. The bulk of Trilateral activity is, like an iceberg, submerged, with only brief descriptions available from annual reports of the individual offices and their websites and conference summaries. The Trilateral website lists the most significant examples of Trilateral cooperation being paperless search capability, common system architecture, electronic filing, harmonization of patent practices, common patent information dissemination policies and exchange of priority documents.[50] Cooperation amongst the three offices also extends to working together on global patent policy issues that are part of treaty negotiation processes and quietly pushing the interpretation of their substantive standards on patentability in directions that see the application of

---

[49] The Trilateral Offices held their first annual conference in 1983. See www.trilateral.net/background/timeline/.
[50] See www.trilateral.net/background/achievements/.

their respective standards produce the same outcomes. Cooperation that begins on matters of technical and administrative convenience, such as the exchange of documentation, over the years runs into cooperation on procedural issues and substantive issues of global patent policy, a tangle of very different types of cooperation that all take place under the name of technical cooperation.

An example of policy cooperation on global patent issues by the three offices is the Trilateral Working Group that is involved in the negotiation of the proposed Substantive Patent Law Treaty that is taking place at WIPO.[51] An example of these offices seeking to create a convergence of outcome in the application of their respective standards of patentability is the project they conducted on the interpretation of the utility/industrial application standard to biotechnological inventions.[52] An example of their cooperation in a new area of patenting is their reaction to the *State Street* decision of the US Court of Appeals for the Federal Circuit.[53] Amongst other things, that case made it clear to patent attorneys that they could claim methods of doing business implemented by means of computer software or over the Internet. Not surprisingly, the number of such applications increased, meaning that the three patent offices had to recruit more examiners.[54] The recruiting and training implications of having to cover new areas of patenting are far from trivial. In 1997 there were twelve examiners in the USPTO working in the patent class relevant to business methods.[55] By financial year 2005 there were 136 examiners and the class itself had expanded to accommodate patenting of tax strategies.[56] Faced by a common problem the Trilateral Offices conducted a study that produced

[51] A discussion paper that shows how the Trilaterals identify differences and work towards common ground is the paper written by the EPO as part of the Trilateral Working Group, 'Substantive Harmonization of Patent Law (SPLT) The European Perspective (2003)', www.aipla.org/Content/ContentGroups/Meetings_and_Events1/International_Symposia1/EPOTrilateral.pdf.

[52] For an analysis see Louise Davies, 'Technical Cooperation and the International Coordination of Patentability of Biotechnological Inventions', 29 (2002) *Journal of Law and Society*, 137, 158–61.

[53] *State Street Bank and Trust* v. *Signature Financial Group Inc.* 149 F.3d 1368 (Fed. Cir. 1998).

[54] Automated business methods form part of US Patent Class 705. In 1998, the year of the *State Street* decision there were 1,425 filings. In 2000 there were 8,058. See www.uspto.gov/web/menu/pbmethod/applicationfiling.htm.

[55] See www.uspto.gov/web/menu/busmethp/transition.htm.

[56] See Statement of James Toupin, General Counsel, US Patent and Trademark Office, Testimony Before the Subcommittee on Select Revenue Measures of the House Committee on Ways and Means, 13 July 2006, available at http://waysandmeans.house.gov/hearings.asp?formmode=view&id=5103.

a consensus statement on the patentability of business method patents.[57] This is also an example of how administrative cooperation in terms of guidelines can produce a convergence effect even though the Trilaterals have different rules on patentable subject matter (under the EPC, business methods as such are expressly excluded from patentability).[58]

The Trilateral period of cooperation amongst the EPO, JPO and the USPTO that begins in the early 1980s marks the beginning of an evolution of a global system of patent administration. Patent offices do not need treaties to create a global system of administrative governance. At the most they simply need memoranda of understanding or just an exchange of notes. The model of global integration that patent office administration might be said to follow is a 'hub and spoke' model. Over time the Trilateral hub has brought its technical systems for exchanging data and for search and examination of applications into greater and greater alignment. At the same time as the hub has become progressively more integrated, patent offices from developing countries have become linked to those systems via 'spokes' of bilateral technical assistance (see Figure 6.1). Two of these offices, SIPO and KIPO, which grew remarkably in the last two decades of the twentieth century (see Chapter 8), have entered the top tier of offices in terms of their systems and the number of filings they receive each year.

Superhighways of cooperation

For the time being the principle that guides the approach of the Trilaterals to cooperation is the principle of mutual exploitation. This means finding ways in which one office can exploit the examination work of another office in order to reduce the amount of work that it has to do on an application that has been filed in both offices. Mutual exploitation allows an office to utilize the work of another office without obliging it to do so. The sovereignty issues surrounding the principle of mutual recognition have led both the USPTO and JPO to conclude that arrangements based on it are some way off. Of the three offices it is the EPO that has the strongest concerns about the application of the principle. Some other European offices like the German PO share its concern. If a PO believes it has high standards of examination and this standard is backed by its

---

[57] See 'Report on Comparative Study Carried Out under Trilateral Project B3b' www.trilateral.net/projects/other_project/.
[58] See Articles 52(2)(c) and 52(3).

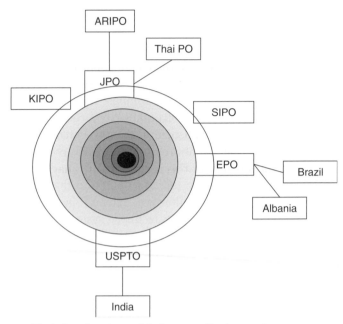

Figure 6.1 The hub and spoke model of patent office integration

domestic industry it will obviously be reluctant to give up sovereignty over its examination system.

The Patent Prosecution Highway (PPH) was an initiative started in July of 2006 in the form of a pilot programme between JPO and the USPTO.[59] The initiative came out of JPO (interview, JPO and interview, USPTO). As we saw in Chapter 5, one potential benefit of the PPH for Japan lies in helping Japanese companies overcome the long queues of applications in the USPTO. The large backlog in the USPTO disproportionately affects Japanese companies which patent heavily in the US market. Typically a Japanese company will lodge an application in the JPO first and a corresponding application in the USPTO. The JPO is the office of first filing (OFF) and the USPTO the office of second filing (OSF). Under the PPH if the JPO allows at least one claim of the application, the Japanese company can then request that the USPTO examine the corresponding US application under the PPH procedure. The USPTO can embark on an accelerated examination of the application in which it gets access to the JPO's search and examination work for the purpose of carrying out its

---

[59] See USPTO Press Release available at www.uspto.gov/web/offices/com/speeches/06–35. htm.

own search and examination. The second office is able to come to a decision about issuance faster than if it carried out a search and examination that did not utilize the work of the first office. The arrangement is reciprocal. If the USPTO is the OFF then the patent applicant can trigger the accelerated examination procedure in the JPO if the USPTO has allowed a claim or claims.

In each case the OFF provides a benefit to the OSF in terms of work savings. The OFF also provides a benefit to its national companies since companies tend to start the patent process in their national office (they may be required to do so). It is for this reason that JPO has embarked on a fast release strategy so that as the OFF it can provide a result to the OSF at the time that office does its work.[60] Free-riding by the second office on the work of the first office does not in this case function as a disincentive for the first office. At the UK PO interview, the UK office like the JPO took the view that under a PPH arrangement it was providing a benefit to applicants who first filed in its office (mainly UK companies). The PPH between the USPTO and JPO has moved to full implementation but as we noted in Chapter 5 its use by applicants has to date been low. This is also true of the PPH arrangement between the Australian PO and USPTO (interview, Australian PO). Whether or not applicants make more use of the system depends in part on the advice they receive about it from their attorneys and whether speeding up the process of application in a foreign country matters to them. Even if the use of PPH arrangements remains low for the time being, these arrangements encourage patent offices to speed up their search and examination processes and to share the results with each other.

The superhighway elite: trust, cooperation and competition

Since the implementation of the patent superhighway between the JPO and the USPTO both offices have moved to build superhighway connections with other offices. The USPTO has PPH programmes in place with the EPO, UK, Canadian, Korean, Australian, Danish and Singaporean patent offices.[61] The JPO has superhighway programmes with KIPO, the UK PO, the German PO and the Danish PO.[62] The growth in these PPH arrangements has been rapid since the USPTO and JPO first trialled such an

[60] See JPO, *Annual Report 2008*, 52.
[61] See www.uspto.gov/main/patents.htm.
[62] See www.jpo.go.jp/cgi/linke.cgi?url=/torikumI_e/t_torikumI_e/patent_highway_E. htm.

arrangement in 2006. Offices want to enter into these arrangements for an understandable reason. An office by increasing the number of PPH arrangements to which it is party increases the number of fast-track procedures that its first examination can potentially trigger, something which applicants may find a useful option. In the case of the JPO and the USPTO it was clear from the interviews that superhighway arrangements would only be put into place with 'trusted offices'. Trust depends on one office coming to understand the examination process of another office through joint projects and examiner exchange. In the case of the superhighway arrangement the search and examination of the first office has to be transparent to the second office. One can see from the list of offices that with the exception of the UK PO and German PO all are ISAs under the PCT with those two offices being in any case capable of meeting PCT standards for qualification as an ISA. If the current pattern is followed patent superhighway arrangements will only emerge between ISAs or offices capable of meeting ISA standards and that represent high patenting destinations (Germany and the UK both being high patenting destinations).

For the time being patent superhighways are cooperative work-reducing exercises. One very busy office can take advantage of the work carried out by another very busy office. These superhighway arrangements may also end up helping to create a common platform that will bring patent offices into much greater competition with each other. The extent of this competition will depend on how much fees are driven down and the benefit in terms of fees that is conferred on the office doing the first examination that serves as the springboard for decisions by other offices. One can imagine a world in which the offices tied together by patent superhighways will, once they have reduced their pendency periods, be forced to compete for the patenting work of multinationals. If all the offices that are part of the network can agree to a set of common quality standards for the network and there are no restrictions on where an applicant may start the application process, then multinationals will choose amongst offices in the network based on considerations of efficiency and cost. It is already the case, for example, that Microsoft, Intel and 3M go to KIPO in preference to the USPTO to start the PCT process (interview, KIPO).[63] KIPO has reduced its pendency period to less than 10 months (see Chapter 8) and its search fee as an ISA (set at US$609 for 2009) for international applications filed in English, is considerably less than the USPTO's fee (set

---

[63] Since 1 January 2006, US citizens and residents can elect to use KIPO as an ISA for PCT applications filed in the USPTO.

at US$2,080 for 2009).[64] The cooperation of today amongst patent offices is helping to lay the foundation for what will probably be an intense competition of tomorrow.

The manual is the message

Another way in which the Trilaterals influence the course of patent administration globally is through the development of guidelines. The EPO, the JPO and the USPTO each have an examining manual containing guidelines for the examination of a patent application.[65] Today, in each office, these manuals have become very long. Their growth reflects the expansion of the patent system and its increase in complexity. The guidelines are there to provide examiners with information about examining procedure, including the effects of court decisions on that procedure.[66] They are a form of instruction to examiners. Examiners come to know the examiner's manual as part of their training and have little incentive to depart from applying it in their day-to-day work. If courts change patent law in some way that affects examination, then patent offices respond by changing the examination guidelines. Examiners are not left to their own devices when it comes to interpreting patent law. These manuals are used to train examiners and to routinize their decision-making so that examiners can evaluate a patent application in about 8 to 25 hours.[67] Subtleties of interpretation do not make it into the examination manual. For example, in a decision of the UK Court of Appeal in 2006, Lord Justice Jacob identified on the basis of the existing case law at least three different approaches to interpreting the exclusion of software programs in Article 52(2) of the EPC, one of those approaches having three variants.[68] This Fu Manchu-like complexity does not make it into manuals because it would be much more demanding of examiners and require them to

---

[64] See PCT Fee Tables at www.wipo.int/export/sites/www/pct/en/fees.pdf.

[65] The Guidelines for Examination in the European Patent Office are available at www.epo.org/patents/law.html. In the US the Manual of Patent Examining Procedure is available at www.uspto.gov/web/offices/pac/mpep/mpep.htm. The Examination Guidelines for Patent and Utility Model in Japan is available at www.jpo.go.jp/tetuzukI_e/index.htm.

[66] Paragraph 3.2 of the Guidelines for Examination in the European Patent Office states that the guidelines 'do not constitute legal provisions'.

[67] This is one estimate for the USPTO. See Federal Trade Commission, 'To Promote Innovation: The Proper Balance of Competition and Patent Law and Policy', October 2003, 10, available at www.ftc.gov/opa/2003/10/cpreport.htm. During the interviews the figure that was most often mentioned was 20 hours.

[68] *Aerotel Ltd* v. *Telco Holdings Ltd and Ors Rev.* [2006] EWCA Civ. 1371.

devote much more time to each application. Manuals are there to help an office run its business model. Even with examiners spending about 20 hours on an application a patent office loses money that it only recovers through renewal fees, assuming that the patent is granted and renewed (see Chapter 1 for a discussion of the business model). In the case of the patentability of software under Article 52(2), the EPO's current examination guidelines essentially do not do any more than re-state the liberalizing approach that was adopted in 1985.[69]

Developing guidelines for new areas of technology can involve a patent office in a costly process, but once those guidelines have been drafted they can have an influence outside of their jurisdiction as other offices will study them and perhaps incorporate what is useful. The Trilateral Offices have to confront the task of drafting guidelines for new areas of technology before other offices because patent applicants working in areas of high technology are likely to apply to one of these offices first since the invention itself will have occurred in one of these jurisdictions and the countries represented by these offices are still the world's most important markets. When it comes to exercising a leadership through the development of guidelines it is these three offices that have all the opportunities, with the USPTO perhaps having the edge because the US innovation system inclines more towards investment in higher-risk technologies.

A good example of the kind of learning processes that Trilateral Offices go through with particular technologies is the USPTO's experience with the requirement that a patent application satisfy the condition of being useful (the utility requirement) in the context of biotechnology. This requirement became a problem in the field of biotechnology because inventors were filing applications for matter such as proteins without really knowing the function of the claimed matter. From the point of view of winning the patent race something had to be put down on the form to satisfy utility. Applicants ended up suggesting general uses such as being useful in further experiments. It took the USPTO about a decade and a half to formulate guidelines that were more or less satisfactory to the biotechnology industry and attorneys. In the late 1980s and early 1990s the USPTO was applying utility in a way that was leading to too many rejections, at least according to the US Biotechnology Industry Organization.[70] After a process of public hearings, formulation and re-formulation of the

---

[69] See Guidelines for Examination in the European Patent Office, Part C, Chapter IV, paragraph 2.3.6.

[70] On this point see Thomas J. Kowalski, 'Analyzing the USPTO's Revised Utility Guidelines', 18 March 2000, *Nature Biotechnology*, 349–50.

guidelines the USPTO produced in 2001 a set of guidelines on utility that seem to have gained a measure of support.[71]

The USPTO's saga over guidelines for utility examination shows how difficult it is for a well-resourced office to develop guidelines that respond to new areas of technology. Most developing-country offices struggle to find qualified biotech patent examiners. They are hardly in a position to develop guidelines. Once a major office has drafted guidelines on the patentability of a new area of technology, a smaller office is likely to see benefits in adopting them. There may be other factors that increase the probability of the take-up of the guidelines by the smaller player. The larger patent office may be a source of the smaller country's patent law and/ or its patent examination manual may have been drafted by members of the larger patent office. Adopting the guidelines becomes a natural process, akin to adopting updates for one's programs from Microsoft.

The process of leadership through guidelines is not confined to a large office leading a small one. Guidelines developed by one Trilateral Office may influence another, leading to a convergence in examination practice. For example, the patentability of computer software was an issue that led the USPTO to develop guidelines allowing for claims over programs, an approach that led the JPO to adopt guidelines that followed this US approach.[72] The European Commission during the late 1990s noting this move by the US and Japan towards the patentability of computer software suggested that Europe do more to increase the patentability of software. The EPO, as we have seen, was already thinking along these lines. Guidelines put out by a lead patent office like the USPTO can thus cascade through other patent systems bringing about various convergences of policy, interpretation and practice.

Of course it helps that all offices are working with the same basic principles when it comes to patentability. Free trade agreements are continuing to push this process of convergence along. The US–Australia Free Trade Agreement, for example, requires both parties to provide that 'a claimed invention is useful if it has a specific, substantial, credible utility'.[73] This

---

[71] See Utility Examination Guidelines, 66 Federal Register, 1092 (5 January 2001). For an earlier attempt see Utility Examination Guidelines, 60 Federal Register, 36263 (14 July 1995).

[72] See 'Promoting innovation through patents: the follow-up to the Green Paper on the Community Patent and the Patent System in Europe', COM(1999) 42 Final, Brussels, 05.02.1999, 13.

[73] See Article 17.9.3.

language picks up the USPTO's utility examination guidelines that were issued in January of 2001.

The diffusion of guidelines drafted by the Trilaterals through the patent offices of the world is another example of the regulatory automation of the patent system. One patent office is not obliged to adopt the guidelines of another. But the world's major patent offices face similar problems and developing-country patent offices face major capacity problems. Once guidelines make it into a patent office's examination manual they become part of decision-making processes in which patent examiners quietly and faithfully follow the routines and instructions prescribed by their manuals.

7

The jewel in the crown

India's Patent Office

Integration

At the beginning of the twenty-first century Brazil, China and India are generally talked about as high-growth economies with China and India in particular set on a path that might potentially see them each chug past the US economy in terms of size.[1] Whatever the future holds these three countries are presently major economic powers using measures such as total GDP.[2] All three countries have a patent law and are investing heavily in the creation of a large modern patent office. Of the three countries China is the most advanced down this path. Its patent office is an International Searching Authority (ISA) for the purposes of the Patent Cooperation Treaty (PCT). The patent offices of India and Brazil, as we saw in Chapter 6, have only just been admitted to ISA status. Both have the potential to increase the size of their offices in the way that China has because both have access to a large pool of low-cost scientific labour.

Before we examine the patent offices of these three countries in more detail we should note that the modernization of their respective offices represents the last step of the integration of these countries into the international patent regime. They are following a historical pattern that we saw in Chapter 3 held true for European powers of the late nineteenth century and early twentieth century in which the modernization of patent offices occurred well after the enactment of patent law. Table 7.1 shows Brazil, China and India's membership of the key treaties in the international

[1] See, for example, 'Dreaming with BRICS: The Path to 2050', Goldman Sachs, Global Economics Paper No. 99, available at www2.goldmansachs.com/ideas/brics/book/99-dreaming.pdf.

[2] See, for example, the table on GDP (adjusted using purchasing power parity factors) for 2006 kept by the World Bank that has China ranked 2, India 4 and Brazil 10. Available at http://web.worldbank.org/WBSITE/EXTERNAL/DATASTATISTICS/0,,contentMDK: 20399244~menuPK:1504474~pagePK:64133150~piPK:64133175~theSitePK:239419,00. html.

Table 7.1. *The patent institution in Brazil, China and India*

	Brazil	China	India
First Patent Law	1809	1912	1856
Modern PO	November 2007	January 1994	November 2007
WIPO Convention	20 March 1975	3 June 1980	1 May 1975
WTO/TRIPS member	1 January 1995	11 December 2001	1 January 1995 (1 January 2005 for pharmaceutical product patents)[3]
PCT member	9 April 1978	1 January 1994	7 December 1998
Paris Convention member	7 July 1884	19 March 1985	7 December 1998

patent framework. We can see that in the case of Brazil and India patent law was acquired while they were colonies and in the case of China while under pressure from Western imperial powers.

The date on which these countries can be said to have acquired a modern patent office is the date on which they were recognized as International Searching and Examining Authorities under the PCT. We saw in Chapter 6 that in order to be an ISA a patent office had to have a sufficient number of examiners, have access to various databases and have in place quality control mechanisms.

India: re-designing a colonial institution

India's first patent law was passed in 1856, but repealed in 1857, the beginning of the Indian Mutiny, because it had not received the sanction of the Crown. After the end of the Mutiny in 1858, the British Crown assumed full power from the East India Company and patent law became

---

[3] Article 65.4 of TRIPS expressly allowed a developing country to delay the application of the TRIPS provisions on product patents for 5 years. Using this and other transitional provisions in Article 65 for developing countries India was able to delay the introduction of these TRIPS obligations for pharmaceutical and agricultural chemical products until 1 January 2005.

part of general colonial administration. A new law was passed in 1859.[4] It required an inventor to petition the Governor-General of India in Council for the grant of a term of exclusive privilege.[5] In granting the petition the Governor General authorized the petitioner to file a specification that described the invention and the manner of its performance. The term of the privilege was 14 years and could be renewed for another 14. Novelty was confined to the UK and India and UK patentees could within 12 months of the grant of their UK patent petition the Governor-General of India for a grant of an exclusive privilege in India.

A consolidated law for the protection of inventions and designs was passed in 1888 and its administration was shifted from the Home Department to the Department of Revenue and Agriculture. The increasing volume of petitions saw the appointment of part-time 'patent secretaries' to examine the specifications. In 1911, a fully revised patent law was passed that established a patent office and a 'Controller of Patents and Designs'.[6] A former examiner of patents from the British Patent Office was appointed Controller. The examination of patents became mandatory, but no examiners were appointed till 1919, when two were appointed. By necessity the task of examining fell to the Controller. From 1931 to 1944 there were five examiners, but by 1946 the number of examiners and assistant examiners had been raised to twenty-six.[7] In 1946 the Indian office received 2,610 applications. We saw in Chapter 4 that in 1930 the UK Patent Office had received almost 40,000 applications and had an examining staff of over 300. The low number of Indian patent applications when compared to the number of applications going through the UK PO suggests that pursuing patents in India was not a priority for many British patentees.[8] British India also formed part of a patent Empire network in which it entered into reciprocal arrangements for the protection of inventions with other Empire countries.

Patent reform became a national priority soon after India became independent in 1947. Two reports on India's patent system followed, one in 1950 which concentrated on the use of compulsory licences (the

---

[4] The details are to be found in James Fraser, *A Handy-Book of Patent and Copyright Law: English and Foreign*, Sampson Low, Son and Co., London, 1860, 64–74.

[5] A copy of the Form of Petition is provided ibid., 65.

[6] A short history of the Indian PO is to be found in Ved P. Mithal, 'Patents in India', 30 (1948) *Journal of the Patent Office Society*, 62.

[7] These numbers are provided ibid., 62, 64.

[8] UK patentees would also have been able to claim in India the priority of the UK application. See ibid., 62, 66.

Chand Patent Enquiry Committee) and a second in 1959 (the Ayyangar Committee Report) which looked carefully at the broad question of how best to design a patent system that served India's economic and social welfare goals.[9]

These two reports together triggered a long process of discussion in India about the content of a patent law that would truly serve India's national interests and crucially the interests of its citizens. As the Indian generic industry was to point out in the early 1990s in its campaign against the Agreement on Trade-Related Aspects of Intellectual Property Rights, 1994 (TRIPS), Indian consumers entered independence having to pay some of the highest drug prices in the world. For evidence the heads of influential generic companies like Dr Hamied of Cipla would point to the findings of a 1961 US Senate Committee headed by Senator Kefauver, which named India as a high-price country for pharmaceuticals.[10] The high prices in India were due to a combination of factors. During the first part of the twentieth century a strong indigenous Indian pharmaceutical industry had not developed.[11] The Chand Patents Enquiry Committee of 1950 found that foreigners used India's product patent regime to block local manufacture and did not establish local manufacturing facilities, preferring to rely on importation.[12] The lack of local manufacturing minimized learning by Indian companies and confined them to mainly formulation of medicines. After independence India was faced with the problem that it had little in the way of indigenous pharmaceutical manufacturing capacity and at the same time the emerging Western pharmaceutical multinationals were forming cartels that raised prices in a number of developing

---

[9] The first report published in 1950 (Report of the Patents Enquiry Committee) was chaired by an Indian Supreme Court Justice, Bakshi Tek Chand, and the second, published in 1959 (Report on the Revision of the Patent Law) was chaired by a retired Supreme Court Justice, Rajagopala Ayyangar. Information provided by the Indian PO, Mumbai branch, 8 February 2005.

[10] See, for example, Dr Y. K. Hamied, 'Patents and the Pharamaceutical Industry: A Review Paper for the International Conference on Patent Regime Proposed in the Uruguay Round', 2,3,4 September 1993, New Delhi. On the views of Indian generic companies generally on TRIPS see 'Submission by IDMA (Indian Drug Manufacturers' Association) before International Conference organised by Forum of Parliamentarians on Intellectual Property & National Working Group on Patent Laws at New Delhi, November 14 &15, 1996'.

[11] Janice M. Mueller, 'The Tiger Awakens: The Tumultuous Transformation of India's Patent System and the Rise of Indian Pharmaceutical Innovation', 68 (2007) *University of Pittsburgh Law Review*, 491, 508.

[12] Sudip Chaudhuri, 'TRIPS and Changes in Pharmaceutical Patent Regime in India', Indian Institute of Management, Calcutta, January 2005, Working Paper No. 535, 29.

countries, including India. The worldwide cartel over broad spectrum antibiotics in which companies like Pfizer and Bristol participated is a well known example.[13] Without indigenous manufacturing capacity, issuing compulsory licences, which would have been a possibility under the 1911 Indian Patents Act, was not really an option. The 1950 Chand Committee also found that India's compulsory licensing provisions were too complicated to be able to be used by local companies.[14]

Together the Ayyangar and Chand reports laid the foundation for the Indian Patents Act of 1970.[15] The 1970 Act was also accompanied by a strategy, which had been publicly advocated by a number of jurists, including former Chief Justices of the Supreme Court of India, of not becoming a member of the Paris Convention for the Protection of Industrial Property,1883 (Paris Convention).[16] The aim was to maximize India's sovereignty over its national patent law.

The 1970 Patents Act is a good example of the way in which a developing country can successfully re-design an institution that was imposed upon it during colonization. The monopoly privileges that the patentee obtained under the 1970 Act were nested amongst a set of regulatory levers, some of which could be pulled by government and some by private actors in order to overcome the anti-competitive effects of a monopoly. So, for example, the central government could, if it took the view that the invention was not available to the public at a reasonable price, apply to the Controller to have a patent endorsed with the words 'licences of right' meaning that the patentee had to grant a licence to any person interested in working the patent.[17] If the parties could not agree terms, the Controller had to settle the terms, but in the case of patents related to pharmaceutical process patents the royalty could not exceed 4% of the 'net ex-factory sale price in bulk'.[18] There were also detailed provisions aimed at encouraging the working of inventions in India on a commercial scale, and to allow individuals to obtain compulsory licences.[19] A separate Chapter of the

---

[13] John Braithwaite, *Corporate Crime in the Pharmaceutical Industry*, Routledge & Kegan Paul, London, Boston, Melbourne and Henley, 1984, 175–90.

[14] See Chaudhuri, 'TRIPS and Changes in Pharmaceutical Patent Regime in India', 29.

[15] References to the Indian Patents Act 1970 are references to the Patents Act, prior to its amendment as a result of TRIPS.

[16] B.K. Keayla, 'New Patent Regime: Implications for Domestic Industry, Research and Development and Consumers', National Working Group on Patent Laws, New Delhi, 1996, 7.

[17] See Sub-section 86(1) and Sub-section 88(1) of the 1970 Act.

[18] See Sub-sections 88(2) and (5) of the 1970 Act.

[19] See Chapter XVI of the 1970 Act.

Act regulated the right of the Indian government to use and acquire patented inventions.[20] The scope of invention was carefully delineated with a considerable number of things excluded from the meaning of invention, including methods of agriculture and horticulture and processes for medicinal, surgical, curative and prophylactic treatment of human beings.[21] Patent claims for substances intended for use as a food, medicine or drug as well as substances produced from chemical processes could not be granted, but claims relating to the processes for manufacture of such substances were allowable.[22] The term 'medicine or drug' was defined in the widest possible way to include, for example, insecticides, germicides, intermediates in the preparation of medicines and substances intended to be used in the maintenance of public health.[23] The patent term for process patents for food, medicines or drugs was reduced from 14 years to 5 years from the date of sealing of the patent or 7 years from the date of patent, whichever one was the shorter period.[24]

It is worth noting that the drafters of the Indian Patents Act of 1970 were not engaging in a frolic of their own. Licences of right were a feature of UK patent law and an amendment in 1919 to the UK's patent law had ruled out the granting of claims to substances produced by chemical processes or intended for food or medicine.[25] As Narayanan points out, the 1970 Act was 'modelled substantially on the UK Patents Act of 1949'.[26] When it came to using a national patent system, India was treading along very much the same path followed by its former colonizer.

A little later more than 20 years after the 1970 Act India found that path blocked. The Uruguay Trade Round of the General Agreement on Tariffs and Trade in which India had been an active participant ended in December of 1993. Amongst the many agreements contained in its Final Act was TRIPS. TRIPS contained a number of important provisions on patents that led the members of the Indian generic industry to conclude that US and European pharmaceutical companies, which had been behind

---

[20] See Chapter XVII of the 1970 Act.   [21] See Section 3 of the 1970 Act.
[22] See Section 5 of the 1970 Act.   [23] See Paragraph 2(l) of the 1970 Act.
[24] See Paragraph 53(1)(a) of the Act.
[25] The UK Patents and Designs Act, 1919 inserted Sub-section 38A(1) into the UK Patents and Designs Act, 1907. This sub-section excluded substances produced by chemical processes or intended for food or medicine from being claimed in a specification except when produced by a special method or process of manufacture. This sub-section was repealed in 1949. Licences of right remain a part of the UK system. See Section 46 of the UK Patents Act 1977.
[26] P. Narayanan, *Intellectual Property Law*, 2nd edn., Eastern Law House, Calcutta, 1997, 17.

the drafting of these provisions, were trying to put them out of business.[27] Amongst other things, TRIPS obliged all members of the WTO to allow patents on pharmaceutical products and it prevented a country from treating one field of technology differently from other fields.[28] India could not, for instance, continue with shorter patent terms for pharmaceutical processes. The Indian generic industry argued that the 1970 Act was the foundation stone of its success. Prior to its enactment the Indian pharmaceutical industry was dominated by foreign multinationals with only two of the largest ten companies in terms of sales being Indian.[29] This foreign domination of the industry was reflected in the patent figures: foreigners held 99% of the 1,704 pharmaceutical patents registered in India between 1947 and 1957.[30] Aside from the 1970 patent law, the Indian generic industry also benefited from importation restrictions and taxes and price controls. Following the 1970 Act, the Indian industry grew quickly and was able to achieve export quality.[31] It was not just pharmaceuticals. The Indian pesticides industry, for example, was another industry that had flourished and become an export industry in the absence of patents on pesticides and chemical intermediates.[32]

Implementing TRIPS is a mandatory part of WTO membership.[33] India after the conclusion of the Uruguay Round faced a clear choice. It could become a member of the newly established WTO and comply with TRIPS or it could stay out of the WTO and retain its patent system. It chose the former.

In the decade that followed the beginning of TRIPS on 1 January 1995, patent law and pharmaceuticals became a major political issue in the Indian Parliament. To some extent, the debate over patent law was a proxy for a bigger debate about India's strategy for dealing with globalization. In the complex currents and eddies of Indian politics, neo-liberal approaches to liberalization and deregulation gained much more traction in public life. The links that Nehru and others had forged in the Cold War era between

---

[27] For the history see Drahos with Braithwaite, *Information Feudalism*.

[28] Article 27(1) of TRIPS.

[29] See Hannah E. Kettler and Rajiv Modi, 'Building Local Research and Development Capacity for the Prevention and Cure of Neglected Diseases: The Case of India', 79 (2001) *Bulletin of the World Health Organization*, 742, 743.

[30] 'Peoples' Commission on GATT: On the Constitutional Implications of the Final Act Embodying the Results of the Uruguay Round of Multilateral Trade Negotiations', Centre for Study of Global Trade System and Development, New Delhi, 1996, 60.

[31] See Keayla, 'New Patent Regime', 11.

[32] Ibid. 11–12.

[33] Article II.2 of the Agreement Establishing the World Trade Organization.

Indian nationalism and socialism weakened as the de-regulatory agendas of Regan and Thatcher began to influence developing-country governments around the world. In 1991 the Congress Party government of P. Narasimha Rao started a period of economic liberalization in India. New interest group voices within the Congress Party and within Indian industry, such as the Confederation of Indian Industry, articulated the case for India to move towards a patent system that favoured the owners of patents, arguing that this would benefit India in terms of access to technology and foreign investment.[34] Step by step India brought itself into full compliance with TRIPS. The reforms over pharmaceutical patents attracted most of the public attention and debate, but in many ways it is the changes to India's Patent Office that signal most clearly the depth of change in India's approach to patents.

The patent raj

TRIPS contains transitional provisions for developing countries in relation to patents of which India took full advantage.[35] Part of the price of delaying the entry of patents on pharmaceuticals and chemicals under the TRIPS transitional provisions for a country was an obligation to establish a temporary system of protection. Basically this involved creating a filing system for patent applications during the transitional period and then providing the term of patent protection that remained once the patent was granted (commonly referred to as pipeline protection).[36] In addition a country also had to create a temporary form of protection known as an exclusive marketing right for products that had been patented and had gained marketing approval in another WTO member country.[37] After a failed attempt to introduce implementing legislation along these lines India found itself on the receiving end of a WTO dispute resolution action brought by the US, an action that the US won.[38] India eventually introduced this temporary system of protection in 1999.[39]

---

[34] Anitha Ramanna, 'Shifts in India's Policy on Intellectual Property: The Role of Ideas, Coercion and Changing Interests' in P. Drahos (ed.), *Death of Patents*, Lawtext Publishing, London, 2005, 150, 161.

[35] Article 65 of TRIPS.

[36] Article 70.8 of TRIPS.   [37] Article 70.9 of TRIPS.

[38] See Panel Report, 'India – Patent Protection for Pharmaceutical and Agricultural Chemical Products', WT/DS50/R, adopted 16 January 1998, as modified by the Appellate Body Report, WT/DS50/AB/R.

[39] Patents (Amendment) Act 1999. A copy of this legislation is available at the Indian Patent Office website at http://ipindia.nic.in/ipr/patent/patents.htm.

In 2002 another amendment to India's 1970 patent law was passed.[40] This amending law brought India's patent law into line with India's membership of the Paris Convention and the PCT. India had joined both treaties in 1998. The strategy of staying out of the international patent framework that had been forged by jurists of Nehru's India had come to an end. There were some sixty-four amendments introduced by the 2002 law, including the lengthening of the patent term to 20 years. A new chapter on compulsory licences was written into the 1970 Act with the provisions on licences of right and the capping of the royalty rate for such licences in the case of pharmaceuticals being omitted.

Under its TRIPS deadline, India had until 1 January 2005 to bring its patent law into full compliance with the patent provisions of TRIPS. The final step meant introducing patent product protection for pharmaceuticals and chemicals. Such product protection had been a feature of India's patent laws under the British Raj. Not surprisingly, the public debates in India over this last stage of TRIPS compliance were heated. In 2005 an amendment was passed that omits the restriction on the patenting of substances intended for use as a food, medicine or drug, or substances produced by chemical processes.[41] With this law India secured its passage to the new global patent raj.

India's patent office: the jewel in the crown

Mithal's description of the Indian PO at the beginning of the twentieth century shows clearly that it was a small operation.[42] The Patent Controller who was appointed in 1912 did not have any examiners to assist him, despite examination being compulsory. In the year of his resignation (1919) the number of applications had reached 1,000. If we assume that the processing, examining and granting of one application took 5 hours (obviously this would allow for only a cursory examination) and the Patent Controller worked every day of the year and did two applications a day he would have been unable to process 1,000 applications in 1 year. Things seemed to have improved by 1946 when there were about 26 examining staff and 2,610 applications, but Mithal gives no information about the size of the backlog.

---

[40] Patents (Amendment) Act 2002. A copy of this legislation is available at the Indian Patent Office website at http://ipindia.nic.in/ipr/patent/patents.htm.

[41] Patents (Amendment) Act 2005. A copy of this legislation is available at the Indian Patent Office website at http://ipindia.nic.in/ipr/patent/patents.htm.

[42] Mithal, 'Patents in India', 62.

After the 1970 Patents Act came into operation in 1972 the amount of patenting by foreign companies in India dropped, dramatically so. Bagchi's study in 1984 showed that in 1968 there were 1,110 applications by Indians and 4,248 applications by foreigners. By the financial year 1979–80, the number of Indian applications was not much different (1,055), but the number of foreign applications had dropped to 1,925. The number of foreign patents in force in India had dropped from 37,816 in 1968 to 14,476 in 1979–80.[43]

We saw earlier just how widely the 1970 Act had defined medicines and drugs for the purpose of excluding such things from patentability, as well as reducing the patent term for processes in these fields. The most obvious explanation for the drop in the number of foreign patent applications is that prior to the 1970 Act the bulk of patenting going on in India by foreign interests was related to pharmaceuticals and chemical products, something the wide exclusion under the 1970 Act largely stopped. In addition, India had raised its standard of novelty to include documentary publication anywhere in the world and raised its patent fees.[44]

The drop in patent applications after the 1970 Patent Act would have provided no incentive to modernize the Indian PO. Things changed with India's membership of the WTO. Foreign companies in the pharmaceutical/chemical field began to show an interest in patenting in India, even before India had implemented the temporary pipeline protection that it was required to under TRIPS and well before it moved to product protection in 2005. In the WTO action that the US brought against India for failing to implement pipeline protection the evidence showed that between 1 January 1995 and 15 February 1997, the Indian PO had received 1,339 applications for pharmaceutical and agricultural products, despite the fact that the Indian PO only had in place an obscure, unpublicized procedure for dealing with patent applications intended for pipeline protection.[45] These applications were an early signal that India could expect to receive many more and that the PO would have to have proper procedures in place for their processing.

---

[43] Amiya Kumar Bagchi with Parthasarathi Banerjee and Utlam Kumar Bhattacharya, 'Indian Patents Act and its Relation to Technological Development in India: A Preliminary Investigation', 19 (7) *Economic and Political Weekly*, 18 February 1984, 287, 293, Table 1.

[44] See Sub-section 13(2) of the 1970 Patents Act. On the rise in fees see Bagchi *et al.*, 'Indian Patents Act', 287, 293.

[45] See 'Report of the Panel, India – Patent Protection for Pharmaceutical and Agricultural Chemical Products', WT/DS50/R, 2.11.

Pipeline protection under TRIPS was only ever going to be a temporary source of work for the Indian PO. The real source of work was, as the experience of the Trilaterals has shown, always going to be the PCT. When India joined the PCT foreigners began to use it to obtain patents in India. Foreigners could designate India in an international application under the PCT as from 7 December 1998. India could only act as a receiving office for PCT applications.[46] Table 7.2 shows that foreigners prefer to use the PCT to file for patents in India rather than filing directly at the Indian PO or using Paris Convention priority (15,467 represents PCT foreign filings in which a PCT application has entered the national phase and 4,571 represents foreigners using other routes to the Indian PO).[47] Applicants from the US, Germany and Japan are the biggest users of the PCT route to India.[48]

Of the 24,505 patent applications that the Indian PO received in 2005–6, 33% were for chemicals, drugs and food.[49] If one adds biotechnology applications to this group this percentage climbs to 39%.[50] Given the low number of patent applications by Indian residents, foreigners would be responsible for most of the patent applications in these sectors.

India's re-integration into the international patent regime through TRIPS has, for the time being at least, produced a situation not unlike the one that prevailed under the British Raj in which much of the patenting was in the drug/chemicals area, with almost all the patents in foreign hands. Reversing this domination through patents was the purpose of the 1970 Act.

Modernization

The increasing number of patent applications that India began receiving as a result of its WTO membership made it clear that it would have to modernize its patent office. Modernization was approved in 1998, but work did not start till 2000.[51] Amongst other things, this meant hiring

---

[46] It achieved ISA status in 2007.
[47] This table is based on the figures in Appendix B in Indian Patent Office, *Annual Report 2005–2006*, 18.
[48] Ibid. 10.
[49] For 2005–6 the number of patent applications were as follows: chemical – 5,810; drug – 2,211; food – 101. See Indian Patent Office, *Annual Report 2005–2006*, 19.
[50] The number of biotechnology applications was 1,525. See ibid.
[51] Indian Patent Office, *Annual Report 2001–2002*, 3.

Table 7.2. *The PCT route in India*

	1999–2000	2005–2006
Total number of applications	4824	24505
Number of national phase PCT applications	269	15467
Residents	2206	4521
Non-residents	2349	4517

more examiners, building new office space and investing heavily in information technology.

The Indian PO is made up of the Head Office in Kolkata with branch offices in Chennai, Delhi and Mumbai. I visited the Mumbai Office in February 2005. At first I thought that the taxi driver had taken me to a derelict building and so an animated discussion ensued in which the taxi driver assured me he had brought me to the right address. Refusing to pay, I went to check this. Picking my way through the hanging wires and pigeons in the dimly lit stairwell, I came upon the sign of the Mumbai PO on the third floor. Hurrying back to the taxi driver I offered an apology and a very healthy tip, both of which were politely accepted. The rest of day was spent talking to examiners in rooms that had not seen paint for a while. Today, if the photo in the 2005–6 annual report is accurate, the Mumbai branch has all the glass and concrete that one would wish upon a modern building. That same annual report announces that India has completed the modernization of all its IP administration. Keeping in mind that the Indian PO has achieved ISA status, the changes in the Mumbai office have been dramatic from the time of my visit, when in essence I saw a branch office of the Indian PO in a pre-modern state.

In 2005, the Mumbai branch had about thirty examiners and was planning to recruit another fifty. Two years prior it had only three examiners. Recruiting examiners has not proved a problem, but retaining them, the Assistant Controller suggested, is more of an issue because of poor public sector salaries. A recurring theme amongst the examiners was the lack of access to databases for the purpose of doing proper searches. They were using free patent searching tools available on the European Patent Office's (EPO) website (esp@cenet was expressly mentioned) and the USPTO's website. The lack of databases, they pointed out, made it difficult to check the work of other offices ('our databases are of no use at the moment', as one of them put it). This in turn meant that they had to give credence to the examination reports being produced by ISAs. Inferior databases heighten the chances that an examiner will adopt a play-it-safe strategy and grant the patent – 'If you reject [the] patent you must be correct. Easier to grant patent' (Indian Examiner, Mumbai branch). The examination reports of large offices like the EPO and the USPTO were described as a useful starting point. As one Assistant Controller put it 'we are getting expertized by reading those reports'.

But at the same time, the Indian examiners were reading the reports of other offices critically, even if they were in an inferior position when it came to searching. Why, they asked me, did the Australian PO grant claims that other offices did not? Caught by surprise I said I didn't know, adding as an afterthought that perhaps they wanted to attract the work (this was followed by nods of agreement).

Reaching ISA status was a clear priority for the Indian PO because it increases its capacity to influence other offices and provides it with more autonomy within the international patent regime. Given that India is now an ISA, the situation with respect to databases must have improved since the time of my interview. India has a memorandum of understanding (MOU) with the EPO, signed in 2006, in which the EPO agrees that it may give India access to its search engine EPOQUE.[52] This would give Indian examiners access to the EPO's subscription databases. These databases are regarded by patent aficionados as being the best in the world. Chapter 2 described how the EPO is using access to EPOQUE as part of its drive to create a global standard of patent searching.

The Indian PO returns the fees it collects to general revenue. Fees have been raised in the last couple of years in order to cover its running costs. As one interviewee put it 'we are moving you can say into profit like a company'. It is also facing a growing backlog of patent applications. In 1992–3, there were almost 8,000 patent applications to be carried forward to the next financial year and in 2001–2 that number had grown to more than 44,000.[53] The strategy for dealing with the backlog is based on a system of examination upon request and increasing the number of patent examiners. A person has 4 years from the date of filing or priority of the application within which to request an examination. Moving to a

---

[52] The MOU was signed on 29 November 2006. A copy can be found at http://ipindia.nic.in/ipr/patent/patents.htm.
[53] See Appendix I of the Indian Patent Office, *Annual Report 2001–2002*, 39.

model of deferred examination in order to deal with a growing number of applications is a strategy that has been tried in other countries, including Germany and Japan, but ultimately it only defers the problem of processing large numbers of applications. We saw in Chapter 5 that in Japan the time in which an applicant has to defer an examination has been reduced from 7 to 3 years. The other strategy is to increase the number of examiners. During the interview in Mumbai, India's target for the number of examiners was said to be 270. According to the 2005–6 Annual Report the Indian PO has a working strength of 179 made up of 140 examiners of patents (and designs) and another 39 staff occupying more senior positions of Controller and Assistant Controller of patents. The success of this strategy obviously depends on recruitment and retention of examiners.

'How can we win?': India's strategy on patents

The reform of India's patent law and the subsequent modernization of its patent office were triggered by TRIPS. But in implementing these changes new policy voices within India have pushed for a more positive embrace of the patent system. So, by way of example, Dr Rakesh Mohan, Secretary, Department of Economic Affairs in the Union Finance Ministry, has suggested that India's new product patent rules will encourage the outsourcing of chemical and pharmaceutical R&D to India.[54] Senior people in the Indian PO take a similar view: 'Indian researchers do research abroad for US companies. They can easily do that research here in India' (interview with Assistant Controller of Patents, Indian PO). Underpinning this thinking is India's large pool of low cost but highly trained scientific R&D workers.[55] Chemical and pharmaceutical multinationals will, the argument runs, want to establish their R&D laboratories in India in order to take advantage of this cheap labour force. R&D centres will spring up like call centres.

There is also the belief that India's existing R&D system is strong enough to be able to support the extraction of patent rents from other countries. At a meeting in 1996 organized by the Department of Scientific & Industrial Research (DSIR), ministers and officials drew attention to the fact that at that time India had 325 national laboratories and R&D institutions, 450 Scientific and Industrial R&D Organizations and 1,250 in-house R&D units

---

[54] See www.ipai.in/product-patent.htm.
[55] India has 120 researchers per million people in R&D. (See *Human Development Report 2005*, UNDP, NY, 2005, 264.) This is a very low ratio, but the size of India's population means that it is a large number overall.

employing around 50,000 scientific and technical personnel. The problem lay in the lack of patents.[56] One survey by DSIR showed in the previous 4 years these 1,250 in-house units had only filed 743 patents, a 'miniscule' effort compared to other powers, including China.[57] The Minister of State made a similar argument pointing out that India had changed its position on patents because it was time for India 'to use the industrial base built up mainly for the domestic market over the preceding 30 years, to move out into world markets'.[58]

These kinds of views are not surprising. After all one of the lessons of colonization that India would have learnt under the British Raj is that the patent system is a rent extraction machine that used correctly allows domestic firms to dominate foreign markets. The reference to China is telling. Once China had signalled that it was reforming its patent system in order to play the patent-based innovation game (discussed in the next chapter), Indian policy elites would have concluded that they had little choice but to prepare for that game as well.

The optimism of India's policy elites about India's bright patent-based future had not made it down to the thirty or so patent examiners in the Mumbai branch at the time of my interview in 2005. In summary, their views were that the globalization of patent standards put developing countries like India in a difficult position. The local pharmaceutical industry was not in a position, they thought, to do sufficient R&D to take advantage of the new system. Many Indian companies could not afford the cost of patent applications. Inequalities of national incomes meant that richer countries were in a better position to afford the costs of patents in India. The system did not benefit small to medium enterprises (SMEs) and even the Indian pharmaceutical industry could not invent new molecules. 'How can we win?' they kept asking.

From bright line rules to shades of grey

One of the features of the 1970 Patents Act prior to its TRIPS-based amendments was that it gave certainty to the Indian generic pharmaceutical

---

[56] 'Welcome Address by Shri Ashok Parthasarathi, Additional Secretary, DSIR', in *Proceedings of the 9th National Conference on In-House R&D Industry: The New Intellectual Property Regime: Implications for Industry and R&D*, Department of Scientific & Industrial Research, Government of India, New Delhi, 1996, 24, 25.

[57] Ibid.

[58] 'Inaugural Address by Shri Bhuvnesh Chaturvedi, Minister of State (Prime Minister's Office and Science & Technology)' in *Proceedings of the 9th National Conference on In-House R&D Industry*, 33, 34.

industry by using a combination of simple rules and automatic regulation. For example, under the 1970 Act, Section 5 simply stated that in 'the case of inventions claiming substances intended for use … as medicine … no patent shall be granted in respect of claims for the substances themselves'. Moreover, the definition of medicines was cast in the widest possible terms leaving little possible doubt about the scope of its operation. A rule that simply excludes a drug from patentability is readily understandable and leaves comparatively little scope for argument. Similarly, a licence of right system, of the kind that India had in its 1970 Act for pharmaceuticals, automates the process of obtaining a licence from the patentee and sets a cap on the royalty. This leaves very little room for litigation strategies to defeat the grant of a licence.

The amendments to the 1970 Act, which implement India's obligations under TRIPS, have resulted in the use of more complex rules and less certainty for generic companies. For example, the 2005 amendment that India passed to the 1970 Act omits Section 5, but inserts a revised paragraph 3(d), the section that deals with exclusions from the meaning of invention under the Act. This paragraph excludes 'the mere discovery of a new form of known substance which does not result in the enhancement of the known efficacy of that substance'. The aim is to prevent pharmaceutical companies from recycling for patentability known molecules in a new form that deliver no real therapeutic gain. Paragraph 3(d) aims to put an end to this kind of practice by excluding it from the meaning of invention. An explanatory note adds that for the purposes of paragraph 3(d), salts, esters, polymorphs, isomers and other things will be considered to be the same substance 'unless they differ significantly in properties with regard to efficacy'.

The rule in paragraph 3(d) is a more complex rule of exclusion because it depends on the meaning of 'enhancement of the known efficacy of that substance' and its operation is also affected by an explanatory note that sets out a test for chemical sameness. In the first instance an examiner will have to interpret this exclusion since a patent can only be granted for inventions within the meaning of the Act. The Indian generic industry like other national generic industries around the world has long complained of the practice of evergreening in which pharmaceutical multinationals find ways to patent slightly revised versions of old molecules.[59]

---

[59] On the views of the Indian Drug Manufacturers' Association see 'Report of the Technical Expert Group on Patent Law Issues', December 2006, 23. For examples of complaints about evergreening in other countries see, Edward Hore, 'Patently

Indian generic companies will be looking to the Indian PO to interpret the exclusion widely since this favours market entry and competition. Pharmaceutical multinationals will be looking to the Indian PO to read this exclusion in the narrowest possible way since this favours exclusivity and monopoly rents. The decision of the Indian PO in which it rejected Novartis' patent application for its brand name drug Gleevec on the basis that it was caught by paragraph 3(d) is precisely the decision that brand name manufacturers fear. Novartis' price for Gleevec in India was around the US$3,000 mark. Indian generic manufacturers were selling a generic version for US$200.[60] Both groups will in essence want to create a supportive interpretive community that reads patent applications in a way that more often than not will produce the correct result (as defined by their business model).

The patent interpretive community is bigger than just patent examiners. It includes judges and patent attorneys. Moreover examiners are at the bottom of the hierarchy of authoritative interpretation. It is courts that have the final say as to patentability.[61] But in practical terms patent examiners are, as it were, the 'grant-keepers'. It is their decisions that in the first instance determine whether or not a patent is to be granted. Very few decisions of the patent office end up being contested in the courts. One estimate suggests that between 1996 and 2000 less than a hundred decisions of the India PO were appealed to the Indian courts.[62] The interpretive examination culture of a patent office matters, crucially so, because in almost all cases the final decision about patentability will be made by an examiner and not a court. The vast patent portfolios that multinationals build globally are built on the backs of examiners' decisions.

Absurd: Evergreening of Pharmaceutical Patent Protection Under the Patented Medicines (Notice of Compliance) Regulations of Canada's Patent Act (2004)', available from the Canadian Generic Pharmaceutical's Association; A. Somogyi *et al.*, 'Inside the Isomers: The Tale of Chiral Switches', 27(2) 2004 *Australian Prescriber*, 24; Aaron S. Kesselheim, 'Intellectual Property Policy in the Pharmaceutical Sciences: The Effect of Inappropriate Patents and Market Exclusivity Extensions on the Health Care System', 9(3) (2007) *The AAPS J E306.*

[60] See Praful Bidwai, 'HEALTH-INDIA: Novartis Patents Case Far From Dead', http://ipsnews.net/news.asp?idnews=38840.

[61] Decisions of the Controller of Patents can be appealed to a High Court of India including a decision of the Controller to refuse an application on the ground that it is not for an invention under the Act – see Sub-sections 15(2) and 116(2) of the amended Patents Act 1970.

[62] Shamnad Basheer, ' "Policy Style" Reasoning at the Indian Patent Office', [2005] (3) *IPQ*, 309, 320, fn. 72.

Developing countries like India that are integrating into the international patent framework present opportunities for the creation of new interpretive communities within patent offices. To begin with developing-country offices themselves create a demand for this training in interpretation, especially in areas such as pharmaceutical product patent protection where they lack experience. During the interview in the Mumbai PO many of the examiners kept coming back to the point that they needed training, especially in the area of pharmaceuticals. We saw in Chapter 6 that the Trilateral Offices offer this training. But at the same time as they do, they build an interpretive community. They instruct developing-country examiners in the interpretation of claims and the making of judgements about the level of inventive step required to satisfy the inventiveness criterion. In the case of India, the USPTO has been prepared to help out by training Indian examiners in the nuanced art of pharmaceutical product examination. At an interview in the USPTO, US officials after drawing attention to this capacity-building exercise noted that it had an element of sensitivity about it (interview, USPTO, 2007). They were hinting at the fact that Indian novices after exposure to US patent examination culture, which itself is based on decades of experience with pharmaceutical product patents, may come to read paragraph 3(d) through the lens of that exposure. And as we saw earlier there is also the fact that the US is the single biggest source of patent applications in India and pharmaceutical/chemical patenting represents, for the time being, the single biggest category of patenting in India. Training of Indian examiners is not, however, confined to pharmaceuticals. The Indian office has also sent examiners to study the US approach to biotechnology applications (interview, Indian patent official, 2007).

The USPTO much like the EPO builds capacity in developing countries that favours the patenting strategies of its respective companies. It is a form of encoded capacity-building in which the aim is to form an interpretive community through patient years of assistance and training. The fact that brand companies lose some cases as Novartis did with Gleevec, although heart wrenching for Novartis, is beside the point. Rather the point is to create a dense technical jurisprudence of rules in which a community of examiners deeply familiar with those rules ultimately comes to 'see' that, for example, changing the particle size of a known drug so as to improve its bioavailability is sufficient to satisfy both the efficacy requirement of 3(d) and the inventive-step requirement.[63]

---

[63] For an unsuccessful attempt by Novartis to argue this in relation to the known drug Oxcarbazepine see the pre-grant opposition filed against Novartis by Ranbaxy

Examiners are not in the process of encoded capacity-building turned into automatons of interpretation in which the right outcome is implanted in them. Rather the technical training opens up for them a world of characterization possibilities in which inventive steps, which from a scientific viewpoint are minor or even trivial, can be seen to be inventive for the purposes of the patent system. Wittgenstein's philosophical aphorism, 'the limits of my language, mean the limits of my world' has real-world grip. By deepening an examiner's knowledge of patent language, as it were, the examiner can begin to see the meaning of invention in a different way. Individual examiners will have professional disagreements about how these characterization possibilities are to be drawn in the case of a given application, but the aim of encoded capacity-building is not to stop these disagreements. These kinds of debates over the application of technical rules help to create and maintain a technical rules-based discourse. Instead the aim is to foster the growth of an interpretive culture, one that (following Wittgenstein's idea) breaks the ordinary language limits on invention and creates a new world in which scientifically trivial innovation becomes patentable invention.

A patent-bright future?

India's entry into TRIPS and the modernization of its PO over the last 5 years or so suggest that it sees the possibility of much greater gains for itself from the system than in the past. Classified as a mega-diverse country it wants a system that helps it to track patent applications that make use of its genetic resources. It has been a key mover in submitting draft amending text on TRIPS that will require patent applicants to disclose the origin of genetic resources over which they are seeking a patent.[64] Similarly, it has been an advocate of the digitization of traditional knowledge resources for the purposes of ensuring that such knowledge forms part of the prior art for the purposes of patent law. The creation in India of a Traditional Knowledge Digital Library led in turn to the development of a Traditional Knowledge Resources Classification system

---

Laboratories and Torrent Pharma held on 16 November 2006 and decided on 4 January 2007. The text of the decision is available at https://www.ipindiaonline.gov.in/patentdecisionsearch/patentsearch.aspx.

[64] The proposed amendment takes the form of a new article in TRIPS – Article 29bis. See document WT/GC/W/564/TN/C/W/41 submitted to the Trade Negotiations Committee on 29 May 2006, by Peru, Brazil, India, Pakistan, Thailand and Tanzania.

so that traditional knowledge resources could be incorporated into the International Patent Classification system.[65]

India's democracy is also vigorous enough to allow passionate public debates to influence patent reform. Patent reform is not a quiet technocratic exercise carried on behind closed doors. My interviews at the Mumbai PO suggested that senior officials were not in favour of retaining India's pre-grant opposition system, preferring instead to rely on post-grant opposition. The move to abolish pre-grant opposition is favoured by multinationals. It was a feature of India's Patent Act in 1970.[66] It had been a part of English law going back to the 1850s, the UK eventually removing it when it joined the European Patent Convention (EPC).[67] Despite a trend for countries to move away from pre-grant opposition, India has retained its pre-grant opposition and added post-grant opposition.[68] Some of India's NGOs have started using pre-grant opposition in the pharmaceuticals area and the Indian generic industry has launched many such oppositions.[69]

It is also clear that India is paving the way for the entry of many more patents into its business culture. It has, for example, introduced a fast-track procedure that will see a patent issued in India in less than 6 months.[70]

---

[65] The 8th edition of the IPC contains classification A61K 36/00 which is described as 'Medicinal preparations of undetermined constitution containing material from algae, lichens, fungi or plants, or derivatives thereof, e.g. traditional herbal medicines'. See www.wipo.int/classifications/ipc/ipc8/?lang=en. On the history of the creation of the Traditional Knowledge Digital Library see V. K. Gupta, 'Traditional Knowledge Digital Library', Sub-Regional Experts Meeting in Asia on Intangible Cultural Heritage: Safeguarding and Inventory-Making Methodologies (Bangkok, Thailand, 13–16 December 2005). For a description of India and WIPO's role in the IPC process related to traditional knowledge see 'Classification Tools Relating to Traditional Knowledge and Biodiversity', Committee of Experts, Special Union of the International Patent Classification, IPC/CE/35/7, 21 September 2004.

[66] See Section 25 of the 1970 Patents Act.

[67] See Clause XII of the UK Patent Law Amendment Act 1852. This clause allowed any person with an interest in opposing the patent to object in writing.

[68] See Sub-sections 25(1) and 25(2) of the amended 1970 Patents Act.

[69] 'A pre-grant opposition has been filed against the anti-HIV drug, Combivir, manufactured by GlaxoSmithKline, a leading pharmaceutical company. The Manipur Network of Positive People (MNP+) and the Indian Network of People Living with HIV/AIDS have lodged the complaint at the Kolkata patent office.' (www.medindia.net/news/view_news_main.asp?x=8969&t=1). Since 2005 domestic pharma companies have filed nearly 150 pre-grant oppositions to patent applications in India (report in the *Economic Times*) see http://blog.ipfactor.co.il/2006/10/25/indian-generic-pharma-companies-delay-patent-protection-by-pre-grant-opposition-proceedings/.

[70] This fast-track process is started by a request for early publication under Section 11A(2) of the amended Patents Act 1970.

Not all companies will necessarily want to fast-track their applications, but the option exists. For multinationals, the cost of patent fees in India would represent a small proportion of the overall cost of their global patenting costs. At the time of the interview in 2005, Indian patent officials put the patent fees for a standard patent at around US$300 and estimated patent attorney fees to be about US$2,000 for a standard application. The more complex rule orientation of the 1970 Act is likely to attract more litigation. Companies like Novartis are unlikely to sit meekly by while the Indian PO issues its rejections of their patent applications in pre-grant oppositions. These multinationals know that the meek shall not inherit the riches of the pharmaceutical kingdom. Indian patent examiners will be given more training by the USPTO and Indian courts will find themselves hearing more cases until a more favourable line of interpretation emerges or the Indian Parliament is persuaded to fix the operation of 3(d) by the usual army of lobbyists. Similarly, India's amendment to Section 3 in 2002 to exclude from the meaning of invention 'a mathematical or business method or computer programme *per se* or algorithms' will see a voluminous patent theology develop around the meaning of *per se*, much as it has around the words 'as such' in the context of the exclusion of computer software programs in the EPC.[71]

More patenting in India and more patent litigation mean that Indian companies will need access to legal services including firms doing patent searches, patent drafting work, patent advising, opposition and litigation work. Patent-based innovation requires high levels of legal servicing. After its entry into the WTO and TRIPS some Indian policy makers drew attention to the fact that India lacked sufficient numbers of people skilled in these areas.[72] Ten or so years down the track it is hard to say to what extent the situation has changed. People within the Mumbai PO were not flattering about the quality of work of the local patent profession, the exception being those legal firms that worked for foreign multinationals. It is a reasonable conjecture that the best patent attorneys in India are likely to be the ones that work for multinationals since they pay the most. Local inventors are, for the most part, left with those that are less able to work the system in favour of their clients. This is a problem for local firms because so much of what ends up in a granted patent is dependent upon the drafting skill of the patent attorney. The great skill of good patent

---

[71] On the different approaches in the context of the EPC see *Aerotel Ltd* v. *Telco Holdings Ltd. & Ors Rev.* [2006] EWCA Civ. 1371.

[72] See the recommendation to create in India a cadre of IP specialists in the *Proceedings of the 9th National Conference on In-House R&D Industry*, 20.

attorneys is to be able to listen to inventors tell their stories of discoveries, take that raw narrative and turn it into something that after a number of years will be accepted by a patent office and sealed as a patent. One examiner put it thus: 'The [patent] agent is inventing for the inventor.'

Developing countries like India, which want to play in the patent-based global economy, need armies of patent attorneys, just as much as they need scientists, since what counts is not invention, but patentable invention. As the pharmaceutical industry has routinely demonstrated one does not need genuine invention to obtain a lucrative patentable invention. The small step of changing the particle size of a known drug in order to be turned into a patentable invention requires some clever drafting of patent claims, a compliant patent office that understands that trivial innovation is patentable innovation and doctors willing to prescribe the patentable version of the drug rather than the generic.

India in raising a patent attorney army has the advantage of English and a large enough market and population in which such differentiated legal services can evolve. Few other developing countries can raise the patent armies needed to set up, defend and extract patent monopoly rents. India will probably have much greater depth in these kinds of services in the next decade.

Can India's patent-based innovation strategy work? Bagchi's 1984 study of India's 1970 Patents Act came to the conclusion that it had not really delivered in terms of innovation in India.[73] Probably by the early 1990s prior to TRIPS coming into operation in India one could say that the Indian generic industry was a success story attributable in part to the operation of the 1970 Patents Act. But here one has to keep in mind Bagchi's point that India was primarily a follower of technology and so the purpose of its patent law was to minimize foreign patenting restrictions on Indian firms.[74] By the time of India's entry into TRIPS, India's policy elites wanted an Indian patent system that would, in the words of Dr Mashelkar, turn India's 'intellectual prowess into knowledge and wealth'.[75] It would, in other words, be Indian firms owning the patent monopolies and extracting the global rents. India's reform of its patent office has been driven by this kind of thinking. To date all that has happened is that foreign patenting levels have risen dramatically especially in the areas of pharmaceuticals and chemicals, the areas which the 1970 Patents Act had excluded from patentability. India's policy elites would no doubt reply that India's current patent strategy is a long-run one.

[73] Bagchi et al. 'Indian Patents Act', 287, 302.   [74] Ibid. 287, 300.
[75] 'Address by Dr. R. A. Maskelkar, Secretary, DSIR and DG, CSIR', in the Proceedings of the 9th National Conference on In-House R&D Industry, 30, 31.

8

The dragon and the tiger

China and South Korea

Patent law in the era of decline, rebellion and war

During the nineteenth century and the early part of the twentieth century China became an increasingly decaying imperial power beset by internal rebellion and conflicts with European colonizing powers. One of these rebellions beginning in 1850 and lasting some 20 years was led by Hung Hsiu-ch'uan. A Christian believer, he declared himself the Heavenly King of the Kingdom of Heavenly Peace and led a rebellion estimated to have cost some 30 million lives. Developing a patent law was not an especially high priority in China during this time. There is a suggestion that amidst the slaughter during the time of the Kingdom of Heavenly Peace a patent law of some kind was proposed by one of the leaders of rebellion.[1]

The Taiping rebellion was one of a number of conflicts in China in the nineteenth century, including the two Opium Wars (the first against the British in 1839–42 and the second against the British and French in 1856–60), a war with France in 1884 that saw China lose control over Indo-China and another with Japan in 1895 that saw China lose Korea and Formosa. With 1900 came the Boxer Rebellion that ended in China making many concessions to the Western powers that had captured Peking and put down the Rebellion. Beginning in the 1860s various attempts were made in China to engage and learn from Western science and technology and in 1898 a patent regulation was passed, but within the broader cycles of rebellion and war that were operating in China its effects were minimal.[2]

---

[1] See William P. Alford, *To Steal a Book is an Elegant Offense*, Stanford University Press, Stanford, 1995, 143, fn. 27.

[2] Liwei Wang, 'The Chinese Traditions Inimical to the Patent Law', 14 (1993) *Northwestern Journal of International Law and Business*, 15, 19.

China's decline came at a time when European imperialism was militarily far superior and looking for opportunities to expand commercially and territorially. China then, as today, was seen as a lucrative export market. Intellectual property issues predominantly in the form of trademark protection for Western goods surfaced in the broader commercial treaty negotiations between China and Western powers, with one such treaty in 1903 between the US and China expressly requiring China to issue patents to US citizens holding patents on the same terms as patents issued to Chinese citizens.[3] Since there was no Chinese patent law or office nothing much came of this. A patent law that applied to Chinese nationals was passed in 1912, the year in which China established a parliament. The Empress Dowager had died 4 years earlier and out of the politics that followed, China emerged with a republic and a president. The parliament was a 'travesty of democracy' with votes 'openly sold and openly quoted on the market' (although perhaps the Chinese were simply anticipating what election campaign financing in democracies would finally produce).[4] Western powers like Britain, Germany and France as well as Japan, with their eyes on the territory and commercial rights they had acquired in China, did nothing to support China's attempt at democratization. The effort by the president, Yuan Shih-K'ai to re-instate dynastic rule in China with himself as emperor failed and with his death in 1916 China entered a period of warlord rule. Peace and political stability were a long time in coming as the Nationalist Party in alliance with the Communist Party first fought with the warlords, then with each other and then with the Japanese during the period of the Japanese invasion (1931–45) and then again with each other after Japan's defeat. This process came to an end when the Communists entered Peking in February of 1949 and the Kuomintang retreated to Formosa, leaving behind a patent law. This 1949 law (a version of which had been prepared in 1944) that built on a patent measure of 1932, appears to have followed a standard Western format of excluding chemicals, food and pharmaceuticals and requiring local working.[5] There is not much evidence of patenting activity under these laws. It appears that no more than a few hundred patents were issued under the 1912 law.[6] Given China's history of more or less perpetual conflict during this period this is hardly surprising.

[3] Alford, *To Steal a Book is an Elegant Offense*, 37–8.
[4] C. P. Fitzgerald, *The Birth of Communist China*, Penguin, England, 1964, 47.
[5] Alford, *To Steal a Book is an Elegant Offense*, 52.
[6] On the number of patents issued see ibid. 42 and fn. 79 on page 145 giving two different estimates.

Despite the fact that there was virtually no patenting activity in China during this time, there was innovative activity. Quite remarkably, China was able to build between 1860 and 1949 a modern chemical industry.[7] The crucial period was the Nanking Decade of 1928–37, a period of brief stability under Chiang Kai-Shek when state-of-the-art methods of manufacture were spread widely in China.

Patents in communist China

One of the many challenges facing a communist state was to develop an approach to the regulation of innovative activity. This was not easy as Marx's theory hardly had much to say that was positive about the use of law. Capitalist law defined rights of ownership over the means of production and was the formal means through which the ruling class extracted surplus value from scientific workers. To the extent that there was a positive theory, it rested on the idea that in communism workers would experience un-alienated labour and that the distribution of the fruits of that labour would be governed by the principle of need.[8] There was also the practical problem that both China and Russia were operating in an increasing internationalized economy dominated by capitalist states bent on expanding the patent system and using it to control the process of technology transfer. In other words, even if one saw international patent law as part of a world capitalist system, one still might need it in order to help processes of technology acquisition and transfer.

Communist Russia had had to confront these kinds of issues after the revolution of 1917. Before then a privilege system for patents had operated in Russia for much of the nineteenth century, with a patent law along the lines of the German model being enacted in 1896.[9] Following the 1917 revolution the Decree of Inventions was signed by Lenin. It eliminated pre-revolutionary law and introduced the broad principles of inventors' certificates.[10] Conventional patent law made a re-appearance in 1924 when Russia enacted a patent law that again followed German law, this

---

[7] For the history see James Reardon-Anderson, 'Chemical Industry in China, 1860–1949', 2 (1986) *Osiris, 2nd Series*, 177.

[8] For a full discussion of the implications of Marx's theories for intellectual property see P. Drahos, *A Philosophy of Intellectual Property*, Dartmouth, Aldershot, 1996, Ch. 5.

[9] See Jan Vojacek, *A Survey of the Principal National Patent Systems*, Prentice-Hall Inc., New York, 1936, 153 and W. A. Van Caenegem, 'Inventions in Russia: From Public Good to Private Property', 4 (1993) *Australian Intellectual Property Journal*, 232.

[10] Van Caenegem, 'Inventions in Russia', 232, 233.

law allowing for the protection of pharmaceutical processes.[11] Another law followed in 1931 under which an inventor could seek a conventional patent or opt for the protection of the invention by means of an inventor's certificate.[12] Under the inventor's certificate system, the holder of the certificate could not commercially exploit the invention, but was entitled to remuneration based on the use value of the invention. A cap was set on the amount of remuneration, but the inventor was given other privileges such as better accommodation and access to better scientific facilities. It was the state that had the right of commercial exploitation, a right that was administered by the exploitation offices that were part of the nationalized industrial enterprises of each industrial sector. This system of dual protection lasted until the break up of the Soviet Union.

The socialist character of this system lies in the fact that the inventor's right of remuneration no longer depends on his ability to exploit the invention in the marketplace. A patent in itself is not a reward, but merely an opportunity to exploit a set of rights in the marketplace. A socially useful invention might not deliver an inventor anything if he does not have the capacity to exploit it and conversely the market might over-reward inventions that are backed by commercially clever tricks and strategies (evergreening by pharmaceutical companies being an obvious example). An inventor's certificate entitled one to remuneration based on the use value of the invention, but the exploitation of the invention itself was carried out by the state. The certificate system is thus consistent with the idea of maintaining the links between the inventor, his labour and a reward for socially useful labour (the principle of unalienated labour), while ensuring that the social benefits of the invention are maximized because the agency carrying out that distribution is interested in social returns and not private returns (the principle of distributing according to need).

The Russian system with its twin model of protection for inventions thus provided emerging communist states with a model that was both consistent with socialist principles and that, by running in parallel with patent law, offered a way of dealing with issues of technology transfer and foreign investment. This system with variations in detail eventually spread to many communist states, including China. In 1950, China adopted a twin-track approach enacting a patent law and an inventor's certificate system.[13] Russia had introduced its German style patent law in

---

[11] Vojacek, *A Survey of the Principal National Patent Systems*, 155.

[12] Ibid.

[13] The Provisional Regulations Governing Inventions and Patent Rights and the Provisional Regulations on Awards of Inventions, Technical Improvements and Rationalization

1924 as part of a process of stabilizing its domestic economy and China in introducing a patent law in 1950 reportedly had a similar goal in mind.[14]

No specialist patent office was created to administer these 1950 laws. Instead they were administered by the Central Bureau of Technological Management of the Finance and Economic Committee of the General Administration of Commerce.[15] Inventors did not flock to the Central Bureau. Only six certificates and four patents were issued between 1950 and 1963.[16] The patent system during this period appears to have fallen into disuse while the certificate system was further refined in 1954 providing for a level of remuneration to the inventor based on the savings in production made by adopting the invention.[17] As the currents that were to propel China into Mao's Cultural Revolution of 1966–76 grew ever stronger, the use of patent rights as a regulatory tool grew ever weaker. In fact no system of incentives for innovation could have worked in a society that was beginning to depict its scientific intellectuals as agents for the subversion of socialism. In 1963 two sets of regulations were introduced, one for technological improvement and the other for inventions.[18] Patents for inventions were discontinued and the previous certificate system replaced by an award system that offered lower levels of financial remuneration based on fixed sums to be paid once. Non-monetary rewards such as access to better medical care remained part of the 1963 scheme. Inventions were declared to be the property of the state. Not much is known about how this system was actually administered, but there is evidence of awards being paid despite the various press polemics against the

Proposals Relating to Production. See David Ben Kay, 'The Patent Law of the People's Republic of China in Perspective', 33 (1985) *UCLA L. Rev. 331*, 343, fns. 47 and 48. Barden Gale states that the Soviet system of inventor's certificates was not introduced until 1954. See Barden N. Gale, 'The Concept of Intellectual Property in the People's Republic of China: Inventors and Inventions', 74 (1978) *The China Quarterly*, 334, 347.

[14] Kay, 'The Patent Law of the People's Republic of China', 343–4.

[15] Alford, *To Steal a Book is an Elegant Offense*, 58.

[16] Kay, 'The Patent Law of the People's Republic of China', 345.

[17] Kay, 'The Patent Law of the People's Republic of China', 346. Article 7 of the Provisional Regulations on Awards for Inventions, Technical Improvements and Rationalization Proposals Concerning Production set out a table that prescribed monetary awards based on a sliding table of percentages for different values that were saved by an industrial enterprise in a 12-month period as a result of adopting the invention. For breakthrough inventions that opened up new fields the table did not apply, the issue of award being settled by the Government Administration Council (see Article 8). An English version of the Regulations is to be found in Albert P. Blaustein (ed.), *Fundamental Legal Documents of Communist China*, Fred B. Rothman & Co., New Jersey, 1962, 523.

[18] Gale, 'The Concept of Intellectual Property in the People's Republic of China', 334, 337.

use of material incentives. Local 'technical innovations units' attached to enterprises appear to have had a role in payments and the diffusion of invention information.[19] During the Cultural Revolution payments for inventions were abandoned.[20]

Opening the door to patents

The open-door policy that the Central Committee of the Communist Party approved in 1978 also signalled the beginning of a new era for the patent system in China. Regulations based on inventor's certificates were issued in 1978, 1979 and 1982, but the real game had shifted towards the development of a patent law a few years earlier.[21] In 1973 Ren Jian Xin, later to become Chief Justice of the Chinese Supreme Court led China's first delegation to the World Intellectual Property Organization (WIPO).[22] After the visit to WIPO, discussion in China of adopting a patent system became more serious. In 1978 China declared its 'Four Modernizations' 10-year plan for agriculture, industry, science and technology, and national defence. Support for a patent law as part of this modernization process came from Deng Xiaoping himself.[23] A patent drafting committee set up in 1979 began studying the patent law of countries such as the US, West Germany and Japan.

One of the major factors for this change in strategy was the realization that China's modernization would depend on foreign trade. Historically both Imperial and Communist China had tended to treat foreign trade with disdain based on a belief in the importance of self-sufficiency. By the 1970s many analysts in China had concluded that access to foreign technology was critical to China's economic growth and that this meant developing foreign trade since China's experiments with self-reliance had failed, one spectacular example being Mao's small-scale industrialization production programme, the Great Leap Forward.[24] Gaining access to foreign technology through foreign trade meant engaging with the patent system since many of the world's most important technologies were

---

[19] Gale, 'The Concept of Intellectual Property in the People's Republic of China', 334, 351 and 353.

[20] Kay, 'The Patent Law of the People's Republic of China', 350.   [21] Ibid. 352.

[22] Andrew Mertha, *The Politics of Piracy*, Cornell University Press, Ithaca and London, 2005, 78.

[23] Alford, *To Steal a Book is an Elegant Offense*, 69.

[24] Y. Y. Kueh and Christopher Howe, 'China's International Trade: Policy and Organizational Change and their Place in the "Economic Readjustment"', 100 (1984) *The China Quarterly*, 813, 814.

the subject of patent protection. Importing technologies related to oil exploration, coal mining, steelmaking, electronics and petrochemicals was critical to China's growth plans. A patent system was thought to have value as a signalling device for the purposes of foreign direct investment. Chinese economists began to lay the conceptual foundations for this change in trade policy by analysing the gains from trade and reconciling a labour theory of value (the foundation of Marxist economics) with the theory of comparative advantage.[25] Aside from this, China's trade negotiation with the US during the 1970s, which began after President Nixon's visit in 1972 and led to a China–US trade agreement in 1979, revealed to China that its entry into the world's trade regime would be affected by the way it handled US intellectual property rights.[26] Led by Wu Heng, the drafting group on patent law produced a report in 1979. In the same year the National Patent Bureau was also established, the Bureau taking on the patent law drafting task.[27] In 1980 the Patent Bureau with responsibilities for the examination of patents was established under the direct administration of the State Council, but managed by the State Science and Technology Commission.[28] Consultations with WIPO about the patent law took place and China joined WIPO in 1980. After 5 years of work and numerous drafts, a bill was produced.

In 1984, the Standing Committee of the Sixth National People's Congress adopted a patent law that become effective in 1985.[29] Its principal features included a 15-year patent term, the exclusion from patentability of pharmaceutical products and substances produced from chemical processes,[30] an 18-month publication rule, deferred examination,[31] pre-grant

[25] For an account of the theorizing see Shu-yun Ma, 'Recent Changes in China's Pure Trade Theory', 106 (1986) *The China Quarterly*, 291.

[26] The trade agreement is the Agreement on Trade Relations Between the United States of America and the People's Republic of China, signed at Beijing on 7 July 1979, available at untreaty.un.org/unts/60001_120000/5/24/00009178.pdf. Article 6 of this agreement opens by stating that both China and the US recognize the importance of the effective protection of patents.

[27] Mertha, *The Politics of Piracy*, 82.

[28] Ibid. 88. According to SIPO's website the Chinese Patent Office was established in 1980. See www.sipo.gov.cn/sipo_English/about/basicfacts/overview/200707/t20070723_182116.htm.

[29] An English translation of this 1984 law is available in Kay, 'The Patent Law of the People's Republic of China', Appendix.

[30] Article 25 excluded food, beverages, flavourings, pharmaceutical products and substances obtained by chemical processes.

[31] Article 35 required an applicant to request examination within 3 years of the date of filing.

opposition[32] and a compulsory licensing system based on a local work-ing requirement.[33] It was a model suitable for a developing country, but China soon discovered that the US had other ideas about what constituted an appropriate set of patent standards for developing countries. During the 1980s and 1990s patents along with other intellectual property rights become the subject of intense bilateral negotiations between China and the US. The basic pattern consisted of US complaints about Chinese stand-ards of protection followed by threats of trade retaliation against Chinese exports to the US market leading to a negotiated settlement of some kind, usually in the form of a memorandum of understanding (MOU) in which China would agree to improve its standards.[34] China was also seeking membership of the WTO and knew that it would have to satisfy the US on intellectual property as part of the process of joining. Naturally the US continued to set the bar of its satisfaction as high as it could.

The MOU of 1992 between China and the US resulted in some signifi-cant changes to China's patent law.[35] In it China agreed to a 20-year patent term, the patentability of all chemical inventions, including product phar-maceuticals and a compulsory licensing provision that followed what was then draft Agreement on Trade-Related Aspects of Intellectual Property Rights (TRIPS) language. It also agreed to try and enact these reforms by 1 January 1993, something it achieved with the Seventh National People's Congress approving amendments to China's patent law in September of 1992. The law came into effect on 1 January 1993. In exchange the US agreed to terminate its investigation under its special 301 trade law proc-ess. The 1993 amendments saw chemical inventions become patentable, the patent term lengthened to 20 years, the removal of pre-grant oppo-sition and the introduction of post-grant opposition. (In subsequent amendments post-grant opposition has been removed.)[36] In a talk given

---

[32] Article 41 allowed any person to oppose the application within 3 months from the date of announcement of the application.

[33] Article 51 obliged the patentee to make the product or use the process in China or author-ize other persons to do so.

[34] Peter Yu, 'Intellectual Property, Economic Development, and the China Puzzle', Occasional Papers in Intellectual Property Law, Drake University Law School, No. 1, September 2007, 11–13.

[35] Memorandum of Understanding Between the Government of the United States of America and the Government of the People's Republic of China on the Protection of Intellectual Property, 17 January 1992, available at http://untreaty.un.org/unts/144078_158780/4/4/12279.pdf.

[36] China's patent law was revised in 2000 and post-grant opposition removed. Under the present law a person may at any time request the Patent Re-examination Board to declare

in 1996 the then Commissioner of Patents, Gao Lulin, described the 1993 reforms as creating 'a favorable legal environment for expanding international trade, promoting technological exchange with foreign countries, and attracting foreign investment' as well as creating 'favorable conditions for China to accede to the World Trade Organization'.[37]

China became a member of the WTO in December of 2001. It entered the WTO after some 15 years of negotiation and having agreed to some 900 pages of legal text. Disputes over intellectual property standards with the US had occupied a disproportionate amount of time in those years and in negotiating those disputes China was in the position of knowing that it would have to satisfy the US before the US agreed to its membership. Its second major amendment to its patent law was adopted by the People's Congress in August of 2000, a little more than a year before it joined the WTO. It brought China's patent law into closer alignment with TRIPS and met the promises that China had made to the WTO Working Party that had been established in 1987 to oversee its accession to the WTO.

China continues the process of adjusting its patent system, but it does so as a WTO member and while disputes between the US and China over intellectual property continue they are disputes between two players of equal bargaining power. The third amendment to China's patent law that was approved in December of 2008 reflects a process of sovereign adjustment to China's economic context. So, for example, China has adopted the absolute novelty standard to be found in the European Patent Convention (EPC) moving away from the US standard of relative novelty. It has made it easier for inventors in China to seek patent protection abroad by removing the requirement that an inventor first file in China, but like the US it has imposed a foreign filing licence requirement. It has redrafted its compulsory licence provisions maximizing the capacity of the government to issues such licences under the standard to be found in TRIPS. The US has consistently argued for minimal compulsory licensing powers of government. China has also included a disclosure of origin obligation with respect to inventions relating to genetic resources, an obligation that

---

the patent invalid. See Article 45 of the Patent Law of the People's Republic of China. The number of requests for invalidation forms a tiny fraction of the number of patents granted in any one year and an even smaller fraction of the total number of granted patents. For example in 2006 there were 356 requests for invalidation. In the same year SIPO granted almost 58,000 patents – see www.sipo.gov.cn/sipo_English/laws/annualreports/ndbg2006/200707/t20070702_176830.htm.

[37] Gao Lulin, 'New Development of the Chinese Patent System', 7(1) (1996) *World Libraries*, www.worlib.org/vol07no1/lulin_v07n1.shtml#about.

the US has argued should not be a part of patent law. At the same time it has signalled to foreign investors that it takes enforcement seriously by improving enforcement through a series of measures including raising the penalties for patent infringement.

The great leap forward: the State Intellectual Property Office

Today China's State Intellectual Property Office (SIPO) is the third largest office in the world as measured by patent applications received.[38] Only the US and Japan are ahead of it. In terms of formal structure, SIPO is directly under the State Council, the highest executive organ in China with responsibilities in crucial areas such as finance, national defence and the economy. In its short history SIPO has been relocated several times within China's overall administrative structure leading one analyst to argue that it has not yet developed a strong political base and influence.[39] As we shall see below it certainly has developed technical competence.

SIPO has experienced large-scale growth over a short period of time with both domestic and foreign patent applicants contributing to that growth.[40] Japan and the US, as earlier chapters have shown, have had a much longer institutional history of patents, going back to the end of the eighteenth century in the case of the US and the end of the nineteenth century in the case of Japan. China's institutional history perhaps can be said to begin with its 1950 regulations but given that the patent provisions fell into abeyance it is more realistic to pick either 1980, the year that SIPO was established, or the 1984 patent law as the starting point. On other measures the growth of China's use of the patent system is also impressive. For instance, China became bound by the Patent Cooperation Treaty (PCT) on 1 January 1994 and since then has risen rapidly as a country from which PCT international applications originate.[41]

As always with patent statistics there are qualifications. China's figure for 2007 of 5,470 international PCT applications, which places it seventh, is a long way behind the US which is ranked first with 53,147 applications. Worth noting also is that China's ranking is disproportionately dependent

---

[38] *The WIPO Patent Report*, 2007 edn. See Chart B3 available at www.wipo.int/ipstats/en/statistics/patents/patent_report_2007.html#P173_14118.

[39] Mertha, *The Politics of Piracy*, 90.

[40] For some figures that show this very rapid growth see www.sipo.gov.cn/sipo_English/laws/whitepapers/200805/t20080506_395881.htm. In 2007 domestic patent applications formed about 62% of the 245,161 applications.

[41] See PCT, *Yearly Review 2007*, WIPO, Geneva, 10, Table 3.1.

upon the patenting activity of one company. In 2007 the Chinese multi-national, Huawei Technologies was ranked fourth in terms of PCT applications with 1,365 applications published in 2007.[42] Huawei's current international filing dominance is also true domestically. In 2006 it filed almost 6,000 applications, more than double that of the next domestic company.[43] While published applications in a given year do not match the applications filed (international applications are generally published 18 months after filing) WIPO's PCT data shows that in a number of developed and developing countries PCT activity is disproportionately concentrated in one or two large companies. Chinese universities are also applying for patents in the kinds of numbers that US universities do.[44] Just like India and Brazil, China is following a regulatory model that sees universities and research institutes being integrated into a pro-patent culture. How much all this patent filing activity represents an actual growth in innovation in China as opposed to growth in patents is hard to say. One recent analysis paints a bleak picture suggesting that when the patent statistics for China are more closely scrutinized they show that Chinese patent law has had little impact on domestic innovation with foreigners dominating key high-technology sectors.[45]

SIPO has grown rapidly for the simple reason that the government sees patents as part of its overall strategy of economic growth through trade. Once Chinese exporters received the benefits of lower tariffs as a result of WTO membership, dealing with private tariffs in the form of patents became important in terms of managing China's export markets. More and more Chinese firms, for example, have become involved in patent litigation in the US market, fighting patent infringement cases in order to defend lucrative export markets.[46] Having a patent office that has state-of-the-art searching expertise and databases along with an expert patent examination workforce in key technology sectors has come to be seen in China as a necessary part of international business.

[42] Ibid. 12.

[43] See the table at www.sipo.gov.cn/sipo_English/laws/annualreports/ndbg2006/200707/t20070702_176830.htm. Huawei's patenting strategy may have been influenced by IBM, itself a big patent filer and which provided Huawei with management consulting services for a number of years.

[44] David Cyranoski, 'Property Rights Go East', 438, *Nature*, 24 November 2005, 420.

[45] Deming Liu, 'The Transplant Effect of the Chinese Patent Law', 5 (2006) *Chinese Journal of International Law*, 733.

[46] For example, in 2003 Cisco commenced patent litigation against Huawei Technologies. See http://newsroom.cisco.com/dlls/corp_012303.html. For a description of the US patent litigation to which the Chinese Battery Association has been a party see Robert Westbrook, 'China's Fight for Legitimacy', *IP Law and Business*, February 2006, 14.

SIPO has moved to garner capacity-building resources from as many sources as possible as quickly as possible. It has sought cooperation with WIPO, the Trilateral Offices and educational institutions that might be in a position to help with training in patent law.[47] The areas it has targeted are the automation of its systems, patent documentation and examiner training. Its annual reports reveal an extensive bilateral cooperation programme that takes in many patent offices including the US, Austria, Brazil, Bulgaria, France, Israel, Japan and Korea. SIPO appears to be an MOU signing machine with every annual report revealing yet another set of MOUs for the year. But as we have seen it is in the exchange of examiners and examiner training that real trust is built between offices. Two patent offices have played a crucial long-term role in developing SIPO's capacity. The German PO began cooperating with SIPO in 1981 and that cooperation continues today (interview, German PO, 2008).[48] The European Patent Office (EPO) has provided examiner training.[49] At one stage in the history of SIPO the bulk of Chinese examiners had been trained by the EPO (interview, EPO). In 1997 the two offices signed a treaty on the transfer of the EPO's EPOQUE search system to SIPO.[50] Similarly, the EPO's 1995 Annual Report describes an ongoing programme of technical cooperation focussing on 'automation projects, basic and further training for personnel, exchange of documentation and the supply of information products'.[51] As we saw in Chapter 2, the EPO's agenda is to promote its version of patent examination quality through a sharing of the technical tools of search analysis. But it is also clear that the Chinese PO through its cooperation with the EPO and the German PO wants to match the quality standards of these two offices.

On the patent documentation front, SIPO has a global collection strategy (for example, in 2001 it received 3,450,000 full-text patent specifications from 28 countries).[52] Just as importantly it has been investing in

---

[47] For example, its 2003 Annual Report refers to the 10 years of cooperation between it and John Marshall Law School in the US and the fact that some seventy SIPO employees have received training at John Marshall. See www.sipo.gov.cn/sipo_English/laws/annualreports/ndbg2003/200412/t20041214_37375.htm.

[48] On current cooperation between the German PO and SIPO see German Patent and Trademark Office, *Annual Report 2007*, 81–2.

[49] www.sipo.gov.cn/sipo_English/laws/annualreports/ndbg2000/200202/t20020227_34014.htm.

[50] EPO, *Annual Report 1997*, 41.

[51] See EPO, *Annual Report 1995*, 62.

[52] www.sipo.gov.cn/sipo_English/laws/annualreports/ndbg2001/200204/t20020426_34018.htm.

building up its collection of non-patent information. Moreover this information appears to be being used in targeted ways. Large generalized patent databases are not of especial interest to individual users who obviously are interested in the patent landscape in their given industry. Interestingly, SIPO appears to be building such specialized databases, its 2001 Annual Report stating that it 'had established over 100 specialized databases for 20 enterprises, including Haier Group, Military Medicine and Science Institution, Chunlan, Jinling etc.' It had established 'Yanglin Agriculture Patent Database for the China intellectual property information center of Yanglin'.[53] Developing specialized industry patent databases is a strategy that was adopted early in the twentieth century by US companies.

SIPO's intense investment in capacity building has paid off in various ways. It was admitted as an International Searching Authority (ISA) in 1994, meaning that it is a player in the top tier of patent offices that will dominate the emerging system of global patent administration. In 2007 it became one of twenty offices to accept full electronic filing of PCT applications. SIPO along with the Japanese PO and the Korean Intellectual Property Office (KIPO) form the Asian Trilateral and now have regular Trilateral Policy dialogues.[54] At a technical level the three offices are focussing on cooperating in the automation of their systems.

SIPO is part of a tiered administrative structure in which patent bureaus operate at the provincial government level to deal with issues of infringement and enforcement as well as playing a role in training, the diffusion of patent information, advising on patentability issues and encouraging Chinese enterprises to file for patents and to take up patented technologies. These local administrative authorities for patents and other intellectual property rights have been established in China's thirty-one provincial governments with powers of administrative enforcement.[55] But it is only SIPO that carries out the examination of patents. One of the principal advantages of this administrative structure of enforcement is that it is cheaper than the option of using the courts to settle disputes (interview, SIPO). This provincial level of patent bureau management is itself a layered structure with bureaus being divided into first tier, second tier and third tier, with

---

[53] www.sipo.gov.cn/sipo_English/laws/annualreports/ndbg2001/200204/t20020426_34018.htm.

[54] www.sipo.gov.cn/sipo_English/laws/annualreports/ndbg2003/200412/t20041214_37375.htm.

[55] See www.sipo.gov.cn/sipo_English/about/Administration/200707/t20070719_178243.htm.

first-tier offices operating with the most autonomy and power. This decentralized and federal-like level of patent administration allows the provinces to compete at the level of patent administration, with, for example, the Sichuan province investing in its patent bureau (ranked as a first-tier patent bureau) as part of a strategy to attract investment in the region, especially from foreign sources.[56] All other things being equal, provinces that offer foreign companies a strong enforcement service through their local administrative and judicial bodies are likely to do better in terms of investment. Large gaps in capability exist amongst the provincial patent bureaus (interview, SIPO). Another example of regulatory competition in China's multi-tiered level of patent bureau administration comes from Hong Kong. The Hong Kong Intellectual Property Department administers a patent law that is separate from mainland China, despite the fact that Hong Kong is a Special Administrative Region of China. The Hong Kong PO is not an examining office. Rather it re-registers patents that have been granted by SIPO, the UK PO or the EPO in which the UK has been designated for grant.[57] Despite being a registration-only office Hong Kong officials at the interview suggested that there was growth potential for their office if they concentrated on enforcement issues since many goods on their way to export markets travel through Hong Kong.[58] Registering a patent in Hong Kong potentially broadens enforcement options for patent owners.

Once China joined the PCT, the number of patent applications travelling via the PCT began to increase. Today about half of the applications that China receives from foreigners comes through the PCT pipeline.[59] SIPO began to experience the kinds of workload problems that other much more established offices were experiencing (interview, SIPO). The solution was the familiar one of opting to recruit more examiners. At first the aim was to recruit people who had had at least 5 years experience in the relevant technical field, but the urgency of the problem gave way to having to recruit graduates. The majority of graduates being recruited have at least a masters degree. Patent examiners operate on a higher pay scale than other civil servants, but the workloads are heavy and overtime pay options appear limited. Training for new recruits is short (about

---

[56] For a full discussion of this level of provincial patent administration see Mertha, *The Politics of Piracy*, 90–100.

[57] See Section 3 of the Patents (Designation of Patents Offices) Notice (HK).

[58] Interview, Intellectual Property Department of Hong Kong, December 2005.

[59] WIPO, *Patent Report 2007*, 46.

4 months) because of the need to get new examiners working. Further training opportunities take the form of short courses. Life for new examiners appears to consist of steep learning curves and long hours in order to deal with a seemingly never-ending queue of applications. In 2007, SIPO's workforce of examiners stood at almost 2,700.[60] First-action pendency data is not clear from the annual reports, but the time taken to examine an application in 2007 after request appears to be around 26 months.[61] In terms of the backlog WIPO's data shows that for 2005, SIPO had a little over 200,000 applications pending examination.[62]

Workload problems mean that SIPO, like other major offices, has an interest in cooperating with other offices in terms of the exploitation of examination results produced by those offices. At the same time there is a certain amount of wariness in accepting the examination results of other major offices. 'It is not so easy to share and accept examination results [of other offices]' (interview, SIPO). The interview suggested that the patent offices of different countries still have different interests, although exactly what these might be was not clearly articulated. The translation of patent documents into Chinese was one practical difficulty that was expressly mentioned. China has not been a participant in patent superhighway arrangements in the way that Japan and the USPTO have been. So while cooperation is seen as important it is a careful and prudent cooperation that keeps an eye on building China's capacity to do its own examination work.

The Asian Trilaterals

China, Korea and Japan constitute the Asian Trilateral Offices. Their first meeting took place in Tokyo in September of 2001.[63] Both collectively and individually these three offices have become a force for the spread and harmonization of patent law in the Asia Pacific region. All three are ISA offices for the purposes of the PCT.[64] Cooperation with IP offices from Association of Southeast Asian Nations (ASEAN) countries is a priority and in some cases has gone as far as recognition of an office's examination results. So, for example, a patent registered in Korea will be accepted without examination in Singapore and Malaysia.[65] Amongst themselves, the Asian Trilaterals have agreed to examiner exchanges and the electronic exchange of priority documents. The mutual exploitation of examination results is at the 'road map' stage.[66]

[60] SIPO, *Annual Report 2007*, 30.
[61] Ibid.
[62] WIPO, *Patent Report 2007*, 38.
[63] KIPO, *Annual Report 2001*, 38.
[64] KIPO began to function as an ISA in 1999.
[65] KIPO, *Annual Report 2004*, 39.
[66] SIPO, *Annual Report 2007*, 71.

With Japan as a common member of both the Asian Trilaterals and the Trilaterals, the two Trilateral groups held a meeting in 2007 aimed at improving the efficiency of their examination systems and to harmonize their office systems, a harmonization much easier to effect than the harmonization of patent law.[67] These five offices also constitute the top five offices in terms of the filing of patent applications.

All three Asian Trilaterals devote resources to spreading IP consciousness and awareness to as many segments of society as possible. KIPO's national programme of setting up inventions clubs in secondary schools is an example.[68] Aside from this missionary work, KIPO also offers Korean companies practical assistance in terms of navigating a world full of patent shoals. Its 2001 Annual Report, for example, describes a patent mapping service that it offers to Korean companies free of charge.[69]

The tiger office

The rise of SIPO and Japan's prominence as an economic and patenting power can cause one to overlook the rise of KIPO, a rise that took place after the Second World War when Korea became free of a brutal Japanese occupation that had followed its annexure by Japan in 1910. After the Second World War, Korea was divided into two distinct political entities that were to become key sites of military and political conflict in the Cold War period. In 1946 Philip Siggers, a US patent attorney, arrived in Seoul and became an advisor to the South Korean Bureau of Patents that had been established in January of 1946.[70] The Bureau was housed in a building with no water, no sewer connection and one inefficient small wood-burning Japanese stove for heat. The patent law which had come into operation in October of 1946 had been drafted by an army officer. Prior to that Korea's patent law consisted of what the Japanese had imposed. Siggers after examining the 1946 law concluded that it was too complicated for the Korean office to administer and recommended a total revision. The office had almost no resources. Aside from some copies of Japanese patents there were no prior art materials and a paper shortage meant no documents could be published. No examinations took place and nor were patents granted (surprisingly there seem to have been a small number of applications). In Sigger's words,

---

[67] KIPO, *Annual Report 2007*, 11.   [68] KIPO, *Annual Report 2001*, 31.

[69] See KIPO, *Annual Report 2001*, 31–2. The patent map website is www.patentmap.or.kr/.

[70] Siggers' description of his experience can be found in Philip E. Siggers, 'The Nursing of an Infant Patent Office', 30 (1948) *Journal of the Patent Office Society*, 531.

'Few Koreans know there is a patent office or have any conception of an invention or the purpose of a patent system.'[71]

Some sixty years later KIPO can claim to be the most efficient patent office in the world. It has reduced patent pendency to slightly less than 10 months and has become the first port of call for some US multinationals when it comes to starting the PCT process.[72] It probably has the most advanced electronic system of all the patent offices in the world with the application process, notification of examination results, payment of fees and aspects of the opposition procedure all being handled online. The high degree of electronic automation has been one of the reasons that it has been able to bring down the pendency period. The change from the destitute office that Siggers describes in 1946 is a classic rags-to-riches story.

These days there is a lot more public knowledge about the patent system in Korea than there was in 1946. Patents and other intellectual property rights are seen by Korean policy makers as being a key component of an economic growth strategy. During the 1980s Korea found itself on the receiving end of US trade pressure over its intellectual property standards. A bilateral agreement between the two countries in 1986, which became an important precedent for the US, was something of a turning point for South Korea. It began to reform its intellectual property laws and pay more attention to the enforcement of those laws. Korean policy makers realized that with TRIPS, patents would simply be part of the rules of the global business game. Playing the role of resister seemed futile. Today securing patents and engaging in patent litigation is seen as part and parcel of the global high-technology businesses in which multinationals compete. In a 2005 interview, the Commissioner of Patents Kim Jong-Kap described the business world as being in a 'patent war', something that had led KIPO to establish a support centre for Korean businesses which had intellectual property rights abroad to defend.[73]

Aside from its investment in smart electronic systems, KIPO has been able to build a high quality patent examination workforce. At the time of the interview in 2005 I was told that 67% of examiners had a PhD (the total number of examiners was about 700). Recruiting highly qualified staff is not the problem that it is in many other countries. Government jobs

---

[71] Ibid. 531, 542.   [72] KIPO, *Annual Report 2007*, 8.

[73] See www.kipo.go.kr/kpo2/user.tdf. KIPO has established the Centre for Overseas Protection of IPRs. This centre provides free advice to Korean companies and subsidizes the costs of litigation in countries where an infringement of Korean intellectual property rights has taken place. See KIPO, *Annual Report 2007*, 45.

remain sought after and KIPO offers good conditions of employment. By way of illustration I was told that in the last recruitment round there was a ratio of twenty persons for one position. Whether having so much highly qualified scientific talent locked up in patent examination work is a good innovation strategy is a question worth asking, but in any case it gives KIPO obvious benefits in terms of the services that it can offer.

Like the Japanese PO, KIPO has gone down the path of outsourcing patent searching in order to relieve the burden on its examiners and improve its pendency period. In 1996 it began to outsource some of its patent searches to the Korean Intellectual Property Institute (KIPI) and more recently has allowed private contractors to bid for search work.[74] The quality of outsourced search reports is checked following a Japanese system in which KIPO's examiners check the results of some outsourced searches, especially in cases where the outsourced search produces no prior art. Where prior art is found the KIPI suffers a penalty. KIPO takes the view that this is an effective means of quality control.

Running a high-quality search system of the kind that KIPI does is a costly exercise, beyond the capacities of most developing countries.[75] KIPI has a search force of about 350 working across all the important areas of technology, including mechanics, chemistry and electronics.[76] Those searchers also have to have foreign technical language skills in order to be able to read, for instance, the patents registered in the US or Japan. In order to be able to find relevant prior art those searchers also have to have access to a range of databases that contain the technological and patent documentation of the world's principal markets where patenting takes place, most obviously the EU, Japan and the US. All of this has to be backed by an investment in continual training and ever-smarter electronic systems that can keep pace with the demand for searches being generated by patent applicants.

The sophistication and quality of KIPO's operation means that it can form its own judgements about the quality of work of other offices. KIPO does study closely what other offices do, especially the Trilateral Offices, but the decisions of the EPO are not influential in KIPO in the way that they are in, for example, the Vietnamese PO. There is no preset commitment to

---

[74] KIPI, *Annual Report 2006*, 6.
[75] According to KIPI's Annual Report for 2007 its expenditure for 2007 was KRW50.6 billion and its income was KRW51.5 billion. A simple currency conversion into US dollars without any adjustments sees KRW50 billion become US$49.6 million.
[76] KIPI, *Annual Report 2007*, 8.

the decisions of one office. KIPO draws its own conclusions when it comes to patent examinations. It is also an office that is keen to expand its sphere of influence, especially as an ISA under the PCT system. At the time of the interview it was an ISA for India, Indonesia, Mongolia, the Philippines and Singapore, but had plans to continue to expand that list (India in any case has become an ISA). My interviews in New Zealand and Thailand revealed that KIPO had been there offering its examination services. By expanding its workload it also expands its revenue. KIPO is entirely self-funded from its fees. Its combination of efficiency and volume of work means that it operates with a healthy profit, allowing it to establish a Korea Funds-in-Trust at WIPO in July of 2004 to bankroll various patent-related projects in developing countries.[77]

Like other patent offices it is engaged in a trust-building process. In KIPO's case this began regionally by developing joint search programmes with China and Japan and then exchanging information about the results of the searches. Amongst other things, this exercise helped the three offices to identify the kinds of databases that examiners were using and how examiners were applying standards of novelty and obviousness. These early exercises showed that examiners from different offices were not finding much of the same prior art in relation to the same application, but I was assured the results were still better than similar exercises carried out by the Trilateral Offices. In any case it is through these kinds of exercises that the three Asian offices are building trust and preparing for a world in which there will be one application and one examination that will be recognized more or less everywhere. As we saw earlier, close regional cooperation with Japan and China has produced the Asian Trilaterals. The obvious natural step is to formalize cooperation between the Trilateral Offices and the Asian Trilateral Offices. We have seen that a meeting amongst the five offices that constitute the two Trilaterals took place in 2007 and that superhighway arrangements are being put in place amongst them. KIPO has superhighway arrangements in place with the Japanese Patent Office (JPO) (in operation) and the USPTO, and it is also moving into a superhighway arrangement with the Danish PO.[78] As we saw in Chapter 6, an efficient office like KIPO will become a more attractive port of first call if it has more superhighway arrangements in place with other patent offices, because that will mean potentially more fast-tracking of patent applications in more patent offices once KIPO does the first examination.

---

[77] KIPO, *Annual Report 2007*, 48.   [78] KIPO, *Annual Report 2007*, 49.

There are a numerous ways in which KIPO is working to make itself more attractive to its corporate customers. Its 2007 Annual Report draws attention to the fact that the office accepts the PCT format for the drafting of specifications, meaning that applicants do not have to rewrite a Korean application for the PCT. A single format that can be used everywhere is one of the key short-term goals of multinational companies seeking a simpler, cheaper patent system and so this step by KIPO is, for these companies, a step in the right direction. Another change in 2007 was to allow applicants up to 18 months in which to revise patent claims. Ringing through KIPO's annual reports is the desire to build a customer-friendly administration.

Like other major patent offices, KIPO has become a significant driver of national innovation policy because for the time being the wider Korean policy community accepts that more patents mean that more wealth will be captured from innovation. My line of questioning about KIPO's influence on Korean industrial and innovation policy suggests that KIPO has both respect and influence. When it comes to developing responses on international intellectual property issues such as patent harmonization KIPO is clearly the lead bureaucracy:[79]

> KIPO is the main agency to decide the basic position of Korea on international issues. After we [KIPO] decide our position internally we collect opinions [of others] and we discuss the issue inter-governmentally.

One cannot be but impressed by KIPO's achievements. It has shown what is possible when one combines sophisticated digital automation with a highly trained workforce. Its current pendency rate of 9.8 months must provoke bouts of pendency envy from the other major offices which are all struggling with rates more than twice that. It has lots of statistical notches on its belt such as its fourth ranking in the world for PCT applications. The scale of its missionary activities in spreading and encouraging the use of patents and other intellectual property rights throughout all levels of the Korean economy and society is matched by few other offices.

The growth in volume of patent applications at KIPO has obviously been dramatic, but ultimately patents are not an end in themselves but a societal path to greater innovation and progress. A question for economists to answer is the nature of the relationship between the increase in patenting in Korea and innovation by Korean companies. Worth noting here is that one company, Samsung, was during the 1990s disproportionately

---

[79] Interview at KIPO, February 2005.

responsible for the increase in patenting in both Korea and patenting by Koreans in the US.[80] One hypothesis about Korea is that it is running a patent system that benefits only a few of its companies and those companies tend to inflate patent application numbers, an inflation that does not correspond to innovation but rather to the strategic behaviour of those companies across patenting jurisdictions (for example, Samsung's domestic patenting strategy is linked to its patenting strategy in the US market).

A related question is how much the investment in patent administration has led to Korean companies owning core technologies. Figures up to 2002 from KIPO show that Korea continued to experience a technology trade deficit because of the lack of ownership of core technologies.[81] Korea's technology trade deficit continues to concern its policy makers and has recently led to a promise from the government to invest more in the development of science and technology.[82] Upon reading this in 2008 I was reminded of a conversation I had over lunch with a KIPO examiner in 2005 after completing my interviews there. The examiner mentioned that she had a PhD from a prestigious US university in molecular biology, which led me to ask whether she had considered working in R&D in Korea. 'Yes,' she said, but went on to explain that there were not so many of those jobs in Korea.

[80] See Sunchang Jung and Keun-Young Imm, 'The Patent Activities of Korea and Taiwan: A Comparative Case Study of Patent Statistics', 24 (2002) *World Patent Information*, 303.

[81] In 2002 the technology trade deficit was US$2.1 billion. Data presented by Byung-jae Lee of KIPO at the WIPO-OECD Workshop on the use of patent statistics, 11–12 October, 2004 available at www.wipo.int/meetings/en/2004/**statistics**_workshop/presentations/**statistics**_workshop_lee.pdf.

[82] 'President Lee Myung-bak said Tuesday (Apr. 29) his new government will invest heavily in the development of science and technology to address the nation's chronic technology trade deficit.' See www.korea.net/News/news/newsView.asp?serial_no=20080429001&part=107&SearchDay=&source=.

9

Joining the patent office conga line

Brazil

Brazil: the nineteenth century

The Portuguese Crown's colonization of Brazil did not produce the kind of colonial administration of patents that the British Crown institutionalized in India. Portugal was itself a comparative latecomer to patent law. Its first patent law appears to be a royal decree of 1837 that set up a registration system for patents in which a description of the invention had to be deposited with the relevant provincial administration of the inventor along with the payment of a fee.[1] In return the inventor received a patent, but without any guarantees as to its validity.

Brazil achieved independence from Portugal in 1822. Prior to independence Brazil had become the centre of the Portuguese Empire as Prince Regent Dom João, fleeing Napoleon, set up court in Brazil in 1808.[2] In 1809 he created the alvará, a law aimed at stimulating industrial activity in an economy dominated by agriculture.[3] Before this law there is some evidence that a European-like privilege system operated in Brazil.[4] This alvará was inspired by the English Statute of Monopolies and followed its basic lines of protection for inventions. Brazil's first constitution of 1824 recognized the right of inventors to a temporary exclusive privilege or remuneration for the use of their invention. This was followed by a law

---

[1] James Fraser, *A Handy-Book of Patent and Copyright Law English and Foreign*, Sampson Low, Son, and Co., 1860, 165.

[2] Theotonio Dos Santos, 'Brazil: The Origins of a Crisis' in Ronald H. Chilcote and Joel C. Edelstein (eds.), *Latin America: The Struggle with Dependency and Beyond*, Schenkman Publishing, Cambridge Mass., 1974, 415, 422.

[3] For the information in this paragraph I am indebted to Mauricio Guaragna, who drew on M. Cruz, *A Entrada do Brasil na Convenção internacional para a Proteção da Propriedade industrial*, Paris, 1883, 1982 and D. Borges, 'Porque o Brasil entrou na Convenção de Paris em 1883', 2 *Jornal do Brasil* 26/09/1982.

[4] Edith Penrose cites one example of such a privilege granted in 1752 in relation to a rice decorticating factory. See Edith Tilton Penrose, *The Economics of the International Patent System*, John Hopkins Press, Baltimore, 1951, 12, fn. 29.

of 1830 that recognized the rights of inventors. Privileges were granted for 5 to 20 years according to the nature of the invention. The 1830 law allowed for the option of a reward for those who introduced an industry from abroad into Brazil, but since the amount was not finalized foreigners were in practice granted patents. Brazil in its 1830 law was like so many European states providing incentives for the importation of inventions.[5]

Brazilian delegates participated in the Paris Conference of 1880 in which a draft version of the Paris Convention for the Protection of Industrial Property (Paris Convention) was discussed; Brazil was one of the fourteen original signatories to the draft treaty in 1883. During the course of the negotiations over the Paris Convention, Brazil had introduced a new patent law in 1882.[6] This law operated on the basis of universal novelty. An invention was considered new if it had not been used, described or published within or outside of Brazil.[7] The term of protection was 15 years, but the state could appropriate the patent on grounds of 'public necessity or utility'.[8] Not surprisingly, given Brazil's participation in the Paris Convention negotiations, the law recognized the priority of foreigners who had been granted a patent elsewhere.[9]

Applications for a patent went to a government department, there being no specially created patent office.[10] There was no examination for novelty or utility, but the government would order the examination of an application if it appeared that the inventor was seeking a patent for an excluded category of invention (for example, an invention that was hurtful to public health or that did not offer practical results) or if the application was for an alimentary, chemical or pharmaceutical product.[11] In all other cases there was no examination.[12] Once the patent was issued the specification was published and the public allowed to make copies. There was no guarantee by the state as to novelty or utility of the invention.[13] A patent could be declared to have lapsed on a number of grounds, including if the patentee did not make effective use of it within 3 years of the date of the patent.[14] In language full of the theme of technology transfer,

[5] Ibid. 73, fn. 28.   [6] The Law of 14th of October 1882.
[7] See Article I, Section 1. An English translation of this law is to be found in Alfred Carpmael and Edward Carpmael, *The Patent Laws of the World, Collected, Edited and Indexed*, 2nd edn, William Clowes and Sons, London, 1889, 46.
[8] Article I, Section 4.   [9] Article II, Section 1.
[10] See Article III. The Secretary of State for Affairs of Agriculture, Commerce and Public Works is mentioned elsewhere in the Act.
[11] For the list of excluded inventions see Article I, Section 2. The provision dealing with limited examination was Article III, Section 2.
[12] Article III, Section 3.   [13] Article III, Section 3.   [14] Article V, Section 2.

'use' was stipulated to mean the 'effective exercise of the patented industry and the supply of the products in proportion to their employment or consumption'.[15]

Brazil's 1882 law is an example of a former colony designing a patent law for its circumstances some 60 years after having achieved independence from its colonizer. Brazil is also one of the few states to have participated in the Paris Convention negotiations in the nineteenth century, the century's single most important treaty dealing with patent rights. Obviously the Brazilian state had concluded that it was important to have a patent law. Like other states, it was careful to preserve the power of the state to acquire the patent and to make sure that there were incentives for the patent owner to work the patent. The law as drafted clearly contemplates the possible grant of patents on chemicals and pharmaceuticals, but it also sets up a system of targeted examination of such patents. Rather than commit to the expensive option of mandatory examination of all patents, Brazil's law selected those patents for examination that could potentially deeply affect state and public interests – food, chemicals and pharmaceuticals. In Brazil today, as we will see later, there operates a modern version of this targeted system of examination for pharmaceuticals.

How much difference did patent law make to Brazil's economy in the nineteenth century? The likely answer is very little. The number of monopoly privileges that were granted, especially to foreigners, did go up after the 1882 law was enacted, but in the overall context of Brazil's economic situation these would have had minimal impact.[16] We know that Brazil was, as measured by wages, a weakly performing economy in the nineteenth century.[17] The economic growth that did occur seems to have been led by exports in the agricultural and textiles sector, but this export growth did not stimulate high levels of technological progress. The lack of technological progress was, at least in part, due to low levels of educational attainment amongst the general workforce. Investment in infrastructure such as railways was low, in part due to the government's difficulty in collecting taxes. Better railways were needed to help overcome Brazil's most serious economic problem of not developing its domestic agricultural

---

[15] Article V, Section 2.2.

[16] In the last 8 years of the 1830 law there were 434 privileges granted (33% of which went to foreigners), whereas in the first 8 years of the operation of the 1882 law, 1,178 privileges were granted. In 1889, 66% of the grants went to foreigners. This information was provided by Mauricio Guaragna.

[17] For a detailed analysis see Nathaniel H. Leff, 'Economic Retardation in Nineteenth-Century Brazil', 25 (1972) *The Economic History Review* (New Series), 489.

sector, where the bulk of the workforce languished on low wages. In such a setting patent law was never likely to stimulate much investment in innovation. There were too many other major economic problems that needed to be addressed. Even though Brazil had design sovereignty over its patent law, a sovereignty which it exercised, its patent system had no real impact on economic growth.

Brazil the leader

Brazil's industrialization gathered pace from the 1930s. By the 1940s domestic manufacturing was firmly established in sectors such as textiles and furniture with imports dominating in the capital goods, consumer durables and chemical sectors. During the 1950s and 1960s Brazil turned to a policy of import substitution aimed at establishing a strong domestic presence in the automobile industry, chemicals, consumer durables and metallurgy.[18] As part of this strategy, the government established public–private enterprises in the areas of transportation equipment, chemicals and steel. The 1960s also saw a more liberal approach taken towards foreign investment, but a more interventionist approach to the question of technology transfer. Brazil began to focus more closely on the need to regulate the transfer of technology to domestic companies from foreign companies on terms and conditions that were consistent with Brazil's goals of improving its own processes of innovation and achieving a measure of technological autonomy.

Predictably the patent system came in for close scrutiny by Brazil and other developing states because the foreign owner of patented technology could use the patent monopoly to obtain a better price for the technology, as well as impose conditions on the use of the patented technology by means of contract.[19] The patent monopoly allowed the owner to maximize the private benefits of the technology transfer process whereas Brazil and other developing countries wanted to maximize the social benefits of the transfer process. Public regulation was used by developing countries to counter the private regulation of markets by largely foreign patent monopolists. The kinds of clauses that Brazil targeted included ones that limited the right of domestic importers of technology to export,

---

[18] For a detailed account see Samuel A. Morley and Gordon W. Smith, 'Import Substitution and Foreign Investment in Brazil', 23(1) (1971) *Oxford Economic Papers* (New Series), 120.

[19] See generally, Michael Blakeney, *Legal Aspects of the Transfer of Technology to Developing Countries*, ESC Publishing Limited, Oxford, 1989, Ch. 3.

production restrictions, obligations to purchase inputs from a given source, restrictions on the right of the domestic firm to improve the technology or requiring the domestic firm to grant ownership of the improvements back to the foreign firm.[20] Brazil well understood, despite the windy rhetoric discharging from Europe and the US about the precious rights of inventors, that the patent system was, in the hands of US and European multinationals, a tool of industrial domination. A state interested in economic development could not ignore the operation of its national patent system any more than it could ignore collecting taxes. In 1961, Brazil brought a draft resolution before the UN General Assembly that drew attention to the problems that the patent system raised for developing countries.[21] This draft resolution explicitly drew attention to problems of the non-working of patents in developing countries, the problems of restrictive clauses in patent licensing contracts and the effect of royalty payments on the balance of payments of developing countries. A much watered-down version of the Brazilian draft was adopted by the General Assembly. Brazil's initiative in the UN signalled the beginning of a period in which developing countries began in various international negotiations to focus much more on the operation and effects of the international patent framework on their economic development, especially on their plans to use the transfer of technology as a source of economic growth. Over the next two decades the issues surrounding patents, technology transfer and the use of compulsory licensing were debated in the UN General Assembly, the World Intellectual Property Organization (WIPO), the Paris Union of the Paris Convention, UNCTAD and eventually, as a result of a US initiative in the 1980s, the General Agreement on Tariffs and Trade.[22] In one way these issues have never gone way and simply find expression in new fora where developed and developing countries meet.

At the same time as Brazil was providing strong leadership on the international front on the issues of patents and development, it reformed its national patent law in order to gain more control over the technology transfer process. The aim behind the regulatory levers that Brazil

---

[20] Jeffrey Scott Handler, 'A Comparative Study of Technology Innovation Policy in Selected NICS', unpublished PhD thesis, Boston University, 1986, 218–19.
[21] For a discussion of the draft see Ulf Anderfelt, *International Patent-Legislation and Developing Countries*, Martinus Nijhoff, The Hague, 1971, 172–4.
[22] For a history and analysis, especially as these issues affected the negotiations over the International Code of Conduct for the Transfer of Technology, the Diplomatic Conference for the Revision of the Paris Convention and the negotiations on the Restrictive Business Practice Code see Susan K. Sell, *Power and Ideas: North-South Politics of Intellectual Property and Antitrust*, State University of New York Press, Albany, NY, 1998.

introduced was to ensure that patent-based technology transfer resulted in technological learning by domestic firms, a learning that could serve as the basis for innovation by those firms. To this end, Law 5,648 of 1970 established the National Institute of Industrial Property (NIIP) (Instituto Nacional da Propriedade Industrial). NIIP was given responsibility for, amongst other things, administering patent law and technology transfer agreements. Under its guidelines NIIP aimed to fulfil some fourteen goals, including encouraging the importation of technology over the importation of goods, the acquisition rather than leasing of the technology, reducing the costs of acquisition and eliminating restrictions on the use of that technology.[23] Technology transfer contracts had to be registered with NIIP. Control of the technology transfer process was reasonably close with different payment ceilings set for different sectors of technology and restrictions on royalty payments where Brazilian companies were in majority ownership by foreign interests. NIIP also had power of approval over contracts with restrictive clauses in them, a power it increasingly utilized during the first part of the 1970s, approving fewer contracts. This regulatory strategy for the transfer of technology ran into compliance problems as local companies made secret deals with foreign technology suppliers and multinationals used Brazilian subsidiaries to transfer technology, a transfer process that NIIP did not have the power to control.[24]

In 1971 Brazil completely revised its patent law (Law No. 5,772 which came into force on 21 December 1971).[25] An extensive list of non-patentable subject matter included substances obtained by chemical processes and pharmaceutical processes and products. The patent term was 15 years and the law operated on the basis of universal novelty for documentary and oral disclosures. A system of deferred examination was adopted, the applicant having 2 years from the date of publication of the application within which to request examination. A third party could also request examination and there was a system of pre-grant opposition. There were also detailed provisions governing assignments and licences. So, for example, assignments and licences had to be registered in order to be effective, they had to provide information as to the conditions of the licence and licences could not contain restrictions as to export. Improvements of the product or process belonged to the licensee rather than the licensor. The law contained provisions that allowed for compulsory licensing,

[23] For the full list see Handler, 'A Comparative Study of Technology Innovation Policy', 231.
[24] Ibid. 235.
[25] A detailed description of this law is available from J.W. Baxter, *World Patent Law and Practice*, 2nd edn., Sweet and Maxwell, London, 1973, 338–46.

including on the grounds of an absence of actual working of the patent in Brazil. Importation was excluded from the definition of working.

In 1996 the Brazilian Congress and President Cardoso of Brazil passed Law 9,279 that repealed the 1971 patent law. This repealing law introduced a revised patent law that met Brazil's obligations under the Agreement on Trade-Related Aspects of Intellectual Property Rights (TRIPS). TRIPS had put paid to both India's 1970 patent law and Brazil's 1971 law. Pharmaceutical products and processes were now once again patentable in Brazil. Brazil, unlike India, did not take advantage of the transitional provisions in TRIPS to delay the introduction of a product patent regime for pharmaceuticals till 1 January 2005.[26] But Brazil more than most developing-country opponents of US and European hegemony over intellectual property standard-setting had been the target of aggressive unilateral trade pressures by the US during the negotiations over TRIPS. It was one of the few countries to suffer retaliatory tariffs over patent issues under US trade law on some of its exports to the US market in 1988.[27]

Brazil's 1996 patent law marks the beginning of its re-integration into an intellectual property regime that continues to be dominated by the US and EU and their brand of knowledge capitalism. Aside from embracing a product patent regime for pharmaceuticals sooner than it had to under TRIPS, Brazil also removed pre-grant opposition and introduced criminal penalties for patent infringement, something not required by TRIPS.[28] It has, however, steadfastly defended its compulsory licensing provisions in the face of US pressure.[29] One of the grounds for a compulsory licence remains a failure by the patent owner to manufacture a

---

[26] The 1996 law had transitional provisions providing for protection of pending applications – see Articles 230 and 231. But the full application of a product patent regime appears to have been dragged out by Provisional Measure No. 2014–1 of 30 December 1999 which qualifies the operation of pipeline protection for patent applications caught by the transitional provisions of the 1996 patent law. This measure also allowed for the deferral of decisions on some product patent applications until 31 December 2004. For a discussion see Rana Gossain and Henry Sherrill, 'Significant Patent Developments in Brazil', 122 (May 2000) *Patent World*, 12.

[27] These retaliatory tariffs on Brazilian paper products, non-benzenoid drugs and consumer electronics items were proclaimed by the US President in October of 1988. See the Section 301 Table of Cases available at www.ustr.gov/Trade_Agreements/Monitoring_Enforcement/Section_Index.html.

[28] Title V of Law No. 9,279 of 14 May 1996 provides for criminalization of patent infringement.

[29] The US sought consultations with Brazil through the WTO dispute resolution process over Brazil's local working requirement as a ground of compulsory licensing. See Brazil – Measures Affecting Patent Protection – Request for Consultations by the United States,

product within Brazil and another is a level of commercialization that does not satisfy the needs of the market.[30] Compulsory licensing has been threatened much more than it has been used, but in 2007 a Presidential Decree granted a compulsory licence over two patents held by Merck over the drug Efavirenz.[31] Under Brazil's HIV/AIDS programme anti-retroviral (ARV) drugs are free and approximately 70,000 people take Efavirenz as part of their treatment.

Brazil is also responsible for an important piece of regulatory innovation in the context of patents and pharmaceuticals. In 1999 it passed a law that made the grant of patents on pharmaceutical products and processes dependent upon the consent of the National Sanitary Surveillance Agency (ANVISA).[32] Patent applications concerning pharmaceuticals are processed by NIIP in the normal way, but the final grant of the patent depends on ANVISA's consent. ANVISA carries out a substantive analysis of the patent application to determine whether in fact there really is an invention and that it is novel.[33] ANVISA's examiners, who have been given training in patent examination, have rejected patent applications that have been approved by NIIP examiners, something that has led to criticism from the patent attorney profession.[34] Some patent attorney firms have invested in the training of NIIP examiners, only to see some of those examiners' decisions overruled.[35] From a social welfare point of view this Brazilian model is one way in

---

WT/DS199/1, 8 June 2000. Brazil retaliated by bringing its own WTO action complaining about Sections 204 and 209 of US Patent Code. See United States – US Patents Code – Request for Consultation by Brazil, WT/DS224/1, 7 February 2001. In July of 2001 Brazil and the US notified the WTO's Dispute Settlement Body of a mutually agreed solution in which both parties dropped their WTO actions. See WT/DS199/4, 19 July 2001.

[30] See Article 68(1) of Law No. 9,279 of 14 May 1996.

[31] For the details see Rana Gosain, 'In Good Health?: Compulsory Licences', 194 (July/August 2007) *Patent World*, 21.

[32] ANVISA's regulatory jurisdiction over pharmaceutical patent products and processes commenced with Provisional Measure 2.006 of 15 December 1999 and was consolidated in Article 229-C of Law 10.196/2001. It reads as follows: 'The allowance of patents to pharmaceutical products and processes will depend upon the previous consent of the Brazilian Sanitary Surveillance Agency – ANVISA.' The text of this law was provided by Ms Ana Paula Jucá Silva of ANVISA to the author by email on 11 July 2007.

[33] Information provided by Ms Ana Paula Jucá Silva of ANVISA to the author by email on 11 July 2007.

[34] For more details on ANVISA's role from a patent attorney perspective see Rana Gosain, 'A Worthless Investment?: Hurdles to Obtaining Patents in Brazil', 163 (2004) *Patent World*, 13.

[35] On the training of patent examiners by local attorney firms see 'On the Cusp of New Technologies', 113 (October 2001) *Managing Intellectual Property*, 62, 63.

which developing countries can improve the quality of examination in a sector of vital national interest.

Brazil's Patent Office: 'making the IP business much bigger'

The 1996 patent law also amended the 1970 law that had established NIIP. The principal purpose of NIIP has become the enforcement of the rules regulating intellectual property.[36] NIIP retains some control over licensing contracts, but my interview at NIIP revealed that it is a role for which it does not have much enthusiasm. Licensing contracts and technology transfer contracts have to be registered with NIIP in order to be effective against third parties.[37] Improvements made by the licensee remain with the licensee with the patent licensor having a right to preferential access. NIIP can also be called upon to arbitrate remuneration in the case of a voluntary licence where the licensor and licensee fail to agree terms.[38]

NIIP administers a system of deferred examination in which an applicant has 3 years from the filing date in which to request an examination.[39] NIIP also has the administrative power to institute nullity proceedings against a patent on a wide range of grounds.[40] Nullity proceedings may also be requested by a person having a legitimate interest and must be brought within 6 months of the grant of the patent.

At the time of the interview in 2007, NIIP had around 300 patent examiners, most of whom had been recruited over the last few years. Improving salaries had been central to this successful expansion. For the time being NIIP returns its fees to general revenue, but because intellectual property has become a priority area it does not have a problem with its budget. The expansion in examiners was needed to cope with the rise in the number of patent applications, especially in the pharmaceutical sector, the single biggest source of NIIP's backlog of some 110,000 applications. Increasing the number of examiners was also important to NIIP's goal of achieving the status of being an International Searching Authority (ISA) under the Patent Cooperation Treaty (PCT). NIIP wants to build a genuinely expert examination force and so requires at least a masters degree (20% of examiners have a PhD), but at the same time the size of the backlog is putting pressure

---

[36] See Article 240 of Law No. 9,279 of 14 May 1996.
[37] See Articles 62 and 211 of Law No. 9,279 of 14 May 1996.
[38] See Article 65 of Law No. 9,279 of 14 May 1996.
[39] See Article 33 of Law No. 9,279 of 14 May 1996.
[40] See Article 50 of Law No. 9,279 of 14 May 1996.

on the office to make quick use of trainees. Pressure is also coming from the US to do something about the backlog. The US cited the backlog as one reason it was keeping Brazil on its Priority Watchlist in 2005.[41]

NIIP sees the European Patent Office (EPO) as leading the way in terms of examination quality while the USPTO was described as having a 'highly concessive approach', that is, one that concedes a lot to the applicant. The EPO approach is seen as the better one for a developing country like Brazil. As we saw in the chapter on the EPO, there are real doubts about whether the EPO actually delivers quality examination. Many of its examining staff think that it does not. Yet NIIP, like other developing-country patent offices, sees the EPO as a quality operation. Whether NIIP will itself be able to deliver high-quality examination is an open question. Just like India it had a gap in pharmaceutical examination capability, a gap that it has addressed through recruitment. Given that it takes about 4 to 5 years for an examiner to be fully productive, building up pharmaceutical examining expertise will take some time. My question about production quotas for examiners brought the reply that these were 'very high in truth'. On top of this it would appear that some of Brazil's law firms, which represent foreign pharmaceutical interests, have been involved in the training of pharmaceutical patent examiners.[42] This seems a little like letting tax accountants representing the rich train tax officials. These firms would have every incentive to promote the 'concessive approach'. Backlogs, quotas and firms eager to secure patents for their multinational clients all push the individual examiner towards an examination slanted in the direction of granting the patent.

Like all other major patent offices NIIP adopts a model of examination in which a single examiner has primary responsibility for the file, a model which when combined with the kinds of pressures mentioned above cannot realistically lead to real quality of examination. In common with some other jurisdictions Brazil has provision for third parties being able to bring prior art to the attention of the examiner.[43] How much third parties use this provision is unclear, but NIIP seems to place some store by it: 'we rely on public contributions to trust the result [of the examination]'. However, the mere fact that a third party has not submitted information during the examination process means little, since a private party may not want to release prior art information early on in the grant process.

---

[41] See the '2005 Special 301 Report' available at www.ustr.gov/Document_Library/ Reports_Publications/2005/2005_Special_301/Section_Index.html.

[42] See 'On the Cusp of New Technologies', 62, 63.

[43] Article 31 of Law No. 9,279 of 14 May 1996.

NIIP has a regional and international networking strategy. At the regional level it cooperates with all other South American patent offices, including in the sharing of examination reports. The sharing of such reports is understood as being supplementary information. For NIIP doing its own searches is important. PCT reports are used by examiners as a starting point, 'but we search more'. Given the pressures of the backlog one does wonder how much more searching is actually done by individual examiners.

Lying behind regional cooperation is the idea of a regional network of patent offices that perhaps one day will administer a South American patent. In the age of the Internet, my interviewees suggested, there is no need to create a single physical entity such as the EPO. Instead one can have a regional network which has the advantage that it will be much less threatening to the offices of small countries. Networks, in the words of one interviewee, make it 'much easier to equilibrate power relations'. While networks may look to be more egalitarian entities their inner workings often reveal de facto hierarchies and top dogs. NIIP for the time being is the only ISA within South America and that will very likely remain the case, especially if the US agenda of restricting the number of ISAs is successful. The US sees patent regionalism as the most obvious solution to dealing with the transaction-cost problems generated by many national patent administrations. But at the same time the US knows that one South American patent requires levels of harmonization and integration that will be a long time in coming. Various regional trade agreements such as the Andean Community, the G-3 Free Trade Agreement, NAFTA, MERCOSUR, SIECA and the Central America-Dominican Republic-United States Free Trade Agreement are creating regional convergences in intellectual property.[44] The Common Intellectual Property Regime of the Andean Community is an example of a sub-regional approach that does prescribe some standards of patent administration (for example, pre-grant opposition and examination by request).[45] But ultimately these regional agreements assume and operate on the basis of the national administration of intellectual property.[46]

---

[44] For a discussion of the intellectual property standards in the first five agreements see David Vivas-Eugui, *Regional and Bilateral Agreements and a TRIPS-plus World: The Free Trade Area of the Americas (FTAA)*, Quaker United Nations Office, Geneva, 2003.

[45] See Articles 42 and 44 of Decision 486 of the Common Intellectual Property Regime.

[46] For example, Article 40 of Decision 486 of the Common Intellectual Property Regime prescribes an 18-month publication rule, but leaves it to the national patent office to determine the manner of publication.

Much more likely than a treaty establishing one patent office and one patent for South America is an operational integration of national offices. This would still require an office to be the de facto key player on patent examination in the region, an office which has the Iberian language databases and depth of examining staff to carry out a level of examination that other offices in the region would trust and recognize.[47] For a long time the databases and information services of most patent offices in South America can be said to have been patchy at best.[48] NIIP is working with the EPO on improving its databases.[49] Amongst other things, NIIP has been given direct access to the EPO's EPOQUE system. Under conditions of operational integration most other offices in the region would in practice defer to the examination work of the lead regional office. We have seen that some Association of Southeast Asian Nations (ASEAN) countries in practice already rely on the examination work of other offices. This may also be true of some smaller South American countries. Ecuador was reported to have moved to a system of granting patents by reference to grants elsewhere in 1998.[50] The Andean Common Intellectual Property Regime expressly allows national patent offices to use the examination results of foreign offices for the purposes of certifying that the conditions for the invention's patentability have been met.[51] Similarly, the patent offices of Central American countries are in a weak position when it comes to prior art searching, a gap in capacity that the EPO along with the World Intellectual Property Organization (WIPO) and the Mexican and Spanish patent offices sought to fill by setting up a search facility in Mexico.[52] The basic idea was that a portal would be created in which Mexican examiners could place search results that could be utilized by the offices of Central American countries. This particular experiment turned out not to be as successful as the EPO had hoped (interview, EPO). Smaller offices faced by technical systems that dwarf their own and administering a system that is overwhelmingly used by foreigners may, in not relying on the results of foreign offices, be behaving rationally. Mexico itself faced by an increasing flood of applications and limited examination capability introduced into its national law a provision allowing its patent office

---

[47] On the need for patent databases covering Iberian languages see Robert M. Sherwood, Vanda Scartezini and Peter Dirk Siemsen, 'Promotion of Inventiveness in Developing Countries through a More Advanced Patent Administration', 39 (1999) *Idea*, 473.

[48] See, for example, Edwin Urquidi, 'Technological Information in the Patent Office of the MERCOSUR Countries and Mexico', 27 (2005) *World Patent Information*, 244.

[49] On cooperation between the EPO and Brazil see EPO, *Annual Report 2006*, 46.

[50] Sherwood *et al.*, 'Promotion of Inventiveness', 473.

[51] See Article 46.   [52] See EPO, *Annual Report 2006*, 46.

to make use of the examination results of other offices.[53] Even if some smaller offices in South America are perhaps quietly resisting integration, the integration plans for South America are reasonably clear. One or two offices like the Brazilian and Mexican offices, which have been integrated into the technical systems of the EPO, will become trusted regional offices and they in turn will, like the Pied Piper, lead the smaller offices to the right patent examination results.

NIIP is working hard to make itself the trusted office in South America – it cooperates internationally with the USPTO, the EPO, the Chinese Patent Office, the Korean Intellectual Property Office (KIPO) and the Japanese Patent Office (JPO) – all ISA authorities. In NIIP's eyes the only way to create a stable patent regime in South America is to build a regional network and then link that regional network to the international network of ISAs that will administer the system globally. NIIP's organizational goal is to become the trusted regional node and interface between the global and regional systems. Few other offices in South America are in a position to take on this role because, amongst other things, it requires a government to invest in building up a patent office to the level of an ISA.

The Brazilian government has been prepared to make this level of investment. Providing NIIP with a new building and the money to hire lots more examiners represent the final steps in which policies of import substitution and tariffs have been replaced by neo-liberal ideologies of liberalization and competition that hide the extension of an empire of monopoly rights. In a schizophrenia I encountered in other patent offices, NIIP, an office that hands out government-backed monopolies to mainly foreign multinationals, sees itself as part of the free market competition paradigm rather than the agent of foreign monopoly capital. NIIP is far from being the only schizophrenic. All patent offices whisper to themselves that they are part of a pro-competition world, even as they hand out hundreds of thousands of monopoly privileges at a rate that would stagger medieval absolutist monarchs. At a time when government tariffs have come down, the capacity of patent owners to impose private tariffs on world technology markets has never been higher. In Brazil's case, the explanation perhaps lies in NIIP's belief that Brazil can be a winner in the battle of wealth-generating monopolies that will come to cover much of global knowledge economy of the twenty-first century. When I asked whether Brazil could be a winner from patents the reply was: 'If we don't have the environmental condition for this to happen, it won't happen.'

---

[53] Article 54 of the Mexican Industrial Property Law of 1991 (as consolidated).

The strategy then appears to be to invest in a patent office that opens the grant gates, let it play a major role in spreading patent culture through a multitude of training courses, and with the assistance of the US build a court system that really understands intellectual property and hope that a sufficient number of Brazilian firms are able to capture economically significant monopolies. The areas in which this is thought most likely to happen are biofuels and biotechnology more broadly, even though for the time being Brazil does not have a significant share of the world's biotechnology patents.[54] But in a candid moment my interviewees admitted that the patent environment in Brazil was conflicted with not all sectors of Brazilian industry seeing an 'innovation future' for themselves.

It may be that these sceptical Brazilian firms understand that patents are often more about the rule-gaming innovation of lawyers rather than real technological innovation. Just as in other developing countries, when I came to the role of the local profession I was told that the large attorney offices in Brazil spend most of their time bringing foreign patents to Brazil rather than helping Brazilian companies obtain patents in Brazil and abroad. And it is true that attorney firms in Brazil report doing more work for foreign companies, as do attorney firms generally in South America.[55] Brazilian firms may well see an innovation future for themselves, just not a patent monopoly one dominated by multinationals.

NIIP's approach to this problem has been to launch a large training programme in patent drafting and licensing. In cooperation with WIPO it has put some 1,400 university professors through a patent-drafting course. Like other major offices, NIIP has established an IP Academy for the purpose of spreading the basics of intellectual property. There is some evidence that universities in Brazil are beginning to embrace a patent culture. Unicamp, the State University of Campinas, was for the period 1999–2003 Brazil's leading national patent holder with some 191 patents.[56] Through its technology office Inova, it lodged 153 patent applications in a 2½-year period starting in 2004. Like India, Brazil appears to be putting its faith in its research infrastructure to make it a winner from patents. Under Innovation Law 10,973 of December 2004, it is mandatory for government universities and R&D centres to have a technology office to handle

---

[54] Brazil has a 0.2% share of the world's biotechnology patents. See *Compendium of Patent Statistics*, OECD, 2008, 19.

[55] For a report of these happy times see 'On the Cusp of New Technologies', 62.

[56] See Rosana Ceron Di Giorgio, 'From University to Industry: The Brazilian Revolution in Technology Transfer and Innovation, the Case of State University of Campinas', 141(2) (2006) *Les Nouvelles*, 90, 91.

intellectual property licensing.[57] According to one study, Brazil's public sector is responsible for about 80% of the country's R&D, yet the number of patent applications by Brazilian universities remains low, meaning that more can be extracted from them by way of patent applications.[58] There is a limit to how much can be extracted from universities, however. OECD data shows that in countries like Australia, Belgium, China, Spain, the UK and the US, universities contribute between 6% and 8% of PCT applications (this percentage does not distinguish between foreign and resident universities).[59] For the same period in Brazil the university sector was responsible for 5%.[60] Brazilian universities can probably lift their patenting rates, but the main game remains patenting by industry. In world terms for 2005 companies were responsible for 82% of all PCT filings.[61] There is a long march ahead for Brazil's universities. The same is probably true of Brazil's companies. Patenting by Brazilian residents according to the WIPO patent database has remained constantly low, as it has for residents in South American countries generally.[62] The usual pro-patent response to this kind of data is to say that patenting by residents will only increase. Given the very low numbers this is bound to be right.

---

[57] Ibid. 90, 93.   [58] Edwin Urquidi, 'Technological Information', 244, 248–9.

[59] *Compendium of Patent Statistics*, OECD, 2007, 31.

[60] Ibid.   [61] Ibid. 30.

[62] Applications by residents were 1,954 (1985), 2,707 (1995) and 3,821 (2005). See the table on patent application filings broken down by resident and non-resident for Brazil available at www.wipo.int/ipstats/en/statistics/patents/. Generally the pattern in South America has been a low number of patent applications filed by residents. See the WIPO study 'Consequences of the Patent Agenda for Developing Countries', A/39/13 Add. 4, 15 August 2003 at 21.

10

Islands and regions in the patent stream

The force of empire

Montesquieu observed that legal institutions and principles of one country rarely serve another well. Laws, he argued, depend on political institutions and before one nation decided to adopt the law of another 'it would be proper to examine beforehand whether they have both the same institutions and the same political law'.[1] Patent systems have not, however, arrived in most developing countries through a careful process of examination and selection by the inhabitants of those countries. The dominant transplant mechanism has been coercion, the military coercion that accompanied processes of colonization of the late nineteenth and early twentieth centuries and then the economic trade coercion deployed by the EU and US in the last quarter of the twentieth century.[2]

Kiribati provides one illustration of how patent systems have spread to developing countries through colonization and empire. The Gilbert and Ellice Islands (now Kiribati and Tuvalu respectively) saw the process of white settlement begin in the 1830s through contact with whalers and copra traders and then the inevitable missionaries. The Islands became a British Protectorate in 1892 and then a colony of the British Crown in 1916. As we saw in Chapter 4 a single patent system for the British Empire was an idea that had been discussed, but what eventuated was a system that gave the UK patent holder a right to register a UK patent in a colony or protectorate of the British Empire that had adopted a law allowing for re-registration of a UK patent. Kiribati became part of this re-registration system.

---

[1] Montesquieu, *The Spirit of Laws* (1748) Book XXIX, Ch. 13.
[2] On the important role of the mechanism of coercion in all kinds of regulation including intellectual property see J. Braithwaite and P. Drahos, *Global Business Regulation*, Cambridge University Press, Cambridge, 2000. On the use of trade coercion see P. Drahos with J. Braithwaite, *Information Feudalism*, Earthscan, London, 2000.

Prior to Kiribati's independence in 1979, British Acts of Parliament of general application applied in its territory. After independence Kiribati passed a law declaring what the laws of Kiribati were and the relationship amongst them.[3] Amongst other things, this law allowed for the operation of UK laws, including statutes of general application in force in England on 1 January 1961.[4] Whether the UK Patents Act of 1949 is part of the applied law of Kiribati depends on whether it can be characterized as a statute of general application.[5] A separate law governs the re-registration of UK patents in Kiribati.[6] This gives the grantee of a UK patent 3 years from the date of issue to register the patent in Kiribati. The patent in Kiribati ceases to be in force when the UK patent ceases.

The number of patents registered in Kiribati is not high. From 1999 to 2005 between two and six UK patents per year have been re-registered in Kiribati.[7] Most of them are pharmaceutical patents. The surprise is that there are any. Why one wonders would a company bother to re-register a patent in one of the poorest nations of the world? When I put this question to one UK patent attorney he suggested that 'some clients want total coverage'.

Kiribati's integration into the patent system is a good example of how in many developing countries a patent law inherited during colonization continues to deepen the integration of that country into the international patent framework. So, for example, the owner of a UK European patent has 3 years in which to apply for the registration of a patent in Kiribati. As we saw in Chapter 4, the re-registration system that was created during British Empire days thus has a new life under the European Patent Convention (EPC). Kiribati also shows that there is hardly a country in the world that has escaped the web of filing routes that has been constructed for the benefit of monopoly capital. A US firm, which would most likely begin the patent process with an application in the US, could, if it wished, use the Patent Cooperation Treaty (PCT) to lodge an application with the

[3] Laws of Kiribati Act 1989.

[4] See Sub-section 7(1) of Laws of Kiribati Act 1989.

[5] This is hardly a pressing issue in Kiribati, but for a discussion of the meaning of the phrase 'statutes of general application' see Jennifer Corrin and Don Paterson, *Introduction to South Pacific Law*, 2nd edn., Routledge Cavendish, 2007, 30–2.

[6] See Registration of United Kingdom Patents Ordinance [Cap 87]. This law refers to the UK Patents Act of 1949. The UK PO website alerts patent owners to the possibility of re-registration. See www.ipo.gov.uk/abroad/abroad-extend/abroad-extend-kiribati.htm.

[7] Information provided to the author by the Australian PO. See also Fiona Ey, 'Institutional Framework and Procedures Regulating Access to Pharmaceutical Products to Address Public Health Problems: Pacific Regional Case Study', Paper prepared for the Commonwealth Secretariat, December 2005, 17.

EPO designating the UK as one of its targets. Once granted a European patent in the UK, it could re-register it in Kiribati.

Other Pacific islands also continue with a re-registration system from days past. Vanuatu, which prior to independence in 1980 was the jointly administered territory of the British and French known as the New Hebrides, along with the Solomon Islands (also a British dependency prior to independence in 1978) have re-registration systems. The systems are much the same, with a UK patentee being given 3 years in which to register a patent for the payment of small fee, the life of the patent being tied to the life of the UK patent.[8] Tuvalu's system also applies to UK patents or European patents designating the UK, with the difference from Kiribati being that its re-registration law picks up the UK Patent Act of 1977 or any succeeding law.[9] Nauru's system allows for the registration of patents from Australia, the UK and the US and has an opposition procedure.[10] Samoa has a patent law that allows a patent owner from any foreign country to re-register the patent.[11]

Despite the irrelevance of the patent system to these small island economies the patent rules inherited from the colonial past have an operational inertia in their legal systems. They serve as the basis for other rule changes. For example, Vanuatu in 2008 amended its re-registration system to allow for the re-registration of patents that have been granted in the EU member countries.[12] Vanuatu also shows that countries can, if they so choose, take advantage of their sovereignty over patent administration to devise systems that meet their own cultural and economic concerns. The protection of traditional knowledge of indigenous communities and the effect of patent rules upon the goal of protection has been a major talking point in various international fora for at least a decade.[13] A model law for the protection of traditional knowledge in Pacific island countries has been drafted.[14] Vanuatu in 2003 passed a patent law that provides for a

[8] See Registration of United Kingdom Patents Act [Cap 179] (Solomon Islands) and Registration of United Kingdom Patents [Cap 80] (Vanuatu).
[9] Registration of United Kingdom Patents Ordinance (Tuvalu).
[10] Patents Registration Act 1973 (Nauru). Formerly a German colony, Nauru became a dependency of Australia after the First World War. It became independent in 1968.
[11] See Sub-section 9(1) of the Patents Act 1972 (Samoa).
[12] See Registration of United Kingdom Patents (Amendment) Act No. 14 of 2008 (Vanuatu).
[13] See Chidi Oguamanam, *International Law and Indigenous Knowledge*, University of Toronto Press, Toronto, 2006.
[14] For a discussion see Miranda Forsyth, 'Intellectual Property Laws in the South Pacific: Friend or Foe?', 7 (2003) *Journal of South Pacific Law*, available at www.paclii.org/journals/fJSPL/.

procedure for handling patent applications involving indigenous knowledge, a procedure that begins with the referral of such an application by the Registrar to the National Council for Chiefs.[15] The rest of Vanuatu's patent law follows a conventional path.

The tiny amount of patenting going on in Pacific island countries is hardly likely to let patent bureaucrats there build the kind of offices that one sees in patent capitols such as Munich and Geneva. Samoa receives about two patents annually.[16] Kiribati's re-registration law, for example, specifies the sum of 10 Australian dollars for the privilege of registering a UK patent.[17] Trademark registration is a much more important source of income for Pacific island countries. Given the levels of patenting it would not be rational for small island economies to invest scarce resources in patent examination. This conclusion seemingly leads to the suggestion that they should consider some kind of regional organization for the purpose of dealing with patents. Regionalization of patent administration we will see a little later has spread to Africa and the Middle East, but whether it serves the needs of developing countries as opposed to the needs of transnational companies is very much an open question. With regionalization will come a much deeper integration into a set of international patent standards that have been deeply influenced by rent-seeking industries such as the global pharmaceutical industry.

New empires

One of the features of the globalization of regulation is that it allows powerful states to impose domestic models of regulation on weaker states in a process of regulatory re-colonization. The patent provisions of the Agreement on Trade-Related Aspects of Intellectual Property Rights, 1994 (TRIPS) are a case in point. The US and EU were able to agree to a set of standards that now function as a set of minimum standards for developing countries that are members of the WTO. These standards oblige developing countries to invest in patent office administration. A state cannot simply pass a patent law for the purposes of having something on its books and then not provide a means for obtaining a patent.

---

[15] See Patents Act 2003 (Vanuatu), Part 12.
[16] Information provided to the author by letter from the Ministry of Commerce, Industry and Labour of Samoa in 2005.
[17] See the Schedule to the Registration of United Kingdom Patents Ordinance [Cap 87], available at www.paclii.org/ki/legis/consol_act/roupo354/. This fee may not be current since fees can be amended by regulation.

Indonesia came close to this situation when after independence in 1945 it became unclear as to whether a patent law of 1911 of the Netherlands East Indies continued to operate.[18] Under this law the examining office was the patent office in the Hague. This raised sovereignty concerns in Indonesia. An Indonesian Ministerial decree issued in 1953 implied that the colonial law was not in force, but in any case even if the colonial patent law continued to apply there was no patent office to process applications. Between 1953 and 1989 some 13,000 patent applications were received in Indonesia and noted in a provisional priority system.[19] Indonesia passed a patent law in 1989 and in August of 1991, the Indonesian PO began to receive and examine applications (interview, Indonesian PO). Today a WTO member that did not provide an administrative process for the grant of patents would rapidly find itself on the receiving end of a WTO action.

TRIPS triggered a massive demand for technical assistance from developing countries in all areas of intellectual property. Unlike the Paris Convention for the Protection of Industrial Property, 1883 (Paris Convention), it produced in developing countries moves to improve patent administration. Indonesia, for example, had according to the World Intellectual Property Organization (WIPO) been a member of the Paris Convention since 1950, but as we just saw it was from 1953 until 1989 happy to let patent applications pile up in an office in Jakarta while it contemplated enacting a patent law.[20] TRIPS and US trade pressure on intellectual property rights drove out this languid approach to patents. In 1997 Indonesia substantially revised its patent law to bring it into line with its TRIPS obligations.

A feature of this regulatory re-colonization through patents is that developing countries bear much of the cost of administration. The case of Indonesia illustrates the point. After 1953 Indonesia had little incentive to invest in its patent office. WIPO's patent data for Indonesia is incomplete, but what data there is shows the usual dominance by foreign patent applicants of the patenting game.[21] Once Indonesia's 1989 patent law came into operation in 1991 there was a dramatic rise in the number of

---

[18] See Christoph Antons, *Intellectual Property Law in Indonesia*, Kluwer Law International, The Hague, London, Boston, 2000, 133–5.

[19] Ibid. 135.

[20] WIPO states that the year of accession is 1950. On the issues of interpretation surrounding the exact year of Indonesia's accession to the Paris Convention see Antons, *Intellectual Property Law in Indonesia*, 46–8.

[21] See the entries for Indonesia in the table 'patent applications by patent office by resident and non-resident' available at www.wipo.int/ipstats/en/statistics/patents/.

foreign applications (for example, in 1991 there were 34 applications by residents compared to 1,280 by non-residents). In order to deal with this increase in numbers the Indonesian PO began to recruit more examiners. At the interview officials said that 'it was very difficult to recruit technical people to become examiners', in part because it was 'not an interesting job'. Starting with six examiners in 1991, the Indonesia PO had grown to about seventy in 2006 (interview, Indonesian PO). Some of the costs of training patent examiners have been met by the battery of training courses and other forms of assistance provided by the EPO, the Japanese Patent Office (JPO) and the Australian PO, but the Indonesian PO has to meet salary costs and importantly it has to find people willing to become examiners. One effect of persuading people to become examiners is that, in the words of a former New Zealand examiner, it 'sucks scientific expertise out of the system'. In countries where scientific labour pools are small to begin with, this is a not insignificant cost. Deploying scarce scientific resources into the rent-seeking machinery of the patent system cannot be part of a productive economic growth strategy, especially not one that takes seriously the idea that productive human capital is at the core of economic growth.

The training that examiners from the Indonesian PO receive from other offices (the EPO was mentioned as a significant provider) also comes with potential costs. As with other developing-country patent offices that I interviewed, the training produces a form of automated regulatory decision-making. Indonesian examiners look to see how the EPO or USPTO has decided an application. Other offices that have this kind of influence in Indonesia are JPO, the Chinese PO and the Korean PO. In the case of patents there is a potential cost if the developing-country patent examiner is automatically following the low quality output of developed-country examiners. Low quality patents in developmentally important sectors of a country's economy such as pharmaceuticals, information technology and business methods will have an effect on competition and local firms in those sectors. The whole point of the patents is to exclude competitors.

There is a high degree of regulatory automation in developing-country patent offices. In the case of the Indonesian PO the patent examiner's manual was drafted with the assistance of the EPO. This was followed by training in the use of the manual. Automation is not confined to patent office procedures. At least in the eyes of the Indonesian PO, the few local patent attorneys with a viable practice in Indonesia function 'just like couriers' having very little input into the applications they forward to the Indonesian PO from their foreign clients.

The fees raised from the patenting process can also be used by a developing country to meet the costs of running a patent office. The regular multinational users of national patent systems have consistently argued that the fees collected from applicants should be used to improve the service to applicants. On this issue, the Indonesian PO has been encouraged and assisted by the EPO to become an independent budgetary entity. At the time of the interview, the Indonesian PO returned the fees it collected to general revenue, a percentage of that being returned to the office. But there were plans to become independent. When it came to the question of who was entitled to the money the officials I spoke to had a clear view: 'we think that this is our money' (interview, Indonesian PO). The spread of the business model approach (see Chapter 1 for a description of the model) to running a patent office is encouraged in developing countries by the major developed-country patent offices and WIPO because it makes the local patent office more independent in terms of its ability to service patent applicants, most of whom are foreign. It also integrates these offices more deeply into the global private governance network. In exchange for budgetary autonomy, the local office enters into new kinds of dependencies. Its greater dependence on fee income means, for example, it has less incentive to question the claim formats that come before it. Its advice on patent policy is more likely to be pro-patent. As in other developing countries it is the Indonesian PO that provides advice to the government on patent policy.

Electronic systems in the Indonesian PO have been improved. There are no longer five examiners to one personal computer. It has brought its backlog under control. If the office does run into problems it has the option under its patent law of requesting the assistance of examiners from other patent offices.[22] It administers a patent law that more or less passes muster with the United States Trade Representative (USTR) in its annual Special 301 reports. The bulk of USTR's criticism is directed at Indonesia's efforts in the areas of copyright and trademarks.

The regulatory colonization of Indonesia's Patent Office has reached an impressive level of automation. In 1997 Indonesia joined the PCT, the treaty that serves as a conveyer belt, carrying hundreds of thousands of foreign patent applications into developing countries around the world. Indonesian inventors make little use of the PCT system with applicants of Indonesian origin filing worldwide, nine PCT international applications in 2007.[23] Most of Indonesia's foreign patent applications arrive via

---

[22] See Sub-section 50(1) of Law no. 14 of 2001 on Patents.
[23] PCT, *Yearly Review 2007*, WIPO, 34.

the PCT.[24] Examiners in Jakarta with the help of EPO training follow an EPO drafted manual that sees them follow the decisions of the EPO and the other major offices. Disagreement with these decisions is rare. The decision tree in the Indonesian PO is much the same as the one that was described in Chapter 4 for Vietnam. At the time of my visit the examining manual was being redrafted. Was this a time to be considering its effect on national interests, I asked? 'No', came the reply, national interests were 'not for the manual, when it comes to the manual we don't think of national interests'. Much as in other developing-country patent offices the manual is there to be followed. Yet at the end of the interview the patent examiners told me that pharmaceutical patents were creating problems in Indonesia and solicited my views on the operation of what is known as the WTO's paragraph 6 solution.

New missionaries

TRIPS is but one part of the WTO's raft of agreements. Once TRIPS came into operation, the WTO secretariat had neither the resources nor the expertise to help developing countries draft intellectual property laws and establish the administrative organizations and judicial authorities needed to make those laws operational. What was being demanded of developing countries through TRIPS standards was a large-scale institution building exercise in which complex laws had to be put on the books and then be made to work as a system by means of administrative and judicial processes, information technology, and technically trained people who knew the rules, the processes and the IT systems. All this had to be done in the context of a developing-country's national legal system, cultural values, and business practices and traditions. To add urgency to this task TRIPS imposed deadlines on developing countries through what were euphemistically called 'transitional provisions'.[25] So, for example, developing countries were allowed to delay the implementation of TRIPS until 1 January 2000, five years after the agreement establishing the WTO came into force.[26] Here it is worth reminding ourselves of the history of patent offices in Western states that we covered in Chapter 3, a history that shows

---

[24] According to the Indonesian PO's website for 2006 there were 3,805 patent registrations via the PCT compared to 282 domestic registrations and 519 foreign direct registrations. The statistical table describes these figures as patent registrations. See www.dgip.go.id/ebscript/publicportal.cgi?.ucid=2663&ctid=55&id=1010&type=0.

[25] See Part VI of TRIPS.   [26] See Article 65.2 of TRIPS.

that Western states took many, many decades to establish procedures of patent office administration once they had passed patent laws.

Confronted by a task that would have made Hercules turn pale, the WTO signed an agreement with WIPO in 1995 in which WIPO agreed to provide legal-technical assistance to developing countries. WIPO was in a much better position than the WTO to do this kind of technical work. It was a specialist organization solely dedicated to spreading the faith of intellectual property. It had experience in working with developing countries. It had drafted model intellectual property laws, including patent laws that it thought suitable for developing countries, and it could draw on its large community of experts and consultants to help developing countries implement the models.[27] Importantly, WIPO was also in a position to fund this work. We saw in Chapter 1 that WIPO administers the PCT system and receives in that capacity the international filing fee. For example, its PCT fee income for 1998 was about 147 million Swiss Francs and in 1999 it was about 160 million.[28]

A WIPO document of 1999 provides the detail of WIPO's technical assistance activities during this period. These included the preparation of 136 draft laws on intellectual property for countries and providing commentary on another 130 draft laws received from developing countries. Thirty-four countries successfully automated their intellectual property offices. Meetings of various kinds organized by WIPO concerning TRIPS-related issues took in some 23,800 government officials. Table 10.1, extracted from one of four WIPO annexes describing its work, provides a small sample that illustrates the specialized patent training that WIPO provided as part of its TRIPS legal-technical assistance programme.

There are a number of reasons why WIPO's missionary work achieved success in many developing countries. To begin with there was the simple question of cost. Establishing new systems of intellectual property, especially a patent system, is costly. The costs varied according to country. Not every developing country planned to commit the US$19million that India reportedly committed to modernize its patent office. For the most part there were estimates about the costs. The World Bank put forward a figure of between US$1.5 to $2million for poor countries to upgrade their administrative systems for intellectual property in general, but then questioned whether this was money well spent given that developing

---

[27] A pre-TRIPS example of a model law is the WIPO Model Law for Developing Countries on Inventions (1979).

[28] These figures are from its published Annual Reports available at www.wipo.int/about-wipo/en/report.html.

Table 10.1. *Extract from WIPO's Awareness Building and Human Resources Development Activities (Inter-regional) for 1998* [29]

02/03/98 – 10/03/98	'Streamlining Search and Examination Procedure'	Munich, Geneva	Saudi Arabia, Argentina, Armenia, Bangladesh, Belarus, Brazil, Colombia, Cuba, Egypt, Georgia, Ghana, India, Kenya, Kyrgyzstan, Philippines, Moldova, Sudan, Swaziland, Tajikistan, Thailand, Ukraine, Uruguay, Vietnam, Zimbabwe, EAPO
23/03/98 – 27/03/98	'Use of CD-ROM Technology for Patent Information and Search'	Berne, Geneva	Saudi Arabia, Brunei, Cuba, Jordan, Kenya, Malaysia, Mongolia, Nigeria, Panama, Tanzania, Vietnam, Zimbabwe
30/03/98 – 02/04/98	'Use of CD-ROM Technology for Patent Information and Search'	Vienna/EPO	Same as above
16/04/98 – 26/04/98	FICPI South East Asian Drafting (SEAD) Training Course	Singapore	
18/05/98 – 22/05/98	WIPO/INPI Course on IP for the Portuguese-Speaking Countries of Africa	Rio de Janeiro	Angola (2), Cape Verde (2), Guinea-Bissau (2), Mozambique (2), Sao Tome and Principe (2)

[29] For the whole table see WIPO's Legal and Technical Assistance to Developing Countries for the Implementation of the TRIPS Agreement from January 1, 1996 to March 31, 1999, Annex IV, PCIPD/1/3, April 28, 1999.

Table 10.1.

02/06/98 – 12/06/98	Training Course on Trademarks for Asia and Pacific	Hull	China, India, Indonesia, Malaysia, Philippines, Korea, Sri Lanka, Thailand, Vietnam
08/06/98 – 19/06/98	The WIPO Academy, Session in English	Geneva	Albania, Bangladesh, Bhutan, Bosnia and Herzegovina, China, India, Indonesia, Malaysia, Nepal, Pakistan, Philippines, Sri Lanka, Thailand, Vietnam, OAU

countries had so many other more urgent priorities combined with scarcities in technically trained people.[30] With the real costs of TRIPS compliance uncertain, developing countries were prepared to take help from wherever they could get it, so none turned WIPO's missionaries away. There were also incentives of a more personal kind for patent offices of developing countries. They were small, under-equipped organizations, paying poor salaries in which developing-country governments had not invested. Many of these offices saw a chance to acquire resources from a wealthy international organization and so they listened to the sound of patent money.

The Malaysian PO, for example, was an office that was unable to recruit patent examiners (interview, Malaysian PO). With the help of WIPO and the EPO it has transformed itself. Today it is part of the Intellectual Property Corporation of Malaysia, managing its own budget and having a pay scale that is roughly 20% higher for its employees than for a comparable government job. It no longer has recruitment problems.

For countries that were not members of the WTO and wanted to be, there were strong incentives to take advice and help from WIPO. Vietnam was one such country. It had applied for WTO accession in 1995. The accession process involves the WTO establishing a working party to oversee the process of accession. In Vietnam's case a Working Party was

---

[30] *Global Economic Prospects and the Developing Countries*, World Bank, Washington, 2002, 136.

established on 31 January 1995. It worked over Vietnam until Vietnam's accession in 2007. During this period Vietnam's intellectual property laws came under forensic scrutiny from the working party.[31] With the EU, Switzerland and the US on the working party nothing less on intellectual property could be expected.[32] It made sense for Vietnam to take help from WIPO because WIPO was working with the WTO to prepare developing countries for the implementation of TRIPS and its experts were advising countries on that basis.

Cambodia was another example of a country seeking WTO accession. It had started the process in 1994 and gained accession in 2004. Like Vietnam it faced a WTO working party that included the US and the EU.[33] Cambodia, as a least-developed country, had in the first instance until 1 January 2006 to implement TRIPS.[34] The accession documents show that it passed a number of intellectual property laws before then including a patent law in 2002 that was promulgated into law on 22 January 2003.[35] In Cambodia's case the patent law was based on WIPO's model patent law and WIPO also had input into the drafting of the law, something that Cambodia drew to the attention of the WTO Working Party.[36] In order to bring itself into full compliance with TRIPS, especially on the administrative and enforcement side, it sought and was granted by the working party an extension of the transition period to 1 January 2007. A more significant achievement was that it was able to exercise its right under paragraph 7 of the Declaration on the TRIPS Agreement and Public Health to delay the application of its patent law to pharmaceuticals.[37]

There are two distinct aspects to WIPO's role in the WTO accession process. The first relates to the detailed content of the patent law system that WIPO was drafting for countries and/or advising them on. WIPO

---

[31] See, for example, the 'Report of the Working Party on the Accession of Viet Nam', WT/ACC/VNM/48, 27 October 2006, available from the WTO's website.

[32] The full list of members can be found in WT/ACC/VNM/1/Rev.23, 25 October 2005.

[33] The full list of members can be found in WT/ACC/KHM/1/Rev.6, 23 July 2003.

[34] See Article 66.1 of TRIPS.

[35] Cambodia notified the working party of its legislation in WT/ACC/KHM/7/Rev.2, 3 March 2003.

[36] See Report of the Working Party on the Accession of Cambodia, WT/ACC/KHM/21, 15 August 2003, para 168. For the background of the patent law see the statement by Mr Ly Phanna of Cambodia's Intellectual Property Division, Ministry of Commerce at www.moc.gov.kh/laws_regulation/development_of_cambodia's_ipr.htm.

[37] Article 4 of the Law on the Patent, Utility Model Certificates and Industrial Designs excludes pharmaceutical products as provided for in Article 136. Article 136 states that pharmaceutical products shall be excluded from patent protection until 1 January 2016 as allowed under the Declaration on the TRIPS Agreement and Public Health.

experts might steer countries into going beyond TRIPS standards in order to guarantee safe passage past the EU and US and into the WTO. Of course, irrespective of WIPO's advice on legislation there was nothing to stop WTO members from pressing developing countries to go beyond TRIPS standards. In the final analysis, the accession process is a bargaining process, albeit a highly unequal one in which the US and EU sit on private WTO committees as inquisitors into the efforts of war-torn and least-developed countries like Cambodia to meet their high intellectual property standards. For example, Cambodia in exchange for being given one extra year in which to fully implement TRIPS agreed to a standard on the protection of pharmaceutical test data not required by TRIPS, as well as a standard that linked the protection of patents to the process of marketing approval of medicines, an area not covered by TRIPS.[38] For the most part developing countries for understandable reasons have had little success in contesting the detailed standards of intellectual property law and for the most part have ended up with Western models. WIPO has played the role of modelling agency, albeit with increasing sophistication. Its model patent law does take into account the fact that developing countries can suspend the operation of patent law in relation to pharmaceuticals. Cambodia's patent law follows the drafting approach of this WIPO model.

A second and in many ways much more important role that WIPO has played has been in the regulatory automation of developing-countries' systems of patent administration. This role has not been confined to acceding countries and it is not a role exclusive to WIPO. The Trilateral Offices have, as we have seen, also been crucial players. WIPO has also been at the core of this process of automation through its administration of the PCT system, endless training courses in patent-related matters and provision of software and hardware to patent offices.

My fieldwork in the Vietnamese PO revealed a similar situation to the one that I found in the Indonesian PO. The PCT had come into operation in Vietnam in 1993 and according to officials 80% of patent applications come into Vietnam via the PCT (interview, Vietnamese PO). This is consistent with WIPO's data which shows a rapid rise in the number of patent applications from 1993 onwards. As we saw in Chapter 4, the lead patent office for Vietnam in terms of influence is the EPO. Vietnamese patent examiners will follow the EPO's practice and guidelines on patenting.

---

[38] See Report of the Working Party on the Accession of Cambodia, WT/ACC/KHM/21, 15 August 2003, para 205.

Basically if the patent is accepted in the EPO it will be accepted by the Vietnamese examiner.

Cambodia offers an instructive contrast to Vietnam when it comes to regulatory automation of patent systems. Both Cambodia and Vietnam have become integrated into the international patent treaty framework with one critical difference. Cambodia is not yet a member of the PCT. It does have a patent office that accepts applications, but the number of applications is very low.[39] The lesson is fairly clear. Developing countries that want to avoid truckloads of patents showing up on the doorstep of their patent office, because, for instance, they fear the effects of pharmaceutical patenting should not join the PCT or delay for as a long as possible. Paris Convention membership is less of a problem because it does not automate the application process. It merely confers a right of priority on an applicant. This right, however, requires an applicant to coordinate a worldwide national application process if worldwide protection is the goal. The PCT by contrast has administrative machinery that allows an applicant to make one application that can be turned into as many national applications as the applicant chooses. Once developing-country examiners are trained to follow the opinions and reports of the International Searching Authorities (ISAs) that process the international application, the process of obtaining a patent in those countries becomes highly automated. Cambodia will join the PCT and like many other developing countries it will rely on PCT examination results to run its system (interview, Cambodian official).

On a final note it is worth observing that there are potentially important links between the micro-processes that occur in patent offices on a daily basis and the bigger macro-processes of development in countries such as Vietnam and Cambodia. Both countries have to deal with a range of diseases for which medicines are needed, including an HIV/AIDS epidemic. The careful examination of pharmaceutical applications makes a lot of sense since the impact of granting a patent on, for example, an HIV/AIDs medicine in a developing country will be much greater than granting a patent on some new method of dampening vibrations in a tennis

---

[39] It appears that in 2007 there were thirteen patent applications. This statistic was obtained from the EC-ASEAN Intellectual Property Rights Cooperation Programme website. See www.ecap-project.org/asean_ip_legislation_international_treaties/cambodia.html. WIPO does not have entries for Cambodia for 2007. An email inquiry to the Cambodian PO produced an email reply on 15 August 2008 that reported that the office had thirty-five foreign applications before it. It also indicated that the office was in a stage of 'capacity development' with examiners being sent abroad for training.

racquet. The automation of decision-making about pharmaceutical patents is full of dangers.

The case of Vietnam illustrates that once a country adopts an automated approach to the grant of patents, patents including pharmaceutical patents will begin to arrive in large numbers. Almost certainly, pharmaceutical patenting will become one of the most significant areas of patenting. We saw that this was true for India, for example. Patent statistics for Vietnam are not readily available, but at the time of my visit to the Vietnamese PO in 2004 officials informed me that patenting in Vietnam went back to a decree of 1981. According to the figures they gave me 12,000 patent applications had been received of which almost 3,000 related to the pharmaceutical field.[40] The Vietnamese PO also had before it forty-six applications for patents on HIV/AIDS treatments, two applications relating to tuberculosis and eleven relating to malaria. A study sponsored by the Ford Foundation and the World Health Organization (WHO) found a number of granted patents to foreign companies covering twenty-two antiretroviral (ARV) drugs in Vietnam.[41] According to the ECAP website, which provides limited information on patenting in Vietnam, for the period 2002–6 the Vietnamese PO granted 120 patents to applicants of Vietnamese origin and 3,452 to foreigners.[42]

The picture that emerges in Vietnam is that patenting is based on the PCT process, heavily dominated by foreigners with pharmaceutical patenting being the single biggest area of patenting. My visit to the Vietnam Pharmaceutical Companies Association shed no further light on the number of pharmaceutical patents in Vietnam. Vietnamese generic companies, I was told, do not do much patent searching, but this was changing. There was a lot of concern about TRIPS implementation. Information about TRIPS and pharmaceutical patents was being provided to the Vietnamese Association by the International Pharmaceutical Research and Manufacturers Association, the international peak body of pharmaceutical multinationals.

---

[40] There were a total of 12,028 patent applications with 1,754 for Class A61 and 1,214 for A61K. Interview, Vietnamese PO, Hanoi, 23 June 2004.

[41] 'Affordable ARV Therapy for People Living with HIV/AIDS in Vietnam: Legal and Trade Issues', Hanoi, June 2004. The authors are Jakkrit Kuanpoth and Le Hoai Duong. The study, which used a Vietnamese law firm to do a patent search, found some thirty patents covering twenty-two ARV drugs. While in Vietnam I was shown twenty patent documents by WHO officials and asked for advice on how they affected the WHO's plan to import generic ARV drugs from India.

[42] See www.ecap-project.org/asean_ip_legislation_international_treaties/vietnam.html.

One of the last people I interviewed in Vietnam was the Minister for Health.[43] The price of pharmaceuticals in Vietnam was a major concern it emerged and the government was thinking about how to grow the generic industry. That evening as I strolled through the streets reflecting on the interviews and the difficulties that would face Vietnamese generic companies operating in the highly patent-regulated markets of the twenty-first century, I came upon Ho Chi Min's tomb. It reminded me that North Vietnam armed with little more than a will of steel had defeated a blustering weapons-laden superpower. Throwing off US pharmaceutical hegemony should surely be an easier task.

Cambodia for the time being has made it easier for its generic companies than has Vietnam. Pharmaceutical product patents, the single biggest obstacle for generic manufacturers, have been excluded until 2016. Cambodia has not yet joined the PCT and so it appears that very few applications from foreigners are finding their way to Cambodia.[44]

Regional automation

One way in which to automate the process of granting patents is for countries to club together and create one office that administers one procedure for grant of patents in all the members of club. We saw in Chapter 4 that the EPC establishes this kind of arrangement for its members. The possibility that states would want to make such arrangements is recognized in the Paris Convention and the PCT.[45] Importantly, the rights of priority that are gained under one treaty are also recognized by other treaties. By recognizing priority rights obtained under other treaties, a network of filing routes is created (see Chapter 2). One of the characteristics of treaties dealing with patents is that they add to the rights of patent applicants while being careful not to eliminate existing options. The role of the Paris Convention, the oldest multilateral treaty on industrial property, in maintaining a network of filing routes remains profoundly important and subsequent multilateral treaties have been careful to avoid the possibility of any erosion of rights that persons have under the Paris Convention. The more countries that join the Paris Convention, the PCT and that participate in regional arrangements, the larger the reach of the filing route network created by these treaties. Trade

---

[43] Meeting with Minister of Health, Hanoi, 25 June 2004.
[44] Another benefit of this is that Cambodia will have fewer patents to deal with under the system of mailbox protection that it must provide under TRIPS for patents until 2016.
[45] See Article 19 of the Paris Convention and Article 45.1 of the PCT.

agreements that the US and EU negotiate with developing countries will generally have as a standard clause an obligation on the parties to join the Paris Convention and the PCT. Cambodia as part of its WTO accession package agreed to join the PCT.

The creation of regional patent organizations is a critical part of the regulatory automation of the patent system. If, for example, there was no European patent system a US applicant would still have a right of priority under the Paris Convention, but would have to pursue that right of priority separately in each European state that was a member of the Paris Convention, a time-consuming and costly exercise. Regional patent organizations offer convenient one-stop shops. They also mean that states have to engage in some degree of patent harmonization, since the single grant procedure cannot work efficiently if the examiner has to work with, for example, twenty very different national patent laws. Finally, regional patent offices become natural allies of companies on issues of patent harmonization since ultimately it makes the task of administering a regional system easier.

To date five regional organizations exist: two in Africa, one in Europe, one in Eurasia and one in the Middle East (see below). Aside from this formal regionalization there are also degrees of informal regionalization when it comes to patent office leadership. So, for example, the Australian PO will do much of the examination work for the New Zealand PO as well as for some Pacific island countries in those cases where they request examination services from it. So, while the Australian office is not a regional patent organization like the EPO, it is an important regional agent and resource for countries. Other offices aspire to have this kind of regional influence. The Indian PO, for example, would like to exercise this kind of influence in its own region, doing work perhaps for Nepal and Sri Lanka (interview, Indian PO). In some regional groupings where there is not yet a regional patent organization there is discussion of its prospect. For example, within the Association of Southeast Asian Nations (ASEAN) region the possibility of a regional patent office was expressly raised in a cooperation agreement signed by ASEAN members in 1995.[46] The idea of a regional patent office has been suggested for Pacific island countries.

---

[46] Article 1.4 of the ASEAN Framework Agreement on Intellectual Property Cooperation, Bangkok, Thailand, 15 December 1995 states that 'Member States shall explore the possibility of setting up of an ASEAN patent system, including an ASEAN Patent Office'. For a discussion of cooperation on intellectual property in the ASEAN region see Michael Blakeney, 'The Legal Regulation of Technology Transfer: Arrangements within ASEAN' in Christoph Antons (ed.), *Law and Development in East and Southeast Asia*, Routledge Curzon, London and New York, 2003, 341.

Regional trade blocs such as the Andean Community and MERCOSUR are producing convergences in patent standards amongst their members making it easier, at least in principle, for national offices to rely on the work of other member offices in administering those standards. In the absence of a regional patent office, one or two offices may emerge as leaders of a regional network of patent offices, that leadership having in part been facilitated by a trade and integration agreement that has brought about a convergence of patent standards. Chapter 9 suggested that this was a possibility for South America.

Regional patent organizations

African Regional Intellectual Property Organization, 1976
Members (16): Botswana, Gambia, Ghana, Kenya, Lesotho, Malawi, Mozambique, Namibia, Sierra Leone, Somalia, Sudan, Swaziland, Tanzania, Uganda, Zambia and Zimbabwe.

Eurasian Patent Organization, 1994
Members (9): Armenia, Azerbaijan, Belarus, Kazakhstan, Kyrgyz, Moldova, Russian Federation, Tajikistan and Turkmenistan.

European Patent Organization, 1973
Members (35): Austria, Belgium, Bulgaria, Croatia, Cyprus, Czech Republic, Denmark, Estonia, Finland, France, Germany, Greece, Hungary, Ireland, Iceland, Italy, Latvia, Liechtenstein, Lithuania, Luxembourg, Macedonia, Malta, Monaco, Netherlands, Norway, Poland, Portugal, Romania, Slovakia, Slovenia, Spain, Sweden, Switzerland, Turkey and United Kingdom.
    States to which a European patent can be extended (3): Albania, Bosnia and Herzegovina, and Serbia.

Organisation Africaine de la Propriété Intellectuelle, 1962 (African Intellectual Property Organization)
Members (16): Benin, Burkina Faso, Cameroon, Central Africa, Chad, Congo, Cote d'Ivoire, Equatorial Guinea, Gabon, Guinea, Guinea Bissau, Mali, Mauritania, Niger, Senegal and Togo.

Gulf Cooperation Council Patent Office, 1992
Members (6): Bahrain, Kuwait, Oman, Qatar, Saudi Arabia, United Arab Emirates.

The most important of these regional patent organizations is the European Patent Organization (discussed in Chapter 4). Through the arm of the EPO, the European Patent Organization provides assistance of various kinds to these other regional patent organizations. Many of the countries that are members of these regional patent organizations are not especially large markets and so are not priority countries from the point of view of a global patenting strategy. Nevertheless, we can see from the membership of these regional organizations that a large number of developing countries have been administratively integrated into the patent system. The possibility of these countries becoming patent havens has been eliminated.

The Gulf Cooperation Council (GCC) was the product of an agreement in 1981 amongst the six Arab states that had common market and defence objectives. The GCC established a patent law in 1992, followed by some implementing bylaws in 1996. The Patent Office of the Gulf Cooperation Council is an example of a regional patent office that is highly dependent on the help and work of other patent offices. In 1998 the GCC PO began to receive patent applications, but delays in bringing the patent law into TRIPS compliance did not see patents being granted till 2002.[47] Before the GCC PO only Saudi Arabia and the United Arab Emirates had a patent office. The GCC PO receives comparatively few applications – a little over 5,000 patent applications had been received in total by 2005.[48] A patent granted by the GCC PO applies in all the GCC member states on the terms specified by the patent law adopted by the GCC. Matters of infringement are heard by the legal authorities of the state in which the infringement occurred. Worth noting is the fact that applicants have 12 months in which to claim the priority of an earlier application 'filed in any state or regional office'.[49] This allows for multiple routes into the GCC PO.

The PO of the GCC lacks experienced examiners and so has training agreements in place with the Austrian, Japanese and Swedish Patent Offices. With the exception of the Japanese Patent Office (JPO), these offices will also do search and examination for the GCC PO. Like other examiners in other developing-country patent offices, the examiners in the GCC depend on free databases and search tools as well as the published reports of other offices, especially ISAs under the PCT. In his analysis of the GCC published in 2006 Mohammed Al-Hajeri pointed out that members of the public could not properly search GCC patents because

---

[47] Mohamed F. Al-Hajeri, 'The Gulf Cooperation Council (GCC) Patent Office', 28 (2006) *World Patent Information*, 14.

[48] www.gcc-sg.org/eng/index.php?action=Sec-Show&ID=62&W2SID=3439.

[49] See Article 7.1 of the Patent Regulation of the Cooperation Council for the Arab States of the Gulf (2006).

of the lack of publicly available databases containing all the relevant information.[50] As in other developing countries, the disclosure obligation under the patent social contract is not being properly implemented. Patenting by locals in these countries is very low and foreign patenting tends to concentrate in the oil and gas sectors.[51]

The degree of automation for patenting in these countries is high. Most patents will arrive in the PO claiming the priority of a patent application somewhere else in the world. It will either be examined by a foreign office at the request of the GCC PO or the GCC examiner will follow the examination report of another office.

The basic story of these countries is a slow, but ever-deepening integration into the international patent framework. All are members of the WTO and with the exception of Kuwait all are members of the Paris Convention. Three are members of the PCT – Bahrain, Oman and the United Arab Emirates. The US through its trade monitoring and enforcement system keeps a watchful eye on the progress of these countries, chiding Kuwait for example in 2008 for not updating its intellectual property legislation.[52] The US also has these countries on its free-trade assembly line, some having moved along the line further than others. So, it has signed trade and investment framework action plans with Kuwait, Qatar and Saudi Arabia, launched Free Trade Agreement (FTA) negotiations with the United Arab Emirates, concluded negotiations with Oman and signed an FTA with Bahrain that has entered into force.[53] Typically US FTAs require the parties to join the PCT.

What is true of these GCC countries is also true of the broader Arab group of states. The legal systems of Arab states have continued to receive higher and higher standards of intellectual property through those states signing various trade and investment agreements with the US and the EU.[54] The EU especially has been a leader in bringing TRIPS-plus standards to the Arab world.[55] Patent offices in these countries overwhelmingly service the needs of foreign applicants. The number of applications is low. The Egyptian PO, which was established in 1951 and is one of the largest

[50] Al-Hajeri, 'The Gulf Cooperation Council (GCC) Patent Office', 14, 15–16.
[51] Ibid. 14, 17.
[52] See the 2008 Special 301 Report available at www.ustr.gov/Document_Library/Reports_Publications/2008/2008_Special_301_Report/Section_Index.html.
[53] See www.ustr.gov/Trade_Agreements/Regional/MEFTA/Section_Index.html.
[54] See the table of agreements in Mohammed El Said, *The Development of Intellectual Property Protection in the Arab World*, The Edwin Mellen Press, Lewiston, New York, 2008, 180–1.
[55] Ibid. 191–4.

offices in the region, received in 2003 a little over 1,100 applications and in 2004 it received 545 applications.[56] Like many developing-country patent offices it was faced with having to upgrade its operations after TRIPS in order to deal with areas that were new to it, such as pharmaceutical patenting.[57]

Political elites in these countries have been happy to give in to higher standards of intellectual property in exchange for trade and assistance deals, calculating no doubt that these higher standards do no immediate harm to their countries. One can debate this in the context of certain sectors such as pharmaceuticals.[58] Political elites in the Arab world are consigning their countries to a world of automated regulation in which judgements about the patentability of knowledge made in a few key patent offices will flow to the states of the Arab world via their patent offices, if patent owners so choose. This is their structural legacy to their citizens.

The origins of the Eurasian Patent Organization (EAPO) can be traced back to the break up of the Union of Soviet Socialist Republics (USSR) in 1991. On 8 December 1991 the three founding states of the USSR – Belarus, the Russian Federation and the Ukraine – signed the Minsk Accord. It dissolved the USSR as a subject of international law and declared that the USSR no longer existed as a geopolitical reality. The dissolution of the USSR and the creation of the Commonwealth of Independent States (CIS) in its place raised a complicated succession of law problems. In the case of patent law, the effect of the Minsk Accord on the establishment of the CIS was to leave most of the former Soviet Republics without a patent law, because Article 11 stated that laws of third states including the former USSR were not to apply to the signatories.[59] In the words of the EAPO website, 'the single patent space was broken'.[60] Russia, however, decided to apply a Soviet patent law of 1991. In its final decade, the USSR had decided to move in the direction of adopting a conventional patent system, passing a patent law in 1991 that abolished inventors' certificates.[61] Not only were the former Soviet Republics without patent law, but

---

[56] These figures are available from www.egypo.gov.eg/inner/english/News_Info_3.html.

[57] For the cost estimates see UNCTAD, The TRIPS Agreement and Developing Countries, United Nations, New York and Geneva, 1996, 23–4.

[58] See Hamed El-Said and Mohammed El-Said, 'TRIPS, Bilateralism, Multilateralism & Implications for Developing Countries: Jordan's Drug Sector', 2 (2005) *Manchester Journal of International Economic Law*, 59.

[59] William van Caenegem, 'Inventions in Russia: From the Public Good to Private Property', 4 (1993) *Australian Journal of Intellectual Property*, 232.

[60] See www.eapo.org/eng/information/history.html.

[61] For the history see van Caenegem, 'Inventions in Russia', 232.

Gospatent, the State Committee for Invention and Discoveries that processed applications for inventors' certificates and patents, ceased operations in December 1991. In Russia's case it was reincarnated as Rospatent at the beginning of 1992. Faced by this patent law void, the Republics of the CIS began to make arrangements to apply existing USSR patent law until they had developed their own.[62]

Officials from Gospatent anticipating the problems that would arise in the patent field from the dissolution of the USSR had begun talks in 1990 about the possibility of establishing a single patent system for what would be the independent states of the former USSR. Following the dissolution of the USSR, talks by CIS states about a single system along the lines of a European Patent Organization model continued. This regional approach to patents was strongly supported by the USPTO. The US also added some enticement by dangling MFN status before the independent republics in exchange for them reforming their intellectual property systems.[63]

The fall of the Soviet Empire notwithstanding, a regional patent system for the countries of the CIS emerged with surprising speed. A draft Eurasian Patent Convention (EAPC) was signed by nine states in 1994 and the Convention came into operation on 12 August 1995.[64] The Eurasian PO was located in Moscow and began operations in January of 1996. The sovereignty of participating states to develop their own national patent systems is expressly preserved by the convention.[65] In those cases where the Eurasian PO has rejected an application, the applicant can convert it into a bundle of national patent applications.[66] Despite the tumultuous times, the various former Soviet states moved quickly after independence to establish their own patent offices.

The EAPC does not cover the same territory covered by the former USSR. Uzbekistan is not a member and while Georgia and the Ukraine signed the Convention they did not ratify it. But these three states have patent offices and can be reached by means of the PCT route. The three Baltic Republics of Estonia, Latvia and Lithuania were not involved in the processes that led to the convention, but all three have become members

---

[62] Laura A. Pitta, 'Intellectual Property Laws in the Former Soviet Republics: A Time of Transition', 8 (1992) *Santa Clara Computer and High Technology L. J.*, 499, 502.

[63] Ibid. 499, 501.

[64] Azerbaijan, Belarus, Georgia, Kazakhstan, Kirghiz, Moldova, Russian Federation, Tajikistan and Ukraine. See www.eapo.org/eng/information/history.html.

[65] Article 1.1 and Article 22.1 of the EAPC.

[66] Article 16 of the EAPC.

of the European Patent Organization. So, in short, while the former republics of the USSR are not part of the one patent space, they are all part of *a* patent space.

Foreign applicants can enter the Eurasian PO by using the priority of the Paris Convention or using PCT procedures. Without going into details, it is a simpler system than that to be found under the EPC. The Eurasian system is a unitary system in which the granted patent automatically applies in all the states that are party to the convention and applicants have really only to be concerned with the Russian language, meaning that translation costs are kept to a minimum. Despite its simplicity, the Eurasian PO is not flooded by applications. In 2007 it received 2,692 with 2,212 of those coming via the PCT route.[67] In terms of the national patent offices that form part of the Eurasian zone, Rospatent, the Russian PO, is the most important. It is an ISA for PCT purposes, but its workload is small compared to other PCT offices, receiving only 0.5% of PCT international applications that were filed in all ISAs for 2007.[68]

For the time being the states of the former USSR are territories of low patenting activity. Foreigners dominate these low levels with applicants from the US representing a little more than 20% of all applications in 2007.[69] Pharmaceuticals and organic chemistry have been easily the two biggest areas of patenting activity.[70] The important point is that foreign companies have the option of patenting in the Eurasian patent zone using a regional system that is user friendly.

In the case of Africa, colonization produced Anglophone, Francophone and Lusophone systems of law. African colonies acquired, in one form or another, the patent law of their colonizer. The result, as Mgbeoji has put it, is 'a gaggle of IP laws and institutions in Africa which, in several instances, are a verbatim reproduction of IP laws in the colonial states'.[71] During colonial times, the simplest mechanism used was to directly apply the law of the colonizing power. So, for example, in the case of French colonies a decree of 1848 simply applied the French patent law of 1844 to France's colonies.[72] In the case of British colonies in Africa, the

[67] Eurasian Patent Organization, *Annual Report 2007*, 15–16.
[68] WIPO, *PCT Yearly Review 2007*, 23.
[69] Eurasian Patent Organization, *Annual Report 2007*, 17.
[70] Ibid. 18.
[71] Ikechi Mgbeoji, 'TRIPS And TRIPS-Plus Impacts in Africa' in Daniel J. Gervais (ed.), *Intellectual Property, Trade and Development*, Oxford University Press, Oxford, 2007, 259, 266.
[72] Decree of 21 October 1848, Regulating the Application of the Patent Law of the 5th of July, 1844 to the French Colonies. For the text see Alfred Carpmael and Edward Carpmael,

re-registration system became an important means by which UK patents could be transmitted to African colonies. For example in Nigeria even after its independence in 1960 it was only possible to obtain patent protection by registering a UK patent.[73] This position was changed in 1970. Generally patent law was simply not a priority in British colonial Africa, with evidence of any actual patent administration taking place being hard to find.[74] Colonization seeded intellectual property norms in Africa, but for the most part those norms existed on paper without the backing of administrative systems. After independence most African countries remained tied to a reception of intellectual property norms from the colonizing power and in the second part of the twentieth century became progressively more integrated into the international patent framework. Some very limited administrative capacity in patent administration has been created in Africa, but this is not capacity-building that will enable African states to pursue an autonomous patent regulatory agenda. Why Western powers would create this small-scale capacity in Africa is a question for which an answer is suggested at the end of this section.

The two regional patent organizations in Africa reproduce colonial divisions of the past. The African Regional Intellectual Property Organization (ARIPO) represents English-speaking African countries and the Organisation Africaine de la Propriété Intellectuelle (OAPI) represents French-speaking ones. One of many effects of colonization in Africa was to set African colonies upon the path of intellectual property protection, a path they have continued to roll along after independence. As a result many African countries provide relatively high standards of patent protection, even though many are classified as least-developed.[75]

ARIPO was created with the assistance of the United Nations Economic Commission for Africa and WIPO.[76] Following the creation of ARIPO

The Patent Laws of the World, Collected, Edited and Indexed, 2nd edn., William Clowes and Sons, London, 1889, 183.

[73] See J. W. Baxter, *World Patent Law and Practice*, 2nd edn., Sweet and Maxwell, London, 1973, 316.

[74] Adebambo Adewopo, 'The Global Intellectual Property System and Sub-Saharan Africa: A Prognostic Reflection', 33 (2002) *University of Toledo Law Review*, 749, 750.

[75] For example, many African LDCs provide patent protection for pharmaceutical products even though they could claim the benefits of TRIPS transitional provisions. See Phil Thorpe, 'Study on the Implementation of the TRIPS Agreement by Developing Countries', Study Paper 7, Commission on Intellectual Property Rights.

[76] On the role of WIPO see www.aripo.org/index.php?option=com_content&view=article&id=19&Itemid=53. Agreement on the Creation of the African Regional Industrial Property Organization (ARIPO) (as adopted by the Diplomatic Conference for the

in 1976, a Protocol on Patents and Industrial Designs was adopted in 1982 (referred to as the Harare Protocol).[77] Under the Protocol, ARIPO is empowered to grant patents on behalf of the contracting states.[78] Applications to ARIPO have to designate the contracting states in which a patent is sought. The ARIPO system operates on an opt-out basis. If ARIPO decides to grant the patent then it will take effect in the designated states unless, using the procedures of the Harare Protocol, a contracting state notifies ARIPO that the patent cannot take effect under its national law.[79]

The operation of the Harare Protocol is fully integrated with the PCT. So, for example, an international application under the PCT can designate ARIPO as the relevant office. This means that one can reach the member states of ARIPO (with the exception of Somalia) by designating ARIPO in a PCT application. Direct national filing is another way into most members of ARIPO. There is also the option of filing in ARIPO itself. Claiming formats for first and second medical indications are standardized under the implementing regulations to the Harare Protocol, the regulations specifying the phrases to be used. It is a good example of the process of regulatory automation. Whether a regional patent organization in Africa should open the door to pharmaceutical patenting in this way is another matter. Under the Harare Protocol, ARIPO is meant to undertake substantive examination or to arrange it. It is a small office with about thirty staff and two or three examiners. Essentially it, like most developing-country offices, has to rely upon the reports generated by the PCT system. Its growth and competency is dependent upon its ability to capture resources from the wealthy players in the system such as WIPO or the EPO. In 2007 it signed a cooperation agreement with China's State Intellectual Property Office (SIPO).

For French colonies, the French National Patents Right Institute acted as the patent authority. After the independence of these colonies an agreement known as the Libreville Agreement was signed in 1962 that was then revised and signed at Bangui in 1977 (referred to as the Bangui Agreement).[80] This regional agreement is an example of deep

---

adoption of an Agreement on the Creation of an Industrial Property Organization for English-Speaking Africa at Lusaka (Zambia) on 9 December 1976.

[77] Somalia is the only ARIPO member not to have adopted the Harare Protocol.

[78] See Section 1 of the Protocol on Patents and Industrial Designs Within the Framework of the African Regional Industrial Property Organization (ARIPO), 1982, as revised.

[79] See ibid. Sections 3(6) and (7).

[80] Agreement Relating to the Creation of an African Intellectual Property Organization, 1977. The Agreement was revised again in 1999.

harmonization in that each member agrees to apply a common set of patent provisions and the grant of a patent by OAPI takes effect as a grant under the Bangui Agreement.[81] Under this agreement there is no bundle of national applications. Instead OAPI grants one patent valid in all the members of the Bangui Agreement. As in the case of the Harare Protocol, the Bangui Agreement is integrated with PCT procedures.

Neither African regional system is much used by patent applicants. WIPO's patent data shows very little activity taking place in either regional office. Patenting traffic generally in African countries is very low. It is clear that South Africa is the dominant patenting destination and that the PCT is the main route into Africa. According to WIPO's data the South African patent office received 5,781 PCT national phase entries in 2006, with 564 for Algeria and 30 for Kenya.[82] There was no data available for most other African countries. WIPO's patent data for 2005 paints a similar picture with, for example, Nigeria, which is sometimes described as the Giant of Africa, having 14 patents in force in 2005.[83] There is a question about the reliability of patent data in many developing countries. WIPO officials pointed out to me that many developing-country patent offices do not always provide WIPO with the information that it needs to keep its statistics up to date. Some of the European patent officials I interviewed suggested that some patent office systems in African countries were not operationally smooth affairs, these patent offices perhaps not even knowing what was actually on patent in their countries. Many patent offices in Africa like those in Pacific island states are run by individuals who might also have responsibility for other business registration systems.[84] Of course, if the patent system itself is a socially inefficient machine serving a few rent-seeking foreigners, then leaving this machinery in a dilapidated state may well be a socially efficient strategy from which some developed countries might learn.

One patent god

Why, one might ask, has so much effort been made to bring some of the world's poorest countries into the global patent fold? The answer has

---

[81] See ibid. Articles 4.1 and 8.4.
[82] See *World Patent Report: A Statistical Review*, 2008, WIPO, Geneva, 65, Table A2.
[83] *WIPO Patent Report 2007*, WIPO, Geneva, 49, Table 2. Mgbeoji states that the Nigerian PO issued 1,458 patents to foreigners and 986 to residents for 1999–2002. See Mgbeoji, 'TRIPS and TRIPS-Plus Impacts in Africa', 259, 280.
[84] Mgbeoji, 'TRIPS and TRIPS-Plus Impacts in Africa', 259, 293.

cost and discipline dimensions. The cost of automating the operations of these offices is relatively small. Training examiners to follow the decisions of the Trilateral Offices and giving them information technology systems to do it is not expensive. This, one has to remember, is not training to produce autonomous capacity, but rather to simply mimic the leader. The half a million dollars that it was estimated that the Egyptian PO would need to upgrade its facilities is small change for a multinational and in any case multinationals do not foot these bills.[85] Very often the cost is met out of overseas development assistance budgets of rich countries.

Just as important is the question of interpretive discipline. Chris Arup has argued that WTO agreements like TRIPS open the door to a rich world of 'inter-legality' in which local legal traditions meet global norms, potentially leaving those norms open to a variety of interpretations.[86] The possibility of variety is real, just as real as the desire of local people everywhere to solve problems in their own way. A variety of standards has been the history of patent law in Western countries. In Africa the development by the Organization of African Unity of a model law to protect the rights of local communities and farmers in respect of their biological resources is one example of community-based problem solving in a world of inter-legality.[87] This kind of problem-solving is precisely what the multinational users of the patent system do not want. They operate business models that demand universal standards of patentability and universally common interpretations of those standards. Africa remains for the West a rich source of raw materials including biological materials. In the case of these materials there are also systems of traditional knowledge that show how this raw material might be turned into products for Western markets. When it comes to the patentability of such materials there can only be one patent god. The mission of these multinationals is to ensure that the world of inter-legality does not dissolve into many different worlds of local interpretation that compromise the universalization process. This

---

[85] See UNCTAD, *The TRIPS Agreement and Developing Countries*, United Nations, New York and Geneva, 1996, 23.

[86] Christopher Arup, *The World Trade Organization Knowledge Agreements*, 2nd edn., Cambridge University Press, Cambridge, 2008, 6–9.

[87] For a discussion of the model and its impact in Africa see Johnson A. Ekpere, 'The African Union Model Law for the Protection of the Rights of Local Communities Farmers and Breeders and the Regulation of Access to Biological Resources' in Christophe Bellman, Graham Dutfield and Ricardo Meléndez-Ortiz (eds.), *Trading in Knowledge*, Earthscan, London, 2003, 231.

means that the operations of developing-country patent offices have to be automated by means of social convention and information technology systems. Lying behind all the endless tedious details of patent office training manuals, exchange programmes, database searching and procedural reform is an agenda of regulatory automation that integrates developing-country offices into a patent empire where the decisions of a few key offices will rule.

11

Reclaiming the patent social contract

A private insider governance network

The twentieth century proved to be the century of innovation in patent bureaucracy and the regulation of markets by patent owners using patenting strategies. Whether this staggering global growth in patent bureaucracy and patent regulation of markets actually caused much important scientific and technological innovation that would otherwise not have occurred, and at a cost that did not outweigh the benefits, is a question to which we will probably never have an answer. More often than not, analysis of the patent system begins with a presumption in its favour: 'High levels of innovation in the United States would seem to be evidence that the intellectual property system is working well and does not require fundamental changes.'[1]

At the beginning of the nineteenth century few European states had patent law and none had recognizably modern systems of patent administration (see Chapter 3). At the beginning of the twenty-first century it is hard to find an example of a country that does not have a patent law of some kind on the books – Timor Leste is perhaps one example. Even in some of the poorest, smallest states such as some of the Pacific islands, there are patent laws on the books that technically, as we saw in Chapter 10, form part of global patent filing routes. No island seems to be without a patent law. Larger patent offices such as the Australian PO trawl the region offering assistance, showing up in places like Palau much to the surprise of officials there. 'We don't invent anything', one Palau official pointed out to me. In the eyes of the patent system this is true. These islands are seen as sites of raw materials where, for example, visiting marine biologists come to take samples to feed the laboratories and patent filing systems of places like the National Cancer Institute in the US.

---

[1] Stephen A. Merrill, Richard C. Levin and Mark B. Myers (eds.), *A Patent System for the 21st Century*, National Academies Press, Washington, DC, 2001, 19.

Patent law and, much more importantly, supporting systems of patent administration now enmesh states and their systems of innovation. The growth of patent bureaucracy has become a self-sustaining enterprise. Patent offices generate fees that they keep or which are returned to them by governments for the purposes of running and spreading patent administration. As we have seen, the major offices at relatively low cost integrate developing-country offices into their systems – the European Patent Office (EPO) drafts examination manuals for developing countries and trains examiners in their use, and the USPTO brings examiners from India and Brazil to its training facilities in Alexandria, Virginia, and helps them understand the art of pharmaceutical examination.[2] In exchange for some manuals and hardware, developing-country offices extend technocratic trust to the large players in the system. A global system of patent governance is being forged at modest cost.

The scope for institutional experimentation with the patent system is much diminished compared to the nineteenth century. No country today can do what the Netherlands did in 1869 and repeal its patent law. Developing countries have even less freedom to operate when it comes to the patent institution. As Thailand has learned, even a modest use of the principle of compulsory licensing in relation to medicines attracts a 'shock and awe' response from the international pharmaceutical industry and its many Congressional apparatchiki. Within developed countries what passes for patent reform is a game of inches concerning, for example, the right level at which to set the standard of inventiveness. But if the patent institution is fundamentally inefficient, this will do little to improve its efficiency, any more than a percentage point drop in agricultural tariffs will help liberalize trade in agriculture.

At some point the need for radical design approaches to the patent system will be taken more seriously by states. Generally speaking, regulatory reform is crisis-driven.[3] Nuclear power plants have to experience meltdown and oil tankers have to spill millions of tons of oil before there are improvements in the regulation of nuclear power and shipping. It is also clear that these disasters must affect the well-off in developed countries. Poor people dying in large numbers in developing countries leads to comparatively little regulatory action by Western policy elites when it

---

[2] For example, the EPO drafted the examination manual for the Philippines Patent Office. Information about the USPTO's training of developing-country examiners was obtained from the USPTO.

[3] For a survey see J. Braithwaite and P. Drahos, *Global Business Regulation*, Cambridge University Press, Cambridge, 2000.

comes to the international patent regime, although these days it does generate a lot of placatory ritualism such as the WTO's so-called Paragraph 6 solution in relation to the access to medicines problems of developing countries.[4]

Over time the patent system's inefficiencies in the innovation and diffusion of medicines will create greater access problems in developed countries. Climate change may also prove to be a rather big exogenous variable for those who guard the patent system with the intensity of zealots. For the purposes of managing climate change, states will want faster innovation and diffusion of alternative energy technologies, plants for food and agriculture and technologies for efficient water use. And, of course, climate change may cause changes in the geographic spread of pathogens and diseases. Colonization by Europeans from about the sixteenth century spread diseases to many developing countries that assisted in, for example, the conquest of the Aztec empire.[5] Climate change may enable those countries to return the favour of new disease burdens. The patent system in its present form is a risk factor, rather than a tool of risk management for handling these kinds of large-scale changes and crises. The system has an appalling track record in producing medicines for tropical diseases.[6] In the case of avian bird flu the World Health Organization (WHO) recommended the stockpiling of oseltamivir (Tamiflu), a drug that was under patent. As a result, the patent system produced an outcome where the highest-risk countries had the smallest stockpiles and the lowest-risk countries the biggest.[7]

Today's globalized patent institution was never designed by states as a tool for the management of risk. Historically speaking, the principal players that have most influenced the evolution of the current system of governance have been the big business owners of patents, the patent attorney profession and the lead states in terms of patenting. At the end of the nineteenth century, the lead patenting states (US, UK, Germany and France) took the decision to support the patent system not for reasons of public welfare but because of its importance to state power (see Chapter 3). Since

---

[4] For an analysis see P. Drahos, 'Four Lessons for Developing Countries from the Trade Negotiations Over Access to Medicines, 28 (2007) *Liverpool Law Review*, 11.

[5] R.A. Weiss and A.J. McMichael, 'Social and Environmental Risk Factors in the Emergence of Infectious Diseases', 10(12) (2004) *Nature Medicine Supplement*, S70, S72.

[6] Thirteen of the 1,223 new chemical entities between 1975 and 1997 related to tropical diseases. See Zafar Mirza, 'WTO, TRIPs, Pharmaceuticals and Health: Impacts and Strategies', 42 (1999) *Development*, 92, 95.

[7] Buddhima Lokuge, Peter Drahos and Warwick Neville, 'Pandemics, Antiviral Stockpiles and Biosecurity in Australia: What About the Generic Option?', 184(1) (2006) *Medical Journal of Australia*, 16–20.

that time patent systems have become ever more sophisticated systems of private taxation serving the interests of a few large users (see Chapter 1). At the beginning of the twenty-first century most states, with one or two notable exceptions, are not bent on war. They want economic development. But increasingly they realize that they must be careful that this economic development does not cause environmental systems to begin tipping like dominoes. The warnings and analysis of the International Panel on Climate Change have gained the attention of most governments around the world. But predictably, as in so many negotiations before, intellectual property rights and technology transfer issues are causing divisions amongst states.[8] More than ever states need a patent system that diffuses innovation and serves global risk management goals rather than beggar-thy-neighbour trade agendas.

Patent systems in their present form represent deep concentrations of power and dominance in which networks of big businesses, patent attorneys and patent offices cooperate to produce an insider governance of the system. The global patent office network that has been described in the preceding chapters is not one that is devoted to benign technocratic management 'enhancing the ability of States to work together to address common problems'.[9] As we have seen patent attorneys and patent offices have over the decades colluded in the development of patent claim drafting techniques to overcome publicly mandated restrictions on patentability (see Chapter 2). The USPTO, the EPO and the Japanese Patent Office (JPO) formed the Trilateral Offices club in the 1980s to steer the system in ways that were responsive to the needs of the big business users (see Chapter 6). These three offices operate within international fora like the World Intellectual Property Organization (WIPO) to push patent treaty harmonization agendas that developing countries oppose. The Trilaterals circumvent this opposition by integrating developing-country patent offices into their systems and training their examiners to follow their examination decisions (see Chapters 4 and 10). Through technocratic cooperation they bring about a process of invisible harmonization (see Chapters 1 and 6). In the name of capacity-building they foster simple imitation. No state, no matter how poor, is left without the benefits of this capacity assistance (see Chapter 10). The patent office network is a pervasive network that

---

[8] See Summary of Views Expressed During the Fourth Session of the Ad Hoc Working Group on Long-Term Cooperative Action under the Convention, FCCC/AWGLCA/2009/3, 18 March 2009.

[9] Anne-Marie Slaughter, 'The Accountability of Government Networks', 8 (2001) *Indiana Journal of Global Legal Studies*, 347.

over time has come to dominate the national level of policy approaches to patents, with members of the network representing states in patent treaty negotiations as well as bilateral and multilateral trade negotiations that cover intellectual property. Its members share a common business model that has made them dependent on their big business customers. They have largely abdicated their responsibilities to their respective publics under their respective national patent social contracts.

The words of one senior insider are worth quoting at length:

> However, it is remarkable that considerations on the benefits of patent protection for the world community or individual economic areas are lacking to a large extent. Tons of paper are produced but the results are very poor. The concerns of the developing countries and transitional countries are not responded to seriously, particularly the formerly frequently asked question about an effective transfer of technology, or the present demands for the integration of the assets of those countries into the patent system and international trade. Rather, serious discussions are taking place about strategies on how to by-pass developing countries and transitional countries, which could lead to a closed shop of a few giants.[10]

There are, of course, public accountability mechanisms for patent offices. As we have seen in preceding chapters, they are part of public service department structures and the heads of patent offices are ultimately answerable to politicians, such as the ministers who in parliamentary systems are responsible for government departments. However, the formal mechanisms of public accountability that operate here are meaningless. Patent rules do not get decided at the ballot box. Tax, law and order, and health services are the stuff of election campaigns. Patents are not. The patent system is so densely technocratic that politicians do not take the lead on patent policy unless an industry lobby dictates a clear direction, as did the industry lobbies that led the US Congress and the Executive in the process of bringing about the Agreement on Trade-Related Aspects of Intellectual Property Rights (TRIPS).[11] The real accountability of patent offices lies with the private governance network of the large businesses that dominate patent applications. It is no surprise that the interviews showed that every patent office is in constant communication with its business users. Every patent office proposal for reform is carefully scrutinized by the patent attorneys

---

[10] Jürgen Schade, 'Europe and the International Community of States on the Path Towards a Common Patent Strategy', 38 (2007) *International Review of Intellectual Property and Competition Law*, 517, 520. Dr Schade is the President of the German Patent and Trade Mark Office.

[11] See P. Drahos with J. Braithwaite, *Information Feudalism*, Earthscan, London, 2002.

that represent the large players. The business networks that surround patent offices are amongst the most watchful and expert in the world.

The displacement of public accountability mechanisms by private networked power is, in the case of patent offices, not a new phenomenon. Business networks have been co-evolving with patent offices for at least a hundred years (see Chapters 1, 2 and 3). Public accountability mechanisms are the convenient front men of legitimacy. They help hide the fact that an organization created to represent the public under a social contract has become deeply intertwined and absorbed by a private governance network. The customer mentality that pervades patent offices makes their role in the network seem perfectly natural. The symbiotic relationship which has developed between patent offices and big business users and the depth of their networked communication with each other mean that genuinely welfare-enhancing reforms of the patent system are, for the most part, likely to fail. Ministers are too ignorant or too worried about offending the global end of the corporate world to be serious about reform. Patent offices know that if they repeat the litany that more patents equal more innovation, most politicians are simple-minded enough to believe it. The few others who are sceptical about the efficiency of patent monopolies nevertheless listen when, for example, a large pharmaceutical company screams that the right to delay and divide patent applications is a precious natural right needed for R&D purposes.

A counter network of outsiders

The basic problem of the patent system can be simply stated. Standard-setting and administration of the system is dominated by a globally integrated private governance network. This network has made the patent social contract largely meaningless. More rule-based reform of the system will simply see this private governance network continue to bend the process of rule-making to its own ends. What is needed to counter the power of this network is another network made up of outsiders to the patent system. The only way to counter the power of one network is with another network. The outsider network needs to have the technocratic skill to confront the insider network. Confrontation has to be constant and detailed. Each patent rule change proposed by the insider network to serve its private interest should be tracked and fought by an outsider network serving the public interest. The thousands of patent grants that daily pour out of the major patent offices must be assessed for social harm and ways found to eliminate the most damaging patents or to contain their effects.

General accountability mechanisms such as ministerial responsibility cannot provide the kind of close oversight that is needed of patent office decision-making. Instead, there has to be a long-term strategy based on building a counter network to the private governance network that has absorbed patent offices. This counter network should be guided by the separation of powers principle, something we discuss in the next section. The basic idea is to contest the power of the private network at every point where key decisions are made and where possible to create veto rights or checks over patent office decisions. An example of a veto model is the Brazilian model in relation to pharmaceutical patents where examiners in the Brazilian PO do not have the final say over the grant of a pharmaceutical patent, a model we discuss in the next chapter. An example of a checking mechanism is the external audit mechanism for patent quality that is proposed later in this chapter.

The future of the patent social contract depends on the formation of an outsider governance network. There are many outsiders – government departments such as health departments and environment departments, competition law authorities, civil society organizations, technology movements interested in patent-free innovation (for example, the free software movement), science researchers who still subscribe to public-good values, university administrators who still have some sense of the public-good mission of universities, companies on the receiving end of patent bullying and litigation, indigenous groups fighting biopiracy, farmer groups opposed to patent locks on seed varieties, and many others. There are many more outsiders than there are insider beneficiaries of the patent system. One of the fundamental problems facing outsiders is a basic lack of information about the patent holdings of the few powerful beneficiaries of the system. Information about granted patents is public information, but it is not available in publicly useful ways that enable the forensic scrutiny of those patents by interested outsiders. Exposing and isolating those patent holdings in ways that are accessible to the many interested outsiders is a first step. The transparency register proposal discussed later in this chapter presents a model of enforceable transparency for this purpose. Revealing concentrated power in a democracy begins the process of separating that power. Exposure of power by itself is not enough. States interested in reclaiming the patent social contract have to help to create the veto and checking systems that will enable outsiders to deal with the patents that cause social harm. Many outsiders have the technical knowledge and the interest in confronting the private governance network that runs patent systems. However, few can afford the costly battlegrounds of courts. States need to create low-cost tools that will help outsiders to create a contest of networks.

Before moving on to outline some tools of engagement, it is worth asking whether there is the political leadership that is needed to take on the sophisticated private governance network that rules the patent system. Here it is worth pointing out that competitive political environments will from time to time create circumstances in which politicians will have incentives to act in the public interest and contribute to the building of an outsider network to regulate the patent system. Later in this chapter we will see that the Australian Parliament passed an amendment to its Therapeutic Goods Act that addresses the problem of patent gaming by brand pharmaceutical companies. This legislation was pushed through by an opposition that was in a position to control the Australian Senate at a time when the Australian government was seeking to implement the US–Australia Free Trade Agreement. Contained in the Agreement were provisions affecting Australia's Pharmaceutical Benefits Scheme (PBS).[12] The PBS was widely regarded as the gold standard for regulating the patent monopoly prices of pharmaceuticals. But the PBS was also disliked by the US pharmaceutical industry and so it took the opportunity of the free trade negotiations to begin the process of dismantling it.[13] A small group of academics and activists pointed to the potential cost implications of this for medicines under the PBS.[14] Their warnings were picked up by the media and there followed a mass public concern about the future of the PBS.[15] The opposition leader Mark Latham donned the cape of the people's health champion. Announcing that he would not let 'dodgy' patents limit people's access to medicines under the PBS, he tabled amendments that aimed to deter pharmaceutical companies from patent gaming behaviour.[16] These amendments were passed.[17]

[12]   See Annex 2-C Pharmaceuticals, US–Australia Free Trade Agreement.
[13]   For the details see Peter Drahos, Buddhima Lokuge, Tom Faunce, Martyn Goddard and David Henry, 'Pharmaceuticals, Intellectual Property and Free Trade: The Case of the US–Australia Free Trade Agreement', 22 (2004) *Prometheus*, 243.
[14]   See, for example, Peter Drahos, Thomas Faunce, Martyn Goddard and David Henry, 'The FTA and the PBS', A submission to the Senate Select Committee on the US–Australia Free Trade Agreement, available at www.aftinet.org.au/campaigns/US_FTA/henrydrahossenatesub2.htm.
[15]   Particularly important in bringing the attention of the public to the issues was the documentary 'A Bitter Pill' that was broadcast by the ABC Four Corners on 2 August 2004.
[16]   See www.abc.net.au/7.30/content/2004/s1169988.htm.
[17]   See US Free Trade Agreement Implementation Act 2004, Schedule 7.

The outsider network for patent governance that needs to be built will not be built overnight. But broader political interest in the patent system has advanced much further than anyone would have predicted two or three decades ago. From time to time politicians will have incentives to act as the people's champion when it comes to fighting patent monopolies. Good ideas for the outside regulation of the system will be put in place and an outsider governance network will continue to evolve.

The separation of powers principle

The design principle that can re-shape the insider governance described in the last section and that matters most to the future evolution of the patent system is the principle of the separation of powers.[18] It is an important idea in the Western political tradition, perhaps the most important. Conceived of broadly, in the way that it is in *The Federalist Papers*, it requires power to be divided and regulated by a system of checks and balances. Institutional designers guided by it must work towards limited and decentralized structures of power, or to borrow Madison's description of its application to public and private affairs: 'the constant aim is to divide and arrange the several offices in such a manner as that each may be a check on the other – that the private interest of every individual may be a sentinel over the public rights'.[19] Many principles of governance and regulation, such as the principles of transparency, accountability and audit, serve this fundamental political value.

Systems of patent administration have grown dramatically and in ways that have seen the rise of networked power. It is true that the traditional patent powers, the EU and the US, have been joined by Japan first and more recently China and Korea. But as we have seen, the network remains a hierarchical network and even though its dominant core has been expanded its pro-patent values and goals have not changed. The first step in genuine patent reform is to break up these concentrations of power, to flip the system from insider governance to a networked governance that contests patent-based technocratic expertise by drawing on innovation expertise from many communities of innovators. The remainder of this

---

[18] On the importance of the principle to regulatory theory see John Braithwaite, 'On Speaking Softly and Carrying Big Sticks: Neglected Dimensions of a Republican Separation of Powers', 47 (1997) *University of Toronto Law Journal*, 305.

[19] James Madison, Alexander Hamilton and John Jay, *The Federalist Papers* (Isaac Kramnick ed.), Penguin, Harmondsworth, 1987, 320.

chapter discusses regulatory ideas that draw on the principle of a separation of powers and are aimed at making the system more responsive to communities of innovators.

New insiders for insider governance

Patent offices typically have policy committees or advisory committees. These committees usually have a heavy representation from business and the patent attorney profession. If there is broader representation it is usually token. Insiders have little incentive to raise critical questions or issues in the development of patent office guidelines. Rather, the focus is on productive efficiency, on making it easier, cheaper and faster to obtain patents. Questions of fundamental principle do not get raised. For example, biotech patent attorneys and patent offices have little incentive to ask whether, as a matter of legal principle, purified biological materials substantially identical to those that occur in nature actually do cross the threshold of 'invention' so as to be eligible for the grant of a patent. Both parties have a financial incentive not to do so. Biologists working in public research institutions may have different views of the invention threshold. Similarly, drugs that have been patented as a combination of left- and right-handed molecular structures are being re-patented by pharmaceutical companies as either left- or right-handed drugs.[20] The real question that society wants an answer to is not whether this is inventive as a matter of patent law jurisprudence, a jurisprudence that has been paid for by decades of pharmaceutical company litigation, but rather whether it is innovative as judged by the community of experimental pharmacologists, a community which tends to look for genuine leaps in therapeutic benefits rather than clever marketing strategies. In a world of networked governance, power grows less out of the barrel of a gun and more from the long occupation of a seat on a key committee. It follows that one element of a strategy to dismantle the insider governance of patent systems is to look at the composition of the committees that guide the development of patent office systems. Patent office committees need to be connected less to the patent attorney profession and more to communities of innovators or groups like economists who understand the social costs of patent intervention in the marketplace. One way in which to build this connection is to put significant numbers of members from these communities on patent office committees.

---

[20] See A. Somogyi, F. Bochner and D. Foster, 'Inside the Isomers: The Tale of Chiral Switches', 27(2) (2004) *Australian Prescriber*, 47.

An external audit check

Well-resourced patent offices have internal procedures for checking the work of examiners (for example, the EPO has a Quality Audit Directorate). It is also true that the Trilateral Offices have devoted considerable resources to improving their internal procedures for checking patent quality and have developed process measures of patent quality. In many developing-country patent offices I interviewed, the Thai PO being one representative example, there was no real system of checking the quality of examination work. The head of an examination section would review some of the work of the section. The story in the Thai office was the familiar one of training by the EPO with Thai examiners following the examination decisions of EPO and USPTO examiners. One argument might be that Thai examiners by doing this are gaining the benefit of the USPTO's and EPO's quality standards and systems. But this raises the issue of whether the quality systems of developed-country offices will necessarily meet Thailand's needs.

The experience of Thailand with the didanosine (ddI) patent, which is an important AIDS medicine, suggests that patent offices have to be careful about the quality standards that they choose to follow. It also shows that there should be other regulatory mechanisms in place for generating information about the quality of patents. The patent on a better oral dosing formulation of dideoxy purine nucleosides was a broad formulation patent and issued to Bristol-Myers Squibb on 22 January 1998, with the company also successfully pursuing a formulation patent in the US.[21] Claims over the way an active ingredient is formulated are accepted by many patent offices, including the EPO. Even old drugs such as paracetamol continue to be the subject of formulation claims in the EPO.[22] The likelihood of such a formulation claim being allowed by a patent office depends on how strictly one applies the requirement of an inventive step.[23] One effect of the issuance of the ddI patent in Thailand was that Thailand's Government Pharmaceutical Organization had to stop production of a generic version of ddI. Doubts about the validity of the patent led to a civil society campaign that included litigation to revoke the patent. The case settled in December

---

[21] See US patent No. 5,880,106. Thailand's experience with the ddI patent is described in 'Regional Report: The ASEAN-Rockefeller Foundation Project on Intellectual Property Laws Review and Capacity Building on Intellectual Property Rights Related to Public Health in the ASEAN Region', ASEAN Secretariat, 2005, 267–71.

[22] See European Patent Application 07112327.7, Injectable liquid paracetamol formulation, filed 12 July 2007.

[23] For an argument that most formulation claims are likely to lack an inventive step see Carlos Correa, 'Guidelines for the examination of Pharmaceutical Patents: Developing a Public Health Perspective', ICTSD, WHO, UNCTAD, Geneva, 2007, 6–7.

2003 and Bristol-Myers Squibb withdrew the patent. Fighting this one patent involved a large number of government and civil society actors in Thailand and dragged on for almost 6 years to produce a result in which the company simply withdrew the patent. The key issues on which civil society wanted a court ruling, issues concerning the circumstances of the patent's grant and its validity, were never ruled upon by a court. These kinds of patent litigation exercises require many civil society activists to coordinate and find resources to fight a case over a period of years. Thailand has historically had a vigorous NGO health movement and is one of the few developing countries in which a national civil society health movement could have mobilized in this way. Moreover, the reality is that this was a fight over just one formulation patent of doubtful validity. The example also shows the importance of having independent sources of information about the quality of patents in a country. During the litigation the Thai Patent Office came in for criticism because it intervened in the litigation in ways that favoured Bristol-Myers Squibb.[24] This behaviour is consistent with the broader argument in preceding chapters that developing-country patent offices have over a long period of time been steadily integrated into a private governance network. By virtue of this integration they will be disposed to behave in ways that are likely to be pro-patent and, in the case of developing-country patent offices, that favour the rent-seeking practices of multinationals.

One way in which to combat the regulatory capture of patent offices is through the external audit of granted patents. Each year a committee of independent experts would target some key areas of patenting (for example, pharmaceuticals, software, biotechnology, nanotechnology) and audit the quality of a sample of patents in that area. This committee (labelled the External Patent Audit Committee (EPAC) in Figure 11.1) would report its findings to a body independent of the patent office, such as, for example, a parliamentary committee. Legislators and ministers in many countries generally do not understand the extent of the regulatory capture of patent offices and tend to be excessively reliant on them for advice, advice that tends to be of a predictable kind. External audit mechanisms for patent offices would catalyse different information flows about patents to legislators, something needed in many, if not most, countries.

This audit mechanism could potentially be combined with other strands of governance to form a powerful tool of nodal governance. Courts and opposition procedures would continue to act as quality filters, but as we saw in Chapters 1 and 2 these filters only reach a small number of patents.

---

[24] See 'Regional Report: The ASEAN-Rockefeller Foundation Project', 270.

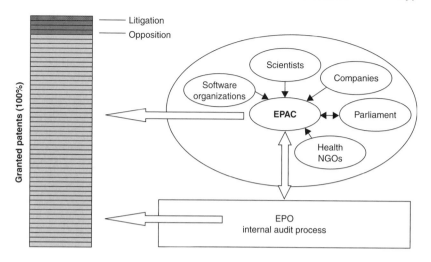

Figure 11.1 Patent quality: an external audit check

An EPAC would provide an additional filter. Companies, for example, encountering patent thickets could feed information to an EPAC so that it could focus its resources on problem areas. Patent offices would, of course, continue with their own internal audit procedures, but in the knowledge that an independent body would also be conducting audits of their work. Importantly, and EPAC would also be an independent source of technical information for legislative bodies. The power of an EPAC to lead through suasion would itself be enhanced by appointing to it scientists with major international reputations who were prepared to defend the public good mission of science and who understood the dangers of low quality patents to that public good mission. So, for example, John Sulston, a Nobel Prize winner in Physiology or Medicine, has written about the dangers of patent office practice in the context of the patents on gene sequences.[25] Scientists like Sulston who understand where real innovation in molecular biology lies and the ways in which individuals in a community of innovators depend on each other's work to advance knowledge could, through an EPAC, foment a more public and rigorous scrutiny of patent office practice and its impact on innovation systems. National legislatures would be amongst the beneficiaries of the information flows about patents and innovation that could be catalysed by a high-profile EPAC.

---

[25] See, for example, John Sulston, 'Intellectual Property and the Human Genome', in Peter Drahos and Ruth Mayne (eds.), *Global Intellectual Property Rights: Knowledge, Access and Development*, Palgrave Macmillan, Hampshire, 2002, 61.

Taking transparency seriously

The patent social contract justification recognizes the cumulative nature of innovation.[26] Inventor D will be better off if Inventors A, B and C have made their inventions public and Inventor E will be better off if Inventors A, B, C and D have made their inventions public and so on. Keeping inventions secret means that inventors have less information and tools with which to solve problems. Yet, as we saw in our discussion of the patent social contract in Chapter 1, the patent system currently does a very poor job of making information available to downstream inventors. A lot of information does not make it into patent specifications and the information that does is crafted in patent drafting language that is often of little use to scientific experts. Sometimes finding patents in the first place may be difficult. During the course of fieldwork I interviewed generic companies in Australia, Canada, Malaysia, the Philippines, Vietnam and Thailand and all of them described a world of ever more elaborate patent strategies:

> The patent issue is becoming exponentially more complex. There are patents around patents. There is less innovation from Pharma. They must extend patents around their basic products. No company can walk away from the compound (CEO of an Australian generic company).
> There is second generation evergreening of patents with a much bigger family creation of patents taking place (Australian generic company).

Litigation was one answer to this problem:

> Only very aggressive litigation in Canada has been effective in dealing with linkage. Generics only get on the market after very aggressive litigation (interview, Canadian generic pharmaceutical association – linkage refers to provisions that link the registration of medicines to the patent system).

In Malaysia and the Philippines finding patents was a problem, with some companies writing to the patent owner in an attempt to clarify the position (interviews with members of the Malaysian and Philippines generic associations). Even though the medicines markets are small in these countries there is evidence of gaming behaviour. One Malaysian generic company provided me with a file on a medicine that had been patented in the US, the patent having expired in 2001. Generic companies had entered the US market. The US brand company had obtained a certificate for utility

---

[26] A cumulative model of innovation is thought to be true of many areas of high technology such as biotechnology. See Adam B. Jaffe and Josh Lerner, *Innovation and its Discontents*, Princeton University Press, Princeton, 2004, 64.

innovation under Malaysian law, giving it protection there until 2006 and the option of further protection until 2011. The Malaysian generic's application for the registration of its generic version had been rejected by the Malaysian National Pharmaceutical Control Bureau because of the certificate. Seeking advice from a Malaysian law firm the generic company received a letter containing the usual impenetrable legal prose that concluded with 'you could attempt to invalidate the Utility Innovation'.

It is not only developing-country companies that get the benefit of this kind of assistance from the legal profession on patents. A complementary medicines company I interviewed in Australia had dropped a vitamin product from its range in Australia because of a US formulation patent, on the basis of legal advice from its lawyers. Its general manager said of the advice: 'to be frank I view it as arse-covering'. An Australian patent had not been applied for by the US company at the time of my interview.

From the point of view of the patent social contract, the uncertainty being generated by the patent system is not acceptable. The whole point of the patent social contract is that patents are meant to disclose invention information in order to enable competitors to enter a post-patent period of market competition. Obviously this cannot happen if relevant patents cannot be found in the first place or too many uncertainty-generating patents are found. The patent social contract creates a very practical obligation for patent offices. They have to provide search systems and databases that will enable interested members of the public to find patents. Importantly, this is an obligation that rests with patent offices and not the market. Patent offices are, as has been stressed, society's agent. They are in the best position to know which patents have been granted and which have not because they are the granting agency.

The obligation of patent offices is not just simply to publish the patent specification. This would be to construe the obligation passively. The purpose of the patent social contract is to diffuse invention information. Simply to publish invention information in a patent office gazette is not the same as working towards actively spreading invention information. Turning patent offices from passive publishers into active diffusers of information requires patent offices to begin approaching their task much more like public libraries: finding creative ways to engage with very diverse user communities. The diffusion obligation of the patent office is not an obligation that is owed to a few wealthy corporate users of the patent system, but rather it is an obligation to society and to the many groups that are affected by monopolies over invention information. Patent offices obtain invention information from inventors by virtue of the operation of the law. Under the social contract they should provide it as a public good. Moreover, they should provide that information in ways that are useful to different user groups, ways that do not depend on patent searching expertise but rather more generalized skills of database searching. To date efforts in this direction have largely remained symbolic. The USPTO, for example, did make the text of 1,500 HIV/AIDS-related patents available online.[27] This is a step in the right direction but patents on many other needed medicines remain hidden in the system.

The beginnings of a much better approach to patent publishing transparency is to be found in the tables and datasets that have been developed by the US Department of Agriculture for patents in the area of agricultural biotechnology.[28] Amongst other things, these show the top 100 companies in terms of patent ownership and provide basic details of the patents that they hold. The data shows that as of 2002, ten companies owned more than 40% of US agricultural biotechnology patents.

Why is it that patent offices are not much more active on the issue of patent transparency? Patent offices themselves have complicated relationships with commercial providers who obviously do not want patent offices investing in search systems that provide patent information as a public good and in a user friendly way.[29] These commercial providers make their living because patent offices fail to provide search systems that would allow members of the public a meaningful exercise of their rights to access invention information, rights that they hold by virtue of the patent social contract. In the past when patent offices have sought to improve patent information delivery services they have encountered criticism from private providers of those services. For example, the EPO's esp@cenet is a free search system designed for general public use. In Europe the industry association that represents private patent information providers has suggested that esp@cenet might be a market threat.[30] Oddly enough, the interviews showed that a number of developing-country patent offices (for example, the Indian, Indonesian and Malaysian Patent Offices) were using it or had used it. This is one example of how such offices are not in a position to check the work of developed-country patent offices which have much more sophisticated systems at their disposal.

Alarmed by the global transparency that the Internet and its search algorithms might deliver to publics around the world, the commercial

[27] See www.uspto.gov/web/offices/com/speeches/98–20.htm.
[28] See www.ers.usda.gov/Data/AgBiotechIP/.
[29] Richard Jefferson, 'Science as Social Enterprise: The Cambia BiOS Initiative', 1 (2006) *Innovations*, 13, 28.
[30] See www.patcom.org/.

providers of patent information services organized themselves into trade associations in Europe, the US and Japan, and then formed the Trilateral Alliance. The Alliance tracks and negotiates with the major patent offices the patent information that the public will be allowed to have for free.[31] Just as in the international patent standard setting game, the Trilateral Offices, when it comes to charting policies for the patent information game, find themselves being shadowed by a globally organized industry Trilateral (see Chapter 6 for a discussion of the Industry Trilateral for patent standards). In Europe the large commercial providers of patent information services, such as Derwent, are part of an industry association called the Patent Committee (PATCOM). PATCOM's website makes it clear that in PATCOM's view the EPO should limit its free offerings of patent information to the public: 'Should they [patent offices] not concentrate on providing the raw data, and maybe stay with rudimentary public sites.'[32] In the US, the private patent information providers have formed the Coalition for Patent and Trademark Information Dissemination and this Coalition keeps a careful eye on the USPTO's website, negotiating with the USPTO over any proposals it has for improving its website services to the public.[33] In Japan, patent information providers formed the Patent Information On-line Service Council. Like its European and US counterparts, this trade association has forged close links with the JPO to ensure that the market position of Japan's patent information providers is protected.[34]

In theory it should be possible to have a technology platform that searched all the world's patents, allowing users to organize that information in various ways (around ownership, technologies, countries etc.). The algorithms that run Google and Wikipedia would seem to suggest that we can achieve global levels of transparency for patent and invention information. As Richard Jefferson has observed, current levels of patent opacity really only serve the interests of patent law firms and patent database providers that 'accumulate billable hours by providing the same information over and over for different customers, and charging full fees to update them periodically'.[35] Jefferson's organization, CAMBIA (the Centre for Application of Molecular Biology in Agriculture), has shown

---

[31] On the work of the Trilateral Alliance see www.patcom.org/.

[32] See www.patcom.org/.

[33] For a discussion of the role of the Coalition see Joseph L. Ebersole, 'Patent Information Dissemination by Patent Offices: Striking the Balance', 25 (2003) *World Patent Information*, 5.

[34] For a discussion see Yutaka Wada, 'Recent Developments in Japan's Intellectual Property Industry', 27 (2005) *World Patent Information*, 31.

what is possible when it comes to creating global patent transparency. Its Patent Lens system allows for simultaneous searching of USPTO, Patent Cooperation Treaty (PCT), European and Australian patent information, including information about patent families in many countries. Patent Lens is a free service, available to anybody with an Internet connection.[36] If one small organization in Australia can advance the cause of global patent transparency as a public good this far, then perhaps patent offices are not trying very hard to do the same. The current level of patent opacity does not serve innovation or goals of risk management. Those working on, for example, water technologies ought to be able to call up, in the time that it takes to do a search on Google, the patent maps and analyses that will affect their plans for such technologies. Global patent transparency is the foundation upon which other reforms of the patent system have to be built.

One reply to the argument that patent offices should become active diffusers of patent information as a public good is to say that the market provides these services through the countless commercial patent searching and advisory services that are available. But this reply misses the point. Costly market-based services only create a private transparency for their clients. Under the social contract the patent office has an obligation to work towards public transparency and diffusion. In that role it should be doing things that private agents do not. Currently patent offices offer free search tools for the purposes of searching their patent databases. Offering someone a search tool to access patented information, however, is not the same as actively promoting the transparency and diffusion of patented invention information.

We have seen that the patent system is, in effect, a system of private taxation. The details of this system of taxation, as with any system of taxation, need to be fully transparent. Patent offices should therefore track and publish the patent portfolios of patent owners, especially those with large patent holdings. The size of the patent-based fiscal empires of multinationals should be made socially transparent. This is, after all, information that belongs to the public. Patent offices are in the best position to develop this kind of transparency, which is the kind that commercial services will never deliver, any more than tax havens will publish the tax affairs of those using their services. Putting it simply, anyone should be able to go to a patent office website and see the complete patent portfolio

[35] Richard Jefferson, 'Science as Social Enterprise: The Cambia BiOS Initiative', 1 (2006) *Innovations*, 13, 28–9.

[36] www.patentlens.net/daisy/patentlens/patentlens.html.

of a Microsoft or Pfizer in the country of that patent office, the degree of concentration of ownership of crucial technologies associated with that portfolio, and information about the licensing and assignment of those technologies. Scientists working in, for example, publicly-funded agricultural research institutes should be able to go to databases that communicate all the invention information relevant to their area and that provide a full picture of the granted patents around agricultural technologies. This is a minimum baseline of transparency that patent offices should meet. Those in the patent information market would be forced to provide higher-quality interpretive services. Patent offices should develop these kinds of databases in cooperation with user groups or other interested government agencies, but it is the patent office that has the primary responsibility under the patent social contract for diffusing patent information and so it is the patent office that bears responsibility for developing the databases. Simply offering free search tools designed for general public use or the occasional specialist database in an area like HIV/AIDS amounts to little more than organizational dissembling about a patent office's true obligations under the patent social contract.

During my interviews, a few patent offices conceded that they probably could do better in terms of diffusing invention information, but the overall impression was that the ideal of the patent social contract had assumed a rhetorical life, a flashy bit of language fit for the seminar room but not something that was relevant for the client-driven business life of a patent office. We saw in Chapter 1 that patent offices, through public sector reforms, have been increasingly turned into business agencies. As a result society now faces a classic principal-agent problem in which the interests of the agent no longer fully match society's interests. Patent offices increasingly think in terms of business opportunities and less in terms of providing public goods. Patent offices, the UK PO and the Austrian PO being examples, set up commercial arms to their operations to run services like, for example, the express search service run by the Austrian PO in which at relatively low cost clients get rapid feedback on the novelty and inventiveness of their invention. Patent offices are more likely these days to be thinking about the commercial services that they can provide rather than the public good functions that they ought to be providing because of this business mentality. Making transparent, for example, the patent portfolios of the multinationals that are their best customers is not something that patent offices will willingly risk.

Following the argument put forward at the beginning of this chapter that what is needed is a counter network to contest the decisions of the private governance network of which patent offices have become a part, the next section outlines another possible element of that counter network.

Transparency registers

Modern large-scale patenting creates large-scale rule complexity that leads to uncertainty. Companies are often not sure that they have found all the patents relevant to a product on which they are working. They frequently have doubts about the scope of the patents they have found. Patents, unlike blocks of land, do not come with settled boundaries. These kinds of uncertainty are especially dangerous from the point of view of the public management of risk, as the recent experience with Roche's patents and licences over oseltamivir illustrate. Roche's reluctance to disclose the patent situation in each country left public health officials confused as to what or what was not permissible in terms of the manufacture and importation of oseltamivir, the drug that the WHO has recommended as a frontline tool for dealing with an outbreak of avian bird flu.[37]

In order to deal with the complexity and uncertainty that is deliberately generated by the gaming behaviour of sophisticated players within the patent system, simple bright-line rules are needed.[38] One way to do this would be for regulatory agencies to establish patent transparency registers in areas of technology where there were serious risk management issues, and transparency concerning the patent situation was, to borrow the words of TRIPS, necessary 'to protect human, animal or plant life or health or to avoid serous prejudice to the environment'.[39] The scope of the transparency register's operation would be a matter for a regulator to decide as part of a risk assessment exercise. A register could target, for example, research tools in biotechnology, particular classes of drugs, specific plants or genes, or technologies of major importance in mitigating or adapting to climate change. The use of registers would not, in other words, be confined to a particular type of technology. Companies would be required to use the registers to make a full disclosure of the patents

---

[37] Buddhima Lokuge, Peter Drahos and Warwick Neville, 'Pandemics, Antiviral Stockpiles and Biosecurity in Australia: What About the Generic Option?', 184 (2006) *Medical Journal of Australia*, 16.

[38] For a philosophical defence of simple rules for dealing with complexity see Richard A. Epstein, *Simple Rules for a Complex World*, Harvard University Press, Cambridge, 1995.

[39] Article 27(2) of TRIPS.

and patent applications surrounding the targeted technology. Other companies would be able to rely on the register knowing that there were no other hidden surprises for them. In addition, the registers would require the disclosure of information relating to ownership and licensing. This information is in practice difficult to track down. Private clearing-house mechanisms have failed to provide this information in any systematic way.

The cost to a company of not disclosing on a transparency register a patent that it should have disclosed could be some form of estoppel that would prevent it from enforcing that patent. Some companies might respond by flooding the transparency register with patents. In the pharmaceutical sector it is clear that a transparency register would force the disclosure of a large number of patents. For example, the European Commission in a recent inquiry found that a single blockbuster medicine could have up to 1,300 patents or patent applications surrounding it and that many of these patents are applied for towards the end of the period in which the first patent expires.[40] Since companies are rational actors, a deterrence mechanism could be used to overcome this potential problem of flooding a transparency register. A patent put on the register containing claims that could not be shown to have reasonable prospects of enforcement by a court in an infringement action could be taken off the register. Procedures for removing patents from a transparency register would be swift and administrative in nature. They could be triggered by a regulator or a third party. If it were later proved that the patent owner had no reasonable basis for believing the patent or some of its claims to be enforceable, severe financial penalties could be imposed on the company. Patent attorneys would also be the target of prosecution since it would be they who had drafted the patent claims for patents on the register. Section 26C of the Therapeutic Goods Act 1989 (Australia), for example, imposes a maximum penalty of $10 million on companies in order to deter them from using patents of doubtful validity as part of a strategy of preventing or delaying the registration of generic drugs. Much higher fines than these are needed, as well as criminal penalties.

In order to get the patent back on the register the patent owner would have to show that it had reasonable grounds for believing the patent to be valid. Once a patent was back on the register, its owner would be allowed

[40] European Commission, 'Pharmaceutical Sector Inquiry: Preliminary Report 28 November 2008', 150, available at http://ec.europa.eu/competition/sectors/pharmaceuticals/inquiry/preliminary_report.pdf.

to enforce it, including for acts of alleged infringement that took place between the patent's removal from the register and its restoration to it. The normal private law situation, in other words, would exist. The primary purpose of the register would be to force disclosure of a company's patents around a key technology and to deter it by means of the criminal law from using patents of doubtful validity to interfere in processes of public research or market competition in relation to that technology. Severe penalties and criminal sanctions would be used as deterrents to gaming behaviour. After the first few prosecutions, companies and their attorneys would think much harder about the patents they placed on the register.

Transparency registers would only need to be created by regulatory agencies in fields of technology where it was important to reduce the social costs of the uncertainty and complexity being orchestrated by patent owners. The key to the success of transparency registers would be to keep the rules that establish them simple and to place the onus of disclosure and judgement about patent quality on the person with the best information to make that disclosure and those judgements, namely the patent owner. The experience of the US with its Orange Book system for regulating the relationships amongst generic companies, brand-name companies, pharmaceutical patents and drug registration suggests that registers based on complex rule-intensive procedures will create more opportunities for rent-seeking behaviour.[41] A transparency register would simply require a company to disclose all the patents around a particular technology. Failure to put a patent on the register would mean that the company would not be able to enforce the patent. Placing low-quality patents on the register would have to run the gauntlet of a quick administrative procedure for their removal. The criminal law would be used to punish gaming behaviour.

Transparency registers could also be complemented by provisions that allowed governments to recover losses that they had sustained as a result of the gaming behaviour of companies. The Therapeutic Goods Act 1989 (Australia), for example, establishes the principle that a court can award the Commonwealth government compensation for any damage it has suffered as a result of an interlocutory injunction being granted to a patent owner for a patent infringement proceeding that ultimately has no reasonable prospect of success.[42] The foundational principle that crime should not pay has seen governments around the world enact criminal

---

[41] See Federal Trade Commission, 'Generic Drug Entry Prior to Patent Expiration', 2002.
[42] See Sections 26C and 26D.

and civil forfeiture laws to confiscate the proceeds of crime.[43] Civil forfeit-ure laws operate on the basis of the balance of probabilities and a reversal of the usual onus of proof, that is on the person challenging the forfeit-ure order. There is every reason for governments to begin thinking about legislation dealing with the proceeds of patent gaming. The sums of money involved are vast. For example, the European Commission found that in the period 2000–7 the cost of delaying the entry of generics amounted to about €3 billion.[44] Most of the delay was due to patent gaming.

A national regulator setting up a transparency register in one country might also provide a spillover benefit to a regulator in another country. Competition law authorities in the US, for example, might be interested in the use of patents granted in other jurisdictions that adversely affected competition in the US market. Information that was generated through the establishment of transparency registers in Australia or Europe might help US regulators.

Judgements about the quality of patents on the transparency register, in most cases, would not be hard to make. The fact that generic companies have prevailed 73% of the time in patent suits under the Orange Book sys-tem suggests that for a significant number of patents the judgement about their quality is relatively straightforward.[45] The European Commission in its study found, when it looked at the litigation between generic and ori-ginator companies concerning the many secondary patents surrounding the basic drug, that generic companies won almost 75% of the cases that went to final judgement.[46] The Commission also obtained evidence that originator companies deliberately used patents known to be of doubtful validity to slow down the entry of generic companies into the market. Currently, however, there are incentives for originator companies to obtain such patents (especially in many developing countries where the prospect of patent litigation is less) and no real costs in doing so. Creating transparency registers would be one way of changing the cost–benefit calculation for companies when it came to pursuing low-quality patents. Imposing criminal sanctions on the members of the patent attorney profession would be an important part of this strategy. They are crucial players in helping pharmaceutical companies to game the system in much

---

[43] Julie Ayling and Peter Grabosky, 'Policing by Command: Enhancing Law Enforcement Capacity Through Coercion', 28 (2006) *Law and Policy*, 420, 430.
[44] See European Commission, 'Pharmaceutical Sector Inquiry', 8.
[45] See Federal Trade Commission, 'Generic Drug Entry', 16.
[46] European Commission, 'Pharmaceutical Sector Inquiry', 189.

the same way that tax accountants and lawyers help companies to evade taxes. This line of argument is expanded in the next section.

The argument that in some jurisdictions, such as the US, transparency registers are not needed because companies have private sophisticated searching techniques for patents is not an argument against transparency registers.[47] This argument does not apply to many local companies in developing countries that do not have access to these searching techniques. But even in the US there are many more groups interested in patent transparency than just companies. Obligations of patent transparency and disclosure lie at the heart of the patent social contract. The transparency demanded is a social transparency, not private windows of transparency only available to the well-heeled. Health NGOs, citizen groups, regulators and those working in public policy should not have to bear the costs of remedying the uncertainty generated by the gaming behaviour of patent owners. Transparency registers are one way in which to reduce this uncertainty.

Finally, it is worth noting that transparency registers might gain support from politicians in charge of health departments. Politicians that oversaw the successful implementation of transparency registers to speed up legitimate generic entry into pharmaceutical markets would be making large savings to health budgets. More politically tradeable esteem might also flow to politicians who were able to preside over the successful use of transparency registers to recover money from pharmaceutical companies caught gaming the system. In the pharmaceutical context, there is the possibility that transparency registers might help to catalyse calculations on the part of politicians that served the public interest.

'The ticket clippers': regulating the patent attorney profession

It would be impossible to run the patent system without the patent attorney profession. Every examiner dreads the inventor who is convinced that he has invented something major such as the perpetual motion machine and is prosecuting his own patent application. During the interviews the word 'nightmare' was used more than once to describe such cases. All the developed-country patent offices that were interviewed agreed that a competent patent profession was critical to running a patent system.

---

[47] For the suggestion that companies in the US do not need the notice function of the Orange Book because of private search techniques see Federal Trade Commission, 'Generic Drug Entry', 54.

Patent officials from developing countries identified a lack of patent attorney expertise as one of the reasons that locals did not use the patent system. Patent attorneys and examiners participate in a dance in which both are highly familiar with the technical steps, and both know that if the steps are followed there is a good chance that the dance will lead to the grant of a patent.

Maintaining good relations with the profession was a priority for all the developed-country patent offices that were interviewed. All have systems of regular communication in place with the profession, these systems involving committees or fora in which meetings between patent officials and representatives from the profession take place. Senior patent officials use the opportunity of regular meetings with the profession to float ideas and proposals for reform in order to get informal feedback and reaction from representatives of the profession. Patent offices also survey patent attorneys in order to assess customer satisfaction. In many cases the patent office, the Canadian PO and the New Zealand PO being examples, is involved in the process of qualifying patent attorneys.

Even if maintaining close and cooperative relations with the profession is a high priority for all the developed-country offices I interviewed, one cannot say that all the offices were enchanted by the profession. Patent offices see a profession that in many jurisdictions is a tightly controlled monopoly squeezing rents out of business, often in exchange for comparatively little service – 'a real bunch of ticket clippers' as one of my interviewees put it.

Patent offices also understand better than anybody that it is patent attorneys who drive the gaming of the patent system. It is they who advise companies on patenting strategies. It is the patent agents who are the source of 'creative' claims-drafting that slips past the restrictions in law on patentable subject-matter. And it is they who make applications longer, with more and more claims. All the developed-country patent offices interviewed said that the complexity of applications had increased. This in turn makes more work for examiners. At the interview with the UK PO it emerged that the office had attempted to deal with the problem through a voluntary code of practice, but according to the senior examiners I spoke to there is little evidence that the code had changed the drafting practices of patent attorneys. The only advantage to the code was that it gave an examiner some basis for negotiating claims with the patent attorney. There was also the suggestion that this broad claiming strategy was in part being driven more by US practitioners than those based in the UK, one examiner pointing out that where the application is from a US client, the UK patent attorney is generally told to file the application as received by the attorney.

Perhaps the US is the centre of an aggressive patent-drafting culture, but without a study of the patent professions of the major patenting countries it is hard to say. A more plausible hypothesis is that in a globalized economy with patent attorney firms servicing large foreign firms, there are strong incentives for those attorneys to do all that they can in order to get their clients the best monopoly weapon. In historical terms, the German pharmaceutical industry used aggressive patenting strategies to establish worldwide cartels.[48] The aggressive use of patents is a tradition not confined to the US.

In the EPO, attempts to regulate the number of claims by imposing a claim fee for claims in excess of a certain number have seen the profession counter with the single claim divided into many parts (interview, EPO). Examiners, facing very large backlogs, would in interviews report these kinds of gaming strategies with a certain air of resignation and weary detachment. And yet, formally at least, some patent offices possess regulatory powers over the patent attorney profession and so are potentially in a position to develop an 'enforcement pyramid' strategy to deal with gaming behaviour by members of the profession.

In developed countries, the regulation of patent attorneys generally involves a combination of the patent office and a specialized body that represents members of the patent attorney profession and articulates rules of professional conduct (for example, a body like the UK's Chartered Institute of Patent Attorneys). A professional body that represents lawyers in general may also be part of the regulatory structure, although in a number of countries a patent attorney need not have qualified as a lawyer in order to be a patent attorney (for example, Australia and the UK). Some patent offices will have, under their national law, the power to de-register a patent attorney, but in many countries the professional body that represents patent agents is involved in setting standards of conduct and disciplinary procedures.[49] Generalizing somewhat, patent agents in many countries do enjoy considerable self-regulation. In other areas of regulation, regulators armed with an ultimate sanction like deregistration have developed a regulatory approach that begins with dialogue, but ends with some sanction of incapacitation such as prison and/or deregistration if the regulatee proves

---

[48] Drahos with Braithwaite, *Information Feudalism*, 55–6.

[49] The Director of the USPTO has the power to exclude or suspend attorneys. See 35 U.S.C. 32. In the UK, the Secretary of State has the power to order the removal of a patent agent from the register under the Register of Patent Agents Rules 1990. But it is the Chartered

resistant to all attempts to obtain compliance. The key idea behind the 'enforcement pyramid' is that punishment and persuasion should be linked in a certain sequence that begins with persuasion at the base of the pyramid and ends with the most punitive sanction at the apex of the pyramid.[50]

The cosy networked relationship between the professional body that represents patent agents and the patent office makes the implementation of an enforcement pyramid by a patent office not very likely. As the opening sections of this chapter suggested, what is needed in cases of network capture that has led to a structure of insider governance is an outsider governance network that shadows and contests the decisions of the insider network. The efficacy of an enforcement pyramid depends on finding a regulator other than the patent office to administer the sanctions at the top of the pyramid. An independent regulator is needed to take the profession out of its comfortable zone of self-regulation.

The social cost of patent gaming by patent agents is very large. As we saw earlier, the European Commission's inquiry into the pharmaceutical sector showed that the cost of delaying generic entry into the market from 2000 to 2007, mostly by means of patent gaming, had cost about €3 billion. The social costs of patent gaming do not just occur in the pharmaceutical sector.[51] If patent gaming strategies were seen as unjustified private taxing schemes no-one would doubt that the full force of the criminal law should be applied to the companies and the attorneys responsible. Fines and prison are a standard part of the tax regulator's tool kit when it comes to dealing with gaming problems in national tax systems and defending the integrity of the tax system. Famously it was the then US Bureau of Internal Revenue that put Al Capone behind bars. Every year the major tax jurisdictions send a small number of tax agents to jail for gaming behaviour that amounts to egregious tax evasion. There is no reason in principle why patent agents should not face the same kind of sanction for gaming behaviour that compromises the integrity of the patent system.

Institute of Patent Attorneys that is the most important regulatory actor for patent agents. In Australia there is the Patent and Trade Marks Attorneys Disciplinary Tribunal established under the Patents Regulations 1991. The Director General of IP Australia is a member of the Tribunal.

[50] First put forward in John Braithwaite, *To Punish or Persuade: Enforcement of Coal Mine Safety*, State University of New York Press, Albany, 1985; see also I. Ayres and J. Braithwaite, *Responsive Regulation: Transcending the Deregulation Debate*, Oxford Unibversity Press, New York, 1992; J. Braithwaite, *Restorative Justice and Responsive Regulation*, Oxford University Press, NY, 2002.

[51] For a discussion of the broader costs see Jaffe and Lerner, *Innovation and its Discontents*, Ch. 2.

One reason that patent offices might be reluctant to develop a more robust approach to gaming by the patent profession is the absence of a broader social consensus when it comes to this kind of behaviour. Even if tax offices are not everybody's favourite regulator, in cases where the public purse has been defrauded of hundreds of millions of dollars tax authorities can count on a social consensus that the criminal law should be employed to punish the guilty. There is no reason why the use of the patent system to rob the public should not attract the same kind of moral condemnation.

The problem lies less in the absence of moral consensus about gaming behaviour that costs the public dearly in terms of access to essentials like medicines, and more in ignorance on the part of politicians, policy makers and the general public about the true costs of this gaming behaviour. Things might be different, of course, if these groups understood that the patent system has become a globally networked system of private taxation. Politicians might then be happy to take on patent reform in the way they are happy to take on tax reform. However, with little political leadership on patents, reform is left to the usual suspects – the large multinational users, the patent attorney profession and patent offices. Criminalizing gaming behaviour within the patent system would require a much greater transparency of the social costs of that behaviour, and it would also require a leadership to form some sort of social consensus around the use of the criminal law to proscribe that behaviour. This leadership is hardly likely to come from the patent attorney profession.

Some members of the profession might take refuge in professional ethics, arguing that patent gaming is a professional obligation. In the US, for example, Rule 10.83 of the Code of Federal Regulations for Patents, Trademarks and Copyrights, which is referred to as 'Canon 7', requires a practitioner to 'represent a client zealously within the bounds of the law'. Rule 10.20(a) defines a canon as an 'axiomatic norm'. Canon 7 does impose a duty to seek maximum patent coverage, but it is not an absolute duty. It is subject to the duty of candour to the USPTO and it also requires the attorney to aim for a valid patent.[52] Attorneys can hardly argue that they have an ethical duty to undermine the patent social contract by striving for invalid patents. Ultimately, like so many legal duties, the duty to obtain maximum patent coverage must be applied by reference to a criterion of reasonableness. Patent agents must have reasonable grounds for

---

[52] For a discussion see David Hricik, 'Aerial Boundaries: The Duty of Candor as a Limitation on the Duty of Patent Practitioners to Advocate for Maximum Patent Coverage', 44 (2002) *South Texas Law Review*, 205.

believing that the patent claims they draft will be upheld by a court. Some measure of uncertainty has to be allowed, otherwise patent attorneys will only draft the narrowest of claims. Escaping patent infringement would become too easy. But patent gaming is based on calculations in which it is known to a high degree of probability that particular patent claims will not be upheld by a court. As discussed earlier, both in the US and Europe brand name companies in the pharmaceutical sector consistently lose patent cases involving secondary patents that have been lodged just as the main product patent is about to expire. Patent gaming rests on combining probabilities in which even if there is an 8 in 10 chance of the patent being declared invalid, it makes sense to push on because there is only, say, a 1 in 500 chance that the patent will be tested in court or, if it is, there is a good chance of obtaining a settlement or the loss of the case is outweighed by the profits made in delaying generic entry. It is precisely this kind of calculation that the Australian Parliament was trying to deter when it amended its Therapeutic Goods Act requiring a patent owner alleging patent infringement to lodge a certificate (with penalties for a false or misleading certificate) stating that the owner was bringing the action in good faith and that the owner believed it had 'reasonable prospects of success'.[53] The legislation makes clear that the mere grant of the patent does not satisfy the requirement that the infringement proceeding has reasonable prospects of success.

In short, there is not in the US, and probably not anywhere else, a professional ethical obligation on patent attorneys to game the system in ways that destroy market competition in important areas such as pharmaceuticals. Patent offices could, if they wished, address this problem through a voluntary code of conduct that would have real bite if it were linked to an enforcement pyramid that was based on their powers of deregistration. This would be a much more cost-effective approach to the problem of patent quality because it would be a preventive strategy aimed at changing the behaviour of patent attorneys in order to improve the quality of patent applications at the point of entry into the system. By not improving input quality and then allowing many such applications through their systems, patent offices pass on the costs of doubtful patents to other actors, actors whose costs of fighting poor patent quality are much greater than the cost of such a preventive approach by patent offices. Doubtful patents are cheap to obtain. They are expensive to fight. Faced by the threat of patent litigation many people will pay to make a problem go away rather than

[53] See Sub-section 26C(3)(b) of the Therapeutic Goods Act 1989 (Australia).

fight their way out of it. Those that do fight have a long battle irrespective of whether they win or not.

Patent offices equipped with powers of deregistration could do much more to change the gaming behaviour of patent attorneys. But the fact that many patent offices seek approval ratings from the profession probably makes those patent offices reluctant to move against those who, after all, obtain advances from corporations that are used to paying patent office fees.[54] It may also be that patent offices believe that they can tackle the problem of gaming by improving the quality of examination. Amongst other things, this means making it just as personally cost-effective for an examiner, who is subject to quotas and performance reviews, to reject a patent application if he or she believes there are real validity issues with it as to accept it. But if patent offices believe that they can lift the quality of their own processes to match the gaming behaviour of the profession, they will have to take a closer look at the way in which they treat examiners.

Examiners and patent quality

Improving patent quality through investing in the training of examiners and developing metrics that give examiners more autonomy is a partly travelled road for all the major patent offices. The USPTO, for example, after years of criticism has been striving to create a better work environment for its examiners (interview, USPTO). A full study of the actual working conditions of examiners was outside the scope of this research. The interviews did suggest two linked factors that affect the quality performance of examiners. Examiners in the words of one interviewee 'must be long stay' and in the words of another: 'You don't get good examination quality until you have years of experience.' Given that I generally interviewed senior people there is an obvious danger of selection error, but experience is certainly relevant to quality. It takes time to get to know the technological literature and to understand the significance of developments in it. One of the reasons that the quality of the USPTO's work is not seen to be as high as that of the EPO's work is the relative inexperience of the USPTO's workforce (see Chapter 5).

---

[54] For an example see the Canadian Intellectual Property Office's National Client Satisfaction Survey for 2008 available at www.cipo.ic.gc.ca/eic/site/cipointernet-internetopic.nsf/eng/wr01511.html.

Developing a long-stay workforce is probably not enough in itself to improve quality, as a long-stay person may also be an unmotivated person, one who no longer invests in building up a knowledge of the prior art or who does not want to enter into negotiating contests with patent attorneys and so applies the test of inventive step in a way that lets too many applications make it to grant. The other factor, suggested by the interview in the German PO, is that the examination workforce as a whole must have an *esprit de corps*, a belief that no one else does patent examination better. Patent offices wanting to improve patent quality have to look at how they can create a long-stay workforce that takes pride in its work.

The ability of a patent office to create a long-stay examination workforce will in turn be affected by the labour market variables of the country in question. We saw, for example, that in South Korea, the Korean Intellectual Property Office (KIPO) has the advantage that there is considerable social prestige attached to government positions. This office said it does not have recruitment problems. Some offices have tended to lose patent examiners to the private sector, the US and UK offices being examples. Other developed-country patent offices have done much, however, in creating a long-stay examination workforce and perhaps an *esprit de corps*. The German PO, for example, garners a lot of recognition for the quality of its work. During the interview at the German PO it became clear that it did not have a problem with retaining examiners. Examiners, by virtue of their employment conditions, find it more or less impossible to go into private practice and if they do move out of the PO, they move to other parts of the German civil service (interview, German PO). A certain labour market inflexibility thus becomes a virtue for the German PO because it enables it to invest in the training of staff knowing that that staff are not likely to walk out the door at the first opportunity. Labour market mobility in the UK, the US and Canada creates problems for their patent offices because in boom times many examiners are likely to shift to the private sector. The German PO recruits people with 5 or so years' experience in industry and then gives them a further 3 years of training using a personal tutor approach in which a senior examiner acts as an individual tutor (interview, German PO). Outsourcing is not seen as an option by the office because of concerns about quality. In the same spirit of independence, it has designed its own electronic system for its examiners, but it has negotiated access to the EPO's EPOQUE system because of its tremendous advantages in searching the non-patent literature. The German PO's relentless drive for quality in examination also has wide stakeholder support. German companies and the patent attorney profession support the German PO's quality standards even if attorneys occasionally grumble about getting patent applications through the patent office (interview, German PO). In Austria, the PO is also confident about the quality of its work, reporting at the interview that its private studies showed that Austrian and German examiners were producing work of the same average quality (interview, Austrian PO). It was clear from the interview that the Austrian PO looked to the German PO as a standard bearer of examination quality. The EPO is another patent office that reported that its examiners tended to stay partly, it was suggested, because the EPO is an international organization and there is therefore kudos in working for it. The EPO does have some recruitment problems, but these in part are due to the fact that the EPO is seeking to find examiners capable of working in three languages in technical areas (interview, EPO).

The danger in all offices is that senior managers will become too focussed on metrics and lose sight of the fact that it is examiners who determine quality. Developed-country patent offices measure, in many different ways, the performance of their examiners. At least in the beginning, those systems were biased in favour of the grant of the patent. Measures of patent quality have proven elusive. As one examiner put it, 'patent quality is far more difficult to measure than things like backlog of unexamined patents, turnaround time, grant rates and so on'. In the German PO there was even more scepticism about a meaningful definition of patent quality: 'Nobody is able to define product quality.' Offices understand the problem of incentives that undermine quality. The Canadian PO has recognized that different technologies require different examination time frames (interview, Canadian PO). It is a mistake to work on the basis of the same number of hours for a disposal for all technologies. Some patent offices have tried to ensure that their quota systems do not penalize examiners for taking decisions that delay grant. The EPO's points system, for example, recognizes that a refusal action by an examiner involves much more work in terms of justification and so awards more points for a refusal action. This is an improvement from the point of view of examiners (interview, EPO). Yet as we saw in Chapter 4, the union representing EPO examiners has continued to argue that examiners are not being given enough time to do quality work. When I put this position to those at the EPO, it was conceded that 'pressure [on examiners] had increased steeply, but examiners have coped somehow'. The critical question, one of them suggested, was how much further examiners could be pushed. In the struggle between productive efficiency and examiner-led patent quality the danger is that the politics around the huge backlogs in patent offices will incline senior managers to squeeze every drop of productivity out of their examiners.

12

Patent administration sovereignty

Nodal solutions for small countries, developing countries

Sovereignty matters

Formally at least, patent administration remains an area of state sovereignty. State sovereignty has been eroded over patent standards, where through multilateral, regional and bilateral trade agreements, many states, most of them developing countries, have moved up to 'international' standards that really are the standards of the US and EU. Even though states largely retain discretion over how to administer a patent system, we have seen that the patent offices of many developing countries are becoming integrated into a system of global governance led by the Trilateral Offices.

The integration of developing-country patent offices into this global governance structure is not necessarily consistent with their national interests. It is not immediately obvious, for example, that a developing country which imports medicines should follow the pharmaceutical examination standards of developed-country patent offices that are prepared to accept the gaming behaviour of patent attorneys in the drafting of patent claims. By doing so a developing country is simply importing that gaming behaviour. It is changing the selection pressures that operate in its markets. We have seen that India and Brazil have taken steps to avoid the quality problems that exist in this area at least. In India, the Indian Patents Act allows the examiner to come to a different view of the patentability of a pharmaceutical product (see Chapter 7), and in Brazil the outcome may be different because the Brazilian pharmaceutical regulatory authority has the power to overturn the Brazilian patent examiner's decision in the case of pharmaceutical patents.

The examples of India and Brazil are examples of what can be done by two very large economies with technical expertise to serve their national interests in the case of patent administration. Most developing countries or even small developed countries do not have these strengths to draw upon.

Even for large developing-country players, however, there is an issue as to whether their patent offices really serve their developmental aspirations. Their offices are a part of the global private governance network of patent administration, a network that ultimately serves multinationals more than it does states. The developmental state literature suggests that one of the historical features of economically successful states is autonomy over administration.[1] Developmental states, argues Bagchi, have the 'ability to switch gears from market-directed to state-directed growth, or vice-versa depending on geopolitical circumstances, as well as combine both market and state direction in a synergistic manner, when opportunity beckons'.[2] This kind of institutional nimbleness can only be achieved through the networked administration of rules. In the context of the patent institution, the developmental state should be tying together the counter network of outsiders described in Chapter 11, a network that would serve the patent social contract and enable the state to respond to the risks and costs generated by the private governance of the patent system.

Turning to the situation of smaller developing countries, the question is whether sovereignty over patent office administration is needed and, if so, how it might be exercised in a world where investing in this administration is beyond the means of smaller players. The first question is relatively easy to answer. Developing countries, small and large, have not been effective in combating the patent standard-setting agendas of the US and EU.[3] Patent office administration is the only means left to them to adjust these international standards to their local circumstances. So even though, for example, the Agreement on Trade-Related Aspects of Intellectual Property Rights (TRIPS) creates an obligation to grant patents on pharmaceutical products, it does not prescribe standards of pharmaceutical product examination that require the issue of low quality patents. This is not an issue confined to the pharmaceutical sector. Countries that are net importers of patented technology have an interest in ensuring that the monopoly rents they pay are for genuinely inventive technologies. This is just as true in sectors such as information technology and energy-related technologies as it is in the pharmaceutical sector.

---

[1] Thandika Mkandawire, 'Thinking About Developmental States in Africa', 25 (2001) *Cambridge Journal of Economics*, 289, 290.

[2] Amiya Kumar Bagchi, 'The Past and the Future of the Developmental State', 2 (2000) *Journal of World-Systems Research*, 398, 399.

[3] P. Drahos, 'Developing Countries and International Intellectual Property Standard-Setting', 5 (2002) *Journal of World Intellectual Property*, 765.

Sovereignty over patent office administration also matters to developed countries. The German PO, along with German industry, believes that high quality patent examination standards best suit Germany's economic circumstances. For this reason the German PO is wary of proposals that might lead to a system of mutual recognition under which one office was formally bound to recognize the examination results of another office. Mutual recognition is seen by the German PO as a sovereignty-robbing principle, while mutual exploitation is seen as a sovereignty-enhancing principle. Of course, the German economy can afford the €225 million budget required to run a patent office that is committed to quality in patent examination.[4]

The costs of defending patent office sovereignty were neatly captured by my interviewees in New Zealand. At the time of my interview, the New Zealand PO was planning to move to a requirement of universal novelty in its patent law. Basically such a shift involves much more searching on the part of the office because it has to assess novelty on the basis of prior art in the world rather than just New Zealand. At that time the NZ PO had about twenty-two examining staff. The question of whether the office would hire more examiners led to the following response: 'We will have trouble finding the resources to do the examination. We don't have masses of PhD people waiting for a job.' Another interviewee observed that maintaining sovereignty over examination 'sucks scientific expertise out of our system'. The NZ PO, it should be noted, is in the top twenty offices in the world in terms of applications.

Dilemmas abound for smaller countries when it comes to the issue of sovereignty over patent examination. New Zealand's approach of having a local novelty requirement lessened the search burden on examiners, allowing them to generate search reports quickly, thereby speeding up the application process. But as one interviewee pointed out, this was hardly in New Zealand's economic interests as a small technology-importing country, because it led to the grant of patents that would not have survived the test of universal novelty. Since most patents enter New Zealand via the Patent Cooperation Treaty (PCT) system there are PCT reports available for New Zealand examiners, with the interviews suggesting that there was considerable reliance on these.[5] But this simply deepens the dependence of a small country on a system dominated by a few large offices and multinational exporters of technology. At the same time, a small developed

---

[4] This figure was provided at the interview with the German PO.
[5] On the volume of PCT applications see WIPO, *Patent Report 2007*, Geneva, 47.

country with limited scientific expertise to deploy does not have the resources to examine the many thousands of patents that are delivered to it by an increasingly automated global patent system. Low filing fees in New Zealand, amounting to little more than 'lunch money for a US company' in the words of one interviewee, mean that the additional cost of adding New Zealand to a filing strategy is low. Keeping up with new technologies and achieving the examination depth of a large office like the USPTO is not possible. Depending on the work of other offices begins to look inevitable.

Outsourcing the patent social contract

One solution being contemplated at the time of the NZ PO interview was to make use of the examination expertise of the Australian PO, a natural step given the history of the regulatory cooperation in general between Australia and New Zealand. The Australian PO acts as one of a number of International Searching Authorities (ISAs) for New Zealand under the PCT.

Arrangements in which a small country patent office contracts another to do examination work are becoming more and more common. These arrangements are not confined to small country offices, as large patent offices like the USPTO and the UK PO also make use of international outsourcing in order to deal with backlog problems. A small country that makes use of outsourcing is the Singapore PO. It sends its examination work to the Austrian, Australian and Danish Patent Offices. Some larger offices are keen to pursue this kind of outsourcing work. Within the Pacific, the Korean Intellectual Property Office (KIPO) has been in hot pursuit of this type of work. The Austrian and Danish Patent Offices are also active in seeking this work.

Outsourcing arrangements amongst patent offices are very much commercial deals. Singapore's use of three offices helps it to obtain a satisfactory price for the examination work. At the time of the interview the arrangement was regarded by Singaporean officials as working well. There were hints from the offices doing the examination work that they would have to think more carefully about their costs. Factors that drive up costs for offices providing outsourcing services are the complexity of applications in particular sectors such as biotechnology, and any divergences in patent law between their own patent systems and the country for which they are providing the service. The offices that do the examination work for Singapore do not gain the benefit of the patent renewal stream of income, which is where all examining offices make their real profits. This

means that offices that do outsourcing work for other offices have to make
the actual examination profitable. The office paying for the examination
work cannot be confident that the patent will be renewed and so paying
large up-front fees for examination becomes problematic.

Obviously these kinds of problems can be overcome or else these outsourcing arrangements would not be in place. The critical issue, however,
is not whether the outsourcing arrangement is commercially satisfactory. Rather it is whether a patent office that outsources examination
does so in a way that is consistent with the patent social contract that
it is meant to serve. A country like New Zealand might come to the
view that it wants a high standard of inventive step that, for example,
rules out the grant of patents on the re-formulation of pharmaceutical
products. Contracting out examination work to the Australian PO runs
risks if that office has a practice of accepting such claims or is generally
liberal in the kinds of pharmaceutical claims it accepts. In fact it would
be hard to find major offices that do not accept claiming formats to allow
for the patenting of naturally occurring substances (claims on purified
versions of the substance are allowed), methods of treatment, combin-
ations of known ingredients, dosage regimes and so on. The Trilateral
Offices represent countries that have major pharmaceutical export interests. Offices like the Australian PO that have business ambitions have
to follow these claiming formats once they are accepted by the EPO and
USPTO. If the NZ PO specified that it wanted a higher level of inventive
step how would it satisfy itself that the patent office it contracted to do the
work was applying this higher level? More generally, how can an office
that outsources work satisfy itself that the work is of a quality that meets
it needs? When I put this problem to the NZ PO the reply was: 'We would
go through a rigorous process of due diligence, the person would have to
demonstrate capacity, quality. There would be regular audits of the work.'
This means that the office doing the outsourcing would have to retain
an examining capability. Once an office lost examination capability, it
would find it difficult to do the audits. It is also not clear that small offices
could find large offices prepared to examine outside of the standards that
benchmarking exercises amongst those large offices had determined to
be the international standards. The multinationals and global industry
associations that track patent office activity are hardly likely to stand idly
by if some patent offices decide to contract for much higher standards
of examination. Instead of contracting out examination, the NZ and
Australian offices could become a joint entity of some kind. The problem
with any such merger of patent sovereignty is how much of a voice the

smaller player retains in the new organization. Would, for example, the smaller player be able to influence examination standards? Most small to mid-size offices have sovereignty concerns: 'In a merger between a big and little player, the little player gets one tenth of the influence' (interview, Canadian PO). On either the contracting-out model or the merger model, the smaller country has to bring its patent standards in line with the larger country and is very likely to lose administrative sovereignty over those standards.

For some countries there would be aspects of patent examination that might prove difficult to outsource. An example of where culture and patent procedure wash into each other is the patenting of biological materials that are linked to traditional knowledge in some way. The NZ PO wants to retain control where the patenting of biological materials is linked to the use of Maori traditional knowledge: 'The Maori issue is very important and not something we would want to be contracting out. In any such [outsourcing] contract the New Zealand Intellectual Property Office would still want to retain responsibility for looking at the implications that are important and unique to us' (interview, NZ PO). A similar type of issue emerged during the course of the interview with the Austrian PO. It was pointed out that Austrian examiners doing outsourcing work for other patent offices need clear guidance on how to apply the exception in patent law that relates to a prohibition on the patenting of an invention that is contrary to morality, an exception that is relevant to areas such as the patenting of stem cell technology.[6]

The outsourcing of patent examination may be a solution for smaller countries, but it does have to be an integrated part of the broader economic and social planning conversations that occur in these countries. Singapore's outsourcing strategy is part of a clear plan for the role that the patent institution plays in its overall economic growth strategy. For Singapore it is better to invest in the creation of a new kind of patent professional, one that is more broadly trained than the traditional patent examiner:

> We want to develop a holistic patent professional, a group of experts who advise their clients on a whole range of matters. Examination is a small part of the patent system and its commercial use. Rather than trying to build up databases and examiners to do just examination when 80% or 90% of patents are filed and examined elsewhere, we want to build a different kind of system (interview, Singapore PO).

---

[6] For an example of this type of prohibition see Sub-section 13(2) of the Patents Act (Singapore).

This strategy in turn fits into a larger one in which Singapore 'is going to move into the IP intensive economy in the next phase of its growth' (interview, Singapore PO). Singapore is a country with a small but highly skilled and educated population. It does not have raw commodity advantages. Turning itself into a destination for high technology investment in sectors such as pharmaceuticals and biotechnology is a feasible plan. Competing with China's factories, scale and labour costs is not. Singapore's approach to the patent system is moulded by its broader economic strategy. Recognizing the reality that pharmaceutical multinationals and biotechnology firms will file first outside of Singapore, Singapore's patent law offers companies a low-cost filing route into Singapore. Patent quality is an issue for Singapore, but not an especially pressing issue. For the purpose of signalling quality it does choose patent offices that are PCT ISAs and it holds regular dialogues with examiners from those offices. It does not, however, have the commitment of the German PO to patent quality. Its commitment is something less than that. It does not have in its patent law pre-grant opposition or a post-grant opposition system of the kind run by the European Patent Office. Instead it has a search and examination procedure for claims that essentially only provides information to a third party requesting the procedure.[7] If the major offices do raise patent quality then, as one interviewee observed, 'if this is achieved at an international level it automatically benefits Singapore'. The strategy, then, is to maintain a dialogue with offices like the EPO on patent quality but not to lead on that issue, to support whatever quality standards emerge but not to move beyond those, while all the time providing a patent environment that is friendly to companies in high technology sectors such as biotechnology and pharmaceuticals in the hope that this will help snare some of the global FDI in these sectors. Singapore's particular model of patent administration does not necessarily transfer well to other countries, but its institutionally integrative approach to patent administration is one many countries could learn from.

Centralized regionalization: making regulatory capture easier

One early hypothesis of this study was that developing countries should think of creating a regional patent office, an institutional solution that has, as we have seen, been adopted in some parts of the world (see Chapter 10).

---

[7] See Section 38A of the Patents Act (Singapore).

The most obvious argument in favour of regionalization is based on cost. Countries which on their own cannot afford to run a patent office can club together and create a regional office that will provide a regional public good for all the members of the club. During the interviews in the Association of Southeast Asian Nations (ASEAN) region, this hypothesis received only lukewarm support from patent offices. This is understandable given that national offices would be worried about their future in any regional arrangement. Despite a 1995 framework agreement proposing an ASEAN Patent and Trademarks Office (see Chapter 10), progress in establishing such an office has been slow. 'Not in my lifetime', observed one senior official from an ASEAN country.

Even if regionalization saves on one set of costs it raises the prospect of other costs. Regionalization means that countries have to embark on a process of harmonizing their patent laws. The process may be a prolonged one, as it has been in the case of the European Patent Convention (EPC), but it is a consequence of creating a regional patent office. The case for countries with very different economies and problems harmonizing their patent laws is not strong. A country like Thailand with a serious HIV/AIDS problem might want to introduce a more rigorous approach to pharmaceutical patenting along the lines of Indian patent law, while an affluent country like Singapore, which is able to afford higher prices for medicines, might want to develop, as it is doing, a much more pharma-friendly patent law.

Another kind of problem insufficiently recognized in the context of regional patent arrangements is the problem of regulatory capture. Patent offices have to deal with some of the world's most powerful companies, companies with a long history of influencing the course of regulation. Creating one regional patent office to represent a group of developing countries means that there is only one office to capture. The existence of many national patent offices makes the task more resource intensive for multinational users. For developing countries interested in regional arrangements it is better to think of arrangements that are administered by a network of national patent offices. This maximizes the potential for a diversity of administrative practice even if the countries involved in the regional arrangement decide on a harmonization of standards. The most dangerous world for states in terms of regulatory capture problems is one in which there is a regional harmonization of laws and a central office that creates a harmonization of practice, with no national offices to create a countervailing practice.

Finally, for developing countries thinking about a regional patent system it is worth noting that in the existing regional patent arrangements, states have been careful to maintain aspects of sovereignty over their patent system. Regional arrangements have been more built on top of national systems rather than replacing those systems. For example, the Eurasian Patent Convention (EAPC) that was discussed in Chapter 10 expressly protects the right of members to establish national offices and the member states have all taken advantage of that right. The proposal in Europe to create a Community Patent by means of Council Regulation is another example of the way in which regional systems coexist with national systems. Under the proposal, a Community patent would automatically apply throughout the member states of the Community and if declared invalid would lapse for the whole Community.[8] But the Community patent would be an autonomous system that would coexist with national patent systems and the European patent system.

Aside from the problem of regulatory capture, the creation of a regional patent office also brings with it, as most of my European interviewees politely described it, governance issues. As the number of countries joining the European Patent Organization has increased, its group politics have become more complicated. Whether or not the European Patent Organization has become ungovernable, as a few of my interviewees wondered, there is little doubt that the price of increasing membership is an increase in coalitional politics. Trust, as we saw in Chapter 4, can become a problem in a regional arrangement. The EPO is probably more trusted outside of Europe than inside it. The strength of regionalization lies in the fact that it networks neighbouring countries to produce regional public goods. The question, however, is whether an international organization is needed in all cases to bring networked regional goods into existence. Perhaps there is another way.

Nodal governance

During the course of the European fieldwork a question that I regularly put to interviewees was whether the EPO regional model was a model that others might follow. The replies were along the lines of 'perhaps', 'possibly' and so on. One senior interviewee, though, suggested that 'a good model for all countries is to do more networking'. The EPO, he went on to point out, was created in the absence of a world where technologies offered so many opportunities for networking amongst countries at the national level, and in such a world it was an open question as to whether

<hr>

[8] See Article 2(1) of the Proposal available at ec.europa.eu/internal_market/indprop/patent/index_en.htm.

one should invest in the creation of a regional office. It is right to say that it is countries that should be doing the networking rather than patent offices. Patent offices are assiduous networkers. But as we have seen this patent office networking has produced an insider governance led by the Trilaterals, and to a lesser extent the Asian Trilaterals, that serves private interests more than it does public ones.

The integration of patent offices into the private global governance network for the monopoly control of knowledge is part of a process of nodal governance that has been used to globalize intellectual property rights more generally. In broad terms, nodal governance is an adaptive response to the problem of information that confronts governance of all kinds, but especially networked governance.[9] Governance requires information. The dramatic proliferation of new types and new scales of networks enabled by information technology mean that the information needed for governance is dispersed through a multiplicity of networks, many of which operate independently of each other. No one network, public or private, has information omniscience. One response of actors to this complexity is to find ways to link networks to produce new structures of governance. The globalization of intellectual property saw pharmaceutical multinationals create new networks and organizational nodes to represent those networks within the US and then link those nodal networks to others in Japan and the EU and then eventually into developing countries. This networking process brought with it more information and more capacity to pull a lever of executive action because a node with executive power such as the United States Trade Representative had become convinced of the rightness of so doing. Nodes in the networked world are organizational centres in time and space from which the actions of governance flow.

Patent offices are important nodal centres, but they are centres that are integrated into a private governance network. Within this private nodal governance network there is a hierarchy in which the offices at the top lead those of lower rank and are also responsive to the wishes of the multinationals that dominate the use of the patent system. The challenge for states is to use their sovereignty over patent administration to make patent offices part of public nodal governance networks, so that patent offices regulate in ways that complement rather than undermine the public policy

---

[9] For a discussion of nodal governance see P. Drahos, 'Intellectual Property and Pharmaceutical Markets: A Nodal Governance Approach', 77 (2004) *Temple Law Review*, 401; Scott Burris, Peter Drahos and Clifford Shearing, 'Nodal Governance', 30 (2005) *Australian Journal of Legal Philosophy*, 30.

goals of states in areas such as health, renewable energy and information technology. States that continue to let patent offices operate as agents of private governance will find that their policy objectives in such areas may be undermined by this agency. So, for example, Chinese negotiators showing up at the negotiations over the Kyoto Protocol and demanding a deal over the cost of renewable energy technologies for the purposes of climate change mitigation and adaptation are not assisted by a Chinese PO that is helping to entrench a global position in which the EU, the US and Japan own 77% of renewable energy patents.[10]

We have seen that patent offices have developed strong connections amongst themselves, as well as with their major corporate clients and patent agents, but they have remained detached from the possibilities of exploiting the networked governance of the outside world. One reason is that communities of innovators subscribe to standards of innovation that, if translated into a legal standard of inventive step, would see a steep decline in the number of granted patents. The search for prior art in patent offices, with some exceptions that will be discussed in a moment, remains very much a closed affair. An issue I discussed with all offices was that of search strategies and teamwork in patent searching. In developing countries, the basic position was that individual examiners did the examination work with comparatively little oversight. As we have seen, developing-country examiners would usually be relying on the results that an ISA had generated under the PCT. In developed countries, patent offices essentially worked with a single-examiner model. In some offices in some examining divisions there might be team meetings to discuss search strategies, junior examiners might work with senior examiners as part of their training, but at base it was about individual examiners being responsible for particular files. Those individual examiners are skilled in using the International Patent Classification system to search the patent literature. It is harder for them to search the non-patent literature.

The single-examiner model used by patent offices to do their searching contrasts strongly with the collaborative and networked research environments in which many scientific researchers now operate.[11] Put simply, this model of patent examination could surely be strengthened if it

---

[10] See *Compendium of Patent Statistics 2008*, OECD, 21.
[11] See Paul A. David and Louise C. Keely, 'The Economics of Scientific Research Coalitions: Collaborative Network Formation in the Presence of Multiple Funding Agencies', in Ado Geuna, Ammon J. Salter and W. Edward Steinmueller (eds.), *Science and Innovation: Rethinking the Rationales for Funding and Governance*, Edward Elgar, Cheltenham, UK, 2003, 251.

found ways to utilize the flows of knowledge in the world's many scientific networks and research communities. The world of networked governance offers many possibilities for improving the quality of examination. One can get a sense of the possibilities of networked governance from the Peer to Patent Project being trialled by the USPTO for software patent applications. This project connects examiners and members of the public through patent Wikis for the purpose of creating an open review process for patent prior art.[12] The aim is to see whether giving members of the public the opportunity to search for documents in relation to a patent application and make comments on the application and the documents they have found will improve the first action decisions taken by an examiner. Peer to patent does not replace the single-examiner model of decision-making, but rather enhances the search power of that model by allowing members of the public to participate in the search process. Searching the non-patent literature in the case of software patent applications is a recognized problem. Finding ways for examiners to make use of software communities in order to track down relevant prior art makes a great deal of sense. The preliminary results from this project are encouraging, with over 70% of examiners wanting peer-to-patent examination to become part of the patent office's practice.[13] Amongst other things, it is clear that this method turns up prior art that examiners would not otherwise have been able to find.

One important issue is whether the major patent offices will use the peer-to-patent model of examination in areas other than software. Patent offices generally carefully assess the level of support by key industry players for new initiatives. At the interview in the USPTO in 2007, my interviewees suggested that there was industry uncertainty about peer-to-patent review. Would Microsoft, not the most adored company in the software community, become a special target of networked review? IBM is a major supporter of the project as it relates to software patents. Many of IBM's technical researchers signed on as reviewers for the purposes of the pilot project.[14] With the support of such industry heavyweights the

---

[12] See http://dotank.nyls.edu/communitypatent; Beth S. Noveck, '"Peer to Patent", Collective Intelligence, Open Review, and Patent Reform', 20 (2006) *Harvard Journal of Law & Technology*, 123.

[13] See 'Peer to Patent: First Anniversary Report', The Center for Patent Innovations, New York Law School, 2008, 6, available at http://dotank.nyls.edu/communitypatent/P2Panniversaryreport.pdf.

[14] See http://domino.research.ibm.com/comm/research.nsf/pages/d.compsci.patent.revolution.html.

USPTO is prepared to continue with piloting peer-to-patent examination for software and extend it to business method patents where software usually also plays a role.[15] The success of the peer-to-patent model has seen other patent offices such as the Japanese Patent Office (JPO) and the UK PO begin their own trials. For examiners in the software field, the peer-to-patent project is attractive because it helps them to search the world's non-patent literature in order to decide whether the criterion of universal novelty has been met. It takes some of the pressure off a mission impossible that probably is impossible: 'Give us some useful stuff instead of screaming about the unpatentability of software, give us some bullets' (interview, UK PO). Whether the peer-to-patent model will be used in sectors of technology such as pharmaceuticals and biotechnology will very much depend on the reaction of industry leaders in those sectors.

In the meantime the main game for the world's major patent offices is dealing with their massive backlogs. The basic strategy here is to employ more examiners and enter into various work-sharing arrangements with other 'trusted' offices. It is a Fordist response – create a giant integrated patent global assembly line and run off millions of patents for the world's technology markets. Developing countries become part of the assembly line through membership of the PCT and the training of their patent offices by developed-country patent offices.

Quality initiatives like the peer-to-patent project that are accepted by the major patent offices may potentially benefit developing countries. Applications not granted in the major offices might be looked at more carefully in developing-country offices, especially where the developing-country's patent law required an applicant for a patent to provide information to the developing-country's patent office about that applicant's foreign applications.[16]

But for developing countries it is important to keep in mind that the history of the patent institution has been that of a few major developed countries and multinationals shaping it for their own economic ends. During the interviews it became clear that senior patent officials continue to see the patent institution in national terms. Europe's smaller patent offices believe they have a vital role to play in serving their national companies. Amongst developed-country patent offices there are different views of patent quality that link back to beliefs about the importance of patent quality to their domestic industries. The German PO, and probably the EPO, sees patent

---

[15] See www.uspto.gov/web/patents/peerpriorartpilot/.
[16] Imposing such an obligation on an applicant is allowable under TRIPS. See Article 29.2.

quality (as produced by rigorous examination rather than badges of quality like ISO accreditation) as being more important, for example, than do the Australian, UK and US offices. For this reason the German PO is wary of the application of the principle of mutual recognition to examination results. Developed-country multinationals with a long experience of the patent system continue to shape it, including quality initiatives to suit their own global commercial agendas. IBM's support for the pilot of the peer-to-patent model was crucial. Here it is worth recalling that IBM, more than any other company, from the 1980s onwards led the world into the era of software patenting after having opposed such patents during the 1960s.[17] It adds about 3,000 patents to its US patent portfolio each year.[18] A model like peer-to-patent used selectively for some of its patent applications may serve as a useful signalling device to others about the quality of its patent portfolio. For many people, such as those in the free software movement, the patenting of software is a bad idea in principle because it does not help innovation.[19] Companies like IBM will simply use peer-to-patent to add a quality hue to their patent portfolio, thereby deepening their dominance over information technology standards and software development and threatening models of software innovation that do not depend upon building large patent portfolios. In short peer-to-patent may simply be the road to greater patent dominance by a few.

For developing countries, the main message of history is to defend sovereignty over patent administration and look to design systems that adjust global patent principles to their local economic and social context. Quality initiatives like the peer-to-patent examination model are potentially useful for developing countries, but they also emerge out of a US innovation context in which mature industry leaders like IBM have matchless knowhow in being able to use the patent system to further their global commercial interests. Staying with the example of software development for a moment, there is an argument for developing countries to experiment with innovation systems that do not depend on large patent portfolios, one reason being that their domestic companies are unlikely to be able to compete on equal terms in innovation systems where patent portfolios are needed.[20] For developing countries it may be more

---

[17] P. Drahos with J. Braithwaite, *Information Feudalism*, Earthscan, London, 2002, 170–1.

[18] See www.uspto.gov/web/offices/com/speeches/02-01.htm.

[19] See http://endsoftpatents.org/.

[20] For a discussion of the advantages of open source innovation in both software and biotechnology see Janet Hope, *Biobazaar: The Open Source Revolution and Biotechnology*, Harvard University Press, Cambridge, Mass., 2008.

important to concentrate on prioritizing models of patent administration that have a commitment to protecting innovation quality as opposed to patent quality. In such models, patent administration would become dispersed amongst networked communities of innovators rather than having a central privatized regulator in the form of the patent office calling all the shots on patent grants using a single-examiner model. In any case, as we have seen in preceding chapters, it is in reality not the national patent office of a developing country that calls the shots, but the Trilateral Offices that lead this global network for the governance of knowledge.

Patent administration in developing countries has to begin with the realization that the knowledge assets and innovative capabilities of countries are tremendously varied.[21] Nodally networked governance offers developing countries numerous possibilities for linking patent administration more specifically to their own local innovation contexts rather than simply accepting models that come out of the EU and US. Through nodal governance developing countries have at least the opportunity of adjusting patent standards to produce a level of protection that is 'just right' for the firms and industries that make up key sectors of their economy.[22] The next section discusses the Brazilian model of pharmaceutical patent examination. It provides one concrete example of how a developing country is approaching the problem of examination in the pharmaceutical sector using a network design in which the final node of decision-making power is not the patent office.

Public nodal governance in patent administration

In 1999 Brazil passed a measure that made the grant of patents on pharmaceutical products and processes dependent on the consent of the Brazilian National Sanitary Surveillance Agency (ANVISA).[23] Patent applications concerning pharmaceuticals are processed by Brazil's PO in the normal way, but ANVISA scrutinizes them for compliance with the requirements

---

[21] Fulvio Castellacci and Daniele Archbugi, 'The Technology Clubs: The Distribution of Knowledge across Nations', 37 (2008) *Research Policy*, 1659.

[22] For a detailed analysis of the theory of the firm and how the 'just right' design of intellectual property laws can contribute to the efficiency of the firm see Dan L. Burk and Brett H. McDonnell, 'The Goldilocks Hypothesis: Balancing Intellectual Property Rights at the boundary of the Firm', 2 (2007) *University of Illinois Law Review*, 575.

[23] The measure was consolidated in Article 229-C of the Law 10.196/01. It reads as follows: '229-C The allowance of patents to pharmaceutical products and processes will depend upon previous consent of the Brazilian Sanitary Surveillance Agency – ANVISA'.

of patentability. If ANVISA concludes that the patent application fails to meet one or more of the criteria of patentability, it can withhold its consent to the grant of the patent in which case the patent cannot issue.[24] For the purpose of making judgements about patentability criteria such as the requirement of an inventive step, ANVISA has established a technical group of experts that understands pharmaceutical innovation.

The Brazilian model is worth close study by other developing countries. It is a preventive strategy that avoids the high costs of testing the validity of patents that have been granted. It is also a good example of nodal networked governance. It brings together public health expertise, pharmacological expertise and patent examination expertise, but in a way where the node of decision-making power is more likely to attend to the goals of the patent social contract. It links patentability criteria in the area of pharmaceuticals to the goal of welfare-enhancing innovation in the health sector. We saw in Chapter 7 that one of the real concerns with pharmaceutical patenting is with patent offices granting patents over essentially trivial advances that serve the gaming strategies of large pharmaceutical companies. The reasons for this have to do with the incentive settings that face patent offices, the narrow training of patent examiners and the fact that examiners are not in an institutionalized dialogue with independent public health researchers who can assess what constitutes therapeutically significant innovation in the pharmaceutical field. Involving independent public health experts in the process of patent administration is one way of helping to ensure that the patent social contract works properly in the health sector.

Where a major economic power like Brazil develops a national initiative of this kind, it has the potential to become a public good for other countries in the region. Patenting in South America and Central America is low. According to the World Intellectual Property Organization's (WIPO) data for 2005, the Brazilian PO received 20,005 applications, Argentina 5,266 and Ecuador 591.[25] The Brazilian PO is the only South American office in the world's top twenty, with a ranking of thirteenth according to the number of patent filings for 2005.[26] It makes sense, therefore, for countries in South America to begin thinking about a networked approach to patent office administration. But it is worth repeating

---

[24] Information provided to the author by Ms Ana Paula Jucá Silva of ANVISA in a paper titled 'ANVISA and pharmaceutical products and process patents', on file with author.

[25] See www.wipo.int/export/sites/www/ipstats/en/statistics/patents/xls/wipo_pat_appl_from_1883_table.xls.

[26] WIPO, *Patent Report 2007*, 12.

the earlier point in this chapter that this should not simply amount to the creation of a regional office because this makes the task of regulatory capture that much easier for experienced multinationals. Instead, smaller developing countries should concentrate on creating counter-gaming networks that can respond to any gaming behaviour within their own patent system. If, for example, the bulk of the 591 patents that were applied for in Ecuador turn out to be from foreign pharmaceutical companies, and this is part of a consistent pattern, then Ecuador has an interest in developing an approach to patent quality that targets pharmaceutical patenting. It makes sense to see if Brazilian and Ecuadorian public health officials can find ways to share data on the patenting of pharmaceuticals. Other smaller countries in South and Central America might also take an interest in such an information-sharing arrangement. In the beginning countries would be taking advantage of Brazil's greater capacity, but the advantage for Brazil would be that it was spreading a regulatory approach to patent quality and creating a coalition of countries willing to defend against chest-beating trade threats that erupt from time to time from the US and EU on patents and pharmaceuticals.

In integrating themselves into the networks around patent administration, small developing countries need to identify the technocratic mentality of the nodes that steer the network. Currently, developing countries are part of a global patent office network that delivers pre-packaged analysis of patent applications favouring the rent-seeking objectives of business rather than the patent social contract. For example, the EPO's and the Mexican PO's creation of a portal to allow the patent offices of Central American countries to access the examination work of Mexican examiners (see Chapter 9) is a network that might simply act as a transmission belt for a low standard inventive step and therefore low quality pharmaceutical patents into Central American countries. The Brazilian approach to pharmaceutical patent examination offers a clear alternative. Improving patent administration in the pharmaceutical sector is important for all countries, but there may also be sectors that are of particular importance to individual countries. Foreign firms that run cartels of various kinds (for example, the flower industry or the vitamin industry) will often have arrangements in developing countries for the locals to collect raw materials for processing.[27] Foreigners can lodge process and product patents

---

[27] I am indebted for this insight to Dr Ana Carolina Roa Rodríguez, a former PhD student of mine who conducted fieldwork in Peru, Bolivia and Columbia looking at, amongst other things, the flower industry in Columbia.

in the developing country where the raw materials are being collected in order to create a barrier to entry for local firms which might have ideas about moving up the value chain. The fact that there are only a small number of patents in a developing country does not mean that those few patents are not having an economic impact or that the country has no real interest in improving its system of patent administration.

Nodal governance networks on patent administration can be assembled by smaller developing countries in other ways that would benefit them. The patent law of some developing countries permits the use of outside examination expertise. Thailand's patent law contains such a provision and allows the result to be treated as an examination for the purposes of patent law.[28] Similarly, at the time of my visit to the Vietnamese PO, there was a decree that gave the PO 'the right to request the opinion of specialized bodies and experts working in the relevant fields'.[29] Smaller patent offices, for reasons that we have discussed, tend to look to the examination expertise of the major offices. A patent office from a small country like Laos, which was setting up at the time of interview in 2004, is from the very beginning encircled by WIPO's assistance in the form of model laws, hardware gifts and a troupe of consultants. The patent office of Laos was simply planning to accept the examination results of other offices or to seek their services if it needed an application to be examined. Once surrounded by these established 'expert' networks it is hard to think creatively about new approaches.

But small players like Laos could draw on a much wider pool of expertise beyond that of patent examiners in major offices and bring in scientific expertise from universities, research institutes and other organizations. There is no reason why a small country could not for the purposes of its patent system create technology-specific pools of expertise. If the expertise was not available in-country it could look for this expertise in other countries, especially from developed countries where publicly-minded retirees might be more than happy to contribute their expertise. The fees for this kind of work could be much lower than that charged by the commercial arms of developed-country patent offices.

Countries would only need to build technology pools in sectors that mattered to their economies and where it was important to ensure high standards of patent quality. Developing countries could share the costs

---

[28] See Section 25 of the Patent Act B.E. 2522 (Thailand).
[29] Article 21, Decree on Industrial Property, Hanoi, 24 October 1996: as amended 1 February 2001.

of creating such pools. These costs would be modest because, as KIPO has demonstrated, the entire patent application process can be handled electronically. This kind of nodal governance approach is also sovereignty enhancing. States would not be giving up sovereignty to a regional patent office. They would only enter into joint technology pools where their economic interests were roughly aligned. For example, Malaysia and Indonesia might agree to form such a pool in the pharmaceutical sector, while Singapore for the reasons described earlier would be likely to continue with its own networked outsourcing approach. Even the most under-resourced countries could make use of technology pools, if the need arose. Very few patents are registered in Pacific island countries but the need for patent quality might still arise in some circumstances. For example, Papua New Guinea, which has an HIV/AIDS problem, might find that it was receiving patent applications for treatments for HIV/AIDS. These patents might complicate its purchase of cheaper generic treatments. Rather than simply registering these patents on the basis of grants elsewhere, it could seek out a technology pool that was servicing the needs of other developing countries in the pharmaceutical sector. Such a pool would mean that it would no longer be dependent upon the Australian PO's expertise concerning these kinds of patents.

Not raising one's head above the parapet: lost opportunities in a world of nodal governance

Left to their own devices the patent offices of small countries and developing countries will probably not exploit the world of nodal governance. Patent officials from these countries, for the most part, see opportunities to acquire more resources from the rich offices and no downsides in deepening the integration of their countries into the global private governance network of patent administration:

Patent official, Pacific island country: 'We are planning to join the PCT.'
Drahos: 'Why?'
Patent official: 'The PCT will generate more applications and more fees for the patent office.'
Drahos: 'What if more pharmaceutical patents are registered and cause problems for your population in terms of access?'
PAUSE…
Patent official: 'We haven't thought of that.'

Integration is cheaply bought by the rich offices. For the cost of a few computers, database programs and some training the small players become sites of automated compliance.

Deals over technical assistance largesse are done at various international meetings like the Asia-Pacific Economic Cooperation's (APEC) Intellectual Property Experts Group where, to the background drone of the usual set WIPO speech about the importance of patents to the future of civilization, the large players cement relations with representatives from smaller developing-country patent offices with offers of assistance and training. Back home, developing-country patent officials discover little real political interest in the workings of their office. Ministers find the area too technical. Patent officials are left to get on with it. They face the practical problem of having to make the patent law at least minimally operational. No-one wants to preside over an office that is seen by the outside world to be a complete shambles. In the past officials could assume that outsiders would be unlikely to lift the veil on the operations of their office. Today they cannot. If they are from a country going through the WTO accession process, their patent system will be scrutinized. If US companies trade in their markets, reports about their patent system will make it into the office of the United States Trade Representative. So they enter a network that gives them off-the-shelf institutional solutions for their problems. Once in the network, they become part of its international meeting circuit where they join in the deal-making for more computers and training visits to the large offices.

The global patent governance network takes the form of a dangerous hierarchy in which more and more patent offices are becoming dependent on the work quality of a small group of offices. This dependency is justified on the basis of productive efficiency. What is ignored by developing countries that are allowing sovereignty over patent administration to slide away in this manner is that nodal governance networks offer the means to adapt international standards for the constitution of patent monopolies to local contexts. These standards are really the standards of the US, the EU and Japan. The Vietnamese PO that automatically follows the guidelines put out by the EPO on pharmaceutical examination is following guidelines crafted for a European context. A crucial question is whether these guidelines, which serve to interpret and implement the creation of grants of monopoly, are the guidelines that Vietnam should be using given its institutions and economic stage of development. Representatives from Vietnam's generic industry described their industry as made up of many small players with no real powers of R&D and reliant upon the importation of active ingredients from China and India (interview, Vietnam). It is worth noting that countries like India, China, Canada and Greece that have developed successful generic industries have done so because the patent environment has been weak enough to allow the industry to grow. Vietnam has no choice but to accept the patent standards dictated to it by the EU and the US if it wants free trade agreements with them, but it does not have to accept their guidance as to how those standards are to be interpreted and administered. Examiners in the Vietnamese PO can insist on a higher inventive step than their counterparts in the EPO and they do not have to accept the patent claims in the pharmaceutical sector that the EPO does.

Rather than following the EPO-drafted manual and the EPO training, they could be developing an approach to pharmaceutical examination that is relevant to Vietnam's health system and economic stage of development. But they are not. Where there should be flexible and adaptive nodal governance networks fighting the gaming behaviour of multinationals and shaping global monopoly standards to local contexts, there are instead dangerously automated hierarchical networks. Within these hierarchical networks developing-country examiners serve as tradesmen installing monopoly products that have rolled off production lines elsewhere in the world. Their examination manuals are like installation manuals setting out the technical specifications and procedures that they have to follow.

Many developing country examiners understand the dangers of the automated process, but believe that there is little that they can do about it. When, for example, I put it to a Philippines patent examiner that the Philippines need not follow the EPO's approach to method-of-treatment claims, the response was that 'no developing country examiner would raise their head above the parapet in that way'. The personal strategy is to keep one's head down, accept the bit of training that is paid for by the patent fee income of the rich offices and follow the list of allowable claiming formats for pharmaceutical compounds in the EPO-drafted examiner's manual, irrespective of the consequences in the Philippines. And those consequences do arrive.

In listening to generic companies in the Philippines I heard a familiar story. There were difficulties in searching for patents at the Philippines PO and it was better to get a number of independent searches done in order to maximize one's chances of picking up all the relevant patents. The generic companies were finding patent claims, in particular, for antibiotics for which the basic product patent had expired. My visit to the Bureau of Food and Drugs revealed the usual gaming behaviour:

> Every day these companies ring the Bureau to remind them of their patent rights (interview, official, Bureau of Food and Drugs, Philippines).

And the Bureau's solution?

> In order to placate the wishes of companies the Bureau of Food and Drugs will ask an applicant [the generic company] to get clearance from the Intellectual Property Office (interview, official, Bureau of Food and Drugs, Philippines).

The need to get a clearance from the patent office creates an incentive for big pharmaceutical companies to apply for patents in order to force a contest over the patents. An examiner from the Philippines PO asked to do a search would turn up the patents with their EPO-approved claiming formats and report back to the Bureau that there were patents. The Bureau would not grant the generic company the certificate of registration it needs to sell its product until its patent dispute with the large pharmaceutical company has been resolved. As we saw in Chapter 11, the Canadian generic industry takes the view that only aggressive litigation can work to break down these patent barriers. Is litigation an option in the Philippines?

Finding real experts in patent litigation in Manila is a problem and the few to be found tend to work exclusively for large foreign companies (roundtable interview with generic manufacturers in the Philippines).

The Philippines has some of the highest prices for medicines in the region (interview, Director, National Drug Program). Attempts by the government to import cheap medicines from Indian generic companies had led to threats of litigation against it for patent infringement (interview, Director, National Drug Program). A Health Department official, perhaps because he thought it important that I meet some of the faces behind the statistics, arranged a meeting with a group of women running an access-to-medicines campaign called 'Cut the Cost – Cut the Pain'. They knew about the problems of the patent system and I had no insights for them. They told me about the cost of medicines – 50 pesos a day for tuberculosis treatment. A family of six might have an income of about 250 pesos a day.

Somewhat ironically, it was my interviewees in the EPO who stressed the importance of strong patent examination for developing countries. Upon further questioning this turned out to mean patent examination that protected local industries from low quality foreign patents. The interview in the German PO revealed the same territorial thinking about patent administration. In both the EPO and the German PO, high quality examination is seen as being important to European firms. These interviews were a reminder that for all its sophisticated evolution and globalization, the patent system, at least in the eyes of some, retains elements of its territorial protectionist heritage. To a large extent, however, the competition among developed-country patent offices on quality issues is a game of nuances. It can hardly be otherwise when the EPO, the JPO and the USPTO pumped out over 300,000 patent grants in 2007. Their principal purpose is to continue to swell the patent portfolios of the multinationals that want to be able to use those portfolios for defensive and offensive purposes in whatever part of the globe they decide is strategically important. Developing-country offices have been trained to serve in the global rollout of these portfolios. Whether these offices will ever have a role beyond this depends on how willing developing-country governments are to take back some control over patent administration.

INDEX